Friday, Oct. 21

Dear Jim —

To a superb thinker and writer, and a great friend.

Frigates and attack submarines are great. However, economic sanctions are often selected, in lieu of military force, or as supplement to it, when diplomacy is not sufficient. Hopefully this book will point the direction toward a wiser legal system for selecting among, and then implementing, sanctions

My best,
Barry

P.S. To avoid this being overly serious, see p. 200.

INTERNATIONAL ECONOMIC SANCTIONS

INTERNATIONAL ECONOMIC SANCTIONS

Improving the haphazard U.S. legal regime

BARRY E. CARTER
Georgetown University Law Center

The right of the
University of Cambridge
to print and sell
all manner of books
was granted by
Henry VIII in 1534.
The University has printed
and published continuously
since 1584.

CAMBRIDGE UNIVERSITY PRESS

Cambridge

New York   New Rochelle   Melbourne   Sydney

Published by the Press Syndicate of the University of Cambridge
The Pitt Building, Trumpington Street, Cambridge CB2 1RP
32 East 57th Street, New York, NY 10022, USA
10 Stamford Road, Oakleigh, Melbourne 3166, Australia

First published 1988

Printed in Canada

Library of Congress Cataloging-in-Publication Data
Carter, Barry E.
International economic sanctions : improving the haphazard U.S.
legal regime / Barry E. Carter.
p. cm.
Bibliography: p.
Includes index.
ISBN 0 521 34258 9
1. Economic sanctions, American. 2. United States – Foreign
relations administration. 3. Economic sanctions. I. Title.
KF1976.C37 1988
341.7′54 – dc19   88-10868
                                                        CIP

British Library Cataloguing in Publication Data
Carter, Barry E.
International economic sanctions : improving
the haphazard U.S. legal regime.
1. International economic sanctions.
International law
I. Title
341.7′5

ISBN 0 521 34258 9

To my mother and father,
Ethel and Byron Carter

Contents

vii

Contents

Contents

TABLES

CHARTS

ix

Preface

The use of economic sanctions by one country against another for foreign policy purposes has generated considerable interest in recent years. In this book I seek to contribute to the discussion and the literature in three principal ways.

First, the book provides a comprehensive analysis of the U.S. laws for imposing economic sanctions for noneconomic foreign policy reasons. Much of the previous literature has consisted of empirical, nonlegal studies of the effectiveness of one or more sanctions. The recent, excellent work by Gary Hufbauer and Jeffrey Schott is the leading example.

Past studies of the U.S. laws have usually focused on a single kind of economic activity, such as exports, rather than on the full range of possibilities. This range includes controls on a variety of government programs, on exports from the United States, on U.S. imports, on private financial transactions, and on assistance by international financial institutions.

The narrow focus of previous legal studies might reflect the fact that many of the relevant laws have purposes other than the imposition of sanctions. For example, an important purpose of the import laws is to protect certain U.S. industries. The narrow focus of past studies might also reflect the specialization of U.S. laws and of many lawyers and legal scholars.

Whatever the cause, this limited view ignores the reality of situations in which sanctions are imposed or at least considered. The United States should, and does, often choose from among the wide range of possible economic sanctions, frequently tailoring a specific mix for a particular situation.

Second, this book highlights and documents the President's haphazard authority under the existing laws. As we shall see, his power to impose different types of sanctions varies considerably. These wide variations have only occasionally been recognized in the literature, in part because of a failure to analyze the many laws in a comprehensive fashion. But these differences can have important implications, such as skewing the President's choice of sanctions or leading to questionable declarations of a national emergency.

Third, I make several recommendations designed to encourage the creation of a comprehensive and, one would hope, wise legal regime for imposing economic sanctions in the future. The proposals are both long and short term. Building on careful studies and recent legislative developments, some of the proposals are quite detailed and could be implemented quickly. Other recommendations are more tentative. For these, further research and analysis seem necessary before deciding on the details. To broaden and enrich the thinking about possible ways to proceed, this book includes a brief analysis of aspects of the statutory framework in the United Kingdom, Germany, the European Economic Community, and Japan for imposing economic sanctions.

A final note: This book generally discusses in full any relevant developments through February 1988. In addition, I was able to note briefly any significant developments through May 1988, such as President Reagan's declaration of a national emergency against Panama and his veto of the omnibus trade bill. Full discussion of the developments after February, however, was not possible because of publishing deadlines.

Acknowledgments

This book has emerged from my general interest in the interaction between foreign policy and the law (both domestic and international). Many people, too numerous to mention, deserve thanks for giving me the opportunities to study this subject in an academic setting or to grapple firsthand with it in various positions in the U.S. Government.

The more direct genesis of this book is a course that Arthur T. Downey and I created and taught together for several years. Having met while on Dr. Henry Kissinger's National Security Council staff, we decided to develop a course that combined our interests and knowledge. Entitled International Economic Coercion and the Use of Force, the course led us to collect extensive materials and refine our thinking. Mr. Downey's knowledge and ideas were invaluable to me in developing my own thoughts. He also read and commented upon an entire draft of this book, certain parts of it more than once, which led to many improvements. Let me quickly add, however, that we have often disagreed on many of the possible changes in the laws.

The students in our course deserve thanks for joining in our sometimes freewheeling efforts to advance our understanding of the issues. Thanks also go to several research assistants who either helped us with the course or worked with me on the book. Deserving special mention for their research, analysis, and writing skills are Craig Albert, Hugh Grambau, Marian Hagler, David Laufman, Daniel Lawton, Anthony Majestro, Ines Radmilovic, and Craig Zimmerman.

A number of other people read all or parts of various drafts of the book and offered valuable comments. Those outside the Georgetown University Law Center include Kenneth Abbott, Madeleine Albright, Kathleen Ambrose, Ian Fagelson, John Jackson, Paula Newberg, L. Edward Shaw, and Phillip Trimble. Readers at Georgetown included Samuel Dash, Richard Diamond, Timothy Dickinson, Steven Goldberg, Charles Gustafson, David McCarthy, and James Oldham.

Acknowledgments

The supportive environment at Georgetown Law Center has been very gratifying. In addition to the comments of the many readers, I appreciate the helpful insights of faculty colleagues who attended my luncheon presentation of the main themes of the book. I am also grateful for the help of Dean Robert Pitofsky, who provided two summer grants and allowed me to adjust my teaching schedule. In the law library, Ellen Schaffer made the wide-ranging research much easier with her excellent knowledge of the materials. When she was unavailable, Patricia Tobin and the reference librarians ably filled the gap. In the Law Center's Technical Support Services, Charles Barnes, Brenda Butler, Brenda Greenfield, Margaret Pooley, and Frank Tam deserve particular mention for their hard work and devotion to the manuscript.

Versions of parts of this book have appeared elsewhere. A version of Chapter 11 on the laws of U.S. allies appeared in the *N.Y.U. Journal of International Law and Politics*, vol. 19 at page 865 (1987), with the title "Looking for a Better Way: The Sanctions Laws of Key U.S. Allies." A considerably shorter discussion of the U.S. laws and my recommendations appeared in an article with the same title as this book in the *California Law Review*, vol. 75 at page 1159 (1987).

Finally, I want to thank the people at Cambridge University Press. Special thanks go to my editor, Mary Nevader, for her rigorous but supportive contributions and to Brigitte Lehner and Andrew Schwartz for ably shepherding this manuscript through to publication.

I

Introduction

Against a broad range of target countries, the United States is resorting increasingly to economic pressure as a major tool in its foreign policy. Recent examples include

- a variety of trade and investment sanctions against South Africa;
- financial and other sanctions against Panama;
- wide-ranging measures against Libya;
- a trade embargo against Nicaragua;
- continuing controls on high-technology exports to certain countries;
- sanctions against Poland and the Soviet Union (including the grain embargo and the ill-fated attempt to stop exports of pipeline equipment); and
- the ban on trade and the freezing of assets during the hostage crisis in Iran.

Other countries have also used economic sanctions for foreign policy purposes, although the United States employs them most often.

This frequent use reflects the special utility of economic sanctions, at least on first impression. Sanctions do not involve the violence and destruction of armed force, yet they provide a nation's leader with the appearance, and often the reality, of taking decisive steps. They are also more acceptable in the international community than is the use of force. At the same time, they are usually more concrete than diplomatic protests or other diplomatic moves.

Considerable debate continues about the effectiveness of economic sanctions. Today's conventional wisdom questions whether they work. Detailed studies suggest, however, that, despite significant failures, sanctions have been successful in some situations. For example, U.S. sanctions helped topple Haiti's Duvalier in 1986, Uganda's Idi Amin in 1979, Chile's Allende in 1973, and the Dominican Republic's Trujillo in 1961. The threat of U.S. sanctions also helped discourage South Korea from buying a nuclear fuel reprocessing plant from France in 1975–6. Although the evidence is still unclear, comprehensive U.S. sanctions probably helped free the hostages from Iran in 1981, and U.S. and allied controls on high-technology exports to the Soviet Union may substantially impair Soviet military potential. Similarly, sanctions against South Africa, by the United States and other countries, appear to be having an impact on the economy and the political climate there.

What has yet to be analyzed comprehensively are the U.S. laws for imposing sanctions. This book presents such an analysis. An important starting point is to demarcate the broad range of possible economic sanctions. They can roughly be grouped into five categories, as limits on (1) U.S. government programs, such as foreign assistance and landing rights; (2) exports from the United States; (3) imports; (4) private financial transactions; and (5) international financial institutions.

In the absence of a declared national emergency, present U.S. laws for imposing these sanctions are at best haphazard. For example, the laws make it relatively easy for the President to limit the U.S. Government's bilateral programs, such as cutting off economic assistance to Nicaragua. The President also has broad discretion to cut off almost all exports. In contrast, restricting imports is legally much more difficult. Similarly, the President has little legal control over foreign loans by private U.S. banks, and even less control over international financial institutions.

Since passing new legislation in a timely fashion is often difficult or even impossible, the existing laws can strongly influence the President's choice of sanctions, frequently in a way that is not in the best interests of the United States. For instance, if the President wants to impose economic sanctions for foreign policy reasons, the present laws encourage him to resort to export controls, where he has relatively unfettered authority, rather than to impose import controls or to restrict U.S. bank lending, where his powers are limited. Yet in certain situations, import sanctions or restraints on private credit would be more effective and cause less harm to U.S. industry and workers than would export controls. Indeed, export controls can often be the economic version of shooting oneself in the foot.

If the President does not want to have his choice of sanctions skewed by these laws, he can declare a national emergency under the International Emergency Economic Powers Act (IEEPA). This statute gives him sweeping powers over exports, imports, and private financial transactions.

Congress passed IEEPA in 1977 to reduce casual resort to "national emergencies." That goal, however, has not been met. The criteria for invoking IEEPA are vague and the major provision for congressional review was gutted by an adverse Supreme Court decision. IEEPA's flaws have become increasingly evident in light of President Reagan's questionable declarations of national emergencies and use of IEEPA powers against Nicaragua, South Africa, and Libya.

The present bias toward either applying export controls under the nonemergency laws or declaring a dubious national emergency under IEEPA is not the only possible legal framework for structuring U.S. laws governing economic sanctions. Many of the present laws were passed primarily for other purposes and without any serious consideration of the best legal regime for imposing sanctions. For example, many import laws are aimed at protecting U.S. industries, and the banking laws focus on the protection of domestic depositors, borrowers, and investors.

The comprehensive analysis of the laws that follows strongly suggests the need for constructive changes. Moreover, recent developments demonstrate that reform is possible. For example, the 1985 Export Administration Amendments Act places a few limits on the President's broad discretion over exports. Also, the 1985 foreign aid law included provisions that authorize the President to prohibit almost all imports from Libya and other countries that support terrorism. And the 1986 sanctions against South Africa contain a variety of specific restrictions on certain U.S. exports, imports, loans, and investments involving South Africa. These developments, however, are all very limited in scope. Comprehensive legislative changes are still needed.

Even a preliminary look at the laws of major U.S. allies for imposing economic sanctions indicates the possibility of other approaches. It appears that the U.S. President is more hamstrung by the present limits on his authority than are the leaders in the United Kingdom, Germany, and Japan.

Of course, since present U.S. laws for international trade and finance do serve many purposes, reform must be undertaken carefully to avoid unintended results. For instance, if the President's authority to impose import sanctions were expanded, would U.S. domestic industry pressure the President to use the new laws for protectionist purposes? Would the U.S. steel industry discover human rights violations in South Korea or Taiwan and seek a ban on steel imports from those countries? Also, could certain proposed sanctions – such as limits on private bank credit – be effectively enforced? If the President were able to prohibit new loans to Poland, would the money simply pass through West European banks to Poland, at a slightly higher interest rate?

To address these issues, Chapter 2 provides a brief treatment of past sanctions, the possible purposes of sanctions, and their effectiveness. Chapters 3 through 10 then examine the present U.S. legal regime for employing economic sanctions for foreign policy purposes. Chapter 3 starts with a useful overview of the nonemergency laws and then considers the laws governing a variety of U.S. government programs. Chapters 4 through 7 explore the nonemergency laws for exports, imports, private financial transactions, and international financial institutions, in that order. Of special note are the recent changes in the export laws that provide – in very limited situations at present – for protecting the sanctity of existing contracts, for compensating injured exporters, and for prohibiting certain controls on agricultural products beyond sixty days unless Congress approves them. Chapter 8 then analyzes some miscellaneous laws, namely the antiboycott laws and the UN Participation Act.

Chapter 9 examines the present U.S. laws for declared national emergency, including the recent uses of IEEPA. The possible powers of the President beyond the statutes are considered in Chapter 10. Chapter 11 is a brief analysis of the laws of major U.S. allies for imposing sanctions.

Chapter 12 builds on the previous chapters to address major alternatives for change. As will be detailed there, the wisest course among the options would be to increase, in carefully structured ways, the President's nonemergency authority to limit imports and private financial transactions, while decreasing his authority to control exports. This approach would allow the President to select the most effective set of sanctions for a given situation, rather than to have his choices skewed by current U.S. laws. This approach would also reduce the President's incentive to resort casually to national emergency powers, and would thus pave the way toward trimming his ability to employ those sweeping powers.

SCOPE OF THE BOOK

Economic sanctions can be defined as coercive economic measures taken against one or more countries to force a change in policies,[1] or at least to demonstrate a country's opinion about the other's policies.[2] The terms "economic boycott" and "embargo" are often used interchangeably with "economic sanction."[3] The nation or nations that impose the sanctions

[1] See *Webster's Third New International Dictionary* 2008–9 (1981) ("sanctions"); D. Losman, *International Economic Sanctions: The Cases of Cuba, Israel, and Rhodesia* 1–3 (1979).
[2] See, e.g., C. Krauthammer, "Sanctions: One Country's Opinion...," *Wash. Post,* Aug. 30, 1985, at A23, col. 1.
[3] E.g., *Webster's,* supra note 1, at 264 ("boycott"), 738–9 ("embargo"); Losman, supra note 1. The word "boycott" has an interesting history. It came into use during the nineteenth century when absentee English landlords owned much property in Ireland. Captain Charles C. Boycott was an agent in County Mayo, Ireland, who collected the rents for absentee landlords. When he refused to reduce the rents, the community retaliated by ostracizing him, economically and socially. He could not endure his isolation and returned to England. Losman, supra note 1, at 2–3.

4

are sometimes termed the sender(s), and the object or objects of the sanctions are sometimes called the target(s).

The focus of this book is the use of economic sanctions for foreign policy purposes. Here foreign policy is defined broadly to encompass national security considerations. As a result, it includes economic sanctions ranging from those intended to influence the target country's policies in relatively limited ways (e.g., human rights, terrorism, or nuclear non-proliferation) to ones designed to destabilize the government or to stop a military adventure.[4]

This definition of foreign policy, however, does not include the use of economic sanctions for economic purposes. Such use admittedly could fit into a broad definition of foreign policy. In trade disputes or negotiations, the United States (like other countries) often takes or threatens to take various economic steps to protect itself or at least to enhance its bargaining power. For example, the United States might threaten to impose tariffs or quotas as a way of inducing foreign companies to raise their prices or of pressuring the target country to accept a voluntary restraint agreement on its industry's sales to the United States. Though interesting and important, the use of economic sanctions for such economic purposes is beyond the scope of this book. It brings in a host of other situations, raises new and difficult issues, and often involves different laws. As a result, this book focuses on economic sanctions for noneconomic foreign policy purposes.[5]

In considering these particular sanctions, the emphasis here is on the relevant U.S. laws, including the relevant international agreements in which the United States is involved, such as the General Agreement on Tariffs and Trade (GATT). The discussion also addresses possible presidential powers beyond those granted in the statutes.[6]

---

[4] As discussed in Chapter 4, at notes 33, 64–75, those who framed the 1979 and 1985 Export Administration Acts (EAA) tried carefully to define and distinguish between "foreign policy controls" and "national security controls." That distinction, however, does not run through all the law of economic sanctions, and is still not entirely clear even in the U.S. export laws. Both types of EAA controls will be subsumed in this book's broad definition of foreign policy.

[5] The book does, however, consider occasionally the use of economic sanctions against expropriation of U.S. business. This is because expropriation cases are often part of a larger political dispute between the United States and another country, such as Chile under Salvador Allende.

[6] For GATT, see Chapter 4, Section E (export controls), and Chapter 5, Section C (import controls). For possible extrastatutory powers, see Chapter 10.

This book does not analyze the question of the legality of international economic coercion under customary international law. The frequent use of these sanctions by the United States and many other countries constitutes persuasive evidence that no clear norm exists against them in customary international law.

Article 19 of the Charter of the Organization of American States does, however,

As detailed in the next chapter, there is already a substantial literature on the history of sanctions and extensive empirical scholarship regarding their effectiveness. In contrast, the literature has not previously included a comprehensive overview and analysis of the U.S. laws for imposing the range of possible economic sanctions or a consideration of alternative legal regimes.[7] Presumably this has resulted partly from the traditional focus of legal scholars, government officials, and practitioners on individual parts of the puzzle — that is, government programs, export laws, import laws, or banking law.[8]

Given the already difficult task of analyzing the U.S. law on economic

provide the following: "No State may use or encourage the use of coercive measures of an economic or political character in order to force the sovereign will of another State and obtain from it advantages of any kind." 2 U.S.T. 2394, T.I.A.S. No. 2361 (1948). See also Article 18, id. Moreover, especially in the 1960s, occasional UN resolutions have inveighed against the use of economic pressures. E.g., Declaration on the Inadmissibility of Intervention Into the Domestic Affairs of States, G.A. Res. 2131, 20 U.N. GAOR, Supp. 14 (A/6014), at 11 (Dec. 21, 1965).

Nevertheless, the frequent use of sanctions and the weight of opinion argue against any violation of international law. For example, in its case against the United States before the World Court, Nicaragua asserted that the United States had violated the principle of nonintervention with its cutoff of economic aid, its 90% reduction of the sugar quota for Nicaragua, and then its comprehensive trade embargo. (These measures are discussed in more detail in Chapter 5, at notes 68, 69, and Chapter 9, at note 49.) Although the World Court ruled that the United States had violated customary international law by training and arming the contras, the majority opinion nevertheless concluded on the economic sanctions, "[T]he Court was merely to say that it is unable to regard such action on the economic plane as is here complained of as a breach of the customary-law principle of non-intervention." *Military and Paramilitary Activities in and against Nicaragua (Nicar. v. U.S.A.), Merits, Judgment,* 1986 I.C.J. 14, 126, reprinted in 25 I.L.M. 1023, 1079 para. 245 (1986). See, e.g., A. Shihata, "Destination Embargo of Arab Oil: Its Legality under International Law," 68 *Am J. Int'l L.* 591 (1974); but cf. T. Farer, "Political and Economic Coercion in Contemporary International Law," 79 *Am. J. Int'l L.* 405 (1985).

[7] The literature provides brief references to the comprehensive approach. For example, Professor Kenneth Abbott discusses laws other than export laws in the introduction to his major and excellent article on export laws: "Linking Trade to Political Goals: Foreign Policy Export Controls in the 1970s and 1980s," 65 *Minn. L. Rev.* 739, 741 n.1 (1981). Gary Hufbauer and Jeffrey Schott have two short references to the statutory framework in their impressive empirical analysis of economic sanctions: *Economic Sanctions Reconsidered: History and Current Policy* 28, 59–60 (1985).

The U.S. General Accounting Office does have a list of alternatives to the use of foreign policy export controls in its report *Export Controls: Assessment of Commerce Department's Foreign Policy Report to Congress* 12–13 (Aug. 1986), based partly on my analysis, which I provided to the report's authors in an interview.

In a recent book, Professor Elizabeth Zoller looks at a variety of U.S. laws, but it is a different mix and she addresses another and narrower objective — enforcing international law. *Enforcing International Law Through U.S. Legislation* (1985).

[8] In each of these areas, there is considerable literature on the particular laws, including some on their use with economic sanctions. See the materials cited in Chapters 3–10.

sanctions, this book does not delve into state and local laws that are intended to provide economic levers for foreign policy purposes. State and local governments have a long and active history of trying to influence other countries through laws or other steps, such as efforts against the Arab boycott and more recently against apartheid in South Africa. The laws include restrictions on the government's purchasing goods from the target country (even from U.S. companies doing business there) and restrictions on the entity's investing its cash reserves or pension funds in U.S. banks or corporations that have operations in the target country. Indeed, state and local efforts appear to have been a significant factor recently in the decision by many U.S. banks and corporations to change their business practices in South Africa, or even to reduce or terminate their activities there.[9] Nevertheless, state and local laws often differ substantially in their approach and coverage from the federal laws, and they raise unique constitutional issues.[10]

Nor does this book consider in any depth the alternatives to economic sanctions. Sanctions fall somewhere in the middle of the spectrum of possible actions for promoting U.S. foreign policy interests. The most coercive steps are the use of military force, covert actions, and the threat to use force.[11] Generally less coercive are such diplomatic measures as expulsion of some of the target country's diplomatic personnel, recall of the ambassador, a formal diplomatic protest, and suspension of cultural exchanges.[12]

Even with these limits on scope, a careful examination of the U.S. laws governing the use of economic sanctions for foreign policy reasons remains complex. The following chapters attempt to provide some clarity and insight.

[9] See, e.g., *Wash. Post*, Oct. 24, 1986, at F1, col. 3; *N.Y. Times*, Sept. 9, 1986, at 1, col. 5.

[10] See H. Fenton, "State and Local Anti-Apartheid Laws: Misplaced Response to a Flawed National Policy on South Africa," 19 *N.Y.U. J. Int'l L. & Pol.* 883 (1987); see also Note, "State and Local Anti-South Africa Action as an Intrusion upon the Federal Power in Foreign Affairs," 72 *Va. L. Rev.* 813 (1986). Contrary to some of the conclusions in the two articles cited, this author sees a constructive and constitutional role for some state and local activity.

[11] See, e.g., C. von Clausewitz, *War, Politics, and Power* 254–68 (Gateway ed. 1962); G. Allison, *Essence of Decision: Explaining the Cuban Missile Crisis* (1971); B. Blechman and S. Kaplan, *Force Without War: U.S. Armed Forces as a Political Instrument* (1978). The boundaries between the different types of sanctions – military, economic, and diplomatic – are often unclear. For example, see the later discussion of arms sales in Chapter 4, Section C.

[12] E.g., W. Christopher, *Diplomacy: The Neglected Imperative* (1981); C. Maynes, "Logic, Bribes, and Threats," 60 *Foreign Pol'y* 111 (Fall 1985); D. Acheson, *Present at the Creation* (1969).

2

Overview of the history and effectiveness of sanctions

Economic sanctions for foreign policy purposes have had a long and controversial history.[1] They were employed in ancient Greece[2] and made an early appearance in American history.

In one of the well-known steps leading to the American Revolution, the colonists resorted in 1765 to a boycott of English goods in response to the Stamp Act and raised the famous cry of "No taxation without representation."[3] The British repealed the Stamp Act the next year, but followed in 1767–70 with the Townshend Act to cover the salaries of colonial governors and judges. The colonists again retaliated with a boycott that eventually led to the Boston Tea Party of 1774.[4]

The use of sanctions then became part of the tradition of the United States. Hoping to avoid war with England or France in late 1807, President Thomas Jefferson successfully urged Congress to enact a thoroughgoing trade embargo. It prohibited American ships from leaving for foreign ports and banned the carriage of American goods by other vessels. Encountering virulent domestic opposition, the embargo was ended in March 1809. In 1811, however, the United States stopped trade with Great Britain in response to British orders limiting U.S. trade with France.[5] The War of 1812 followed.

---

[1] An extensive discussion of economic sanctions before 1945 is beyond the scope of this book. For a more thorough treatment see the sources cited in this chapter.

[2] The best-known example was Pericles' decree of 432 B.C. limiting the entry of products from Megara into the markets of Athens in response to Megara's territorial expansion and its kidnapping of three women. Aristophanes suggests that the decree played a major role in the start of the Peloponnesian War. See C. Fornara, "Plutarch and the Megarian decree," 24 *Yale Classical Stud.* 213 (1975); see also R. Ellings, *Embargoes and World Power: Lessons from American Foreign Policy* 17–18 (1985).

[3] J. Miller, *Origins of the American Revolution* 109–163, esp. 123, 150 (1962).

[4] Id. at 268–73, 345–50.

[5] The British revoked their orders, but unaware of this the United States declared war two days later, starting the War of 1812. S. Morison and H. Commager, 1. *The*

The history and effectiveness of sanctions

A. FROM 1918 THROUGH WORLD WAR II

Until 1918, countries generally used economic sanctions as a complement to military hostilities. The creation of the League of Nations after World War I, however, generated new hope and enthusiasm for economic sanctions as an alternative to the use of force. Article 16 of the League's charter provided that all League members were to cease all economic intercourse with any other member that resorted to war.[6] While trying to sell the League to the American people, President Woodrow Wilson proclaimed:

> A nation that is boycotted is a nation that is in sight of surrender. Apply this economic, peaceful, silent, deadly remedy and there will be no need for force. It is a terrible remedy. It does not cost a life outside the nation boycotted, but it brings a pressure upon the nation which, in my judgment, no modern nation could resist.[7]

Two early successes by the League against smaller powers in the 1920s[8] further encouraged supporters of sanctions.[9] However, the League itself and hopes for the peace-keeping powers of economic sanctions were

---

Growth of the American Republic 394–402 (5th ed. 1962); R. Renwick, *Economic Sanctions* 4–7 (1981) (Paper 45, Harvard Studies in International Affairs). See generally L. Sears, *Jefferson and the Embargo* (1966).

[6] Article 16 (Sanctions of Pacific Settlement) provided in pertinent part: "1. Should any Member of the League resort to war in disregard of its covenants under Articles 12, 13 or 15, it shall *ipso facto* be deemed to have committed an act of war against all other Members of the League, which hereby undertake immediately to subject it to the severance of all trade or financial relations, the prohibition of all intercourse between their nationals and the nationals of the covenant-breaking State, and the prevention of all financial, commercial or personal intercourse between the nationals of the covenant-breaking State and the nationals of any other State, whether a Member of the League or not."

[7] See *Wilson's Ideals* 108 (S. Padover ed. 1942).

[8] In 1921, the League's threat to impose sanctions under article 16 was a factor in Yugoslavia's decision to give up attempts to seize territory from Albania. Similarly, the League's threat in 1925 led Greece to withdraw from its occupation of Bulgarian territory. G. Hufbauer and J. Schott, *Economic Sanctions Reconsidered: History and Current Policy* 124–31 (1985).

[9] For example, a panel of distinguished American business leaders and academics recommended in 1932 that the United States, which was not a member of the League, take the lead in calling upon other nations to enter into an agreement or treaty with emphasis on the use of economic sanctions. It would provide, in the event of actual or threatened hostilities, for multilateral consultations with a view toward an arms embargo and "such further economic sanctions and concerted measures, short of the use of force, as may be determined to be appropriate and practical under the circumstances of any given case." The chairperson of the committee was Nicholas Murray Butler, President of Columbia University. Other members included John Foster Dulles, later to be President Eisenhower's Secretary of State, and Silas Strawn, President of the U.S. Chamber of Commerce. *Boycotts and Peace: A Report by the Committee on Economic Sanctions* 8 (E. Clark ed. 1932).

severely damaged by the League's weakness in response to Italy's invasion of Ethiopia in October 1935.

The League of Nations approved an arms embargo and other trade and financial sanctions against Italy. After much-publicized vacillating and negotiating, however, the League failed to embargo exports to Italy of the vital commodities of petroleum, coal, steel, and pig iron. Moreover, non-League countries like the United States and the Soviet Union did not adhere to the sanctions, and many League members, including Germany, were less than punctilious in observing them. The selective sanctions had some economic impact on Italy, but they did not deter the Italian aggression. Addis Ababa fell to Mussolini in May 1936, and the League discontinued its sanctions in July.[10] Some experts argued that the sanctions had not been the comprehensive ones envisioned by the League's founders, but had only been selective and poorly observed. Nonetheless, the public perception was clearly that sanctions had failed.[11]

During World War II, however, economic sanctions proved useful. The trade embargo against Europe and Japan and the Allies' preemptive buying of strategic materials from neutral countries played at least a modest role in the defeat of the Axis countries. Japan, especially dependent on imports from across the seas, was particularly vulnerable.[12]

B. SANCTIONS FROM 1945 ON

Since World War II, economic sanctions have been used frequently and for a variety of purposes. Indeed, countries employed economic sanctions for foreign policy reasons in at least ninety-one cases from World War

[10] For good accounts of the Italian case, see Renwick, *supra* note 5, at 9–24; H. Feis, *Three International Episodes: Seen from E.A.* 195–283 (Norton ed. 1966).

[11] Feis, *supra* note 10, at 274–5, 282–3; D. Losman, *International Economic Sanctions: The Cases of Cuba, Israel, and Rhodesia* 5 (1979). As Losman reports: "In September 1938, at the prodding of China's representative, sanctions were imposed on Japan for bombing Chinese cities. By this time, however, the weakness and inability of League boycott efforts were so patent that the sanctions were almost immediately rescinded, an action taken after the British suggested that the League merely express its sympathy to China and drop the entire matter." Id.

[12] D. Acheson, *Present at the Creation* 19–38 (1969); M. Domke, *Trading with the Enemy in World War II* (1943); Hufbauer and Schott, *supra* note 8 at 8, 155–70; K. Knorr, *The Power of Nations: The Political Economy of International Relations* 140 (1975); W. Medlicott, *The Economic Blockade* (2 vols. 1952). Some observers have concluded that the 1940–1 embargo by the United States and several other countries against Japan was taken as a challenge by Japan that helped lead to its attack against the United States. E.g., H. Feis, *The Road to Pearl Harbor* 109 (1950).

II through 1984, according to the comprehensive study by Gary Hufbauer and Jeffrey Schott.[13]

The United States leads the world in its use of economic sanctions for foreign policy purposes. Of the study's ninety-one cases, the United States employed sanctions sixty-two times, either alone or with other countries.[14] Other frequent users of sanctions include the United Kingdom, with twelve post–World War II episodes. The British uses included, for example, the trade and financial embargo against Argentina during the war over the Falkland Islands; financial and trade sanctions against Idi Amin's Uganda from 1972 to 1979, in cooperation with the United States; and financial and trade sanctions against Rhodesia from 1965 to 1979, in cooperation with the United Nations. The Soviet Union was also active, with ten episodes, often against recalcitrant satellites, and so were the Arab League and its members, with four uses of its petroleum power.[15]

The remainder of this book focuses on the U.S. uses of sanctions since World War II because their recent vintage usually means that they carry more lessons for the present and future. This is partly because these sanctions were invoked under laws that are the same as or similar to current laws.[16]

---

[13] Hufbauer and Schott, supra note 8. This 753-page study was done under the auspices of the Institute for International Economics in Washington, D.C. It has several overview chapters and then provides the abstracts of the authors' analyses of a total of 103 cases of economic sanctions with foreign policy goals, beginning with the economic blockade of Germany in World War I. The study's definition of "foreign policy goals" is similar to the broad use of "foreign policy reasons" in this book. Compare id. at 2 and 29–30 with the discussion at the end of Chapter 1, this volume.

Hufbauer and Schott recognize, for understandable reasons, that the study "probably omits many uses of sanctions imposed between powers of the second and third rank." Id. at 3. The authors note that these "cases are often not well documented in the English language, and we did not have adequate resources to study source material in foreign languages." The study also "may have overlooked instances where sanctions were imposed by major powers in comparative secrecy to achieve relatively modest goals." Id.

In addition, the United States has resorted to economic sanctions several times since the study's 1984 cutoff. Examples include the following: a suspension of U.S. assistance to Haiti from November 1987 through the present (May 1988) as well as the prior suspension of aid to that country in early 1986; a ban on almost all imports from Iran from October to the present; the current freeze on most U.S. foreign assistance to Panama that began in July 1987 and the other, more recent sanctions; and steps to limit travel to Greece and Lebanon after the 1985 hijacking of a TWA airliner. Moreover, the continuing U.S. sanctions against Nicaragua, South Africa, and Libya in 1985–8 are expansions of "episodes" in the study.

[14] See id. at 7, 13–20. The totals at page 7 of the study are corrected to include only post–World War II sanctions.

[15] Id.

[16] Exclusion of the earlier cases avoids the special U.S. legal situation during war-

International economic sanctions

1. The purposes of sanctions

There are three broad rationales for imposing sanctions:

- seeking to influence a country to change its policies or even its government;
- punishing a country for its policies;
- symbolically demonstrating opposition to the target country's policies to many possible audiences – such as constituencies in the sender country as well as audiences in the target country, other potential target countries, or allied countries.[17]

More than one of these rationales can be involved in the decision to employ a sanction or set of sanctions in a particular situation. For example, the widening U.S. sanctions against South Africa stem from a mix of all of them. The sanctions involve an effort to influence South Africa to change its apartheid policy, a dose of punishment, and a symbolic statement to several groups of U.S. opposition to apartheid.

Anyone attempting to delineate the exact rationales can encounter serious problems. In the United States, the sanctions might be imposed by the President on the basis of his existing statutory discretion, or through a new law passed by Congress and signed by the President, or under a new law enacted by Congress over the President's veto. Besides the fact that there are different possible combinations of key actors, it is very difficult to divine the intentions of Congress with its many members. It is even difficult to determine the exact rationale of a President with his many goals and constituencies.

Further confusing the analysis is the reality that sanctions are sometimes resorted to because "something" has to be done, and sanctions appear in the situation to be the least objectionable alternative. As noted earlier, alternative actions include a range of steps, such as applying diplomatic pressure and using (or threatening to use) force. In a particular situation, however, diplomatic pressure might not appear decisive enough, but the use of force might seem extreme.

Besides the broad theories or rationales suggested earlier, a sender country generally has more *specific foreign policy motives* for impos-

---

time and reflects the fact that present U.S. laws, especially on government programs and exports, bear little relation to pre–1945 laws.

[17] E.g., General Accounting Office, *Export Controls: Assessment of Commerce Department's Foreign Policy Report to Congress* 5 (1986); see also K. Abbott, "Coercion and Communication: Frameworks for Evaluation of Economic Sanctions," 19 *N.Y.U J. Int'l L. & Pol.* 781 (1987); K. Abbott, "Linking Trade to Political Goals: Foreign Policy Export Controls in the 1970s and 1980s," 65 *Minn. L. Rev.* 739, 798–857 (1981).

ing sanctions. Hufbauer and Schott categorized these objectives as follows:

a. "Change target country policies in a relatively modest way (modest in the scale of national goals, but often of burning importance to participants in the episode)." These goals include slowing nuclear proliferation, promoting human rights, fighting terrorism, and resolving expropriation claims.
b. "Destabilize the target government" and, in doing so, change its policies.
c. "Disrupt a minor military adventure," as illustrated by the United Kingdom's sanctions against Argentina over the Falkland Islands dispute.
d. "Impair the military potential of the target country," as illustrated by sanctions by the United States and its allies against the USSR and its allies.
e. "Change target country policies in a major way (including the surrender of territory),"[18] as illustrated by U.S. efforts in 1981–4 to end martial law and obtain internal reforms in Poland.

Again, more than one specific foreign policy objective can underlie a set of sanctions. For example, the recent U.S. efforts against Nicaragua are ostensibly designed to promote human rights, destabilize the Sandinista Government, and disrupt the Nicaraguan support of rebels in El Salvador.

2. Measuring effectiveness

Assessing the effectiveness of sanctions has its own set of hurdles. To begin with, the frequent ambiguity over the rationales and objectives of a use of sanctions makes it difficult to determine the starting point for measuring whether the use has been successful. Even if the real goal is discernible, there are still questions about how to determine the extent to which the sanctions contributed to the desired outcome. For example, if a sanction is designed to influence a country to change its human rights policies, is the sanction successful if the country releases ten political prisoners, but leaves ten more in jail, and only partly modifies its state of emergency?

There have been numerous studies of the effectiveness of one or more recent uses of sanctions.[19] The Hufbauer–Schott study, which ably draws

[18] Hufbauer and Schott, supra note 8, at 29.
[19] Some of the better studies include Hufbauer and Schott, supra note 8; Losman, supra note 11; M. Doxey, *International Sanctions in Contemporary Perspective* (1987); Renwick, supra note 5; Ellings, supra note 2; D. Baldwin, *Economic Statecraft*

on previous scholarly work, is the most comprehensive. It evaluated the effectiveness of sanctions against the five specific foreign policy objectives listed earlier.[20] To measure "success" the study examined two issues: "the extent to which the policy outcome sought . . . was in fact achieved," and "the contribution made by sanctions to a positive outcome." The policy outcomes were measured "against the *stated* foreign policy goals of the sender country." Of course, this meant that the study did not take into account domestic political purposes.[21]

Despite the difficulties of measuring effectiveness, it does appear that economic sanctions are more often "successful" than current conventional wisdom recognizes. As discussed below, for Hufbauer and Schott's sixty-two cases since 1945 in which the United States was one of the sender countries, the success rate was about 37 percent.[22]

3. Effectiveness as a function of purpose

The U.S. success rate varies according to the foreign policy objective being pursued.

a. Relatively modest changes in policy. The United States has frequently employed economic sanctions since World War II to achieve modest policy goals. One important use has been trying to *limit the spread of*

(1985); *Economic Coercion and U.S. Foreign Policy: Implications of Case Studies from the Johnson Administration* (S. Weintraub ed. 1982); S. Ayubi, R. Bissell, N. Korsah, and L. Lerner, *Economic Sanctions in U.S. Policy* (1982).

[20] When a use of sanctions was found to have more than one objective, the sanction was categorized according to the most difficult objective. Where two objectives were judged equally important, however, the case was analyzed under both categories. Hufbauer and Schott, supra note 8, at 32.

[21] Id. Hufbauer and Schott employed a numerical calculation for measuring success. To measure the policy outcome, they assigned values on a scale of 1 (failed outcome) to 4 (successful outcome). To measure the contribution of the economic sanctions, they assigned values on a scale of 1 (zero or negative contribution) to 4 (significant contribution). They then multiplied the two assigned numbers together, giving values ranging from 1 to 16. A score of 9 or higher was viewed as a "successful" outcome. Id. at 33.

The two scholars recognized that their study did not consider domestic political purposes, but concluded that there was no literature by which to evaluate these motives systematically. Id. at 32.

[22] See id. at 80. As noted earlier, the study did not include the U.S. actions against Haiti in 1987–88 and in early 1986, Iran in 1987–8, Panama in 1987–8, or Greece and Lebanon in 1985. See supra note 13. Also, the sanctions against Ethiopia were rated unsuccessful, but the outcome now appears to be successful. See infra text accompanying note 38. The success rate for all 103 cases in the study (from 1914 on) was 36%, very close to the post–1945 rate for the United States. See Hufbauer and Schott, supra note 8, at 80.

nuclear weapons, which became an increasingly important U.S. foreign policy objective in the 1970s.[23]

Economic sanctions have occasionally succeeded in furthering non-proliferation policy. For example, in 1975–6, Canada and the United States threatened financial and export sanctions to persuade South Korea not to buy from France a reprocessing plant that could have been used to make weapons-grade nuclear material.[24] Similarly, the United States delayed some shipments of nuclear power reactors and fuel to Taiwan in 1976–7 in a successful effort to stop the Taiwanese from reprocessing spent fuel.[25] However, U.S. restrictions on the export of nuclear fuel and technology to South Africa, India, Argentina, Brazil, and Pakistan did not persuade those countries to accept full multilateral safeguards, and the restrictions sometimes had serious diplomatic repercussions.[26]

The traditional American belief in *human rights* found renewed expression in congressional initiatives beginning in 1973 and then in strong presidential involvement during the Carter Administration in 1977–80. The congressional actions, detailed later, included inserting provisions in foreign assistance bills calling on the President to deny economic and military aid to countries that engaged in gross violations of internationally recognized human rights. Congress also enacted amendments that denied or reduced assistance to specific countries. In addition to strong public proclamations, the Carter Administration began denying foreign aid on a case-by-case basis to several countries.[27]

All of these activities made human rights a much more important issue on the international agenda. As for specific effects, U.S. reductions in military and economic assistance helped to increase respect for human rights in Brazil in 1977–84.[28] Also, the successful U.S. trade ban of 1978–9 against Uganda was intended to improve human rights there, as well as to destabilize Idi Amin.[29] Nevertheless, in more than ten other cases,

---

[23] The United States signed the Treaty on the Non-Proliferation of Nuclear Weapons in 1968. 21 U.S.T. 483, T.I.A.S. 6839. The Nuclear Non-Proliferation Act was enacted in 1978. See the discussion in Chapter 4, Section B. See generally L. Spector, *The New Nuclear Nations* (1985); *Nonproliferation and U.S. Foreign Policy* (J. Yager ed. 1980).

[24] Canada and the United States did this by tightening their own financial terms on nuclear sales to the South Koreans and by the United States threatening to block entirely some of its sales of nuclear reactors to the South. Hufbauer and Schott, supra note 8, at 505–7.

[25] Id. at 540–3.

[26] See the relevant case studies in id.

[27] See discussion in Chapter 3, Section B.

[28] Hufbauer and Schott, supra note 8, at 579–82.

[29] Id. at 455–60.

the U.S. cutoff of military assistance or other steps apparently had only limited effects.[30]

Combating *international terrorism* has been another of the modest, though increasingly important, goals of the United States in its use of economic sanctions. Starting in the 1960s, terrorism became a serious problem for this country and many others. The United States reacted with a number of measures – for example, increasing security at airports and embassies, assigning more intelligence resources to the problem, and entering into international agreements to combat hijacking and other terrorist acts.

The U.S. government also employed economic sanctions, cutting off various financial assistance programs and imposing some export controls, against countries that were designated as supporting terrorism.[31] It is not clear, however, whether these selective sanctions had much effect in the 1980s on the policies of two of the principal target countries – Syria and Libya.[32]

Sanctions might have had some influence in 1985 on Greece's decision to take steps to limit terrorist activities within its borders. On June 14, Arab terrorists hijacked TWA flight 847 after takeoff from Athens airport. The United States issued a travel advisory on June 19, warning American citizens of the inadequate security at the Athens airport.[33] The publicity surrounding the hijacking and the travel advisory led thousands of tourists to cancel flight reservations to and from the airport. After

---

[30] These include U.S. sanctions against Poland in 1981–4, Bolivia in 1979–82, Argentina from 1977 to 1983, El Salvador in 1977–81, Guatemala from 1977 on, Paraguay in 1977–81, Ethiopia from 1976 on, Uruguay in 1976–81, Kampuchea in 1975–9, Chile from 1973 on, South Korea in 1973–7, and the Soviet Union on several occasions. See the relevant case studies in id.

Some observers have argued that human rights goals were not met partly because the Carter Administration did not try hard enough. For example, Professor Stephen Cohen, a former Deputy Assistant Secretary of State for Human Rights in the Carter Administration, concludes that at least on decisions regarding reductions or cutoffs of security assistance, "the Carter administration exhibited a remarkable degree of tentativeness and caution, so that its pursuit of human rights goals was anything but 'single-minded.'" S. Cohen, "Conditioning U.S. Security Assistance on Human Rights Practices," 76 *Am. J. Int'l L.* 246, 264 (1982).

[31] Useful discussions of international terrorist activities and the steps the United States has taken to combat them include K. Abbott, "Economic Sanctions and International Terrorism," 20 *Vand. J. Transnat'l L.* 289 (1987); *Public Report of the Vice President's Task Force on Combatting Terrorism* (Feb. 1986); J. Murphy, *Punishing International Terrorists: The Legal Framework for Policy Initiatives* (1985). See also the relevant discussion in Chapters 3, 4, 5, and 7.

[32] See, e.g., Hufbauer and Schott, supra note 8, at 453–4, 620–5.

[33] The hijacking followed several months of efforts by the U.S. Government and others to get the Greek government to improve security at the Athens airport.

Greek officials agreed to make major improvements in security, the United States canceled the travel advisory.[34]

Then, in reaction to Libya's apparent support of terrorists who fired on civilians at the Rome and Vienna airports in December 1985, President Reagan tightened the sanctions against Libya by imposing a comprehensive trade embargo and asset freeze.[35] (In April 1986, the United States bombed Libya after receiving further evidence of its support of terrorist activity, including the bombing of a disco in West Berlin frequented by U.S. servicemen.) The results of these measures are still uncertain.

Another modest policy goal of U.S. economic sanctions has been to resolve *expropriation* claims. The United States has long been strongly opposed to other countries' expropriating the properties of U.S. companies unless there is "prompt, adequate, and effective compensation."[36] Employing sanctions in reaction to expropriation is often part of a broader U.S. policy, discussed later, of trying to destabilize the target government. This occurred, for example, with Allende in Chile in 1970–3, Goulart in Brazil in 1962–4, Castro in Cuba from 1960 to the present, and Mossadegh in Iran in 1951–3.

In any event, it appears that the United States has been successful in an impressive eight of its nine uses of sanctions against expropriation. The continuing effort against Cuba is the only unsuccessful case.[37] The

---

[34] *N.Y. Times*, July 23, 1985, at A3, col. 1; see *Newsweek*, July 1, 1985, at 16. Since flight 847 eventually landed in Beirut and the hijackers were not punished, President Reagan also banned flights to and from the United States by Lebanese airlines, as well as flights from or destined for Beirut airport. The announced goal was to get the incapacitated Lebanese Government to turn over the hijackers of the TWA flight and to improve security at the Beirut airport. The Lebanese Government has not turned over the hijackers, though it has apparently increased security measures at the airport. *N.Y. Times*, July 3, 1985, at A12, col. 1. See discussion of the applicable U.S. laws in Chapter 3.

[35] See discussion in Chapter 9, at notes 57–60.

[36] E.g., Statement of President Reagan on International Investment Policy, 19 *Weekly Comp. Pres. Doc.* 1214 (Sept. 13, 1983); Statement of President Nixon Concerning the International Minimum Standard, 8 *Weekly Comp. Pres. Doc.* 64 (Jan. 19, 1972); see 22 U.S.C. § 2370(e)(1); see also P. Trimble, "Foreign Policy Frustrated – Dames & Moore, Claims Court Jurisdiction and a New Raid on the Treasury," 84 *Colum. L. Rev.* 317, 367 nn.220–1 (1984). This policy reflects the traditional U.S. respect for private property, the existence of the constitutional standard of just compensation for public takings in the United States, and the fact that many U.S. companies and individuals have substantial foreign investments.

[37] In addition to the Ethiopian and Iranian cases discussed next, the successful cases are Chile in 1970–3, Peru in 1968–74, Brazil in 1962–4, Ceylon in 1961–5, Egypt in 1956 (joined by the United Kingdom and France), and Iran in 1951–3. Hufbauer and Schott, supra note 8. Note that Hufbauer and Schott rated the Ethiopian case unsuccessful at the time their book went to press in 1984. Id. at 548.

most recent success seems to be that against Ethiopia. Ethiopian expropriation of U.S. business interests triggered sanctions starting in 1976. After little progress was made initially, the United States signed an agreement with Ethiopia in December 1985 in which Ethiopia provided $7 million in settlement for all claims by U.S. nationals.[38]

Although most observers rate them a success, the role of U.S. sanctions against Iran during 1979–81 in resolving an expropriation dispute and in obtaining the release of the American hostages remains uncertain. The comprehensive sanctions, including the freeze of about $12 billion in Iranian assets, presumably had some influence, particularly since Iran was attacked by Iraq and was in need of money and spare parts. It is not yet clear, however, what finally led Ayatollah Khomeini to come to terms with the United States.[39]

b. Destabilizing governments. The United States has enjoyed frequent success in its use of sanctions to destabilize foreign governments.[40] The U.S. suspension of $26 million in foreign assistance, as well as its diplomatic maneuvers, apparently contributed to Duvalier's downfall in Haiti in February 1986.[41]

Other successful efforts include the toppling of Uganda's Idi Amin in 1979, Chile's Allende in 1973, and the Dominican Republic's Trujillo in 1961. Indeed, it would appear that, in the fifteen cases in which the United States has applied economic sanctions since 1945, it has been successful in ten episodes and unsuccessful in two. Three cases – against Panama, Libya, and Nicaragua – continue.[42]

[38] The Compensation Agreement and related documents are reproduced at 25 *Int'l Legal Materials* 56 (1986). For a history of the episode, see *Kalamazoo Spice Extraction Co. v. Provisional Military Government of Socialist Ethiopia*, 616 F. Supp. 660 (W.D. Mich 1985); Hufbauer and Schott, supra note 8, at 544–9.

[39] See R. Carswell and R. Davis, "Crafting the Financial Settlement," in *American Hostages in Iran* 232 (P. Kreisberg ed. 1985); see also H. Saunders, "Beginning of the End," in id. at 290–2. Hufbauer and Schott rated the Iranian sanctions a success, giving them a score of 3 on a scale of 1 (none) to 4 (significant) that measured their contribution to the policy result. Id. at 635.

[40] Other measures, such as covert action and military operations, have usually accompanied the use of such sanctions.

[41] *N.Y. Times*, Feb. 27, 1986, at A3, col. 1. See Chapter 3, "Abuse of human rights" at note 47.

[42] The other six successful efforts were Somoza in Nicaragua in 1979, Ian Smith in Rhodesia in 1979, Goulart in Brazil in 1964, Diem in South Vietnam in 1963, Prince Souvanna Phouma and General Phoumi in Laos in 1960–2, and Mossadegh in Iran in 1951–3. The two failures were Sukarno in Indonesia in 1963–6 and Castro in Cuba from 1960 on. Hufbauer and Schott, supra note 8, at 6, 43–4, 50–3, and the relevant case studies.

Note that Hufbauer and Schott did not include the U.S. effort against General Noriega of Panama or the Duvalier episode in Haiti since their study was completed

The history and effectiveness of sanctions

The study of U.S. successes and uses of sanctions by other countries leads to the further conclusion that sanctions having an immediate impact are the most effective. It also helps to target a country that is much smaller than the sender country. Moreover, a government that is already plagued by significant economic problems and political turmoil is more easily destabilized than other governments.[43]

c. Disrupting military "adventures." Since 1945, the United States has resorted to imposing sanctions ten times to disrupt military adventures.[44] Notable successes include U.S. opposition to the expansionist policies of Egypt's Nasser in Yemen and the Congo in 1963–5, as well as the U.S. opposition to the British–French invasion of Egypt in 1956.

Overall, the use of U.S. sanctions since 1945 to disrupt military adventures has succeeded three times and failed six times, with one close case.[45] Generally, since the goal is clear-cut, the episode is either a definite success or an obvious failure.[46] In all three successful cases, the target country was either an ally (England, France, Netherlands) or a neutral country (Egypt) before the sanctions were imposed. Failures were often marked by prior hostile relations, such as with the Soviet Union or China.[47]

d. Impairing the military potential of the target country. Almost all economic sanctions are intended in some general sense to weaken the

---

before the events. They did identify another case – in which the United States applied sanctions against Argentina starting in 1944. This took place during World War II and so is not counted here. Id. at 171–89. Also, these two scholars count the sanctions of the Organization of Eastern Caribbean States against Grenada as including the United States. However, the sanctions were in effect for only a few days before the military invasion of Grenada in October 1983, and it is unclear what economic sanctions the United States actually applied. As a result, this book does not count the Grenada episode as one involving U.S. economic sanctions. Id. at 749.

[43] Id. at 86, 83, 44.

[44] These are defined as military actions on a smaller scale than the two world wars.

[45] In addition to the two successes involving Egypt, the United States deterred the Netherlands in 1948–9 from forcibly resisting Indonesian independence. The failures include U.S. sanctions against the Soviet Union over its invasion of Afghanistan in 1980–1, against Kampuchea in 1975–9 to deter Vietnamese expansionism, against Turkey over Cyprus in 1974–8, against India and Pakistan over Bangladesh in 1971, against Cuba for its expansionist policies starting in 1960s, and against China from 1949–70 for extending its control over the mainland and for invading Korea. The "close case" involved U.S. reductions in aid to Indonesia and other threatened sanctions during 1963–6 to discourage Sukarno's support for rebel forces in Malaysia. Although Indonesia finally withdrew its support, the U.S. sanctions did not play a decisive role. Id. at 44–5, 52–3, 81, and relevant case studies.

[46] Accompanying measures such as covert operations and military action generally are not decisive in determining success or failure. Also, the presence of international cooperation was not usually determinative. Id. at 45.

[47] Id.

target country. However, a distinction can be made between those sanctions with political goals, like combating proliferation or destabilizing a government, and sanctions that are meant to limit the long-term military potential of the target country.[48]

The latter usually involve competition between major countries.[49] Since 1945, often with various allies, the United States has used sanctions six times with the primary purpose of impairing an opponent's military potential. The principal use has been the continuing controls that the United States and its CoCom[50] allies have imposed since 1948 on the export of strategic materials (including high-technology products) to the Soviet Union and its East European allies.[51]

Responsible analyses and opinion differ about the effectiveness of these sanctions against the Soviets. To begin with, there are significant differences over the estimated dollar costs of these sanctions to the Soviet Union and to the United States.

As for the cost to the Soviets, Hufbauer and Schott apparently estimate that the annual cost of the U.S. and allied controls on high-tech trade has been less than $1.7 billion per year in recent years.[52] Other studies

[48] This distinction is similar to the one between national security controls and foreign policy controls written into the recent Export Administration Acts, discussed in Chapter 4, Section A.

[49] This competition often occurs during war or when war is threatened. For example, the United States and its allies employed sanctions during World Wars I and II, with positive results. See earlier discussion, in Chapter 2, Section A.

[50] CoCom is the abbreviation for the Consultative Group and Coordinating Committee for Multilateral Export Controls, which was created secretly in 1949. It now consists of sixteen countries, the fifteen NATO countries (not including Spain and Iceland) and Japan. See discussion in Chapter 4, Section A.1, on exports.

[51] Other uses include similar export controls against China since 1949; a trade embargo against North Korea since 1950; export limits, then a complete trade and financial boycott, against North Vietnam starting in 1954; and increased export controls on high-tech goods and other sanctions against the Soviet Union over Afghanistan in 1980 and then over Poland in 1981. Hufbauer and Schott, supra note 8, at 45, 54–5, 68, 80, and relevant case studies.

Hufbauer and Schott conclude that these uses of economic sanctions have been "distinctly unsuccessful." Id. at 68. This conclusion, at least with regard to the high-tech sanctions, seems to demonstrate some of the limits of any empirical study on the effectiveness of sanctions. See generally Baldwin, supra note 19, at 235–51.

[52] This even includes the additional controls in response to Afghanistan and Poland. The last figure Hufbauer and Schott provide for the cost to the Soviets of the general CoCom controls against the Soviet Union and East Europe is an annual average of $1.19 billion for the period 1970–81. Hufbauer and Schott, supra note 8, at 218. They also estimate that the additional U.S. high-tech controls imposed because of Afghanistan cost the Soviets $24 million per year. Id. at 663. Finally, they estimate the annual cost of the Polish sanctions on the Soviets at $480 million. Id. at 708.

For their methodology of estimating the cost of sanctions, see id. at 60–1, 103–6. The study concedes that it "tried to err on the side of overestimating the economic impact of sanctions on target countries." Id. at 63.

have taken different analytical approaches.[53] A 1986 Pentagon study estimates that the denial of Western technology to the Soviet Union would cost the Soviet military between \$4.6 billion and \$12 billion during 1986–96.[54]

With respect to the cost to the United States, the sender country, Hufbauer and Schott did not try to "calculate the actual costs of sanctions to sender countries." [55] Instead, they generalized that sanctions intended to impair military potential "invariably" impose a "significant economic burden" on the sender.[56] In contrast, the 1986 Pentagon study found that the denial of high-tech exports *benefited* the United States and its allies by reducing defense expenditures that would be needed to counter Soviet developments. The savings were estimated to be \$5 billion to \$13.2 billion for 1986–96.[57]

Both the Pentagon and Hufbauer–Schott studies gave little weight to two other potentially important considerations. First, as several other experts have emphasized, at some point strict export controls on high technology can have a chilling effect on innovation and the flow of ideas in this country. Second, even if the Soviets obtain access to more technology, other impediments there restrict the full use of this technology. The Soviets, for example, have sometimes failed to make the necessary internal management reforms.[58]

---

[53] For a careful recent study of U.S. export controls for national security reasons, including an expert's cost calculations, see National Academy of Sciences Panel on the Impact of National Security Controls on International Technology Transfer, *Balancing the National Interest* (1987). See also U.S. Department of Defense, *The Technology Security Program* (1986).

Recent developments have reinforced questions about the effectiveness of the CoCom controls. Most prominent have been the large sales of propeller-milling equipment to the Soviet Union by Toshiba Corporation of Japan and Kongsberg Vaapenfabrikk of Norway. American officials have said that the propellers produced by this high-technology equipment have allowed Soviet submarines to run more quietly, and thereby make detection more difficult. Companies in other Western countries were apparently involved in these and other high-technology sales to the Soviets. See, e.g., 4 *Int'l Trade Rep. (BNA)* 1317 (Oct. 28, 1987), *N.Y. Times*, Oct. 22, 1987, at D2, col. 5.

[54] U.S. Department of Defense, supra note 53, at 11, 18.

[55] Hufbauer and Schott, supra note 8, at 38. "Instead, we have drawn from the case abstracts a rough sense of the trade or financial loss incurred by the sender...." Id.

[56] Id. at 68. More specifically, the study estimated the costs at 3 on a scale of 1 (net gain) to 4 (major loss). Id. at 219, 665, 711.

[57] U.S. Department of Defense, supra note 53, at 11, 18.

[58] Scholarly articles and intellectual interchange at conferences and other meetings between U.S. experts and foreigners can generate new developments, yet such sharing of ideas could well be limited by strict controls. E.g., R. Schmitt, "Export Controls: Balancing Technological Innovation and National Security," *Issues in Science and Technology* 117 (Fall 1984); National Academy of Sciences, *Scientific Communication*

On balance, putting aside the specific issue of whether the high-tech controls are "successful," they do impose some costs on the Soviet Union and likely reduce demands on U.S. defense spending. Moreover, U.S. concerns about the Soviet military threat ensure that U.S. policy will require these controls, or at least some variant of them, for the near future.[59]

e. Other major policy changes. This last catchall category encompasses sanction cases seeking major changes other than destabilization of a government or the impairment of military potential.

The United States was the lead sender country in only three cases: against Poland in 1981–4, in order to end martial law and obtain a number of internal reforms; against the Arab League since 1965 for its boycott against Israel; and occasionally against Israel since 1956, in order to change its policies.[60] In addition, the United States has participated in the UN sanctions against South Africa. Indeed, as detailed later, the United States has imposed controls that are broader than the UN sanctions. President Reagan substantially expanded these controls in September 1985, and then Congress passed even more comprehensive sanctions in October 1986.

and National Security 41 (1982); see Office of Technology Assessment, *Technology and East–West Trade: An Update* 75–84 (1985).

As for Soviet problems, see T. Gustafson, *Selling the Russians the Rope? Soviet Technology Policy and U.S. Export Controls* vi, 71–3 (1981).

[59] There are considerable pressures, though, for some lessening of U.S. export controls on high-technology goods, as exemplified by the 1987 report of the National Academy of Sciences Panel, supra note 53. See also 4 *Int'l Trade Rep. (BNA)* 127 (Feb. 4, 1987); *N.Y. Times*, Jan. 14, 1987, at D1, col. 3. Controls on the export of oil and gas equipment to the Soviet Union were relaxed in January 1987. 52 *Fed. Reg.* 2500 (1987). Other controls, including those on personal computers, were relaxed in January 1988. 53 *Fed. Reg.* 2582 (1988).

What impact the serious and widely reported diversion by Toshiba and Kongsberg, discussed supra note 53, will eventually have on U.S. controls is still uncertain as of May 1988. In December 1987, some new statutory limits were imposed on purchases by the U.S. Department of Defense from Toshiba and Kongsberg and any of their subsidiaries. See 5 *Int'l Trade Rep. (BNA)* 17, 18 (Jan. 6, 1988).

Congress passed a major trade bill in April 1988, the Omnibus Trade and Competitiveness Act of 1988, H.R. 3, 100th Cong., 2d Sess. [hereinafter the April 1988 Trade Bill]. President Reagan, however, vetoed the bill in May. It seems unlikely that Congress will override his veto. Whether some or any of the provisions in the bill will be enacted in other legislation in 1988 is uncertain as of May 1988. The bill vetoed by the President did include several proposed reforms of export controls, including those on high-technology goods. E.g., §§ 2411–33. It also included further sanctions directed at Toshiba and Kongsberg. § 2443.

[60] Hufbauer and Schott, supra note 8, at 29, 46, 54–5, 68, 80, and relevant case studies.

Hufbauer and Schott conclude that all these cases through 1984 were "distinctly unsuccessful."[61] This conclusion further demonstrates some of the limitations of their success standard and of many other measures of "success." Although none of these sanction cases has yet contributed significantly to a positive policy outcome, each has been important for other reasons.

In the case of South Africa, for example, the sanctions have made that country pay an economic price for its apartheid policies and refusal to give independence to Namibia. It is estimated that even the pre-1985 sanctions cost South Africa more than $270 million per year, or about 2.8 percent of its gross national product.[62] More recently, South Africa has encountered serious financial problems as a result of credit restrictions that were first imposed by private banks and then by the U.S. and other governments. Moreover, the UN and U.S. sanctions provide the entire world, including the people of South Africa, with an important symbol of opposition to that country's policies. The debate over these sanctions also serves to educate the American public about apartheid, and thus generates greater opposition to it.[63]

Similarly, U.S. antiboycott legislation is an important symbol of U.S. support for the state of Israel and opposition to religious and ethnic discrimination. Also, it has apparently led some Arab countries to be less energetic in their use of the boycott.[64]

f. Overall. Economic sanctions since the end of World War II have often been "successful." As noted earlier, the United States experienced a success rate of about 37 percent for Hufbauer and Schott's sixty-two cases since 1945.[65]

The success rate, however, varies by the type of goal sought. Taking recent developments into account, U.S. sanctions for destabilization purposes succeeded in ten of fifteen cases (or 67 percent, with three cases undecided), and were successful about 40 percent of the time in their use for so-called modest policy goals. In contrast, U.S. sanctions intended to disrupt military adventures, to impair the target country's military potential, or otherwise to effect major changes in its policies were generally unsuccessful.[66]

The U.S. success rate has declined in recent years, notably in the realm of sanctions seeking modest policy results. Target countries are perhaps

[61] Id. at 68.
[62] Id. at 355.
[63] See discussion of South African sanctions in Chapters 3–6.
[64] See discussion of the antiboycott laws in Chapter 8, Section A.
[65] See text supra at note 22.
[66] See Hufbauer and Schott, supra note 8, the prior analysis in this section.

becoming "more immune" because of two factors. First, the recent target countries have been less dependent on trade with the United States. Second, other countries, such as the Soviet Union, have stepped forward more often to assist the target countries.[67]

4. Relative effectiveness of sanctions by type

An analysis of the effectiveness of sanctions must also consider whether certain *types* of sanctions are more effective than others in achieving their objectives. As noted earlier, economic sanctions can include limits on bilateral government programs, exports, imports, private financial transactions, and lending by international financial institutions. Relative effectiveness can, of course, depend on the circumstances in a particular situation.[68]

For example, if the United States were to impose sanctions against South Korea for human rights violations, import controls might be more effective from an economic standpoint than export controls. The United States imports about 39 percent of all of South Korea's foreign sales. In contrast, U.S. exports total about 21 percent of South Korea's foreign purchases (Table 1). Not only does the United States play a larger role as an importer, but the amount and type of its principal imports from South Korea (manufactured articles and clothes) suggest that the Asian country probably cannot easily change long-established business relationships and find willing buyers in other countries. At the same time, South Korea would probably have less trouble and incur fewer additional costs in finding other suppliers for the goods the United States now exports to it, such as machinery, crude materials, and chemical products. These are generally available in world markets.

Even for those countries where the U.S. plays about the same role, in percentage terms, as an exporter or importer, import controls might still be at least as effective as export controls. For example, the United States imports about 40 percent of Guatemala's foreign sales and exports about 40 percent of its purchases. Guatemala, however, might encounter severe problems trying to sell elsewhere at comparable prices the coffee, sugar, bananas, and other vegetables and fruits that constitute its principal sales to the United States. Trade barriers against agricultural products are widespread, and the countries of the European Economic Community

---

[67] Id. at 81.

[68] This analysis ignores for now the legal and diplomatic problems with the General Agreement on Tariffs and Trade, as well as with U.S. laws. See discussion in Chapters 3 and 4.

provide to their former African colonies special treatment on many of these items.

Similarly, the United States imports a large amount of Chile's copper production, an important revenue earner for that country. Chile would probably find it more difficult to change its long-established relationships with U.S. copper purchases than to find new suppliers for the goods it buys from the United States. Thus, U.S. import controls would likely be more effective than export restrictions.

Any analysis of relative effectiveness should also consider the possible contribution of controls on private credit transactions. For example, as Table 1 indicates, U.S. banks now make a large share of the foreign loans to certain countries, such as South Korea (26 percent), Guatemala (33 percent), and Chile (47 percent). Resort to controls on private credit also might be effective, but there are many potential problems, as will be discussed later.[69]

History provides several concrete examples of the effectiveness of controls on imports and private financial transactions. For example, increased U.S. duties on the Dominican Republic's sugar imports in 1961–2 helped topple the Trujillo regime.[70] Threats by the United States to deny most favored nation status to Romania seem to have encouraged it to relax its emigration restrictions until recently.[71]

As for financial controls, the freeze on $12 billion in Iranian deposits in 1979–81 probably had the greatest impact of all the comprehensive economic sanctions.[72] Similarly, the private decisions by several U.S. banks not to roll over South Africa's short-term loans helped create a financial crisis in that country in August–September 1985. The official U.S. sanctions later included a prohibition on new loans to the South African Government and then on new investment in the country. These financial controls have probably created more problems for South Africa than have any of the other sanctions recently imposed by the United States or other countries.[73]

In short, each use of sanctions should be rooted in a careful analysis of the vulnerabilities of the target country. And export controls are not inherently more effective than import controls or financial controls. Indeed, one of the most interesting conclusions of the Hufbauer–Schott study was that "[t]he multiple regression analysis suggests that financial

---

[69] See Chapters 6 and 12.
[70] Hufbauer and Schott, supra note 8, at 302–7.
[71] See Chapter 5, at notes 88–97.
[72] W. Christopher, "Introduction," in *American Hostages in Iran* supra note 39, at 24; R. Carswell and R. Davis, supra note 39, at 231–4.
[73] See discussion in Chapter 6, Section A.

Table 1. *Illustrative potential target countries*

Country	U.S. exports as % of country's imports[a]	Principal U.S. exports[b]	U.S. imports as % of country's exports[a]	Principal U.S. imports[c]	U.S. banks' claims as % of total bank claims[d]
Chile	20	Machinery and transport equipment (MTE), chemicals, manufactured goods	22	Metals, vegetables and fruits	47
Ecuador	32	MTE, chemicals, manufactured goods	50	Oil, coffee, fish	48
Guatemala	40	Chemical products, MTE, oil and gas	40	Coffee, vegetables and fruits, sugar	33
Honduras	45	MTE, manufactured goods, chemical products	48	Sugar, coffee, fish	NA[e]
Mexico	67	MTE, manufactured goods, chemical products	67	Oil, machinery (electronic)	43
Panama	17	MTE, manufactured goods, chemical products	54	Fish, vegetables and fruits, coffee	36
Philippines	25	MTE, food, chemical products	36	Manufactured articles, clothes	17
South Korea	20	MTE, crude materials, chemical products	39	Manufactured articles, clothes	26
Taiwan[f]	24	MTE, crude materials, chemicals	48	Clothing, manufactured articles	24

[a] International Monetary Fund, *Direction of Trade Statistics: Yearbook* (1987). The percentages, rounded to the nearest 1%, are calculated from statistics for 1986, which are based on dollar values.

[b] Bureau of the Census, U.S. Department of Commerce, *U.S. Exports* (Pub. FT455/1986 Dec. and Annual 1986). Data are for 1986; items are ranked in order of dollar value according to the Bureau's categories.

[c] Bureau of the Census, U.S. Department of Commerce, *U.S. General Imports* (Pub. FT155/1986 Dec. and Annual 1986). Data are for 1986; items are ranked in order of dollar value according to the Bureau's categories.

[d] These percentages for the end of June 1986 were obtained by analyzing published data for total external bank claims and total U.S. bank claims for each country (including both public and private creditors). Country totals were taken from Bank for International Settlements and Organisation for Economic Co-operation and Development, *Statistics on External Indebtedness: Bank and Trade-Related Non-Bank External Claims on Individual Borrowing Countries and Territories at End-June 1986*, Table I at 5–8 (Jan. 1987). U.S. bank claims are from Office of the Secretary, U.S. Department of Treasury, *Treasury Bulletin* (Summer 1986). The data do not include lending from international financial institutions, such as the World Bank.

[e] NA, not applicable.

[f] The 1985 trade figures for Taiwan, rounded to the nearest 1%, are from Council for Economic Planning and Development, Republic of China, *Taiwan Statistical Data Book* 214, 216 (1986).

controls are marginally more successful than export controls, but that import controls are the most successful of all types."[74]

That study regrettably lumped into the general catchall phrase of "financial controls" three of this book's categories of sanctions – U.S. government programs, private financial transactions, and international financial institutions. As detailed later, the U.S. laws for these three categories vary greatly.[75]

In any case, the relative effectiveness of import controls and at least some financial controls suggests that these potential sanctions should be available for use if the circumstances warrant it. Under present U.S. laws, however, export controls are usually much easier to impose than import controls or restraints on private financial transactions, thus skewing the President's options in selecting the most effective sanctions.

5. Costs to the sender country

Apart from measuring the effectiveness of economic sanctions against the target country, it is important to recognize that economic sanctions usually involve some costs to the sender country. The type and amount of costs depend, of course, on the situation and the type of sanctions imposed.

Myriad costs might be involved. Many stem from the indirect effects of sanctions, such as the loss of sales by a supplier when the manufacturer is prevented from making an export sale to a target country. Other costs result from long-term changes in business patterns, which often occur when the target country seeks to minimize the financial effects of future sanctions. An example is the Soviet Union reducing its dependence on U.S. grain supplies by contracting with other foreign suppliers.

These domestic costs of sanctions are rarely calculated in any detail or with much reliability. The cost calculations might not be important to the U.S. policy maker, particularly when the United States is imposing sanctions against a country with a much smaller economy, like Nicaragua. Moreover, there may be considerable incentives for the government *not* to calculate domestic costs. Careful estimates might highlight those costs and exacerbate the government's political problems with domestic constituencies hurt by the sanctions, such as farmers faced with export controls.

At the risk of oversimplification, however, a few general observations

---

[74] Id. at 89. This conclusion applied to all the study's 103 cases. However, it would appear to apply equally well to the 62 cases of U.S. economic sanctions since 1945.
[75] The study's approach reflects the fact that it did not delve into the U.S. laws. In the study's summary chapters, U.S. laws are discussed only twice, and then very briefly. Id. at 28, 59–60.

about the cost of sanctions seem possible. First, terminating or reducing government bilateral programs, such as foreign assistance, can initially *save* the United States money. Such measures may, however, entail indirect costs, such as lost sales to U.S. companies. Foreign recipients of U.S. assistance programs often spend a substantial amount of these funds on U.S. goods and services, sometimes because U.S. laws or regulations require them to do so.

Second, restrictions on imports and private financial transactions might often cost less than export controls, though all these sanctions have their domestic costs. Export sanctions directly cause lost sales for U.S. businesses and lost jobs for employees. The immediate impact might be reduced if other customers are found, but complete substitutability is not ensured, and the alternative sales would presumably be made on less favorable terms (or they would have occurred before the controls were imposed). Export restrictions also create long-term problems for U.S. sales abroad, since they jeopardize the reputation of U.S. businesses as reliable suppliers. Foreign purchasers are tempted to prefer non-U.S. suppliers out of a concern over future U.S. resort to export controls.

As a dramatic example of this, the Caterpillar Tractor Company lost sales and markets as a result of the on-again, off-again restrictions on sales of oil and gas equipment to the Soviet Union. In 1978, the company had 85 percent of the Soviet market for pipelayers, tractors, and special hoists for laying pipelines. Those sales helped Caterpillar dominate the world market. Its exports totaled between $50 million and $100 million per year. After the 1982 export sanctions over the Yamal pipeline, Caterpillar's share of the Soviet market dropped to 15 percent and the share of its principal competitor, Japan's Komatsu, rose to 85 percent. That business apparently helped Komatsu challenge Caterpillar in the world market.[76]

Similarly, the U.S. agricultural embargo against the Soviet Union in 1980 hurt the export sales of U.S. farmers. A careful study concluded that the U.S. share of the world market for grains and soybean products

---

[76] See 130 *Cong. Rec.* S1712 (daily ed. Feb. 27, 1984) (statement of Sen. Danforth); also see Subcommittee on Europe and the Middle East of the House Committee on Foreign Affairs, 97th Cong., 1st Sess., *An Assessment of the Afghanistan Sanctions: Implications for Trade Diplomacy in the 1980's* 72 (Comm. Print 1981) (report prepared by the Congressional Reference Service) [hereinafter House Afghanistan Report]. It should be noted that other factors were also at play here in Caterpillar's declining fortunes, such as the then increasing value of the U.S. dollar.

Dresser Industries has experienced at least as much buffeting. Their exports to the Soviet Union were hampered by a series of controls from 1978 to 1982 – first over dissidents, then Afghanistan, and then the Yamal pipeline. See House Afghanistan Report, supra, at 72–3 (for 1978–80 period), as well as the discussion of the 1982 pipeline sanctions in Chapter 4, Section A.6.

declined as consuming countries expanded their sources of supply and U.S. competitors expanded their production and their exports. In particular, the U.S. share of the Soviet Union's imports of wheat and coarse grain declined sharply from 74 percent in the 1978–9 crop year to 19 percent in 1982–3. The Soviets not only increased imports from Canada, Argentina, and Brazil, but entered into new five-year agreements with them.[77]

Import controls generally involve smaller costs. Since new foreign policy sanctions are usually applied against only one country or a few countries, alternative foreign suppliers frequently exist. As a result, the U.S. purchaser does not have to do without a good, but only faces the increased costs that must be paid to a higher-priced supplier.[78] Although this might mean that the U.S. purchaser has to raise its prices and thus lose some sales of its own product, the cost differences are so small that the resulting losses are marginal.

Moreover, especially if its competitors also have to turn to higher-priced sources of supply, the initial U.S. purchaser should be able to pass on much of the added costs to its customers by raising its own prices. While these customers will then bear some of the costs, their individual burden will probably be a small share of the total domestic costs of import sanctions, because the costs may be spread among many purchasers at different levels of the distribution process.[79]

---

[77] International Trade Commission, *U.S. Embargoes on Agricultural Exports: Implications for U.S. Agricultural Industry and U.S. Exports*, Pub. No. 1461 (Dec. 1983); see House Afghanistan Report, supra note 76, at 47–52. See generally U.S. Department of Agriculture, *Embargoes, Surplus Disposal, and U.S. Agriculture* (1986) (an extensive study on the impact of embargoes).

Since farmers in the United States rely heavily on export sales, the decline in their overseas market contributed to the plight of U.S. agriculture. International Trade Commission, supra, at viii–xi; see Bureau of Economic Analysis, U.S. Department of Commerce, 67 *Survey of Current Business* S-17 (Sept. 1987); 66 id. at S-17 (May 1986) (indicating that U.S. exports of agricultural products declined from $37.8 billion in 1984 to $29.2 billion in 1985 to $26.1 billion in 1986).

[78] Some U.S. suppliers might even benefit from import controls that lead U.S. purchasers to switch to domestic suppliers because a foreign competitor has been blocked out. Of course, while the U.S. supplier will gain sales, the U.S. purchasers will probably be paying a higher price.

[79] It should be noted that import controls can be expensive for domestic consumers. An example is the so-called voluntary restraints by the Japanese on the number of their automobiles imported into the United States. The number has been limited to 2.3 million cars per year from 1985 through March 1989. A study by Robert Crandall of the Brookings Institution estimated that the auto restraints cost the American consumer $26.6 billion in 1985, adding $2,500 to the price of a Japanese car and $1,000 to a U.S. car. *Wash. Post*, Feb. 13, 1986, at 1, col. 1. American automobile manufacturers obviously benefited. They enjoyed larger sales and were able to charge higher prices. As discussed earlier and in Chapter 12, however, import sanctions for

For example, the cost of the cutoff of Iranian oil imports in 1979 and of most Libyan oil in 1982 had only minimal impact on the supplies or price of oil in the United States. Similarly, the 1983 cutback of the Nicaraguan sugar quota was easily offset by increased imports from other countries at no increased price to U.S. consumers.

A more indirect, but potentially significant cost of import controls is the impact on the world trading system, and on GATT in particular. As discussed later, this *is* a problem, though steps can be taken to minimize it.[80]

Controls on private financial transactions also entail costs. The type and amount often hinge on the type of financial control – whether it be on trade financing (for either exports or imports), on general extensions of credit (e.g., large loans to a government), or on foreign deposits or other property in the possession of U.S. entities. Given the complexities of these controls, the potential costs can best be discussed later when alternative proposals to govern their use are considered.[81]

Economic sanctions, then, are often effective. Moreover, controls on imports and private financial transactions might in some cases be more effective than export controls and impose fewer costs on the United States. Yet as the following chapters demonstrate, the present U.S. legal system is decidedly not structured to facilitate the President's use of these various types of sanctions according to their relative effectiveness and cost.

foreign policy purposes would usually be against smaller trading partners and where there are major alternative foreign suppliers.

[80] See discussion in Chapter 5, Section C, and Chapter 12, Section C.2.

[81] See Chapter 12, Section C.3. For more extensive discussion of the costs of sanctions to the sender country, see, e.g., Losman, supra note 11, at 7–19; Hufbauer and Schott, supra note 8, at 64–9.

3

Nonemergency laws: an overview and bilateral government programs

In the absence of a national emergency, a wide variety of U.S. laws authorize or require the President to impose economic sanctions for foreign policy reasons. These laws can be divided into five categories: limits on (1) U.S. government programs, such as foreign assistance and landing rights; (2) exports from the United States; (3) imports; (4) private financial transactions; and (5) international financial institutions.

The order of these categories roughly reflects the relative degree of authority the President has to impose sanctions under present U.S. laws. Generally, he has the most control over the Government's own programs, and he has broad discretion to cut off almost all exports. It is much more difficult, however, for the President to limit imports. Moreover, the U.S. Government usually has little legal control over the foreign lending decisions of private U.S. banks, and even less control over international financial institutions.

A. AN OVERVIEW OF THE NONEMERGENCY LAWS

The differences in the President's authority are striking (see Chart 1).[1] For *bilateral government programs*,[2] the President has almost complete discretion to apply sanctions. He can restrict or eliminate a foreign country's fishing rights, port access, and aircraft landing rights, and he can discourage Americans from traveling to that country with travel advisories and passport restrictions. He can also limit low-interest credit, loan guarantees, and special insurance from the Export–Import Bank (Eximbank), Overseas Private Investment Corporation, and Commodity Credit Corporation. As for foreign assistance, either he can decide not to request funds for a country or he might be able to suspend payments.

[1] These differences are also analyzed in detail in Chapters 3–8.
[2] See first column, Chart 1, and Section B, this chapter.

U.S. government programs

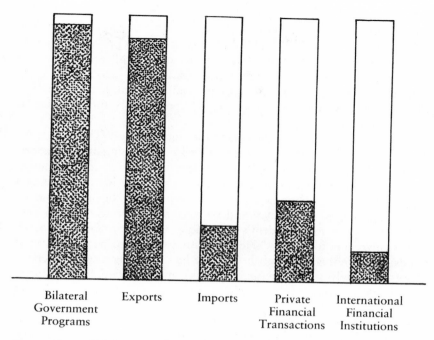

Chart 1. Present U.S. laws: presidential discretion in the absence of a national emergency. This chart highlights visually the variations in the President's authority. Each column represents one type of activity. The *enclosed area of each column* represents all possible transactions for a given activity. For example, the second column represents all U.S. exports. The *shaded area of each column* represents a crude estimate of the percentage of the dollar value the President has discretion to terminate or otherwise limit. For example, given the President's great discretion over exports, almost all of the second column is shaded. In contrast, very little of the import column is shaded because of the President's sparse authority. Note that this chart is meant to be a rough approximation of the President's authority. The first column, for example, includes a wide variety of government programs, and assigning values to them is a very imprecise process.

Minor limits exist on the President's discretion here. Congress could mandate expenditures that the President does not want to make, or it could impose sanctions that he does not request. Most significantly, Congress has the power of the purse, and it can simply not authorize the funds the President seeks. However, in recent years, Congress has generally gone along with the President's aid requests, and usually the President can easily satisfy the conditions that Congress has imposed.[3]

[3] Given the experience with provisions of the foreign assistance act that theoretically limit assistance to countries violating human rights and with the certification requirements for El Salvador in 1981–3, it frankly appears to be very difficult for Congress to use conditions to constrain a determined President. See Sections B.1.a and B.1.b.2.

In the area of *exports*,[4] the President has nearly complete discretion and can stop almost all exports to a particular country or countries. The only significant limitations on his authority are recent provisions that, in very narrow situations, protect the sanctity of existing contracts, compensate existing exporters, and restrict controls on agricultural commodities to sixty days without congressional approval. (As discussed in Chapter 12, it would be wise to extend considerably the coverage of these limitations.)

A sharp shift occurs with *imports* to the United States.[5] The President's discretion is strictly limited. He is confined to exercising an odd assortment of controls – for example, on critical defense materials, on sugar and sometimes beef, on imports from Libya or from other countries that support terrorists or have expropriated U.S. property, or on goods from certain communist countries that deny free emigration to their citizens.

Also limited is the President's discretion over *private financial transactions* involving foreigners.[6] He can restrict the financing of exports of goods or technology, though he already has sweeping powers over the exports themselves. Otherwise, the President has essentially no control over the decisions of banks or other entities to extend credit or transfer funds.

The President has very limited ability to influence any of the *international financial institutions*,[7] such as the World Bank or International Monetary Fund, to impose economic sanctions for U.S. foreign policy reasons. The one exception is the Inter-American Development Bank, where the United States has a considerable voice, including a veto over one small loan fund.

The focus of much of this analysis is the President's existing authority. To begin with, the President effectively controls the entire Executive Branch in deciding to impose economic sanctions for foreign policy purposes. As will be seen, statutes or situations rarely give a federal agency any authority in this area independent of the President. One exception is the International Trade Commission, which on occasion has some independence in deciding whether certain import statutes can be invoked, since its affirmative decisions are a requirement and its members have autonomy because of their long, staggered terms. These import statutes, however, are based on economic criteria and are of little use for foreign policy sanctions.[8]

---

[4] See second column, Chart 1, and Chapter 4.
[5] See third column, Chart 1, and Chapter 5.
[6] See fourth column, Chart 1, and Chapter 6.
[7] See fifth column, Chart 1, and Chapter 7.
[8] See Chapter 5, Section B.5. The President's dominance of the Executive Branch makes sense. Even if one changes the laws, as proposed in Chapter 12, it does not

Congress usually plays a secondary role, essentially one of having passed the basic statutes (such as the export laws) that the President then decides to invoke or not to invoke when a dispute or minor crisis arises. Although the amount of the President's discretion obviously depends on each statute, the discretion given him is usually very broad.

Sometimes Congress is more directly and immediately involved in the decision to impose sanctions. It can limit its authorization of foreign assistance that the President has requested, such as it did for Turkey in 1975–8. It can condition foreign assistance on various criteria (e.g., observance of human rights), but the President has usually been able to find a way to proceed under the statutes as he has wished. Congress now limits the length of export controls on agricultural commodities to sixty days in the absence of a complete export embargo against a country unless Congress approves a longer period by joint resolution, but this is unlikely to affect many sanctions. Moreover, Congress has inserted into a number of laws a variety of consultation and reporting requirements, such as in the 1985 Export Administration Amendments Act, but their incomplete coverage and the exceptions to the provisions enable a determined President to avoid significant constraints.

The *Comprehensive Anti-Apartheid Act of 1986* is a recent and important exception to the secondary role of Congress, as well as to the lack of a comprehensive statutory framework for sanctions. Congress enacted the law in October 1986 over President Reagan's veto, adding one more chapter to the long and tumultuous history of sanctions against South Africa.[9]

The United States first imposed sanctions against South Africa in 1963 with limits on arms sales, partly at the urging of the United Nations. Despite occasional backsliding, the United States increased the type and severity of its sanctions through 1985. Congress was then on the verge of passing major new sanctions, when President Reagan preempted it in September 1985 by declaring a national emergency and invoking his powers under IEEPA. He ordered by regulation most of the sanctions that the legislature was about to pass.[10]

seem advisable to create independent agencies or the like that somehow share authority with the President in this area. The use of economic sanctions for foreign policy purposes seems very much to require a delicate judgment on U.S. objectives, diplomatic considerations, and willingness to bear the costs – the kind of political judgment a President is expected to make, presumably after consulting with his advisers. There are no particularly important technical components in this decision that would argue for requiring quasi-independent expert review.

[9] Pub. L. No. 99-440, 100 Stat. 1086 (codified at 22 U.S.C. §§ 5001–5116 (Supp. IV 1986)) [hereinafter the 1986 Act]. The House of Representatives voted on September 29 to override the veto by 313 to 83, and then the Senate voted 78 to 21 on October 2.

[10] For a discussion of the events surrounding the 1985 use of IEEPA, see Chapter

Congress returned to the subject with the Comprehensive Anti-Apartheid Act of 1986. The statute not only includes several important new measures, but also writes into law most of the sanctions that Reagan had imposed the preceding year. By and large, the statutory provisions are mandatory and precise. The President's discretion is thus considerably confined, though he is still given some flexibility on the details of implementation.

Although its application is limited to South Africa, the 1986 Act takes a relatively comprehensive approach toward the use of sanctions – providing for a variety of controls on bilateral government programs, exports, imports, and private financial transactions.[11] These sanctions will be examined in detail in the appropriate chapters, but it will be useful here to note their broad range.

Among the government programs, the principal provision prohibits the airlines of either South Africa or the United States from taking off or landing in the other country.[12] The Act also codifies a 1985 regulation requiring any U.S. national in South Africa (including U.S.-controlled corporations) to observe the Sullivan Principles, a set of fair employment practices. If the national fails to do so, no U.S. government entity can intercede on behalf of that national "with any foreign government or any national regarding [the U.S. national's] export marketing activities in any country."[13]

9, Sections C and D. For the earlier history, see Chapter 8, Section B (UN Participation Act) and any of a number of histories on the South African sanctions, such as K. Danaher, *The Political Economy of U.S. Policy Toward South Africa* (1985); G. Hufbauer and J. Schott, *Economic Sanctions Reconsidered: History and Current Policy* 347–59 (1985) (with extensive bibliography).

[11] In the continuing resolution for fiscal year 1988, Congress included a new sanction against South Africa – the denial of tax credits to U.S. companies for taxes paid by their subsidiaries in South Africa. The new law prevented the U.S. companies from crediting the taxes paid in South Africa against the companies' tax bills in the United States on a dollar-for-dollar basis, as is generally allowed for taxes paid to other countries. The full impact of this provision is still not clear. *N.Y. Times*, Dec. 25, 1987, at D1, col. 3.

The 1986 Act did not contain any provisions regarding international financial institutions. In 1983, however, Congress had passed and President Reagan reluctantly signed legislation that instructed the U.S. Executive Director of the IMF to oppose actively any IMF funding for any country that practiced apartheid – i.e., South Africa. 22 U.S.C. § 286aa(b) (Supp. IV 1986). See discussion in Chapter 7.

[12] 1986 Act, supra note 9, at § 306.

[13] Id. § 207. These practices, termed the "Code of Conduct," are written into the statute. Incidentally, the provisions regarding bilateral government programs also contained several carrots as well as sanctions. For example, the Act provided $4 million per year for three years in scholarships for "victims of apartheid" (section 201); approved $1.5 million for a human rights fund, including money for "direct legal and other assistance to political detainees and prisoners and their families" (section 202); and directed the U.S. Export–Import Bank to take active steps to extend

The law also adds some export controls. Subject to certain exceptions, the Act prohibits the export of crude oil and petroleum products to all customers in South Africa. And it essentially codifies existing regulations against exporting most nuclear goods or technology, computers, and items on the Munitions List to South African Government agencies.[14]

Even more extensive are the import controls. The Act codifies restrictions that President Reagan had ordered against gold coins, nuclear items, and arms. Moreover, it adds prohibitions against importing uranium, coal, iron, steel, textiles, sugar, and other agricultural products, as well as most items from any South African entity owned, controlled, or subsidized by the South African Government.[15]

Possibly most path breaking are three major restrictions on private financial transactions, since Congress had not often relied much on such measures before. The Act codifies the 1985 regulation against new loans to the South African Government, and it adds an important prohibition against U.S. nationals making "any new investment" in South Africa. It also forbids U.S. banks from holding deposits for the South African Government.[16]

With its wide range of sanctions against South Africa, the 1986 Act demonstrates the possibility of creating a comprehensive statutory framework governing the use of sanctions. The Act, however, is geographically limited to South Africa, provides very little discretion to the President, and required years of effort in Congress and well-publicized events in South Africa to become law.

Other present U.S. nonemergency laws fall decidedly short of a comprehensive approach. The following analysis of these laws illustrates the haphazard nature of the present legal regime that provides the President with greatly varying authority for imposing different types of sanctions. These laws can skew the President's decision making so that he will choose less effective sanctions, or those with greater domestic costs, because they are more easily implemented.

B. BILATERAL GOVERNMENT PROGRAMS

A wide variety of U.S. government programs can be used as economic sanctions for foreign policy purposes. These include bilateral foreign

credit to South African businesses that are majority-owned by South African blacks or other nonwhites (section 204). This last provision amended a prior law that prohibited Eximbank activities in South Africa. 12 U.S.C. § 635(b)(9) (1982).

[14] See Chapter 4, Section D.
[15] See Chapter 5, Section B.1.
[16] See Chapter 6, Section A.

assistance, low-interest credit, loan guarantees, special insurance programs, fishing rights, port access, aircraft landing rights, travel advisories, and passports.[17]

The United States has often restricted more than one of these government programs in a sanction episode. For example, it cut off foreign assistance and low-interest credit to Allende's Chile in 1970–3, and curtailed fishing and landing rights to the Soviet Union after its 1979 invasion of Afghanistan. Moreover, the United States has combined limiting bilateral programs with other types of sanctions, such as controls on exports or imports. As a result, it is hard to measure the impact on the target country of a change in any one of these bilateral government programs.[18]

As detailed in this section, the President usually has nearly unfettered discretion to terminate or curtail bilateral programs. For example, without even consulting Congress, he can stop a target country from receiving Eximbank low-interest loans or can suspend its fishing and landing rights.

Congress can theoretically thwart the President's efforts to use sanctions in some situations. It can oppose his decision not to spend funds that have already been authorized for a specific country, or it can authorize new funds that he does not want.[19] A short-lived example of this

---

[17] This is a potpourri of programs that have the common strain of depending on funding by the U.S. Government, or at least on some critical government approval. Conceivably, some of these programs, such as travel advisories and passports, could be put in the miscellaneous category (discussed in Chapter 8). Exactly how these government programs are categorized, however, does not seem decisive for any of the general conclusions of this book, which focus on exports, imports, and private financial transactions.

[18] Obviously, a target country is more vulnerable to curtailment of these programs if they provide something substantial to the country. Conversely, if the United States is not already giving or allowing something to the target country, there is no leverage in formally taking that benefit away.

[19] In these two situations, the President could decide whether he wanted to rescind or try to defer the authorization. In doing so, he would need to take into account the Budget and Impoundment Control Act of 1974, Pub. L. No. 93–344, 88 Stat. 297 (codified in scattered sections of 1, 2, and 3 U.S.C.).

The Act followed extensive efforts by President Nixon to "impound" authorized funds. For a discussion of the controversy, see, e.g., R. Abascal and J. Kramer, "Presidential Impoundment Part I: Historical Genesis and Constitutional Framework," 62 *Geo. L.J.* 1549 (1974); Abascal and Kramer, "Presidential Impoundment Part II: Judicial and Legislative Responses," 63 *Geo. L.J.* 149, esp. 180–2 (1974) [hereinafter Abascal and Kramer, "Presidential Impoundment Part II"]. See generally T. Franck and C. Bob, "The Return of Humpty-Dumpty: Foreign Relations Law After the Chadha Case," 79 *Am. J. Int'l L.* 913, 944–8 (1985).

The Act imposes major restraints on the President's authority to impound authorized funds. The President may not rescind these funds unless Congress expressly approves the rescision. 2 U.S.C. § 683(b) (1982). Consequently, the President would have to

congressional opposition occurred when Congress appropriated foreign assistance funds for Somoza's Nicaragua in 1977–8 over President Carter's objections.[20]

Political realities make this type of congressional opposition unlikely, however, since the President is presumably proposing sanctions because the target country has done something objectionable to U.S. interests. Even if a majority in Congress were to have a different perspective than the President, there would be considerable pressure not to support some foreign country over the President.

The more likely case is Congress striking out on its own to impose sanctions the President has not requested and might even oppose.[21] This can happen when Congress, for foreign policy or domestic political reasons, becomes more upset about a country's policies than does the Chief Executive. For example, over the objections of President Ford, Congress cut off most military assistance to Turkey in 1975–8 because of its invasion of Cyprus.[22]

seek congressional approval for terminating foreign assistance to a country where Congress had earlier made a specific authorization.

Whether the President can *defer* expenditures is a more difficult question at present. Although the President may defer expenditures to meet contingencies or to achieve greater efficiency in the administration of programs under 31 U.S.C. § 1512 (1982), the Chief Executive may not use this deferral authority to impose his own policy preferences. 31 U.S.C. § 1512(c)(1) (amending the Anti-Deficiency Act, 31 U.S.C. § 665(c)(2) (1970)). See *City of New Haven v. United States*, 809 F. 2d 900, 901 (D.C. Cir. 1987) (distinguishing between policy and programmatic deferrals). See generally Abascal and Kramer, "Presidential Impoundment Part II," supra, at 180 (and sources cited there) (deferrals to meet economic and policy objectives are, in the congressional view, an abuse of impoundment authority).

A separate provision of the 1974 Act allowed policy deferrals subject to the legislative veto by either house of Congress. 2 U.S.C. § 684(b) (1982); 31 U.S.C. § 1513 (1982). However, the Court of Appeals for the D.C. Circuit reasoned that the legislative veto was void in light of *Immigration and Naturalization Serv. v. Chadha*, 462 U.S. 919 (1983). *City of New Haven*, 809 F.2d at 905. It then concluded that the veto provisions could not be severed from the deferral mechanism because Congress would not have given the President such unchecked deferral powers. Id. at 909. Although the mechanism for policy deferrals was therefore held invalid, the court expressly indicated that programmatic deferrals under 31 U.S.C. § 1512 were not affected by its ruling. Id.

[20] Hufbauer and Schott, supra note 10, at 568–9.

[21] There is the potential problem of the President not faithfully following the laws, if only temporarily. This happened with laws restricting U.S. funding and military involvement in the closing days of the Vietnam War. Franck and Bob, supra note 19, at 944–8; T. Franck and E. Weisband, *Foreign Policy by Congress* 30–33 (1979). More recently, serious questions have been raised about White House adherence to the Boland amendment, which restricted the use of covert funds for the Nicaraguan contras. See *Report of the Congressional Committees Investigating the Iran–Contra Affair*, H. Rept. 433, 100th Cong., 1st Sess. 395-407; but see id. at 489–500 (minority views).

[22] Franck and Weisband, supra note 21, at 34–45. See also the Angola case, discussed in Section B.1.a, this chapter.

As the preceding examples suggest, the President's discretion to use bilateral government programs as sanctions has been most limited in the area of foreign assistance programs.[23] Even here, however, his discretion has been considerable. Indeed, Congress has authorized the President to furnish up to $50 million in foreign aid to a country without regard to the foreign assistance laws, if the President determines "that to do so is important to the security interests of the United States" and if he consults appropriate congressional committees in advance.[24] Congress added even more discretion in the continuing resolution for fiscal year 1987, which empowered the President not to spend the funds authorized for a country if he finds that it "is engaged in a consistent pattern of opposition to the foreign policy of the United States."[25]

1. No aid for you: bilateral foreign assistance

In addition to their humanitarian purposes, U.S. bilateral foreign assistance programs have a long history of use as a foreign policy tool. Increases in assistance have often been utilized as the proverbial carrot, and reductions or cutoffs as a stick (i.e., sanction).[26] Restricting foreign assistance as a sanction is evident in the 1985 foreign assistance act, which authorized $12.8 billion in annual spending on programs in fiscal years 1986 and 1987. It contained numerous legislative provisions identifying the recipients and the conditions for giving aid.[27]

---

[23] For an analysis of the President's authority over foreign assistance programs, with conclusions that his discretion is and should be extensive, see D. Wallace, "The President's Exclusive Foreign Affairs Power Over Foreign Aid: Part I," 1970 *Duke, L.J.* 293 and "Part II," 1970 *Duke L.J.* 453. For a different viewpoint, see L. Henkin, *Foreign Affairs and the Constitution* 109–10 (1972).

[24] 22 U.S.C. § 2364 (Supp. III 1985). The ceiling of $50 million is higher if the "country is a victim of active Communist or Communist-supported aggression." Id. The consultation with Congress, including "a written policy justification," takes place with the Foreign Affairs and Appropriations Committees in both the House and Senate. See, e.g., 46 *Fed. Reg.* 27,623 (1981) (furnishing $25 million to Liberia under this provision).

[25] Act of Oct. 30, 1986, Pub. L. No. 99-591, §§ 101(f), 528(b), 100 Stat. 334.

[26] See generally M. Armacost, *Foreign Assistance and the U.S. National Interest,* Dept. of State Current Policy No. 739 (Sept. 11, 1985).

[27] International Security and Development Cooperation Act of 1985, Pub. L. No. 99-83, 99 Stat. 190 (codified at 22 U.S.C. §§ 2251, et seq.) [hereinafter the 1985 foreign assistance act or 1985 act]. This was the first foreign aid authorization bill to pass Congress in four years. Since 1981, the legislation had been caught up in foreign policy disputes between the Senate and House of Representatives. The foreign aid programs had to be funded by stopgap spending bills that Congress hurried through at the beginning of each fiscal year. *Wash. Post,* Aug. 1, 1985, at A8, col. 1. Congress reverted to old habits in 1986 and 1987 when foreign aid was again part of the last-minute funding bills for many government programs for FY 1987 and FY 1988.

In the 1985 act, Congress authorized about $270 million of the $12.8 billion for

Since World War II, U.S. bilateral foreign assistance programs have essentially been of two types: economic and military. In the 1985 act, the largest economic assistance programs included development assistance to help countries establish the basic conditions for economic development; PL 480 funds for food assistance and balance-of-payments support; and the economic support fund, which primarily provides additional economic help to Israel and Egypt. The largest military assistance programs were credits for foreign military sales and grants for the military assistance program.[28]

These programs are employed as sanctions in two general ways. First, aid to a specific country is cut off or reduced. Second, the legislation contains policy (or issue) prohibitions that terminate aid if certain events occur, such as a recipient country expropriating U.S. property or harboring international terrorists. These policy prohibitions frequently make continued assistance contingent upon a presidential certification that a condition does or does not exist.

a. Country-specific reductions. Terminating or reducing foreign aid to a target country is frequently one of the first sanctions the United States imposes. It does this either by simply not appropriating any more funds

voluntary contributions to a variety of "international organizations and programs," such as the UN Development Program (59.65%), the UN Children's Fund (19.3%), the International Atomic Energy Agency (7.2%), and the development assistance programs of the Organization of American States (5.44%). Sec. 402, 22 U.S.C. § 2222 (Supp. III 1985). The United States generally has very little control over how and where these entities spend their funds. Given the relatively small size of this funding and the great number of such entities, this book does not address these programs further. (The discussion in Chapter 7 on assistance to the international financial institutions focuses on the IMF, World Bank, and the regional development banks.)

In addition to foreign assistance programs, the 1985 act included a number of provisions that dealt with a miscellany of foreign policy issues. For example, as discussed in Section B.2 of Chapter 5, section 504 (22 U.S.C. § 2349 aa-8) authorized the President to prohibit almost all exports to *and* imports from Libya.

[28] For an overview of the U.S. programs, see *Foreign Assistance Program: FY 1986 Budget and 1985 Supplemental Request* (May 1985), Dept. of State, Bureau of Public Affairs. For exact details on funding for FY 1986, see the 1985 act, supra note 27, and the Conference Report, H.R. Rep. No. 237, 99th Cong., 1st Sess. 106–7 (1985). As in recent years, the largest recipients of foreign assistance were Israel and Egypt. The act provided $3 billion per year to Israel and $2.1 billion to Egypt. Israel also received $1.5 billion in emergency economic assistance and Egypt $500 million. *Wash. Post*, Aug. 1, 1985, at A8, col. 1.

In the 1986 continuing legislation, Congress cut back Administration requests, but still approved $13.4 billion for FY 1987. Congress earmarked sums for certain countries, such as Israel, Egypt, Cyprus, and the Philippines. Israel was guaranteed $3 billion in military and economic grants and Egypt $2.3 billion. *Wash. Post*, Oct. 17, 1986, at A21, col. 4.

for that country or by explicitly prohibiting funding in the foreign aid legislation.[29]

Cutbacks in foreign assistance have had a major, positive impact in some cases. For example, they were helpful in the generally successful U.S. efforts against Peru in 1968–74 over expropriation of U.S. investments there,[30] and against Brazil in 1962–4 in efforts to resolve expropriation disputes and to destabilize the Goulart Government.[31] With Nicaragua in 1977–9, cutbacks in economic assistance and suspension of military assistance were major U.S. tools in initially protesting the human rights policies of the Somoza Government and then helping to oust Somoza.[32]

---

[29] E.g., 22 U.S.C. § 2370 (1982) (prohibiting assistance to the present government of Cuba). A unique case is the cutoff of aid to Zimbabwe in 1986. The U.S. Department of State announced that no new economic assistance, which had been averaging $20 million per year, would be provided because of that country's "unwillingness to conduct its relations with us according to accepted norms of diplomatic civility and practice." One factor triggering the decision was harsh criticism by a Zimbabwean Cabinet Minister at a July 4 reception at the U.S. embassy, which caused former President Carter to walk out in protest. *Wash. Post*, Sept. 3, 1986, at A15, col. 4; *N.Y. Times*, Sept. 3, 1986, at 1, col. 1.

Angola is also unique. In 1975, Congress passed the Clark amendment, which prohibited "assistance of any kind" for the purpose of promoting the capability of "any nation, group, organization, movement, or individual to conduct military or paramilitary operations in Angola." There was an exception if the President made a report and recommendation to Congress, and Congress enacted a joint resolution approving such assistance. Pub. L. No. 96-533, § 118(a). For the legislative history, see Franck and Weisband, supra note 21, at 46–57. The Clark amendment had the effect, then, of cutting all U.S. covert funding to Angolan rebel groups. As it was, the United States was not sending foreign assistance to anyone in Angola. The language of the amendment, however, was very inclusive and would have prevented any foreign assistance.

The 1985 foreign assistance act, supra note 27, repealed the Clark amendment. Sec. 811, 22 U.S.C. § 2293 note (Supp III 1985). This did not automatically translate into aid for the Angolan Government or guerillas operating there, though the Reagan Administration reportedly began giving covert assistance to the guerillas under Jonas Savimbi. *N.Y. Times*, Feb. 21, 1986, at A31, col. 6. Incidentally, the 1985 law did authorize assistance to insurgent forces in other countries – including humanitarian assistance for the Nicaraguan contras (sec. 722 (g)), aid to the Afghan people (sec. 904, 22 U.S.C. § 2344), and assistance for certain noncommunist resistance groups in Cambodia (sec. 905–6, 22 U.S.C. § 2311).

[30] During the period, the United States cut economic and military assistance from $49.5 million in 1966 and $32.3 million in 1967 to $15.2 million in 1968 and $13.7 million in 1969. Hufbauer and Schott, supra note 10, at 434–8.

[31] United States economic aid dropped from $304 million in 1961 to a total of $174 million in the two-year period of 1962–3. Aid to the Brazilian military, which was viewed as friendly to the United States, stayed roughly constant, from $24 million in 1961 to $33 million for the next two years. After the Brazilian military ousted Goulart in April 1964, the United States substantially increased that year its economic aid to $337 million and military aid to $41 million. Id. at 340–5.

[32] Id. at 568–72.

Reductions in U.S. foreign assistance have also been unsuccessful. Examples include U.S. efforts against Nicaragua from 1981 to the present, and against Turkey from 1975 to 1978.[33]

The President often initiates these reductions in foreign assistance, though Congress has frequently played an active role. As discussed earlier, Congress has sometimes imposed a sanction by denying the President funds that he requested, such as military assistance for Turkey in 1975–8 and for Ethiopia in 1977.[34]

Congress has also affected the President's use of foreign aid by hedging its aid approval with various conditions. Sometimes, this is done for a specific country. For example, Congress hesitantly appropriated foreign assistance for Nicaragua under the Sandinistas in 1980 as President Carter requested, but it was leery of possible Sandinista support for the leftist guerrillas in El Salvador. Congress stipulated that the assistance could be terminated at any time if the President determined that Nicaragua was supporting any violence or terrorism abroad.[35] In April 1981, President Reagan then froze any foreign assistance that had not been already transferred to Nicaragua.[36]

Another example of Congress linking aid to a country with specific conditions was its policy toward El Salvador from 1981 through 1983. Congress required the President to certify every six months that El Salvador had satisfied a long list of conditions. By the end of 1983, these conditions included the following: The country was making a significant effort to comply with internationally recognized human rights; reducing the incidence of torture by its security forces; making continued progress on essential political and economic reforms, including land reform; com-

[33] With Nicaragua, the Carter Administration initially resumed foreign assistance to the new Sandinista Government in 1979–80, though with growing concern about its support for the guerillas in El Salvador. In 1981 the Reagan Administration froze the aid program and terminated any future assistance, while commencing a number of other coercive steps against the Sandinistas. These latest sanctions against Nicaragua clearly hurt the country economically but have not yet led to the overthrow of the Sandinistas or to any major changes in their policies. Part of the reason for the lack of success is probably the increased support that Nicaragua has received from the Soviet Union, Cuba, and Libya. Id. at 671–82.

The Turkish invasion of northern Cyprus in July 1974 triggered a series of suspensions and reductions in U.S. military assistance to Turkey from 1974 through 1978. The sanctions failed to generate a Turkish withdrawal. Though there was no offsetting assistance from the Soviet Union to Turkey, which is after all a member of NATO, the reduction in U.S. aid was less than $100 million and thus a small percentage of the Turkish GNP (about $37.1 billion in 1975). Id. at 491–5.

[34] See preceding footnote regarding Turkey. For Ethiopia, see discussion at p. 46 infra.

[35] Special Central American Assistance Act of 1979, Pub. L. No. 96–257, 94 Stat. 423 (codified at 22 U.S.C.).

[36] 46 *Fed. Reg.* 24,141 (1981).

mitted to holding free elections at an early date; and making good-faith efforts to investigate the murders of certain U.S. citizens in El Salvador.[37] President Reagan certified each time that El Salvador had satisfied the requisite conditions, even though the certification seemed to strain the facts on several items.[38]

b. Prohibitions. Congress has also initiated several policy prohibitions that limit the circumstances in which foreign assistance can be given. Although these prohibitions have often been enacted with a specific country or countries in mind, they have potential impact on other cases. The President usually has accepted these prohibitions and then decided whether to use them within the often broad discretion the provisions leave him. The foreign policy proscriptions include injunctions against aid if certain conditions exist in the target country, such as expropriation of private U.S. investments, abuse of human rights, or harboring international terrorists.[39]

[37] International Security and Development Cooperation Act of 1981, as amended, Pub. L. No. 95-113, § 728, 95 Stat. 1519, 1555-7 (codified at 22 U.S.C. § 2370 note (1982 and Supp. III 1985)). For discussion of the fourth certification on July 20, 1983, see statement of L. Motley, "Fourth Certification of Progress for El Salvador." 83 *Dept. of State Bull.* 82 (Sept. 1983).

Other examples are found in the massive continuing resolution that was enacted in December 1987 for fiscal year 1988. Congress directed that most foreign assistance to Haiti be cut off unless certain democratic processes were followed there. It also conditioned most assistance to Panama upon a certification by the U.S. President that, among other things, progress was being made toward civilian control of that government and that due process of law was being restored. Foreign Operations, Export Financing, and Related Programs Appropriations Act of 1988, Pub. L. No. 100-202 § 569 (Haiti), § 570 (Panama), (1987) [hereinafter 1988 continuing resolution].

[38] See W. Christopher, "Ceasefire Between the Branches: A Compact in Foreign Affairs," 60 *Foreign Aff.* 989, 1002 (1982); Franck and Bob, supra note 19, at 951 n.273. The President then vetoed new legislation in November 1983 that would have continued the certification requirement. White House Statement, Nov. 30, 1983, reprinted as "President Opposes El Salvador Certification Legislation," 84 *Dept. of State Bull.* 88 (Jan. 1984).

[39] Some *other* policy prohibitions for foreign policy purposes include bans on assistance to countries developing nuclear explosives or having communist governments. Several provisions attempt to discourage nuclear proliferation, the first having appeared in 1976. Assistance is prohibited to countries that deliver or receive equipment, materials, or technology for nuclear enrichment or nuclear reprocessing, unless the recipient country has agreed to implement international safeguards or unless the President certifies that certain conditions exist. 22 U.S.C. §§ 2429 and 2429a. (1982 & Supp. III 1985). See also 22 U.S.C. § 2375 (Supp. III 1985) (a provision specifically about Pakistan's nuclear program). None of these provisions regarding nuclear proliferation has apparently been invoked yet. However, as discussed in Chapter 2, Section B.2.a, U.S. threats to change credit terms or to use export sanctions were useful in discouraging some purchases of nuclear equipment by South Korea and Taiwan.

The foreign assistance programs have long contained prohibitions against any as-

1. *Expropriation*. One of the most debated policy prohibitions in foreign assistance law is the sanction against expropriation of U.S. investments. This sanction started with the so-called Hickenlooper amendment in 1962, enacted in reaction to expropriations by Cuba, Brazil, and Ceylon, and when other expropriations were being threatened elsewhere. The amendment mandated that the President suspend foreign assistance to any country that took the property of, or nullified contracts with, any U.S. citizen unless "appropriate steps" were taken by that country within six months to ensure prompt, adequate, and effective compensation.[40]

The amendment was used once in its first ten years – in 1963 to suspend foreign aid to Ceylon for its expropriation of various properties of U.S. oil companies. Partly because of this aid cutoff, the Ceylonese economy deteriorated and the Government was overthrown in 1965. The new, relatively conservative Government soon reached an agreement with the oil companies to provide some compensation.[41]

The amendment was generally viewed, however, as counterproductive to U.S. foreign policy interests. Among other reasons, it gave the President little discretion and played "into the hands of nationalist leaders anxious to score anti-Yankee points by proclaiming that the United States extends foreign aid only to protect its private foreign investments."[42] As a result, the U.S. Government went to considerable lengths not to invoke it in some sensitive situations, such as Peru's expropriation in 1969 of the properties of International Petroleum Company.[43]

Criticism of the amendment from many quarters and only lukewarm

sistance to communist countries, including Yugoslavia and the People's Republic of China. The Foreign Assistance Act of 1961 contained such a prohibition, unless the President made certain certifications. 22 U.S.C. § 2370(f) (1982). The 1985 foreign aid act added a provision that required a less demanding certification – i.e., that the assistance "is important to the national interests of the United States." It did say that the President was to consider as a factor whether the country was "giving evidence of fostering the establishment of a genuinely democratic system, with respect for internationally recognized human rights." 22 U.S.C. § 2370(f) (Supp. III 1985).

[40] U.S.C. § 2370(e)(1) (1970). The current version of the law is provided below in note 44. As discussed in the accompanying text, the only major change has been in the presidential waiver provision. The amendment was named after its chief author, Senator Bourke B. Hickenlooper (R-Iowa). It should not be confused with the second Hickenlooper amendment, 22 U.S.C. §2370(e)(2) (1982), which was designed to overturn the Supreme Court's holding on the act of state doctrine in *Banco Nacional de Cuba v. Sabbatino*, 376 U.S. 398 (1964). The amendment is better known as the Sabbatino amendment.

[41] Hufbauer and Schott, supra note 10, at 324–8. See generally the excellent study on the security of foreign investments by C. Lipson, *Standing Guard: Protecting Foreign Capital in the Nineteenth and Twentieth Centuries* (1985).

[42] R. Lillich, "Requiem for Hickenlooper," 69 *Am J. Int'l L.* 97, 98 (1975).

[43] Id.

support from the U.S. business community led Congress in 1973 to make application of the amendment discretionary rather than mandatory.[44] This did not change the basic U.S. policy, however, that opposed expropriation and called for prompt, adequate, and effective compensation. For example, after Ethiopia expropriated some U.S.-owned properties in 1975 and engaged in other objectionable activities, the President finally invoked the Hickenlooper amendment as one sanction in 1979. United States bilateral aid was suspended, except for humanitarian aid for the victims of the famine there.[45]

The amendment, in its discretionary form, remains on the books. In December 1985 its use was threatened as a possible sanction against Peru's expropriation of a U.S.-owned oil company.[46]

[44] Id. at 98–100. *See Aerotrade v. Agency for Int'l Development, Dept. of State,* 387 F. Supp. 974, 975 (D.D.C. 1974). The revised amendment reads in pertinent part:

> The President shall suspend assistance to the government of any country ... when the government ... –
>
> (A) has nationalized or expropriated ... ownership or control of property owned by any United States citizen or by any corporation, partnership, or association not less than 50 per centum beneficially owned by United States citizens, or
>
> (B) has taken steps to repudiate or nullify existing contracts or agreements ... or,
>
> (C) has imposed or enforced discriminatory taxes or other exactions ...
>
> and such country ... fails within a reasonable time ... to take appropriate steps ... to discharge its obligations under international law toward such citizen or entity, including speedy compensation for such property in convertible foreign exchange, equivalent to the full value thereof, as required by international law ... and the provisions of this subsection shall not be waived with respect to any country unless the President determines and certifies that such a waiver is important to the national interests of the United States. Such certification shall be reported immediately to Congress [22 U.S.C. § 2370(e)(1)].

[45] Ethiopia's other activities included human rights violations and growing ties to the Soviet Union. *Ethiopia: A Country Study* 224 (H. Nelson and I. Kaplan eds. 1981). The United States began cutting back its aid in 1976, and then Congress omitted Ethiopia from the military aid bill in 1977. The Hickenlooper amendment was invoked in 1979. Hufbauer and Schott, supra note 10, at 544–9. Ethiopia and the United States reached an agreement in December 1985 on the expropriation dispute. See supra p. 18.

Iran's expropriation of many U.S.-owned properties in 1979 also occasioned U.S. objections. The Hickenlooper amendment was not invoked, however. The seizure of the American hostages in November 1979 quickly led to a comprehensive set of sanctions against Iran (including suspension of foreign aid), mainly pursuant to the International Emergency Economic Powers Act. See discussion in Chapter 9, Section C.

[46] D. Gellene, "Occidental Petroleum Avoids Seizure in Peru: Belco's Status Unclear," *L.A. Times,* Dec. 28, 1985, sec. CC, at 1, col. 5. Peru still proceeded with the expropriation, but the Garcia Government went to great lengths to explain that

2. *Abuse of human rights.* Usually enacted at the initiative of Congress, several laws have attempted to limit foreign assistance to countries that are in gross violation of internationally recognized human rights. The primary legislative efforts have focused on military aid and arms sales, but there have also been efforts to limit economic assistance to these countries.[47]

The first law was passed in 1973. A nonbinding sense of Congress resolution, it was openly ignored by the Nixon and Ford Administrations. Congress responded with several progressive amendments to tighten the law and reduce the President's discretion.

For military assistance and arms sales, the key provision is amended section 502B, which has changed little since 1978.[48] The critical subsection provides that "no security assistance may be provided to any country the government of which engages in a consistent pattern of gross violations of internationally recognized human rights." An exception is permitted if the President certifies in writing to Congress that "extraordinary circumstances exist warranting provision of such assistance."[49]

With its public commitment to human rights, the Carter Administration terminated security assistance for various periods of time to eight

independent evaluators would set a price on Belco's assets and the Government would make any payments necessary. *N.Y. Times*, Dec. 30, 1985, at D4, col. 5. The valuation process continued at least through early 1987. *Christian Science Monitor*, Apr. 9, 1987, at 22, col. 3.

[47] Haiti is an example of a success. In the 1985 foreign assistance act, supra note 27, Congress required that the President certify certain matters before Haiti could receive economic or military assistance, one matter being that the country was making progress toward improving the human rights situation. Sec. 705, 22 U.S.C. § 2347 (Supp. III 1985). During the final weeks of Jean-Claude Duvalier's rule in January 1986, the Reagan Administration announced that it could not make this certification and withheld about $25 million in funds. This was viewed as an important factor in Duvalier's flight to France on February 7. The Administration certified on February 26 that there was an improvement in the human rights situation and released the aid. *Wash. Post*, Feb. 27, 1986, at A19, col. 4; *N.Y. Times*, Feb. 27, 1986, at A3.

[48] 22 U.S.C. § 2304 (1982). The 1985 foreign assistance act, supra note 27, added a new subsection to section 502B, requiring a presidential report to Congress before funds can be made available to a country after it has been determined that a country may receive assistance because a significant improvement has occurred in its human rights record. Sec. 1201, 22 U.S.C. § 2304(g) (Supp. III 1985).

The most thorough study of the history and use of section 502B is that by Professor Stephen B. Cohen, "Conditioning U.S. Security Assistance on Human Rights Practices," 76 *Am. J. Int'l L.* 246 (1982). Other useful articles include J. Morrell, "Achievement of the 1970's: U.S. Human Rights Law and Policy," *Int'l Pol'y Rep.*, Nov. 1981, at 1; D. Weissbrodt, " Human Rights Legislation and U.S. Foreign Policy," 7 *Ga. J. Int'l & Comp. L.* 231 (1977).

[49] U.S.C. § 2304(a)(2). The section also provides that Congress can request a statement from the Secretary of State explaining why security assistance is being given to a country. Id. § 2304(c)(1)(C).

countries, all in Latin America.[50] One participant in the process terms this record "quite modest" in light of the human rights abuses that existed. He notes the "liberal use" made of the exception for "extraordinary circumstances."[51] On the aid cutoffs that did occur, the evidence about the impact on the human rights policies of the target country is unclear.[52]

The Reagan Administration has yet to invoke section 502B to cut off military aid or arms sales.

For economic assistance, the primary provision is amended section 116. Like section 502B, it prohibits assistance to any country that engages in a consistent pattern of gross violations of internationally recognized human rights. It has an important exception – when "such assistance will directly benefit the needy people in such country." Partly because of its exemption, section 116 has never been invoked to cut off assistance to a country.[53]

3. *International terrorism.* A series of provisions in U.S. foreign aid legislation have potentially limited aid to countries assisting international terrorists. The first limitation appeared in 1976.[54] Many of the present laws were enacted in the 1985 foreign assistance act after the hijacking of TWA flight 847 from Athens. The 1985 statute contains a separate title, "International Terrorism and Foreign Airport Security," with a wide range of provisions. The policy prohibition on terrorism reads in pertinent part:

[50] Argentina, Bolivia, El Salvador, Guatemala, Haiti, Nicaragua, Paraguay, and Uruguay. Cohen, supra note 48, at 270.

[51] Id. Professor Cohen concludes that "the history of section 502B is a case study of executive frustration of congressionally mandated foreign policy and underlines the need, particularly with this kind of legislation, for clearer directives, less discretion, and more assiduous congressional oversight." Id. at 277.

In reaction to the failure of the Nixon and Ford Administrations to use section 502B at all and then, as perceived by some, the limited use of the section by the Carter Administration, Congress passed country-specific legislation. This limited military aid (and also arms sales in two cases) to a number of countries at various times. The countries included Argentina, Brazil, Chile, El Salvador, Guatemala, Paraguay, the Philippines, South Korea, Uruguay, and Zaire. Cohen, supra note 48, at 254–6.

[52] Cohen concedes that a definite answer "is far from easy to obtain." Id. at 278–9. The Hufbauer and Schott study did not consider all of the eight examples in which section 502B was invoked. That study generally concluded that foreign assistance sanctions for human rights purposes had usually been unsuccessful, though it acknowledged some benefit in Nicaragua in 1977–9 and in Brazil in 1977–84. Hufbauer and Schott, supra note 10, at 544–82.

[53] 22 U.S.C. § 2151n(a) (1982); see Morrell, supra note 48. There is a similar provision for terminating the Food for Peace program. 7 U.S.C. § 1712 (1982). As will be discussed later in this section, there are similar human rights provisions dealing with the Eximbank and OPIC and a weaker provision for the IMF.

[54] Pub. L. No. 94-329, § 303, 90 Stat. 753 (codified at 22 U.S.C. § 2371(a) (1982)), amending section 620A of the Foreign Assistance Act of 1961.

(a) The United States shall not provide any assistance under this Act, the Agricultural Trade Development and Assistance Act of 1954, the Peace Corps Act, or the Arms Export Control Act, to any country which the President determines –

(1) grants sanctuary from prosecution to any individual or group which has committed an act of international terrorism, or

(2) otherwise supports international terrorism.

(b) The President may waive the application of subsection (a) to a country if the President determines that national security or humanitarian reasons justify such a waiver.[55]

The President has yet to invoke any of these antiterrorism provisions formally, probably because the United States was not inclined initially to provide foreign assistance to countries that support terrorists.

2. No loans for you: credit, loan guarantees, and insurance programs

The U.S. Government has several large, bilateral programs for providing low-interest credit, loan guarantees, and special insurance programs to promote U.S. exports or foreign investment. The laws provide the President with broad authority to deny access to these programs for foreign policy reasons. Three major programs are those of the Export–Import Bank (Eximbank), the Commodity Credit Corporation (CCC), and the Overseas Private Investment Corporation (OPIC).

a. No more discounts: Export–Import Bank. The Eximbank is a financially self-sustaining agency established to encourage trade in goods and services between the United States and other countries. The Eximbank provides this support through a variety of below-market lending, credit guarantee, and insurance programs. Its primary activities include directly lending to foreign purchasers, extending credit to foreign banks and other institutions to enable them to lend to foreign purchasers of U.S. goods, discounting outstanding private bank loans, guaranteeing export debt

---

[55] 1985 foreign assistance act, supra note 27, at § 503, amending 22 U.S.C. § 2371 (Supp. III 1985). This provision is similar to the 1976 provision. It does add the category of a country that "otherwise supports terrorism" and allows a presidential waiver for humanitarian as well as national security reasons.

The U.S. statute books are fast becoming laden with other laws that prohibit or sharply limit U.S. foreign assistance and other government programs to a country supporting terrorists. For example, in the 1988 continuing resolution, supra note 37, there was a provision against any bilateral assistance to countries that the Secretary of State designated as ones supporting terrorism. Section 576; see also §§ 512, 554 (prohibiting direct and indirect assistance to specific countries, including Libya and Syria).

obligations, and insuring the receivables of U.S. exporters against commercial and political risks.[56]

Eximbank's activities are substantial. In fiscal year 1986, it authorized $557 million in direct loans and another $5,508 million in loan guarantees and export credit insurance. This supported about $6.4 billion in U.S. exports,[57] or about 3 percent of total U.S. exports.

The Eximbank is very responsive to the President of the United States. He appoints the Bank's president, first vice-president, and the three other directors. All their terms are at his pleasure.[58]

American laws do impose a few specific limitations on Eximbank's activities for foreign policy reasons. These include limitations on loans, guarantees, or insurance for the following: products going to a "Marxist–Leninist country,"[59] many exports to Angola[60] and South Africa,[61] and exports that will be used to construct or operate nuclear facilities.[62] Very few of these restrictions are absolute. Rather, the President is given discretion to allow Eximbank activities if he certifies that certain conditions exist or, in the case of some nuclear facilities, if there is a report to Congress.[63]

Beyond the specific limits, the President has much broader discretion under the Chafee amendment, which provides:

[56] Eximbank's charter was extended in 1986 through September 1992. Export–Import Bank Act Amendments of 1986, Pub. L. No. 99-472, § 14, 100 Stat. 1204, amending 12 U.S.C. § 635f (Supp. IV 1986). For a discussion of Eximbank programs, see the Conference Report on the 1986 amendments, H. Rep. No. 956, 99th Cong., 2d Sess. (1986); Eximbank, *1986 Annual Report* (1987); M. Keler, "The Export-Import Bank," 11 *L. & Pol'y Int'l. Bus.* 355 (1979).

[57] National Advisory Council on International Monetary and Financial Policies, *International Finance* 22 (1987) (annual report to the President and Congress for FY 1986) [hereinafter *Int'l Finance FY 1986*]. The Reagan Administration tried unsuccessfully to terminate the direct lending program. *N.Y. Times*, Aug. 17, 1985, at 7, col. 3. David Stockman, former Reagan budget director, testified that almost half of the direct loan financing by Eximbank in 1980–4 went to only five big corporations: Boeing, McDonnell Douglas, General Electric, Westinghouse, and Lockheed. Id. Eximbank reported major losses to Congress in late 1987. 5 *Int'l Trade Rep. (BNA)* 5 (Jan. 6, 1988).

[58] 12 U.S.C. § 635a (Supp. IV 1986). The Senate does advise and consent to the appointment of these two top officials and the other three directors. Id.

[59] 12 U.S.C. § 635(b)(2) (Supp. IV 1986). Also, as provided in the Stevenson amendment, there is a $300 million ceiling on Eximbank loans to the Soviet Union. 12 U.S.C. § 635e(b).

[60] 12 U.S.C. § 635(b)(11) (Supp. IV 1986).

[61] Id. § 635(b)(9). The Comprehensive Anti-Apartheid Act of 1986 waived these limits for South African businesses that are majority-owned by blacks or other non-white South Africans and encouraged Eximbank to use its programs to help these businesses. Id.

[62] Id. § 635(b)(3) and (5).

[63] See the citations above to id. §§ 635 and 635e.

Only in cases where the President determines that such action would be in the national interest and where such action would clearly and importantly advance United States policy in such areas as international terrorism, nuclear proliferation, environmental protection and human rights, should the Export–Import Bank deny applications for nonfinancial or noncommercial considerations.[64]

Though couched in cautionary terms, the provision clearly gives the President the discretion to deny applications for a wide range of foreign policy objectives if he determines that denial would be "in the national interest" and would "clearly and importantly advance" one of these objectives. Presidents have resorted at least three times to this provision – against Chile in 1980,[65] Argentina in 1982,[66] and Syria in 1986.[67] The open-ended nature of the provision is illustrated by its use against Argentina because of the Falklands invasion, a use that fell outside any of the four areas specified in the amendment.

b. No food for unfriendly countries: Commodity Credit Corporation and P.L. 480. A principal activity of the Department of Agriculture's CCC is helping finance exports of U.S. wheat and other agricultural products by extending export credit guarantees for sales in dollars.[68] The CCC credit guarantees insure U.S. exporters (or their U.S. bank assignees)

[64] Id. § 635(b)(1)(B). This 1978 amendment replaced a more demanding 1977 provision regarding human rights. It required the Eximbank to "take into account, in consultation with the Secretary of State, the observance of and respect for human rights in the country . . . and the effect such export may have on human rights in such country." Pub. L. No. 95-143, 91 Stat. 1210 (1977). Pursuant to this 1977 amendment, Eximbank refused to provide direct credit for Chile, Uruguay, and South Africa. Eximbank also initially declined to issue a "letter of interest" supporting a proposed sale of certain goods for a project in Argentina. Partly as a result of these decisions, private and public concerns were raised over the wisdom of the 1977 amendment. Keler, supra note 56, at 362–3.

[65] President Carter suspended Eximbank financing of goods to Chile in November 1980 because that Government refused to extradite three Chilean officials allegedly involved in the 1978 slaying of former Chilean Foreign Minister Orlando Letelier in Washington, D.C. Although Chile did not drop its refusal, President Reagan lifted the ban in February 1981. *U.S. Export Weekly (BNA)*, No. 346, at A-6 (Feb. 24, 1981).

[66] At the outbreak of the war over the Falkland Islands in May 1982, the Reagan Administration ordered Eximbank denial of credit applications for loans to Argentina. 47 *Fed. Reg.* 19,842 (1982). The sanction was removed in July after the conclusion of the hostilities. *N.Y. Times*, July 13, 1982, at A1. The sanction affected six preliminary commitments totaling $230 million in Eximbank loans. Id.

[67] *N.Y. Times*, Nov. 15, 1986, at 4, col. 2.

[68] The program is found at 7 U.S.C. §§ 1691–1736aa (1982 & Supp. IV 1986). The original bill was known as the Agricultural Trade Development and Assistance Act of 1954, Pub. L. No. 83-480, July 10, 1954.

against defaults by foreign banks on sales contracts of up to three years.[69] By providing guarantees against nonpayment due to "all risks," such as insurrection or lack of foreign exchange, the CCC makes it easier and cheaper for the foreign importer to find financing.[70] Total CCC guarantees each year are sizable, amounting to almost $4.2 billion in fiscal year 1986.[71]

The President has almost unlimited discretion in deciding whether, for foreign policy reasons, to cut off a country from CCC credit guarantees.[72] For example, at the start of the Falklands War in April 1982, the Reagan Administration canceled a $2 million unused authorization for export credit guarantees for Argentina and halted any additional authorization.[73] President Reagan lifted the sanction in July 1983 after the war had ended.[74]

The President exercises similar discretion over the so-called P.L. 480 agricultural export programs. These include foreign famine relief and sales for foreign currency that allow developing countries to purchase U.S. agricultural products on concessional terms.[75] President Reagan in-

[69] CCC Export Credit Guarantee Program (GSM-102), 7 C.F.R. §§ 1493.1–1493.15 (1987). The CCC guarantees against loss by the exporter (or his bank assignee) when a foreign bank defaults on its payment pursuant to a letter of credit that the exporter had obtained to ensure payment on the sales contract.

[70] Department of State Press Release, Apr. 30, 1982, reprinted in 21 I.L.M. 683 (May 1982).

[71] *Int'l Finance FY 1986*, supra note 57, at 23.

[72] 15 U.S.C. §§ 714–714g (1982 & Supp IV 1986). The CCC board of directors consists of seven members appointed by the President plus the Secretary of Agriculture, who is a member ex officio and board chairman. Id. § 714g. 7 C.F.R. § 1493.3(b) provides that the CCC assistant general sales manager may reject applications for payment guarantees.

[73] Department of State Press Release, supra note 70.

[74] N.Y. *Times*, July 13, 1982, at 1. The Reagan Administration also used CCC in 1982 in the opposite way – i.e., to avoid putting pressure on another country. The Department of Agriculture allowed the CCC to pay at least one private U.S. bank the interest and principal on payments missed by the Polish Government. The Department changed its rules and did not require banks to declare the loans in default (which could have triggered other defaults against Poland) before the CCC paid. The payments were carried on the CCC's books as accounts receivable.

There were efforts in Congress to prevent the CCC from using its funds for repayments unless the U.S. banks declared Poland in default. These efforts were defeated in both the Senate and House of Representatives. *U.S. Export Weekly (BNA)*, No. 395, at 541 (Feb. 16, 1982).

[75] 7 U.S.C. §§ 1701–27g (1982 & Supp. IV 1986). Section 1703(d) provides that sales shall be made only to those countries the President "determines to be friendly to the United States." Also, no sales "shall be made with any country if the President finds such country is (a) an aggressor, in a military sense, against any country having diplomatic relations with the United States, or (b) using funds, of any sort, from the United States for purposes inimical to the foreign policies of the United States."

voked this authority in 1981 against Nicaragua when he froze Food for Peace aid and canceled a $9.6 million wheat sale to that country.[76]

c. Invest at your own risk: Overseas Private Investment Corporation. The Overseas Private Investment Corporation seeks to promote Third World development by supporting projects that also have positive trade benefits for the United States.[77] Its primary program is insuring U.S. investments in projects against the "political risks" of inconvertibility, expropriation, war, revolution, insurrection, and civil strife.[78] In fiscal year 1987, its total insurance in force was $2.9 billion.[79] OPIC also provides direct financing, loan guarantees, and local-currency loan commitments, but on a much smaller scale. In fiscal year 1987, these totaled about $348 million.[80]

The U.S. President has great discretion in determining whether to extend new OPIC insurance or other programs to a country. He appoints the OPIC president, executive vice-president, and board of directors.[81] OPIC also operates under the policy guidance of the Secretary of State.[82]

Moreover, there are few legislative restraints on OPIC's ability to cut off new insurance or other programs to a country for foreign policy reasons. Most important are two 1978 provisions regarding human rights. First, OPIC is required, in consultation with the Secretary of State, to "take into account" the host country's "observance of and respect for human rights and fundamental freedoms" and the effect of OPIC programs on these rights and freedoms.[83] Since this language is hortatory rather than mandatory, OPIC (and the U.S. President) is left with maximum discretion.

[76] Hufbauer and Schott, supra note 10, at 671–82.

[77] 22 U.S.C. § 2191 (1982 & Supp. III 1985); see Note, "The 1981 OPIC Amendments and Reagan's 'Newer Directions' in Third World Development Policy," 14 *L. & Pol'y Int'l Bus.* 181, 187 (1982).

[78] 22 U.S.C. § 2194 (1982 & Supp. III 1985); see D. Burand, "Civil Strife Coverage of Overseas Investment: The Emerging Role of OPIC," 34 *Fed'n Ins. Couns.* 391 (1984); see Chapter 7, note 1, regarding the World Bank's Multilateral Investment Guarantee Agency (MIGA).

[79] OPIC, *1987 Annual Report* 40 (1987).

[80] 22 U.S.C. § 2194(b), (c); OPIC, supra note 79, at 38–9, 41. Since starting operations in 1971, OPIC not only has been self-sustaining as required by statute, but has accumulated a profit. It reported a record net income of $102 million in FY 1987. 22 U.S.C. § 2191; OPIC, supra note 79, at 2.

[81] 22 U.S.C. § 2193 (1982). Their appointments are subject to the advice and consent of the Senate. Five of the eleven directors are to be officials of the U.S. Government, and the Administrator of AID is ex officio the chairman of the board. Id.

[82] 22 U.S.C. § 2191.

[83] Id. § 2199 (1) (1982 & Supp. III 1985).

Second, section 116 of the foreign assistance laws was made applicable to OPIC. As discussed earlier, this provision prohibits assistance to countries where "a consistent pattern of gross violations" of human rights standards is found. It contains, however, a major exception for cases in which "such assistance will directly benefit the needy people." In addition, the application of section 116 to OPIC was hedged by another exception, allowing OPIC to go forward with a program "if the national security interest so requires."[84] Neither of these two human rights provisions has had much influence on OPIC's decision making. Uruguay is apparently the only country that has been dropped from OPIC's country list for human rights reasons.[85]

3. You can't fish here

The President has essentially open-ended discretion to limit for foreign policy reasons another country's fishing rights near the United States. The only major constraint on this discretion could be an international fishery agreement that the United States may have entered into with the target country.

In the Magnuson Fishery Conservation and Management Act of 1976, the United States extended its jurisdiction by establishing a fishery conservation zone with a breadth of 200 nautical miles.[86] This encompasses an area of approximately 3 million nautical miles off the coasts of the fifty states, Puerto Rico, and all U.S. territories and possessions.[87] Much of this area contains valuable fisheries.

The 1976 Act prohibited foreign fishing within this area,[88] unless three

---

[84] Id. See discussion of section 116 under "Abuse of human rights" in Section B.1.b, this chapter.

[85] Note, "Overseas Private Investment Corporation: The 1978 Amendments and the Future of OPIC," 11 *L. & Pol'y Int'l Bus.* 321, 340–1 (1979).

[86] 16 U.S.C. § 1801–82 (1982 & Supp. IV 1986). The 200-mile fishery conservation zone was established in section 1811. The exact outer limits of the zone had to be negotiated with many neighboring countries who have overlapping boundary claims. Id. § 1822(d). These countries include Mexico, Canada, the Soviet Union, and certain Caribbean nations. For a thorough article on these overlapping boundaries, see M. Feldman and D. Colson, "The Maritime Boundaries of the United States," 75 *Am. J. Int'l L.* 729, 733–4 (1981).

The 200-mile zone is consistent with the 200-mile exclusive economic zone provided for in part V of the UN Convention on the Law of the Sea, opened for signature Dec. 10, 1982, 17 U.N. CLOS III GAOR at 164, U.N. Doc. A/Conf. 52/122 (1984). The United States has not signed or ratified that Convention, which is not yet in effect.

[87] Id. at 734.

[88] 16 U.S.C. § 1821. Actually, this conditional prohibition encompasses not only the fishery conservation zone, but also anadromous species (fish, such as salmon, that spawn in fresh or estuarine waters of the United States and that migrate to the open ocean) and fishery resources on the Continental Shelf beyond the fishery conservation

conditions are met. First, there must be reciprocity – that is, the Secretaries of Commerce and State must be satisfied that the other country has extended substantially the same fishing privileges to U.S. fishing vessels as the United States extends to the other country's fishing vessels. Second, the United States and the other country must have entered into an international fishery agreement. Third, the foreign fishing must be conducted under a valid permit issued by the Secretary of Commerce.[89] These conditions leave great discretion to the President. The first requirement for reciprocity is determined by his appointees. And although the terms of an international fishery agreement often guarantee minimum annual catches, they are negotiated by the Executive Branch and include escape clauses.

As for issuing a permit, the so-called basket clause of the 1976 Magnuson Act implicitly recognizes that the Executive Branch can take foreign policy considerations into account when determining the fishing allocation for a foreign country allowable under the permit. The clause allows the determination to include "such other matters as the Secretary of State, in cooperation with the Secretary [of Commerce], deems appropriate."[90]

Since the Act became effective in 1977, the President has used fishing rights as a foreign policy sanction on four occasions.[91] For example, in 1980, President Carter reduced the Soviet fishing allocations in response to the USSR's invasion of Afghanistan. The Soviets and United States had entered into an international fisheries agreement in 1976, and permits to catch 75,000 metric tons of fish had already been issued to Soviet fishing vessels that had begun operations off Alaska before the imposition of the sanctions. Carter froze the Soviet catch at that level, which was the minimum required under the agreement, rather than allow the Soviets their quota of 435,000 metric tons. This sanction had only a modest impact on the Soviet Union. The gap of 360,000 metric tons is about 4 percent of the Soviet worldwide catch. To offset this shortfall, the Soviets reportedly increased their fishing efforts off their own coasts and in other places.[92]

zone. Id. The United States did not claim exclusive fishery management authority in any of these areas over highly migratory species of fish, such as certain species of tuna. Id. § 1813.

[89] Id. § 1821(a).

[90] Id. § 1821(e)(1)(E)(viii).

[91] *Wash. Post*, April 7, 1988, at A32, col. 1 (recent measures against Japan); prepared Statement of E. Wolfe, Jr., before the Senate Committee on Commerce, Science, and Transportation and the National Ocean Policy Study Committee, July 23, 1985, at 15 (mimeographed version; copy on file at Georgetown University Law Center) [hereinafter Wolfe testimony].

[92] Subcommittee on Europe and the Middle East of the House Committee on Foreign Affairs, 97th Cong., 1st Sess., *An Assessment of the Afghanistan Sanctions:*

4. *Don't dock here*

The President also has great discretion to limit access of a foreign country's ships to U.S. ports. As with fishing rights, the only likely major constraint would be a bilateral maritime agreement, which the Chief Executive is in charge of negotiating in the first place.

Ports are part of the internal waters of the United States. It is generally recognized among countries that a country has sovereignty over its internal waters and complete control over access to them.[93] A number of U.S. laws and regulations regulate access by foreign ships to U.S. ports with the President being given broad discretion to decide on access.[94]

The United States has entered into bilateral agreements with some countries, further defining their rights and the procedures for gaining access. For example, with the Soviet Union, the United States entered into an executive agreement on maritime matters on January 1, 1976.

Implications for Trade and Diplomacy in the 1980's at 93–4 (Comm. Print 1981) (report prepared by the Congressional Reference Service).

A second and third use of the fishing sanction was to reduce Japanese allocations because of a dispute over Japanese adherence to international whaling restrictions. *Wash. Post*, April 7, 1988, supra; Wolfe testimony, supra note 91. The sanction was used a fourth time when President Reagan temporarily denied Poland any fishing allocations from December 1981 to November 1983 because of the Polish Government's declaration of martial law and other measures. *U.S. Export Weekly (BNA)*, No. 389, at 351 (Jan 5, 1982); id., No. 6, at 208 (Nov. 8, 1983).

Incidentally, President Reagan notified Congress on May 31, 1985, that, despite Soviet violations of international whaling restrictions, he would not reduce Soviet fishing allocations. Reagan said that this or other economic sanctions would be ineffective and that U.S. fishing interests would be seriously harmed by Soviet retaliatory action. 2 *Int'l Trade Rep. (BNA)* 766 (June 6, 1985).

Similarly, the Secretary of Commerce declined in 1984–5 to certify that Japan was whaling in violation of the International Convention for the Regulation of Whaling, a certification that would have mandated the imposition of economic sanctions under one of the provisions of the Packwood amendment. 16 U.S.C. § 1821(e)(2)(B) (Supp. IV 1986). In a 5 to 4 decision, the U.S. Supreme Court upheld the Secretary's action as within his discretion. *Japan Whaling Ass'n v. American Cetacean Soc'y*, 106 S. Ct. 2860 (1986).

[93] See, e.g., Convention on the Territorial Sea and the Contiguous Zone of Apr. 29, 1958, art. 1, 15 U.S.T. 1606, T.I.A.S. No. 5639.

[94] Most important is 50 U.S.C. § 191 (1982), which authorizes the President to order wide-ranging actions, including taking possession of foreign ships, whenever he finds that U.S. "security...is endangered by reason of actual or threatened war, or invasion, or insurrection, or subversive activity, or of *disturbances or threatened disturbances of the international relations of the United States....*" (emphasis added). See Department of Commerce, Memorandum on U.S. Port Procedures and Other Matters, 26 U.S.T. 2799 (Dec. 29, 1975), sent to the USSR in connection with the U.S.–USSR Maritime Agreement.

The agreement provided that certain designated ports of each country were open to entry by certain vessels of the other country, subject to four days' advance notice. Though the agreement was for a term of six years, it could be terminated by either party upon ninety days' written notice.[95]

In response to Soviet involvement in the repression in Poland, President Reagan announced in December 1981 that negotiations on a new maritime agreement were being suspended, and that a new regime for port access would be put into effect when the then current agreement expired on December 31.[96] A State Department spokesman later announced that ships covered under the old agreement would have to request entry to a U.S. port at least fourteen days before the intended port call. He indicated that "for the time being there will be a presumption of U.S. denial for port requests by Soviet passenger vessels and freighters, along with a presumption of U.S. approval for port requests by Soviet bulk carriers engaged in the bilateral trade of products not embargoed by the President."[97]

5. Travel restricted: aircraft landing rights, travel advisories, and passports

As with the use of U.S. ports, the President has broad discretion to suspend or cut back the right of foreign airlines to land in the United States. Additional U.S. laws give the President especially broad powers when the foreign country harbors hijackers or has inadequate security at one of its airports.[98]

The basic statutory framework for granting or suspending the landing rights of foreign airlines places the decision making in the Department of Transportation, in consultation with the Department of State.[99] The Secretary of Transportation, a presidential appointee, can amend or cancel foreign air carrier permits "whenever [he] finds such

[95] Agreement between the Government of the United States of America and the Government of the Union of Soviet Socialist Republics Regarding Certain Maritime Matters, Dec. 29, 1975, 26 U.S.T. 2720, 2771, T.I.A.S. No. 8195.
[96] "Statement on U.S. Measures Taken Against the Soviet Union," 18 *Weekly Comp. Pres. Doc.* 1429, 1430 (Dec. 29, 1981).
[97] *U.S. Export Weekly* (BNA), No. 389, at 351, 352 (Jan. 5, 1982); see "U.S. Measures Against Polish Government and Soviet Union," 76 *Am. J. Int'l L.* 379, 384 (1982) [hereinafter "U.S. Measures"].
[98] See statutes discussed below; see also Exec. Order No. 12,547, 51 *Fed. Reg.* 5029 (1986). See generally *Chicago & Southern Air Lines, Inc. v. Waterman Steamship Corp.*, 333 U.S. 103, 109–10 (1948) (according the President broad powers over foreign air carriers).
[99] The Department of Transportation took over from the Civil Aeronautics Board (CAB) on January 1, 1985. 49 U.S.C. app. § 1551(b)(1)(B) (1982 & Supp. III 1985).

action to be in the public interest" – which provides a great deal of discretion.[100]

Complications can arise from a bilateral agreement between the United States and another country that purports to limit the right of the United States to modify or withdraw landing rights. The United States might want to adhere to the terms of the agreement and consequently impose the sanctions more gradually.[101] The President, however, has the power to terminate or suspend the agreement on behalf of the United States if he deems it necessary.[102] For example, when the U.S. Government suspended landing rights in late 1981 for the Polish airline LOT, there was

---

[100] Id. § 1372(f))(1) (1982 & Supp. III 1985). The statutory framework was established when the now defunct CAB made the decision to grant or terminate operating permits to foreign airlines. First, the Board (now Secretary of Transportation) may amend or cancel foreign air carrier permits "whenever [he] finds such action to be in the public interest." Id. Second, in reaching decisions about the "public interest," the Secretary is generally required to consider, among other matters, "the present and future needs of the domestic and foreign commerce of the United States, the Postal Service, and the national defense." Id. § 1302(a)(5) (1982). Finally, decisions by the Secretary to issue, amend, or suspend a foreign carrier's permit are subject to the approval of the President. Id. § 1461(a) (1982).

In 1981–2, the CAB explicitly deferred to the President in suspending the permit of the Soviet airline Aeroflot and the Polish airline LOT to land in the United States. The CAB stated: "Under [49 U.S.C. § 1302(a)(5)], the Board must consider the foreign policy and defense needs of the United States in assessing the public interest. In the circumstances of this case, we are plainly obligated to give the President's assessment of the pertinent decisional criteria great deference." In re foreign air carrier permit of Polskie Linie Lotnicze (LOT), Docket 40339, Order No. 81-12-155 (show cause order), quoted in "U.S. Measures," supra note 97, at 381.

[101] 49 U.S.C. app. § 1502 (1982) provides that the Secretary of Transportation shall act "consistently with any obligation assumed by the United States in any treaty, convention, or agreement that may be in force between the United States and any foreign country or foreign countries."

The special statutes discussed later for dealing with foreign countries harboring hijackers or with dangerous airports specifically include an exemption from compliance with section 1502. See 49 U.S.C. app. §§ 1514–15 (1982 & Supp. III 1985).

In some analogous situations, the United States has chosen to abide by an agreement's provisions. For example, after the Soviet invasion of Afghanistan, President Carter did not terminate either the fishery agreement (see Section B.3, this chapter) or the grain sales agreement (see Chapter 2), but allowed the Soviets only the minimum benefits required under the agreements.

The Comprehensive Anti-Apartheid Act of 1986 mandated a prompt shutdown of air service between the United States and South Africa. However, it also contained language about terminating the bilateral air service agreement "in accordance with the provisions of that agreement." 22 U.S.C. § 5056 (Supp. IV 1986). This apparently led the Department of Transportation to delay revoking landing rights until it finally did so in mid-November 1986. *Wash. Post*, Nov. 15, 1986, at D9, col. 4.

[102] See generally, *Restatement (Third) of Foreign Relations Law of the United States* § 339(b) (1987). President Reagan apparently took this approach in terminating an aviation agreement with Syria in November 1986, although no airlines were then flying between the two countries. *N.Y. Times*, Nov. 15, 1986, at 4, col. 2.

an existing bilateral agreement that gave LOT certain landing rights.[103] Article 15 of the agreement required a one-year notification for termination.[104] Nevertheless, LOT's permit was suspended on the ground that the President had "ample authority" in the circumstances to breach the agreement.[105]

Special statutory provisions give the President broad powers to suspend air service if a foreign country harbors hijackers or fails to take adequate security measures at one of its airports. In the hijacker situation, the President is authorized to act, without notice or hearing, to suspend (1) all flights between that country and the United States and (2) all flights by a foreign air carrier between the United States and any other foreign nation that maintains air service between itself and the country harboring the hijackers.[106]

After the hijacking of TWA flight 847 to Beirut in June 1985, when Lebanon did not cooperate in prosecuting or extraditing the hijackers, the Department of Transportation relied on its general statutory authority to revoke the right of Middle East Airlines, a Lebanese carrier, to serve the United States.[107] President Reagan used the special statute on hijacking, discussed above, to suspend all air service between the United States and Lebanon and to prohibit all sales in this country of tickets that involved service to or from Lebanon.[108]

Reagan also relied on the hijacking statute as one legal basis for terminating in early 1986 all air service to or from the United States by any

---

[103] Air Transport Agreement Between the Government of the United States of America and the Government of the Polish People's Republic, July 19, 1972, 23 U.S.T. 4269, T.I.A.S. No. 7535, and later exchange of notes extending the agreement.

[104] Id. See also Article 4.

[105] In commenting on LOT's argument that the agreement did not allow the President to suspend or terminate it as he did, the CAB's final order stated: "Obviously, the President's action is of the most extraordinary nature, brought about by exceedingly serious world events. Clearly, under such circumstances, there resides in the President and the Executive Branch of the U.S. Government ample authority to suspend application of an Executive Agreement between the United States and a foreign country, whether or not such suspension is provided for under the specific terms of the Agreement. This is a political question which is clearly one for the President. That the President has made such a decision is reflected in his public television speech of December 23, as confirmed by the letters of the Department of State attached to this Order." Order No. 81-12-171, quoted in "U.S. Measures," supra note 97, at 381.

[106] 49 U.S.C. app. § 1514. The triggering events are whenever "the President determines that a foreign nation is acting in a manner inconsistent with the Convention for the Suppression of Unlawful Seizure of Aircraft, or if he determines that a foreign nation permits the use of [its] territory . . . as a base of operations or training or as a sanctuary for, or in any way . . . aids . . . any terrorist organization which knowingly uses the illegal seizure of aircraft or the threat thereof as an instrument of policy. . . ." Id.

[107] N.Y. Times, July 3, 1985, at A12, col. 1.

[108] Id.

Libyan aircraft that included any stop in Libya. This was part of the comprehensive sanctions imposed against Libya after terrorists attacked passengers at the Rome and Vienna airports.[109]

The TWA hijacking also led to extensive provisions in the 1985 foreign assistance act aimed at strengthening and expanding U.S. laws regarding security at foreign airports. In the extreme case, when there is an immediate danger and the public interest requires it, the Secretary of Transportation may immediately suspend the right of any person to operate aircraft to or from that airport.[110] The President is authorized to go even farther. He can prohibit all air carriers from providing service between the United States and any other foreign airport that is even indirectly served by aircraft using the dangerous airport.[111] Moreover, the Secretary of State is authorized to issue a "travel advisory" about a dangerous foreign airport.[112] The airport should be identified through the news media and by prominent displays at U.S. airports.[113]

The President can also attempt to limit travel by exercising his reasonably broad discretion to impose geographic restrictions on the use of U.S. passports. Although the law now prohibits these restrictions in general, it allows major exceptions for "war, . . . armed hostilities . . . or where there is imminent danger to the public health or the physical safety of [U.S.] travellers."[114] The Reagan Administration, for example, invoked this statute starting in 1981 to restrict the use of U.S. passports for travel to Libya.[115]

---

[109] 51 *Fed. Reg.* 875 (Jan. 9, 1986). See discussion in Chapter 9, Section C.

[110] 49 U.S.C. app. § 1515(g). This provision parallels the power of the President, discussed supra at note 106, when a country harbors hijackers. Id. § 1514. In less pressing cases, the Secretary is authorized, after consultation with the foreign government and each air carrier serving the dangerous airport, to suspend or amend the operating authority of any carrier to use that airport. Id. § 1515.

[111] Id. § 1514.

[112] 49 U.S.C. app. § 1515a (Supp. III 1985).

[113] Id. §§ 1515–15a. Each domestic and foreign carrier providing service between that airport and a U.S. airport is required to provide notice to passengers who purchase tickets for transportation to or from that airport. Id. § 1515. Even before this statute, the United States issued a travel advisory on June 19, 1985, warning American citizens of the inadequate security at the Athens airport. The advisory was partly responsible for Greek officials' decision to make major improvements in security. See discussion in Chapter 2, Section B.2.

[114] 22 U.S.C. § 211a (1982). Cf. *Zemel v. Rusk*, 381 U.S. 1 (1965) (upholding a restriction against travel to Cuba even before the 1978 statute cited above); see also *Haig v. Agee*, 453 U.S. 280, 300–1 (1981) (favorably discussing the 1978 statute).

[115] Acting Secretary of State William P. Clark said that the "unsettled relations" between the United States and Libya and "the increased threats of hostile acts against Americans" led him to conclude that there was "imminent danger to the physical safety of" U.S. travelers. 46 *Fed. Reg.* 60,712 (1981), renewed, 52 *Fed Reg.* 46,876 (1987). Similarly, the use of passports for travel to Lebanon was restricted in February 1987. 52 *Fed. Reg.* 3730 (1987).

The practical impact of such geographic restrictions is marginal, however. If an off-limits country is amenable, a U.S. citizen can easily circumvent the restrictions by not using the passport to obtain entry to that country. Americans regularly traveled in this way to Libya after 1981 and before the more thoroughgoing controls imposed under IEEPA.[116]

C. CONCLUSIONS

This survey of major government programs illustrates the President's broad discretion over the use of these programs as economic sanctions. Effective limits on the President's ability to suspend or cut back programs are the exception, and they are essentially confined to foreign assistance programs. There, Congress can conceivably mandate expenditures the President does not want or it can impose sanctions he did not request.

The trend in recent years has been toward even fewer limits on the President's discretion. This might well reflect the considerable popularity of President Reagan, but it is being institutionalized in various statutes. On foreign assistance for particular countries, except for its sporadic opposition to funds for the Nicaraguan contras, Congress has generally not resisted the President's aid requests. In the 1985 foreign assistance act, Congress even repealed the 1976 Clark amendment prohibiting any assistance to antigovernment groups in Angola.[117]

For various policy prohibitions on foreign aid, Congress also appears to be according the President greater discretion. For example, although

---

[116] *N.Y. Times*, Jan. 9, 1986, at A8, col. 1. A U.S. citizen is required to use his or her passport to depart from or enter the United States, unless the President directs otherwise. 8 U.S.C. § 1185(b) (1982). However, once the traveler is clear of the United States, use of the passport is not legally required.

As discussed in Chapter 9, Section C, the 1986 regulations against Libya pursuant to IEPPA make it much more difficult for U.S. citizens to travel there.

Even more limited in its impact than the President's authority to impose geographic restrictions is his authority to revoke the passports of specific individuals for national security or foreign policy reasons. *Haig v. Agee*, 453 U.S. 280 (1981). Revocation does constrain an individual's travel since, as noted above, it is illegal for a U.S. citizen to enter or leave the United States without a passport, unless the President directs otherwise. Although this means that the President's power over an individual is considerable, the Constitution and court decisions effectively limit the President's discretion to only a small group of individuals who present some threat to U.S. national security or foreign policy. Cf. *Haig v. Agee*, 453 U.S. at 302, 306; *Aptheker v. United States*, 378 U.S. 500 (1964); cf. *Kent v. Dulles*, 357 U.S. 116, 125–9 (1958). Moreover, practical politics would limit any President from widespread revocation of passports, which would be much less efficient and would cause many more problems for travelers than geographic restrictions.

[117] *Supra* note 27, § 811.

Congress added limits on most aid to Panama in the FY 1988 continuing resolution and inserted prohibitions concerning terrorism and nuclear proliferation in the 1985 foreign assistance act, the restrictions included the possibility of a presidential certification waiving any aid cutoff.[118] Moreover, Congress allowed the President to make several certifications about progress in El Salvador on human rights and other matters during 1981–3 on the basis of questionable facts, and then did not require a new certification procedure in 1985.[119] Also, there have been only limited complaints about President Reagan generally ignoring human rights provisions, such as section 502B.

The trend toward greater presidential discretion is also evident in the new powers given the President to deal with countries that harbor hijackers or that have inadequate airport security. Similarly, the power to license foreign air carriers was shifted from the quasi-independent Civil Aeronautics Board to the Secretary of Transportation, a presidential appointee.

Congress, however, has not ceded all its gains in influence since the Vietnam and Watergate periods. It continues to add extensive reporting requirements.[120] Congress is also very specific in some of its aid approvals, seeking to define and limit the use of the funds. For example, the 1988 continuing resolution and 1985 foreign assistance act specified what type of aid could go to Haiti and when.[121]

Indeed, Congress on occasion still pursues its own foreign policies. For example, it took the initiative to provide humanitarian assistance to the people of Afghanistan and Cambodia.[122] It also mandated the prompt cutoff of air service between the United States and South Africa. Nevertheless, these congressional initiatives do not seriously constrain the President's generally extensive discretion to use U.S. government programs to impose economic sanctions.

---

[118] 1988 continuing resolution, supra note 37, § 570; 1985 foreign assistance act, supra note 27, §§ 503, 902, 1204.

[119] See Section B.1.a., this chapter.

[120] See, e.g., 1985 foreign assistance act, supra note 27, §§ 702 (c), (d) (El Salvador), 709 (Latin America and the Caribbean).

[121] 1988 continuing resolution, supra note 90, § 569; 1985 act, supra note 27, § 705.

[122] 1985 act, supra note 27, §§ 904–5.

4

Exports from the United States

The President's extensive power over bilateral government programs is almost matched by his control over exports from the United States. This was not the case before World War II. As Professor Harold Berman observed, "Traditionally, the United States Government has restricted exports only in time of war or in special emergency situations. With the end of World War II, however, drastic wartime controls over exports were continued.... "[1] Starting in 1979 and accelerating after the Soviet grain embargo of 1980–1, Congress placed a few limits on the use of export controls and on presidential discretion. Nevertheless, the President today still has sweeping powers to cut off almost all of the U.S. export trade, or any segment of it.

The Export Administration Act (EAA), substantially amended in 1985, provides the principal statutory framework for controlling U.S. exports, which totaled about $253 billion in 1987.[2] Also relevant to certain exports are the Atomic Energy Act of 1954, the Arms Export Control Act, and the Comprehensive Anti-Apartheid Act of 1986. Through the use of these statutes, the United States has shown itself the country most willing to resort to export controls as an economic sanction, rather than rely on import controls or limits on private credit.[3]

---

[1] H. Berman and J. Garson, "United States Export Controls – Past, Present, and Future," 67 *Colum. L. Rev.* 791 (1967) (a classic article on export controls). "In both World Wars the President was empowered to control all exports to all destinations. Otherwise, with rare exceptions... controls upon exports prior to 1945 were limited to war materials or to articles exported to countries with which we were at war or which were at war at others or in which a state of civil strife existed." Id. at n.1. For example, the Neutrality Act of 1939 authorized the President to restrict any exports to countries that were in a state of war. Id. at 791–2.

[2] U.S. Dep't of Commerce, 68 *Survey of Current Business* 5–16 (March 1988).

[3] See discussion in Chapters 2, 5, 6, and 12. See also H. Moyer and L. Mabry, "Export Controls as Instruments of Foreign Policy: The History, Legal Issues, and Policy Lessons of Three Recent Cases," 15 *L. & Pol'y Int'l Bus.* 1, 2 (1983).

International economic sanctions

A. THE EXPORT ADMINISTRATION ACT

The EAA[4] provides no right to export.[5] On the contrary, it prohibits, with few exceptions, all exports from the United States unless they are licensed by the Department of Commerce.[6] The licensing requirement is not burdensome for most exports, which can be shipped under "general licenses." These are Department of Commerce licenses that allow the export of specified goods and technology to certain destinations without any special authorization.[7] For example, grain or automobiles can be exported to Spain or Australia under a general license.

The Executive Branch might decide, however, that greater control over certain exports or over exports to certain countries is appropriate on the grounds of national security, foreign policy, or short supply.[8] In this case, the Executive Branch will issue regulations requiring the specific prior approval of Commerce. This approval is generally known as a "validated license." A validated license can authorize a specific export transaction – identifying the goods or technology, the buyer, the country, and the end use. Alternatively, to simplify the administrative process, some val-

---

[4] 50 U.S.C. app. §§ 2401–20 (1982 and Supp. III 1985).

[5] Courts have traditionally held that there is no right to export. See e.g., *Buttfield v. Stranahan*, 192 U.S. 470, 493 (1904) (upholding an import statute, but noting generally that "no individual has a right to trade with foreign nations"). This is recognized in the EAA's legislative history. S. Rep. No. 169, 96th Cong., 1st Sess. 3–4 (1979); see J. Murphy and A. Downey, "National Security, Foreign Policy and Individual Rights: The Quandary of United States Export Controls," 30 *Int'l & Comp. L.Q.* 792, 823 (1981). See discussion of the limited right to administrative or judicial review under the EAA, in Section A.5.

[6] For a more detailed review of the EAA statutory scheme see, e.g., K. Abbott, "Linking Trade to Political Goals: Foreign Policy Export Controls in the 1970s and 1980s," 65 *Minn. L. Rev.* 739, 745–56 (1981); Murphy and Downey, supra note 5, at 823–6. The principal exceptions to the statute are (1) most exports to Canada for consumption there, (2) certain exports to U.S. armed forces, and (3) exports regulated by another U.S. agency, including defense articles under the authority of the Arms Export Control Act. See 15 C.F.R. §§ 370.3(a) and 370.10 (1987). Controls on nuclear-related commodities and technical data are implemented under both the EAA and the Atomic Energy Act of 1954, as amended by the Nuclear Non-Proliferation Act of 1978 and other statutes. See 15 C.F.R. pt. 378 (1987).

[7] 15 C.F.R. § 371.2(a). Even with a general license, an exporter must file a "Shipper's Export Declaration" and may face other documentation requirements. Id. §§ 386–7; Abbott, supra note 6, at 751.

[8] The focus of the discussion here on export controls is on national security and foreign policy controls. The short-supply controls are designed "to restrict the export of goods where necessary to protect the domestic economy from the excessive drain of scarce materials and to reduce the serious inflationary impact of foreign demand." 50 U.S.C. app. § 2402(2)(C). They generally are not used for foreign policy purposes. There is also an antiboycott section in the EAA. This is discussed in Chapter 8.

idated licenses cover multiple exports for a year or two for specific projects or certain commodities.[9]

If the President, through Commerce, denies an application for a validated license, the exporter's right to administrative and judicial review is very limited. Moreover, an exporter who ships goods without the required license is subject to a wide range of severe penalties – including civil fines, denial of future privileges to export or import, and felony criminal charges.

The basic framework of the EAA and recent trends can best be understood in the context of its post–World War II history, including the amendments enacted in 1985.

1. Before 1979

Most of the strict export controls of World War II were continued from year to year until February 1949, when Congress enacted the Export Control Act. The Act was considered a temporary measure and might have lapsed in 1951. However, with the Korean War and continuing international tensions, the Act was renewed in 1951 and about every three years afterward through 1969.[10]

The 1949 Act was originally designed to achieve two main purposes: first, to prevent vital supplies from being drained away from this country as the world was emerging from a war and experiencing great shortages of many goods; and second, to channel exports to the countries that the United States most wanted to help, such as Western Europe.[11]

A third purpose of export controls assumed growing importance as countries were rebuilt after World War II and as the "Cold War" became colder with the communist coup in Czechoslovakia in March 1948, the Berlin blockade in the summer of 1948, and the invasion of South Korea in June 1950. This purpose was to prevent the Soviet Union and the rest of the "Sino-Soviet bloc" from obtaining any goods or technology that might enhance its military or economic position.[12] The practical result was the denial of almost all U.S. export trade with the these countries.

The NATO allies and Japan either shared this view or were willing to go along with it. The Consultative Group Coordination Committee (CoCom) was created in 1949 by the United States and six European allies to orchestrate the West's efforts to block exports to communist

---

[9] See 15 C.F.R. §§ 372.1–13.
[10] Berman and Garson, supra note 1, at 792.
[11] Id. at 794–5.
[12] Berman and Garson, supra note 1, at 795, 799–803; Murphy and Downey, supra note 5, at 792.

countries. CoCom was expanded in 1952–3 and has come to include all the NATO allies (except Iceland and Spain) and Japan. The organization continues to operate as an informal arrangement, there being no underlying treaty or executive agreement.[13]

The Export Administration Act of 1969 replaced the 1949 Act. The new statute continued the three broad policies that had been used to justify limits on exports – national security, foreign policy, and shortages in supply.[14] The 1969 Act, however, reflected definite changes in U.S. policy toward exports.

First, the United States began to recognize more fully the positive benefits of export trade to economic growth. Support grew for efforts to increase exports rather than to hamper them.[15] The 1969 Act contained, among other things, a statement that it was U.S. policy to "encourage" trade with all countries with which the United States had diplomatic or trading relations and to use U.S. exports "to further the sound growth and stability of its economy."[16]

Second, the goal of nearly total denial of exports to the communist countries was replaced by a narrower conception of national security interests.[17] As a result, although the national security and foreign policy

[13] In addition to the United States, the original CoCom members included the United Kingdom, France, Italy, the Netherlands, Belgium, and Luxembourg. Berman and Garson, supra note 1, at 834–5. For a general discussion of the history and operation of CoCom, see id. at 834–6; C. Hunt, "Multilateral Cooperation in Export Controls – The Role of CoCom," 14 *U. Tol. L. Rev.* 1285 (1983); Murphy and Downey, supra note 5, at 805–7.

[14] Export Administration Act of 1969, Pub. L. No. 91–184, § 3, 83 Stat. 841 (codified at 50 U.S.C. app. § 2402 (expired 1979)) [hereinafter EAA 1969 or 1969 Act]; Abbott, supra note 6, at 746–8.

[15] Murphy and Downey, supra note 5, at 805–7.

[16] EAA 1969, supra note 14, § 3, 50 U.S.C. app. § 2402. In that vein, the 1969 Act, especially as amended in 1977, attempted to provide "an element of due process" for exporters. H.R. Rep. No. 190, 95th Cong., 1st Sess. 13, reprinted in 1977 *U.S. Code Cong. & Ad. News* 362, 374. For example, time limits were established for certain actions on license applications, exporters were permitted in certain cases to respond to questions about their applications, and applicants had to be informed of the statutory reasons for the denial of their applications. Abbott, supra note 6, at 750. Nevertheless, these procedural safeguards were designed only to limit the Executive "to some minimal degree." H.R. Rep. No. 190, supra.

[17] Murphy and Downey, supra note 5. This reflected not only the relatively improved U.S. relations with the Soviets, but also the reality of the United States apparently losing out in the trade benefits. For example, in 1965, U.S. exports to communist countries amounted to $139 million, whereas West European exports to these countries amounted to $4 billion, and total "free world" exports to them were $7.5 billion. This very small U.S. share of East–West trade contrasted with the U.S. share (16%) of total "free-world" exports. Berman and Garson, supra note 1, at 876–7.

criteria for export controls were retained, the 1969 Act eliminated as a justification for limiting exports the consideration that they made a significant contribution to the "economic potential" of an adversary.[18]

The 1970s witnessed a continuation of the developments that had caused the 1969 changes in the export law. In addition, the 1970s saw a dramatic increase in the use of export controls for a variety of foreign policy, as distinguished from national security, purposes. In the past, foreign policy as well as national security had been a consideration in the broad limits on trade with communist countries. Export controls based primarily on foreign policy considerations, however, had been "quite rare"[19] and were limited in their coverage. These controls were essentially of three types: those helping to implement UN actions, such as against Rhodesia and South Africa;[20] those limiting the export of nuclear items; and those designed to maintain stability in volatile regions, such as the Middle East.[21]

The situation changed with increased concern over terrorism and human rights, emanating originally from Congress and then from the Carter Administration. As for terrorism, Congress included in the 1977 amendments to the 1969 Act a policy statement authorizing the President to use export controls "to encourage other countries to take immediate steps to prevent the use of their territories or resources to aid, encourage, or give sanctuary to" international terrorists.[22] The Carter Administration quickly cited this provision to help justify a number of export controls, though they generally were also justified on national security grounds.[23]

Most important to the growth of export controls for foreign policy purposes during this time was the heightened concern for "internationally recognized human rights."[24] Although this general concern was never

---

[18] EAA 1969, supra note 14, § 3. Compare with Pub. L. No. 87-515, 76 Stat. 127, § 3 (1962), amending EAA 1949.

[19] Abbott, supra note 6, at 760.

[20] The Rhodesian and South African controls were also based in part on the UN Participation Act, discussed in Chapter 8.

[21] Abbott, supra note 6, at 760–3.

[22] Export Administration Amendments of 1977, Pub. L. No. 95–52, § 115, 91 Stat. 235 (codified at 50 U.S.C. app. § 2402(8)). This was one of several legislative attempts to combat terrorism. As discussed elsewhere, other efforts included similar provisions in laws regarding foreign assistance and arms exports, as well as ones directing the U.S. directors in several international financial institutions to vote against countries supporting terrorists. See also Abbott, supra note 6, at 767–9.

[23] Abbott, supra note 6, at 770–1. An example of the mixture of reasons for license denials includes the 1978 case of commercial aircraft to Libya. Concerns about regional stability and terrorism temporarily delayed the sale. Id. at 762 n.119.

[24] This concern was also reflected in other legislation regarding foreign assistance,

explicitly written into the 1969 Act, it fathered amendments that limited the export of crime control equipment and that banned all exports to Uganda, and also led to several major regulations and denials of licenses.

Crime control equipment was an early target of concern, rooted in the fear that repressive governments would use this equipment for torture and for suppressing dissidents. In 1974, regulations under the Export Act required a specific (validated) license to export this equipment to communist countries. These regulations were expanded in 1978 to include all countries other than NATO members, Japan, Australia, and New Zealand. Congress then essentially wrote these existing controls into the 1969 Act.[25]

As part of a variety of sanctions imposed by the United States against the genocidal regime of Idi Amin, Congress imposed in 1978 a mandatory embargo on exports to (as well as imports from) Uganda.[26] This constituted the first unilateral U.S. embargo that did not originate from war or similar circumstances. Partly because of the U.S. sanctions, Amin was overthrown in April 1979.[27]

Similarly, as one of its steps against South Africa's apartheid policies, the Carter Administration in 1978 embargoed all exports of U.S.-origin goods and unpublished technical information to any "military and police entities" in South Africa. Although the Administration claimed that it was acting to further both the UN arms embargo and U.S. foreign policy on human rights, the President's authority came from the Export Act of 1969 since the Security Council resolutions involved only the exports of arms and related equipment.[28]

President Carter also imposed in 1978 additional controls against the export to the Soviet Union of most types of the equipment and technology used for the exploration and production of oil and natural gas. Although some equipment and technology had already been limited for national security reasons, the 1978 controls were also imposed to "be consistent with the foreign policy objectives of the United States."[29] A major impetus appears to have been the trial and sentencing of dissidents Anatoly Shcharansky and Aleksandr Ginzburg.[30]

The Export Act of 1969 came up for renewal in 1979 against this

the Export–Import Bank, OPIC, and U.S. participation in international financial institutions. See discussion in Chapter 3, Section B, and Chapter 7; see also Abbott, supra note 6, at 772–7.

[25] Abbott, supra note 6, at 787–90.
[26] Bretton Woods Agreement Amendments Act, Pub. L. No. 95–435, §§ 5(c)–(d), 92 Stat. 1051 (1978).
[27] See discussion in Chapter 2.
[28] Abbott, supra note 6, at 783.
[29] 43 *Fed. Reg.* 33,699 (1978).
[30] Z. Brzezinski, *Power and Principle* 320–5 (1985).

background of often conflicting concerns – the long-standing ones over excessive use of the national security justification and the need for increased exports, as well as the increased willingness by some to use export controls for a variety of foreign policy purposes.[31]

2. *The 1979 Export Administration Act*

In replacing the 1969 Act, the Export Administration Act of 1979 made some major changes.[32] It continues to provide the basic legal framework today for most U.S. exports. (The Export Administration Amendments Act of 1985, discussed in Section A.4, includes some important changes, but it does not alter the essential framework of the 1979 Act.)

Probably the most important advance of the 1979 Act was to divide the provisions on national security controls and foreign policy controls into two separate sections and require that they be treated differently. The basic criterion for national security controls remains whether the exports "would make a significant contribution to the military potential of any other country or combination of countries which would prove detrimental to the national security of the United States."[33] In an effort to narrow the scope of these controls, the Act requires that the Administration take better account of the foreign availability of goods.[34]

For foreign policy controls, the 1979 Act codified and tried to put some boundaries on the major expansion of these controls that began in

---

[31] See J. Bingham and V. Johnson, "A Rational Approach to Export Controls," 57 *Foreign Aff.* 894 (1979). There were also widespread concerns about the cumbersome administrative process in considering license applications. Id. at 902–3.

[32] Pub. L. No. 96–72, 93 Stat. 503 (1979) (codified at 50 U.S.C. app. §§2401–20 (1982)) [hereinafter the 1979 Act].

[33] 50 U.S.C. app. § 2402(2)(A). The Act did give the Defense Department a bigger role in deciding whether to deny license applications on national security grounds. Id. §§ 2403(a)(1) and (c)(2), 2409(g). The Act also found that these controls should "give special emphasis to the need to control exports of technology (and goods which contribute significantly to the transfer of such technology) which could make a significant contribution to the military potential...." Id. at § 2401(8). This emphasis on controlling sensitive technology, rather than on the stated end use of a particular good, reflects the conclusions of the so-called Bucy Report (named after its chairman J. Fred Bucy). *Defense Science Board Task Force Report on Export of U.S. Technology, An Analysis of Export Control of U.S. Technology – DOD Perspective* (1976).

[34] 50 U.S.C. app. § 2404(f)(1) required continuous monitoring of this by the Secretary of Commerce. If the Secretary finds that items are available from foreign sources, he is directed to approve applications for a validated license, unless the President determines that national security requires the export controls anyway. Id. § 2404(f)(2). The Act also directs the President to enter into negotiations with other CoCom members to improve the workings of CoCom. This effort is to include "[a]greement to reduce the scope of the export controls imposed by [CoCom] to a level acceptable to and enforceable by all" CoCom members. Id. § 2404(i)(3).

the 1970s. The Act carried over the basic criterion that controls could be used "to restrict the export of goods and technology where necessary to further significantly the foreign policy of the United States or to fulfill its declared international obligations."[35] The Act, however, includes a list of criteria that the President is directed to consider before imposing export controls for foreign policy reasons.[36] The Act further requires the Executive Branch to take other steps before imposing foreign policy controls.[37] Specific provisions were inserted for exports to countries supporting international terrorism and for crime control instruments.[38]

To encourage regular reconsideration of the need for controls, the Act provides that they expire one year after their imposition.[39] The President could extend the controls on an annual basis, but he would have to notify Congress and determine that the controls still satisfied the initial criteria for imposing the controls.[40]

The Act also includes a number of procedural reforms designed to speed up the licensing process.[41]

3. Experience under the 1979 Act

Effective October 1, 1979, the new Act soon encountered a major test with the Soviet invasion of Afghanistan in late December 1979. In response, President Carter ordered a variety of controls on exports to the Soviet Union. In doing so, he quickly highlighted some of the statute's ambiguities.[42]

---

[35] Id. § 2402(2)(B).

[36] Id. § 2405(b). See the discussion regarding the 1985 amendments in Section A.4.b.

[37] For example, the President is to "determine that reasonable efforts have been made to achieve the purposes of the controls through negotiations or other alternative means." Id. § 2405(d). The President is also required to consult Congress "in every possible instance" (id. § 2405(e)), and the Secretary of Commerce is directed to "consult with such affected United States industries as the Secretary considers appropriate." Id. § 2405(c). See the discussion regarding the 1985 amendments at notes 68–75 infra.

[38] Id. § 2405(i), (j). As amended in 1986, the provision regarding terrorism requires the President to notify certain congressional committees at least thirty days *before* "any license is approved for the export of goods or technology" valued at more than $1,000,000 to any country determined by the Secretary of State to support international terrorism. See discussion in Section C, this chapter. Iran had been designated one of those countries. See 15 C.F.R. § 385.4 (1987).

[39] 50 U.S.C. app. § 2405(a)(2) (1982).

[40] Id.

[41] See Murphy and Downey, supra note 5, at 824–34.

[42] Relatively straightforward was the decision to ban temporarily high-technology exports to the Soviets. In January 1980, Carter directed the Secretary of Commerce to begin a review of U.S. policy on these exports to the Soviet Union, to suspend the

Exports from the United States

Most controversial politically and legally was the President's decision of January 7, 1980, to terminate shipments of agricultural products, including wheat and corn, to the Soviet Union.[43] This decision still allowed 8 million metric tons to be shipped as the minimum required under the U.S.–Soviet grain agreement of 1975, but it cut off the sale of an estimated additional 17 million tons of grain, as well as sales of other agricultural products.[44]

Although this partial embargo had considerable symbolic significance, its economic impact on the Soviets was limited.[45] In the United States, even with some offsetting government programs, the embargo hurt U.S. farmers in the short term and also prompted the Soviet Union to reduce its long-term reliance on U.S. agricultural exports to fill the gap after bad Soviet harvests.[46]

As justification for this embargo, the President cited "national security and foreign policy."[47] This dual justification, however, was contrary to the clear purpose of the 1979 Act, which was intended to draw a distinction between the two grounds. Moreover, the national security basis for limiting all agricultural exports, including chickens and truffles, seemed somewhat strained.[48] In fact, the Administration's own elaborations essentially rested on foreign policy grounds.[49]

issuance of new validated licenses until the review was completed, and to suspend the previously issued validated licenses where the export had not yet occurred. E.g., 45 *Fed. Reg.* 3027 (1980); Subcomm. on Europe and the Middle East of the House Comm. on Foreign Affairs, 97th Cong., 1st Sess., *An Assessment of the Afghanistan Sanctions: Implications for Trade and Diplomacy in the 1980's* 65 (1981) (report prepared by Congressional Reference Service) [hereinafter the House Afghanistan Report]. (This excellent report provides a very thorough, objective study of the Afghanistan sanctions.) On March 18, the Department announced that the review had been completed and that it would begin to review the several hundred or so suspended validated licenses. Id.

[43] President Carter, "Shipments of Agricultural Commodities to the Soviet Union," 16 *Weekly Comp. Pres. Doc.* 32 (Jan. 7, 1980).

[44] See id.; House Afghanistan Report, supra note 42, at 23–52.

[45] House Afghanistan Report, supra note 42.

[46] Id.; International Trade Commission, *U.S. Embargoes on Agricultural Exports: Implications for the U.S. Agricultural Industry and U.S. Exports*, Pub. No. 1461 (Dec. 1983); see K. Schneider, "Russians Ignore Reagan's Offer to Sell Wheat," *N.Y. Times*, Sept. 30, 1986, at 1, col. 2; see discussion in Chapter 2 at note 77.

[47] President Carter, supra note 43.

[48] At a minimum, the national security basis required falling back to the broad rationale in the Export Control Act of 1949, which, as amended, authorized license denials if the President determined that an export made a "significant contribution to the military or economic potential" of an adversary. 50 U.S.C. app. § 2023(a) (1964). However, in the 1969 and 1979 Acts, Congress had eliminated the concept of "economic potential" and had maintained only the narrower standard of "military potential." See Murphy and Downey, supra note 5, at 794, 818.

[49] See Murphy and Downey, supra note 5, at 818; see also *U.S. Export Weekly*

The decision to invoke national security as well as foreign policy was actively debated in the Executive Branch.[50] One unannounced reason was that using foreign policy only would have appeared inconsistent with a campaign statement by President Carter that he would not use food products as a weapon of foreign policy.[51] Moreover, the dual justification made the embargo less vulnerable to challenge for failure to satisfy all the EAA's procedural requirements.[52] Possibly most important, the 1979 Act had provided Congress with authority to veto by a concurrent resolution controls on agricultural exports imposed for foreign policy purposes, but not for national security reasons.[53]

President Carter later used the 1979 Act to further his Olympic boycott. In March 1980, he prohibited exports to the Soviet Union of any goods or technology in connection with the Olympic Games. To the surprise of some observers, Carter then went a step further and also prohibited any payments or transactions that could provide financial support for the Games. The asserted legal authority for these financial controls was tucked away in a provision of the EAA. It authorized controls over "financing" in order apparently to help implement export controls, rather than providing independent authority to control international financial transactions. In any case, this application of the Act demonstrated the President's ability to use the Act expansively.[54]

Many people in Congress and elsewhere were also unhappy over other uses of the 1979 Act. There were complaints, for example, over the perfunctory way that President Carter and President Reagan extended foreign policy controls beyond their one-year termination dates. The renewal requirement was designed to trigger an evaluation of the need for the controls, but the renewals became routine.[55] Similarly, foreign policy controls were expanded or modified with little consultation with Congress. In early 1982, for example, President Reagan trimmed back

(BNA), No. 291, at A–4 (Jan. 22, 1980) (describing confusion over the basis for the embargo).

[50] Telephone interview with Joseph Onek, formerly Deputy Counsel to President Carter (Mar. 14, 1986).

[51] Moyer and Mabry, supra note 3, at 31.

[52] Id.

[53] 50 U.S.C. app. § 2406(g)(3)(1982). The provision also applied to short-supply controls. Id. The provision for a concurrent resolution is now effectively void as a result of the 1983 Supreme Court decision in *Chadha*, discussed in Chapter 9, Section D.2.

[54] 50 U.S.C. app. § 2414. For a more detailed discussion of this incident, see Chapter 6, Section B.

[55] See e.g., Department of Commerce, *Foreign Policy Report to Congress: Jan. 21, 1984–Jan. 20, 1985* (1985); Department of Commerce, "Extension of Foreign Policy Export Controls," 48 *Fed. Reg.* 3359 (1983).

the limits on some exports to South Africa, setting off considerable public dispute.[56]

In June 1982, President Reagan announced an unprecedented broadening of trade controls against the Soviet Union. These controls were imposed on exports of oil and gas equipment and technology and were designed, at least in part, to hamper Soviet construction of the Yamal natural-gas pipeline to Europe.[57] These so-called pipeline controls raised issues of both contract sanctity and extraterritoriality. They encountered strong opposition in Congress, in the U.S. business community, and with many of our allies. Faced with this opposition, including affirmative efforts by several European countries to blunt the impact of the controls on resident companies, the Administration rescinded the controls in November 1982,[58] but the experience left a bad taste with many in Congress and elsewhere.[59]

There were also continuing concerns about sensitive goods and technology getting to the Soviet Union, concerns that were heightened by disclosures in the early 1980s about extensive Soviet efforts to obtain Western technology and of substantial leakage of this technology to the Soviets.[60]

Even before the 1979 Act expired in 1983, unhappiness with the 1980–1 grain embargo led Congress to limit progressively the President's power to impose agricultural embargoes. The first step was a provision in the Agricultural and Food Act of 1981 requiring farmers to be compensated at a generous rate if there were another agricultural embargo against a major purchaser, whether imposed for national security or foreign policy reasons.[61] Congress then tacked onto the Futures Trading Act of 1982

[56] Under the revised controls, goods in a number of export categories (including personal computers, word processors, and electronic copying machines) could be sold to South African government agencies, including the military and police forces, without U.S. export licenses. *Bus. Week*, Mar. 15, 1982, at 39; *Wash. Post*, Feb. 27, 1982, at 1.

[57] 47 *Fed. Reg.* 27,250 (1982); *N.Y. Times*, June 19, 1982, at 1. The controls were a considerable extension of a series of controls that had been imposed against the Soviets during late 1981 and early 1982, ostensibly over the repression in Poland.

[58] 47 *Fed. Reg.* 51,858 (1982).

[59] For a more detailed discussion of the pipeline controls, see Section A.6, this chapter, on extraterritoriality.

[60] Also continuing were the long-standing objections to the snail's-pace administration of the export laws.

[61] Pub. L. No. 97–98, 95 Stat. 1213 (1981) (codified at 7 U.S.C. § 1736j (1982 & Supp. IV 1986)). The statutory requirement is triggered if the export sales of the embargoed commodity to that foreign country during the year before the embargo exceeds 3% of the total export sales of that commodity and if the embargo is not part of an embargo of all U.S. exports to that country. If those conditions are met, the Secretary has to make payments or loans in specified amounts to the producers of the embargoed commodity. The terms would be generous since the calculations

a provision actually limiting the President's power to impose an agricultural embargo. It provides that the President cannot curtail the export of any agricultural product under an existing export sales contract that requires delivery within 270 days of the start of the embargo, unless the President has declared a national emergency or Congress has declared war.[62]

4. Export Administration Amendments Act of 1985

The current 1985 Act had a long and difficult birth. When the 1979 Act expired on September 30, 1983, the Senate and House extended it by joint resolution through October 14. President Reagan then declared a national emergency and invoked IEEPA to continue the export regulations, until Congress reinstated the EAA from December 5, 1983, through March 30, 1984. Reagan then stepped in again with IEEPA.[63]

Reauthorization bills did pass both houses in 1984, but the Conference Committee was unable to reach agreement. Last-minute efforts to compromise failed, and the bills died in the 98th Congress. The legislation was resubmitted in 1985, received speedy consideration, and was signed by the President in July.[64]

The 1985 Act essentially extends the 1979 Act and its basic structure – including the separation of national security and foreign policy controls. However, the 1985 Act does contain several important changes, some designed to limit further the President's power to impose export controls. Most important are the time limit on agricultural embargoes, the tougher steps for imposing foreign policy controls, and the new provision on "contract sanctity."

a. Agricultural embargoes. Reflecting the unhappy experience with the 1980–1 agricultural embargo, the 1985 Act goes beyond even the 1981–2 statutory changes discussed earlier. It prohibits the President from imposing export controls on any agricultural commodity for more than sixty days, unless Congress enacts a joint resolution authorizing the ac-

---

assumed that the farmers would have received a price equivalent to 100% of parity. Id.; see Conference Report, S. Rep. No. 290, 97th Cong., 1st Sess. 208–9 (1981).

[62] 7 U.S.C. 612c–3 (1982).

[63] See discussion in Chapter 9, Section C.

[64] Pub. L. No. 99–64, 99 Stat. 120 (1985) (codified in scattered sections, primarily at 50 U.S.C. app. §§ 2401–20 (Supp. III 1985)) [hereinafter the 1985 Act]. Both houses passed their bills in April 1985, and the Conference Committee ironed out a compromise in June 1985. It was passed by both houses on June 27 and signed by the President on July 12. See J. Harris and J. Bialos, "Congressional Balancing Act Benefits Exporters," *Legal Times,* Aug. 15, 1985, at 17.

tion.[65] Congress, however, left an important exception to this time limit. It does not apply when the agricultural controls "are imposed with respect to a country as part of the prohibition or curtailment of *all* exports to that country."[66] Congress apparently was trying to protect farm interests from being singled out as a tool for embargoes, while also protecting the President's discretion to impose a more comprehensive embargo.[67]

b. Foreign policy controls. The 1985 Act also tightens up the steps the President must take before using foreign policy controls. This change reflected concerns that export controls were invoked too frequently, were often ineffective, and created unnecessary burdens on exporters.[68]

Specifically, the Act first toughens the criteria the President should consider before imposing the controls. Instead of simply charging him to think about certain matters, the Act directs the President to make certain determinations, which include the following:

- "such controls are likely to achieve the intended foreign policy purpose, in light of other factors, including the availability from other countries of the goods or technology proposed for such controls, and that foreign policy purpose cannot be achieved through negotiations or other alternative means;"
- "the reaction of other countries ... is not likely to render the controls ineffective ... or to be counterproductive ... ;"
- "the United States has the ability to enforce the proposed controls effectively."[69]

This requirement that the President make determinations has had only limited impact so far. It apparently has not stopped any new controls from being imposed or any existing controls from being extended. It probably has encouraged, however, more extensive analysis in the Sec-

---

[65] The Act did this by, first, prohibiting the use of national security controls for agricultural products. 50 U.S.C. app. § 2404(g) (Supp. III 1985). Then, it required congressional approval after sixty days for foreign policy or short-supply controls over agricultural commodities. Id. § 2406(g)(3)(A).

[66] Id. § 2406(g)(3)(B) (emphasis added). Note that this provision clearly implies that the President can ban all exports to a country.

[67] See, e.g., The Export Administration Act Amendments of 1983, S. Rep. No. 170, 98th Cong., 1st Sess. 12 (1983).

[68] Id. at 14.

[69] 50 U.S.C. app. § 2405(b). The criteria in the 1979 Act were phrased in a considerably more tentative way. For example, the President was to consider "the probability that such controls will achieve the intended foreign policy purposes" rather than that they are "likely to." Similarly, the President was to consider "the ability of the United States to enforce the proposed controls effectively" rather than the fact that "the United States *has* the ability to enforce" (emphasis added). 1979 Act, supra note 32, § 6(b).

retary of Commerce's annual report on the existing controls.[70] One specific problem is that the tougher requirements regarding the foreign availability of goods have been undercut by the fact that most foreign policy controls are categorized as symbolic – for example, to distance the United States from another country's actions. In these situations, foreign availability is not relevant.[71] In any case, the impact of these and similar requirements for determinations will probably remain very limited until much greater administrative and judicial review is provided for under the EAA.

More importantly, the 1985 Act requires the President to consult Congress and submit a detailed report *before* imposing the foreign policy controls.[72] This stands in contrast to the 1979 provisions requiring consultation with Congress "in every possible instance" and a less complete report after the imposition of the control.[73] The Conference Committee expressed its unhappiness over past consultation with Congress, which had "been perfunctory at best." Specifically noting the constitutional powers of Congress, the Committee hoped that the new consultation requirement would result in "greater deliberation ... by the President" and "in wiser control policies enjoying greater Congressional support."[74]

---

[70] Statement of Secretary of Commerce Malcolm Baldridge before the Subcomm. on Int'l Economic Policy and Trade of the House Comm. on Foreign Affairs 1 (March 19, 1986) (mimeographed copy on file with author). A study by the Government Accounting Office (GAO), however, found that the 1986 annual report still had "certain shortcomings," including the fact that the sections addressing alternative means and enforcement included little explanation and that the sections on economic impact did not explain the limitations on its estimates. GAO, *Export Controls: Assessment of Commerce Department's Foreign Policy Report to Congress* 4 (Aug. 1986).

[71] See GAO, supra note 70, at 6. Note that there are requirements in the 1985 Act regarding foreign availability other than the requirements in 50 U.S.C. § 2405(b), discussed at note 69 above. For example, see id. § 2405(h).

[72] Id. § 2405.

[73] 1979 EAA, supra note 32, § 6(e).

[74] Conference Report, H. Rep. No. 180, 99th Cong., 1st Sess. 57 (1985). "This should result in more meaningful consultation, which is in keeping with article I, section 8, of the Constitution which gives the Congress the power to regulate international commerce. Export control authority is only delegated by Congress to the President, as provided in the Act, and the Congress intends that the President consult with the Congress in the conduct of that delegated authority." Id.

The President is also directed, "at the earliest possible opportunity, [to] consult with the" CoCom countries and any others the President considers appropriate regarding the criteria for imposing the foreign policy controls. 50 U.S.C. app. § 2405(d) (Supp. III 1985). The 1985 Act further requires the Secretary of Commerce "in every possible instance to consult with and seek advice from affected United States industries." Id. § 2405 (c). The 1979 Act was less demanding, requiring that the Secretary

It remains to be seen whether these mandatory consultation and reporting provisions will impose many additional limits on the President's discretion. The Executive Branch can still deny them much substantive impact by undertaking consultation only after making its policy decisions.[75]

c. Contract sanctity. Possibly the most "bitterly contested" provision[76] of the 1985 Act dealt with "contract sanctity" – that is, the power of the President to impose export controls that abrogate existing contracts. It remains to be seen whether all the legislative fireworks produced any significant limits on the President.

Contract sanctity became a widespread issue after the agricultural embargo and the pipeline sanctions. President Carter had stopped some agricultural exports that had not yet been shipped from the United States, which overrode preexisting contracts.[77] President Reagan went even further with the pipeline sanctions. The controls were extended in some cases to prohibit exports from a *foreign* country to the Soviet Union subject to an existing contract, if the goods had been manufactured on the basis of a licensing agreement with any company subject to U.S. jurisdiction.[78] This obviously contributed to the reluctance of foreign buyers and others to rely on U.S. suppliers.[79]

Disgruntled exporters and unhappy allies sought relief, but they encountered the competing concern that the President should be able to act flexibly to protect U.S. interests. The compromise language in the 1985 Act prohibits the President from imposing foreign policy controls on the export or reexport of goods or technology under existing contracts or validated licenses, unless the President determines and certifies to Con-

---

shall consult with such industries as he "considers appropriate." 1979 EAA, supra note 32, § 6(c).

The 1985 Act also puts some backbone into the consultation requirements. If the President wants to impose certain foreign policy controls without consulting Congress (or the allies and affected industries, or without meeting the requirements regarding foreign availability of the goods), he must obtain a joint resolution from Congress, albeit on an accelerated schedule. 50 U.S.C. app. § 2405(o).

[75] See Harris and Bialos, supra note 64, at 18. Even the Conference Committee acknowledged that "on some occasions conditions may require that consultation [with Congress] take place no sooner than shortly before the controls are imposed." H. Rep. No. 180, supra note 74, at 57. Note that the Reagan Administration failed to notify Congress in advance about its arms sales to Iran in 1985–6, in spite of an EAA provision apparently requiring prior notice. See supra note 155.

[76] H. Rep. No. 180, supra note 74, at 58.

[77] See discussion in Chapter 12 regarding liability under the Uniform Commercial Code for buyers and sellers.

[78] 47 *Fed. Reg.* 27,250 at 27,251 (1982).

[79] See H. Rep. No. 180, supra note 74, at 59.

gress that (1) "a breach of the peace poses a serious and direct threat to the strategic interest of the United States," (2) "the prohibition or curtailment . . . will be instrumental in remedying the situation posing the direct threat," and (3) "the export controls will continue only so long as the direct threat persists."[80]

This provision requires a "cause-and-effect" relationship between the proposed contract-breaking control and that control's remedial effect on a situation that directly threatens U.S. strategic interests. The congressional conferees judged "that this constraint significantly narrows, but does not entirely eliminate, the authority of the President to impose controls on exports subject to" existing contracts.[81] In a separate statement, one of the provision's strongest supporters, Senator John Heinz (R.-Pa.), declared that the provision would ban retroactive controls "except in the most extreme circumstances."[82]

Although the concept of contract sanctity is a major new addition to export laws,[83] this provision is likely to have limited impact, especially if the President is determined to steer around it. First, the provision now applies only to foreign policy controls and not national security controls. As demonstrated earlier with the Soviet grain embargo, the President might well invoke the national security ground even when it is arguably not appropriate.

Second, the language of the certification provision allows the President ample room to justify abrogating existing contracts. Against the restrictive language of the conference report and of Senator Heinz, there are other authoritative statements calling for a broad interpretation of the exception for a "breach of peace." Congressman Howard Berman, one of the authors of the exception, would construe it expansively to encompass "a violation or disturbance of the public tranquility and order."[84] Senator William Proxmire, another conferee and the then ranking minority member of the Senate Banking Committee, specifically endorsed Berman's view, which he said was supported by legal history, Supreme Court decisions, and international law.[85]

Contract sanctity has yet to arise in a situation since the 1985 Act.

---

[80] 50 U.S.C. app. § 2405(m). The section actually protects exports or reexports under an existing "contract or agreement" or "under a validated license or other authorization issued under the [EAA]." Id.

[81] H. Rep. No. 180. supra note 74, at 58–9. The conferees go on to note their expectation that "the President [will] adhere to the intent of Congress in implementing this provision and to treat the certification required . . . with the utmost gravity."

[82] 2 *Int'l Trade Rep. (BNA).* 856, 857 (July 3, 1985).

[83] Note the prior provision protecting certain agricultural contracts (of 270 days or less) in the Futures Trading Act of 1982, discussed at note 62 in this chapter.

[84] 130 *Cong. Rec.* H12,167 (daily ed. Oct. 11, 1984).

[85] 131 *Cong. Rec.* S8926 (daily ed. June 27, 1985).

Nevertheless, some commentators have already concluded that "Congress has given the business community a symbolic victory largely bereft of substance."[86]

d. Other changes. The 1985 Act did contain other changes that affected the Executive Branch's implementation of export controls. These include several administrative improvements designed to speed up or to simplify the licensing process. For example, Congress mandated new and stricter deadlines on the Department of Commerce's handling of license applications and certain other requests by exporters.[87]

The 1985 Act also toughened enforcement of the export laws. For example, in reaction to justified concerns that the CoCom system was often a sieve that seemed to stop mainly U.S., and not allied, exports, there were several provisions for strengthening CoCom's controls. These included directing the Executive Branch to negotiate for certain improvements.[88] The Act also toughened the broad array of criminal, civil, and administrative sanctions that can be imposed on violators of the U.S. export laws. Probably the most significant change was to allow import sanctions for any person who violates a national security export control.[89] In the past, such violators could be punished by orders denying their right to export further and by fines and jail terms. It was thought, however, that this import provision would provide another lever for ensuring

---

[86] Harris and Bialos, supra note 64, at 19.

[87] 50 U.S.C. app. §2409 (Supp III 1985). Congress also eliminated U.S. licensing requirements for relatively low technology items being exported to CoCom countries. Id. This eliminated the need for Commerce to process 40,000 to 50,000 export licenses, approximately 40% of its workload. Harris and Bialos, supra note 64, at 17.

The Act also directed Commerce to establish a new "comprehensive operations license, authorizing exports and reexports of technology and related goods...from a domestic concern to and among its foreign subsidiaries, affiliates, joint venturers, and licensees that have long-term, contractually defined relations with the exporter." 50 U.S.C. app.§2403(a)(2). This broad license would avoid the need for many multinational firms to obtain numerous validated licenses for ongoing transactions among their related parts.

The Executive Branch, under prodding from Congress, was taking further steps in 1986–8 to streamline the licensing process. See, e.g., 52 *Fed. Reg.* 5274 (1987); but cf. 4 *Int'l Trade Rep.* 293 (Mar. 4, 1987) (Cong. Bonker says he is skeptical about Reagan Administration efforts to modify export controls). The disclosures in mid-1987 about large sales of propeller-milling equipment to the Soviet Union by Toshiba Corporation of Japan and Kongsberg Vaapenfabrikk of Norway put a damper at least temporarily on the pressures for reform. See *N.Y. Times*, June 12, 1987, at 1. For more recent developments, see Chapter 3, notes 53 and 59.

[88] Among the improvements were seeking agreement to enhance full compliance by all CoCom members, to improve the control list and upgrade the CoCom staff, to adopt uniform and adequate penalties, and to increase on-site inspections. 50 U.S.C. app. § 2404(i).

[89] 19 U.S.C. §§ 1864 (Supp. III 1985).

enforcement of the export controls.[90] It remains to be seen how this new import sanction for enforcement purposes will be used. Given the availability of many other serious sanctions, its use might well be rare. Possibly most important is the fact that this new provision helps open a tiny window to greater use of import controls for at least national security reasons.

5. Continuing paucity of effective administrative or judicial review

The 1985 Act basically left unchanged the lack of any effective administrative or judicial review of the EAA.[91] As a result, the President (or his delegate, the Secretary of Commerce) can require a validated license for any type of export or for exports to a certain country. With very little chance of being successfully challenged in most cases, Commerce can then deny applications for those licenses.

If there is a license denial, the applicant must be informed within five days in writing.[92] Under the 1985 amendments, the applicant may then appeal certain issues to an administrative law judge and may request a hearing.[93] The judge's determination, however, is reviewable by the Secretary of Commerce, a presidential appointee, whose decision is "final and shall not be subject to judicial review."[94] This procedure hardly provides much hope to people objecting to the President's imposition of export controls.

If an exporter, frustrated by a licensing decision or for some other reason, violates the EAA, Commerce has available a panoply of administrative and criminal sanctions. These have been made increasingly more comprehensive and more stringent by successive amendments of the export laws.

The primary *administrative* sanctions now available for violations of the EAA or accompanying regulations, orders, or licenses include (1) the imposition of a civil penalty of up to $10,000 for each violation (or up

---

[90] 131 *Cong. Rec.* S8923 (daily ed. June 27, 1985) (Sen. Garn).

[91] See discussion in this section, however, about the 1985 Act providing new administrative hearing rights, but also making explicit the exemption from judicial review of certain decisions by the Secretary of Commerce. Though now somewhat dated, a thorough and excellent analysis of the enforcement of export controls can be found in Berman and Garson, supra note 1, at 850–76; see also Murphy and Downey, supra note 5, at 823–34.

[92] 50 U.S.C. app. § 2409(f)(3) (Supp. III 1985).

[93] Id. § 2412.

[94] Id. See 15 C.F.R. § 389.2 (1987). This regulation applies to "any person directly and adversely affected by an administrative action (excluding denial or probation orders, civil penalties, sanctions...)." Id. § 389.2(a). The taking of the appeal does not stay the operation of any administrative action unless the Assistant Secretary grants a stay. Id. § 389.2(d). For a major 1988 case, see note 98 below.

to $100,000 for each violation of national security controls), (2) suspension or revocation of the authority of any U.S. person to export goods or technology from the United States,[95] and (3) controls on the importation of goods or technology by any person into the United States.[96] These sanctions can be very draconian indeed, particularly the last two, which could drive an exporter out of business. Under the 1985 amendments, the party charged with a violation is entitled to receive a formal complaint and can contest the charges in a hearing before an administrative law judge.[97] As with license denials, however, the judge's determination shall be reviewed by the Secretary of Commerce, whose decision "shall be final and is not subject to judicial review."[98]

The *criminal sanctions* available are also wide ranging, and the penalties can be steep. For willful individual violators, the maximum penalty is a fine of $250,000 and/or ten years in jail. Corporations or other entities that are in willful violation can be fined up to five times the value of the exports involved or $1,000,000, whichever is greater.[99] In addition, the 1985 Act added a broad forfeiture provision for those that violate a national security export control.[100] Though criminal sanctions necessarily involve judicial enforcement, their more frequent use recently has not led to extensive challenges to the EAA. Moreover, none of the challenges appear to have been successful.[101]

---

[95] 50 U.S.C. app. § 2410(c).

[96] 19 U.S.C. § 1864 (Supp. III 1985).

[97] 50 U.S.C. app. 2412 (Supp. III 1985).

[98] Id. However, a U.S. court of appeals was willing to review the Secretary's reversal of an administrative law judge's decision that there was no EAA violation and the Secretary's imposition of civil sanctions. The court limited the Secretary's discretion. *Dart v. United States*, No. 86–5715 (D.C. Cir. May 31, 1988).

[99] The statutory framework provides for knowing violations (50 U.S.C. app. § 2410(a)) and willful violations (id. § 2410(b)). The 1985 Act expanded the category of knowing violations to include conspiracies and attempts. It expanded the category of willful violations to include persons who have not yet illegally exported goods and technology, but who possess them (1) with the intent to export them illegally or (2) knowing that they would be so exported. The 1985 Act also provides that any person who "takes any action with the intent to evade the provisions of [the EAA] or any regulation, order, or license issued under this Act" shall be criminally liable. Id. § 2410(b)(4).

[100] Id. § 2410(g). It provides that any person convicted of a violation of a national security export control shall, in addition of any other penalty, forfeit to the United States (1) any interest in the goods or tangible items that were the subject of the violation, (2) any other tangible property that was used in the illegal export, and (3) any proceeds obtained directly or indirectly as a result of the violation.

[101] For example, in *United States v. Brumage*, 377 F. Supp. 144 (E.D.N.Y. 1974), defendants were charged with willfully exporting electronic and technical equipment, without a validated export license, to East Germany and Hungary. They challenged as void for vagueness a provision of the EAA regarding exports "for the benefit of any communist-dominated nation." In upholding the provision, the federal district

6. Extraterritoriality

The EAA allows the President considerable discretion to assert extensive jurisdiction in imposing export controls on companies and goods outside U.S. territory. In spite of much recent controversy over the extraterritorial use of these controls, the 1985 Act essentially ignored the extraterritorial issue.[102]

The EAA authorizes the President to control the export of any goods and technology "subject to the jurisdiction of the United States or exported by any person subject to the jurisdiction of the United States."[103] This language is similar in its broad scope to that of the International Emergency Economic Powers Act (IEEPA),[104] and it is not limited in its coverage to only exports from the United States.

Traditionally, the United States imposed controls on three categories of foreign exports: (1) reexports by a foreign company of goods or technology of U.S. origin,[105] (2) reexports of U.S.-origin parts even if included in foreign-made goods,[106] and (3) exports of foreign-origin goods that are the direct products of U.S.-origin technology.[107] This was usually done by requiring foreign buyers to agree before receiving U.S. goods or

court opined, "As a federal statute regulating foreign commerce closely related to foreign affairs and national security, § 2405(b) is entitled to the *highest presumption of validity*." Id. at 150 (emphasis added). Cf. *Briggs & Stratton Corp. v. Baldrige*, 728 F.2d 915 (7th Cir. 1984), aff'g 539 F. Supp. 1307 (E.D. Wisc. 1982)(upholding constitutionality of antiboycott provisions of the EAA and accompanying regulations). Under the Arms Export Control Act and related statutes, challenges have also been unsuccessful. E.g., *United States v. Edler Industries*, 579 F.2d 516 (9th Cir. 1978); *United States v. Van Hee*, 531 F.2d 352 (6th Cir. 1976).

 Criminal sanctions were not resorted to often under the Export Control Act from 1949 to 1969. Berman and Garson, supra note 1, at 863. These sanctions, however, have been used more often since the 1969 EAA. Murphy and Downey, supra note 5, at 830.

[102] Although the 1985 Act left unchanged the key jurisdictional language of the EAA, the effect of other changes might be to raise new disputes over extraterritorial reach. For example, "in connection with the new comprehensive operations license established under [sec. 104 in the 1985 Act 50 U.S.C. app. § 2403(a)(2)], Commerce undoubtedly will require foreign concerns seeking to operate under the license to: (1) submit to extensive pre-license investigations; (2) establish internal control systems; and (3) allow periodic audits and investigations by Commerce." Harris and Bialos, supra note 64, at 18–19.

[103] 50 U.S.C. app. § 2405(a)(1982).

[104] IEEPA gives the President authority with respect to "any person, or with respect to any property, subject to the jurisdiction of the United States." 50 U.S.C. § 1702(a)(1)(1982).

[105] 15 C.F.R. § 374 (1987).

[106] Id. § 376.12. In March 1987, the Department of Commerce clarified and eased the requirements for obtaining the needed U.S. authorizations for shipping foreign products with U.S.-origin content. 52 *Fed. Reg.* 9147 (1987).

[107] Id. § 379.8.

technology not to reexport them nor to export goods that incorporated U.S.-origin parts or technology, without prior U.S. approval.[108] Although such controls are extraterritorial, they have generally been noncontroversial because they were used for national security reasons.[109]

Since 1977, the EAA language could also be read to provide authority to control the exports by foreign subsidiaries of U.S. companies.[110] However, this statutory authority was not used for this purpose until the pipeline sanctions in June 1982.

President Reagan announced these controls partly to hamper Soviet construction of a natural-gas pipeline. Two controls went beyond any previous assertion of extraterritorial jurisdiction under the foreign policy provisions of the EAA.[111] First, the controls prevented foreign subsidiaries of U.S. firms from exporting equipment or technology even though it was of wholly foreign origin. Second, the controls restricted independent foreign companies from exporting foreign-origin products that were made with technology acquired through licensing agreements with U.S. companies.[112] These controls covered, for example, compressors built by a French company (e.g., Creusot-Loire) under a licensing agreement with a U.S. company (e.g., General Electric).

The U.S. policy against the pipeline clashed with that of major European countries that were not opposed to its construction – indeed, some were signing contracts to buy gas from the pipeline and many countries were encouraging their companies to participate in its construction.[113] The attempt by the United States to impose its antipipeline policy on companies operating in, say, France, West Germany, England, and

[108] Id. at pt. 375.

[109] See Moyer and Mabry, supra note 3, at 108–9.

[110] Before 1977, the EAA language was more limited, authorizing the President to control exports "from the United States, its territories and possessions." Congress amended this in 1977 with the broader language presently in the Act. Pub. L. No. 95–223, tit. III, 91 Stat. 1625 (1977). The 1977 legislative history specifically indicates that at least one purpose was to confer authority over foreign subsidiaries of U.S. concerns. The Senate Report said that the amendment was designed "to confer non-emergency authority under the [EAA] to control non-U.S. exports by foreign subsidiaries of U.S. concerns. Such authority has been exercised under the emergency authority of section 5(b) of the Trading with the Enemy Act. Export controls of this kind could [also] be implemented in future emergencies under the authority of [IEEPA]." S. Rep. No. 466, 96th Cong., 1st Sess. 6, reprinted in 1977 U.S. Code Cong. & Ad. News 4540, 4545.

[111] The extraterritorial use of IEEPA and its predecessor for national emergencies, the Trading with the Enemy Act, has occasionally been controversial. See discussion in Chapter 9. For an earlier discussion of the pipeline sanctions, see Section A.3., this chapter. See generally B. Jentleson, *Pipeline Politics: The Complex Political Economy of East–West Trade* 172–214 (1986).

[112] 47 *Fed. Reg.* 27,250 (1982); see Moyer and Mabry, supra note 3, at 70.

[113] E.g. *N.Y. Times*, Mar. 12, 1982, at A6, col. 1.

Italy drew a strong reaction.[114] The European Economic Community and others argued that the extraterritorial extension of the controls was contrary to international law.[115] Governments in some European countries encouraged companies within their borders to honor their contracts with the Soviets. France even issued formal orders directing businesses to continue to perform.[116] As a result, several companies in Europe, including some U.S. subsidiaries such as Dresser-France, found themselves subject to conflicting orders from the United States and from the country where they were located. Several of these companies complied with the directives from their resident countries and performed under their contracts.[117] The United States reacted swiftly by placing the companies that did not comply with the U.S. orders on a "temporary denial" list, which essentially cut these companies off from *all* exports from the United States.[118]

Although no U.S. court ruled definitively on the extraterritorial reach of the controls, at least one European court ruled against it. In *Compagnie Européenne des Petroles S.A. v. Sensor Nederland B.V.*,[119] a Dutch district court decided that Sensor, a Dutch subsidiary of a U.S. corporation, could not be excused from performing a sales contract under Dutch law because of the U.S. export regulations. The court determined that the U.S. regulations had no jurisdictional basis under international law that required the court to take the regulations into account.

The President's decision to rescind the regulations was apparently

---

[114] See, e.g., *Wash. Post*, June 25, at A21, col. 1.

[115] E.g., "European Communities: Comments on the U.S. Regulations Concerning Trade with the U.S.S.R.," reprinted in 21 *Int'l Legal Materials* 891 (1982). The European Community's arguments were persuasive. See also Moyer and Mabry, supra note 3, at 110–16.

[116] *Wash. Post*, July 23, 1982, at A21; see Moyer and Mabry, supra note 3, at 71–82. See also United Kingdom, The Protection of Trading Interests (U.S. Reexport Control) Act 1980, June 30, 1982.

[117] *N.Y. Times*, Aug. 24, 1982, at D1; Moyer and Mabry, supra note 3.

[118] E.g., 47 *Fed. Reg.* 38,710 (1982), as amended by 47 *Fed. Reg.* 39,708 (1982)(Dresser sanctions). Dresser Industries and its wholly owned subsidiary, Dresser-France, attacked the export controls and the penalties against it in the Commerce Department and in the courts. Commerce denied Dresser's petition. 47 *Fed. Reg.* 51,463 (1982). The U.S. district court twice denied Dresser's request for a temporary restraining order against imposing sanctions, finding that Dresser had failed to make the necessary showing of irreparable harm and a substantial likelihood of success on the merits. *Dresser Industries v. Baldridge*, No. 82–2385 (D.D.C. Nov. 4, 1982) (denying request for temporary restraining order); 549 F. Supp. 108 (D.D.C. 1982). Before the court could rule on the merits of the case, the President rescinded the disputed regulations. 47 *Fed. Reg.* 51,858 (1982).

[119] Dist. Ct. at the Hague, Netherlands (Sept. 17, 1982), reprinted in 22 *Int'l Legal Materials* 66 (1983). See also the discussion in Chapter 9 at note 58 about a UK court ruling in 1987 against the extraterritorial reach of IEEPA controls against Libya.

caused by the strong allied reaction, pressures from the U.S. business community and Congress,[120] and the apparent ineffectiveness of the controls since work on the pipeline continued and companies in Europe generally continued to perform under their contracts.[121] Possibly chastened by the pipeline experience, the Reagan Administration has not since asserted such broad extraterritorial jurisdiction, not even in the recent controls pursuant to IEEPA against Nicaragua, South Africa, and Libya.[122] Nevertheless, the broad statutory authority remains unchanged at this point.

B. THE ATOMIC ENERGY ACT

Exports of nuclear materials, equipment, and technology are subject to the extensive regulatory regime established by the Atomic Energy Act of 1954,[123] as amended by the Nuclear Non-Proliferation Act of 1978 (NNPA).[124] The President's authority to stop these exports is essentially

---

[120] Substantial opposition to the expanded pipeline controls arose in Congress. Though unlikely to succeed, the congressional opposition probably put additional pressure on the Administration to back off. Twin bills were introduced in the House and Senate seeking to repeal the specific regulations. On September 29, 1982, the House bill was voted down by a narrow margin – 206 to 203. The Senate did not act on its bill before the fall recess, and the President withdrew the regulations shortly after Congress reconvened. See Moyer and Mabry, supra note 3, at 73. As for business opposition, see, e.g., *Wash. Post*, June 18, 1982, at A1, col. 3.

In January 1987, the Reagan Administration also ended other U.S. controls on the export of oil and gas equipment to the Soviet Union that had been in existence since 1978. 52 *Fed. Reg.* 2500 (1987).

[121] See sources cited in Moyer and Mabry, supra note 3, at 71–3.

[122] See discussion in Chapter 9, Section C. Moreover, the Administration eased the extraterritorial reach of some controls. See supra note 106.

For further analysis of extraterritoriality, including the pipeline controls, see, e.g., Note, "Predictability and Comity: Toward Common Principles of Extraterritorial Jurisdiction," 98 *Harv. L. Rev.* 1310 (1986); K. Abbott, "Defining the Extraterritorial Reach of American Export Controls: Congress as Catalyst," 17 *Cornell Int'l L.J.* 79 (1984); D. Morse and J. Powers, "U.S. Export Controls and Foreign Entities: The Unanswered Questions of Pipeline Diplomacy," 23 *Va. J. Int'l L.* 537 (1983); S. Marcuss and D. Mathias, "U.S. Foreign Policy Export Controls: Do They Pass Muster Under International Law?" 2 *Int'l Tax & Bus. Lawyer* 1 (1984); Moyer and Mabry, supra note 3; S. Marcuss and E. Richard, "Extraterritorial Jurisdiction in United States Trade Law: The Need for a Consistent Theory," 20 *Colum. J. Transnat'l L.* 439 (1981); K. Feinberg, "Economic Coercion and Economic Sanctions: The Expansion of United States Extraterritorial Jurisdiction," 30 *Am. U.L. Rev.* 323 (1981).

[123] 68 Stat. 921 (1954) (codified at 42 U.S.C. §§ 2011–2296 (1976) (before amendment by NNPA)).

[124] Pub. L. No. 95–242, § 2, 92 Stat. 120 (1978) (codified at 22 U.S.C. §§ 3201–82 and scattered sections of 42 U.S.C. (1982)). See generally *Natural Resources Defense Council v. Nuclear Regulatory Commission*, 647 F.2d 1345 (D.C. Cir. 1981); R. Bettauer, "The Nuclear Non-Proliferation Act of 1978," 10 *L. & Pol'y Int'l Bus.* 1105 (1978).

unlimited, reflecting the fact that they could allow the construction of dangerous power plants abroad and could even facilitate the proliferation of nuclear weapons, thereby upsetting the military balance in many regions.

A prospective nuclear exporter must apply to the Nuclear Regulatory Commission (NRC)[125] for an export license. The NRC forwards the application to the Department of State, which begins an Executive Branch review along with the Departments of Defense, Commerce, and Energy and the Arms Control and Disarmament Agency.[126] The NRC is prohibited from granting a license unless the Secretary of State notifies it that the proposed export "will not be inimical to the common defense and security."[127] In the legislative history and in actual practice,[128] this phrase has been generally understood to give the President broad discretion.

Presidents have exercised their authority under the Act to stop nuclear exports or to threaten stoppage, with mixed results. Successes include the U.S. delay of export licenses in 1976–77 to encourage Taiwan to stop reprocessing spent fuel (which can be a prelude to building nuclear weapons). And in 1975–6, U.S. export controls over other nuclear items helped persuade South Korea not to buy a French reprocessing plant.[129]

Very concerned with nonproliferation issues in the 1970s, Congress attempted in the 1978 NNPA to impose some limitations on the President's authority to *allow* exports. (This approach can also be viewed as an effort by Congress to force the U.S. Government to impose economic sanctions in certain situations.) The NNPA added new criteria that the Executive Branch and the NRC were to consider in their export licensing

---

[125] The NRC is an independent regulatory commission that is responsible for a variety of nuclear licensing and regulatory functions, functions that were formerly handled by the Atomic Energy Commission, which was abolished in 1974. 42 U.S.C. § 5841 (1982); Bettauer, supra note 124, at 1111–12. The NRC has five commissioners, who are appointed for five-year terms by the President, with the advice and consent of the Senate. Id. § 5841(b) and (c).

[126] Id. § 2155.

[127] Id. § 2155 (a)(1). If the Executive Branch makes a finding in favor of allowing export, the NRC must still consider the matter. The Commission must consider the same "common defense and security" criterion, among others. Id. § 2133(d). If the NRC is unable to rule on the license application within 120 days after receipt of the Executive Branch judgment or if the NRC rules against the application, NNPA empowers the President to authorize the export upon a finding that not to do so would seriously prejudice the achievement of U.S. nonproliferation objectives or would otherwise jeopardize the common defense and security. Id. § 2155(b).

[128] See, e.g., S. Rep. 1669, 83rd Cong., 2d Sess., reprinted in 1954 *U.S. Code Cong. & Adm. News* 3456; NRDC v. NRC, 647 F.2d at 1364.

[129] See discussion in Chapter 2 at notes 23–6.

decisions, with a heavy emphasis on limiting the proliferation of nuclear weapons.

Probably the most important provision in the NNPA when enacted was the prohibition on exports of nuclear fuel and reactors to nations that did not accept International Atomic Energy Agency (IAEA) safeguards for those exports.[130] The President could waive this prohibition if he determined that it would be seriously prejudicial to U.S. nonproliferation objectives or would otherwise jeopardize the common defense and security. The waiver, however, could be overridden if Congress passed a concurrent resolution within sixty days. This provision almost succeeded in stopping the U.S. export of enriched uranium fuel to India in 1980.[131]

Whatever the past importance of this safeguard provision, the demise of the legislative veto has considerably reduced congressional influence over the presidential determination.[132] Other strict criteria of the NNPA remain, but their effect is to limit the President's authority to *allow* exports. His ability to *prevent* exports remains sweeping.

C. THE ARMS EXPORT CONTROL ACT

As he does with nuclear exports, the President has essentially unfettered power to stop all arms exports.[133] Congress, however, has imposed some limits on his authority to allow them.

The Arms Export Control Act (AECA), enacted in 1976 and amended

---

[130] 42 U.S.C. § 2156.

[131] In a situation with a complicated history of agreements, India refused to accept the required IAEA safeguards. President Carter exercised his waiver authority to approve the shipments. He concluded that failure to ship would be interpreted by India as an abrogation of the existing U.S.–India Agreement for Cooperation, thus releasing India from its obligations under the Agreement (including observance of partial safeguards). Although the House voted decisively to override the waiver, the Senate failed to override it by one vote. L. Spector, *Nuclear Proliferation Today* 350–1 (1984); *Nonproliferation and U.S. Foreign Policy* 331–4 (J. Yager ed. 1980); G. Hufbauer and J. Schott, *Economic Sanctions Reconsidered: History and Current Policy* 598–606 (1985).

[132] See discussion of the *Chadha* case in Chapter 9, Section D.2; K. Dam, "Legislative Veto in Foreign Affairs," *Dept. of State Bull.* 52, 54 (Sept. 1983). Of course, Congress can always pass new legislation to stop the export, but this would require a two-thirds vote in both houses if the President vetoed the legislation.

[133] Controlling arms exports can be viewed as an economic sanction or as a variation on the use of, or threat to use, force. As discussed in Chapter 1, the boundaries between the different types of sanctions – diplomatic, economic, military force – are sometimes indefinite. For a general analysis of arms sales and their role in foreign policy, see A. Pierre, *The Global Politics of Arms Sales* (1982); P. Farley, S. Kaplan, and W. Lewis, *Arms Across the Sea* (1978).

frequently since, is the principal statute governing foreign military sales.[134] Section 38 authorizes the President to "control the import and export of defense articles and defense services."[135] The statute imposes no significant limits on the President's ability to stop exports of these items. The AECA recognizes two types of arms sales: (1) government-to-government and (2) contractor-to-government or commercial sales, whereby private contractors sell directly abroad without the U.S. Government acting as an intermediary. Sales by the U.S. Government are easily controlled by the President.

As for private U.S. manufacturers, exporters, or importers, they are required to register with the U.S. Government and to secure licenses for any such exports or imports.[136] In general, licenses for the shipment to most communist countries of goods or data on the Munitions List will be denied. A general prohibition may also be applied to other countries or areas against which "the United States maintains an arms embargo or whenever an export would not otherwise be in furtherance of world peace and the security and foreign policy of the United States."[137]

The principal examples of the President stopping or slowing arms sales are the sporadic and largely unsuccessful efforts against Israel and Turkey. In attempts to influence Israeli policies, the United States slowed arms shipments in 1969–70, 1975,[138] 1981, and 1982–3. For example, in 1981, the shipment of four F–16 fighter/attack aircraft was delayed for several months after Israel bombed an Iraqi nuclear reactor, and fourteen additional planes were then temporarily delayed after Israel bombed Beirut.[139] Then, in 1982–3, the Reagan Administration delayed further shipments of F–16s because Israel had used American arms in its invasion of Lebanon.[140] These delays presumably put some

---

[134] Arms Export Control Act of 1976, Pub. L. No. 94–329, 90 Stat. 729 (codified in scattered sections of 22 U.S.C.). See 53 *Fed. Reg.* 11, 494 (1988).

[135] 22 U.S.C.A. § 2778 (1979 & West Supp. 1988). The President is authorized to designate those items that shall be considered defense articles and defense services. These items constitute what is called the Munitions List. Id.

[136] Id. at § 2778(b). The President has delegated his export control functions to the Secretary of State and his import control functions to the Secretary of the Treasury. Exec. Order No. 11,958, 3 C.F.R. 79, reprinted at 22 U.S.C. § 2751 note.

[137] 22 C.F.R. § 126.1 (1987).

[138] G. Ball, "The Coming Crisis in Israeli–American Relations," 58 *Foreign Aff.* 231–56 (Winter 1979–80)(regarding both 1969–70 and 1975).

[139] *N.Y. Times*, Aug. 19, 1981, at 3, col. 1.

[140] *N.Y. Times*, Apr. 2, 1983, at 1, col. 3. On July 15, 1982, the Acting Secretary of State, Walter J. Stoessel, Jr., sent a classified letter to congressional leaders in which he noted that, under a 1952 U.S.–Israeli agreement, Israel assured the United States that American military equipment would be used only for international security, "legitimate self-defense," or regional defense. Israel also said "it will not undertake

88

pressure on Israel, but do not appear to have significantly altered its policies.[141]

The Turkish invasion of Cyprus triggered a drawn-out struggle between Turkey, two U.S. Presidents (Ford and Carter), and the Congress over efforts to limit U.S. arms sales and military assistance. The temporary delays did not result in Turkish withdrawal, but were essentially symbolic.[142]

Congress has sought to restrict the President's authority to allow arms exports.[143] In addition to broad policy statements,[144] Congress directs the President not to approve any sale unless certain conditions are met.[145] Unless Congress passes new legislation, however, its only real tool for enforcing conditions was provided by legislative veto provisions. These required the President to report proposed sales or transfers of defense equipment or defense services above certain dollar amounts, and then allowed Congress to stop the sale or transfer if it promptly passed a concurrent resolution.[146] In 1981, Congress came within two votes in the Senate of blocking an $8.5 billion arms package to Saudi Arabia, which included five AWACs early-warning aircraft.[147] With the demise of the legislative veto, however, Congress has lost much of its leverage.

---

any act of aggression against any other state." Citing AECA, Stoessel wrote, "I must report on behalf of the President...that a substantial violation by Israel of these provisions may have occurred." Id. at 2.

[141] See sources cited in the preceding three footnotes; Hufbauer and Schott, supra note 131, at 263–8.

[142] K. Legg, "Congress as Trojan Horse? The Turkish Embargo Problem, 1974–78," in *Congress, the Presidency and American Foreign Policy* (J. Spanier and J. Nogee eds. 1981); Hufbauer and Schott, supra note 131, at 491–5.

[143] As with nuclear exports, this can be viewed either as an attempt by Congress to establish its own sanctions, or as a limit on the President's authority to approve exports as a carrot rather than as a sanction.

[144] E.g., 22 U.S.C. §§ 2751–2 (1982 & Supp. III 1985).

[145] Among the principal conditions are that (1) the sale strengthens the security of the United States and promotes world peace, (2) the recipient country agrees not to transfer the arms to a third country without prior approval of the President, (3) the recipient country agrees to maintain the security of the arms, and (4) the country is otherwise eligible to purchase defense items. Id. § 2753. In addition, the arms must be used for internal security or self-defense, id. § 2754, and the arms cannot be sold to countries that aid or abet terrorism, see infra at notes 153, 154, or that engage in a consistent pattern of harassing Americans, id. at § 2756. Congress also requires a variety of reports from the President. E.g., id. § 2776(b)(quarterly reports).

In December 1987, Congress added a special restriction on the sale of Stinger antiaircraft missiles to any country in the Persian Gulf region, except to Bahrain if the President makes a special certification. Foreign Operations, Export Financing, and Related Programs Appropriations Act of 1988, Pub. L. No. 100–202, § 573 (1987).

[146] See 22 U.S.C. §§ 2776(b)(1), 2776(c)(2)(B), and 2753(d)(2)(A).

[147] N.Y. *Times*, Oct. 24, 1981, at A1, col. 6; see *Wash. Post*, Oct. 28, 1981, at A6, col. 1.

Current regulations treat the former legislative veto provisions only as a "report-and-wait" requirement – if Congress does not forbid the export by passing a new statute within thirty days, the license may be issued. This approach now applies to exports of defense articles or services pursuant to a contract for more than $50 million and of "significant" military equipment in excess of $14 million.[148]

This waiting period does leave Congress with the power to react in a timely fashion, but it also "ups the ante." Rather than being able to stop a sale with a majority vote of both houses on a concurrent resolution (which cannot be vetoed), Congress needs a two-thirds vote to pass a joint resolution and override the likely presidential veto. Congress might still be able to do this. For example, after the Reagan Administration informed Congress of a proposed $1.5 billion arms sale to Jordan, congressional leaders told the White House in early 1986 that Congress would have the necessary two-thirds votes in opposition in both houses. The President then postponed the sale indefinitely.[149]

Although the two-thirds majorities existed at that time, in other situations they are obviously more difficult to obtain. This was evident later in 1986 when the Administration proposed selling $354 million worth of advanced arms to Saudi Arabia. After the House and Senate initially passed a joint resolution by larger than two-thirds margins, the President vetoed the resolution. The House then voted to override the veto, but the Senate failed to do so by a single vote. The sale went through.[150]

The "report-and-wait" requirement is subject to a presidential override, as were the legislative veto provisions. The AECA provides in two

[148] 22 C.F.R. § 123.10(e)(1987). See Dam, supra note 132, at 53. Serious questions have been raised about whether the invalid legislative veto provision is severable from the rest of the AECA. See T. Franck and C. Bob, "The Return of Humpty-Dumpty: Foreign Relations Law after the *Chadha* Case," 79 *Am. J. Int'l L.* 912, 931 n.127 (1985). The authors note that the statute "contains no severability clause, and its legislative history, though somewhat ambiguous, tends to reveal that it would not have been passed, and its broad authority would not have been delegated, had the legislative veto provision been known to be inoperable. Certainly, the purpose of the legislation was to limit, not to unleash, presidential authority to export arms." Id. Nevertheless, as discussed above, both the Executive Branch and Congress are proceeding as if the rest of AECA is still valid. Cf. *Alaska Airlines v. Brock*, 107 S. Ct. 1476 (1987) (legislative veto provision of Airline Deregulation Act held severable).

[149] *Wash. Post*, Feb. 1, 1986, at A14, col. 1. In a more recent case, the Reagan Administration withdrew the proposed sale of 1600 Maverick air-to-ground missiles to Saudi Arabia after 67 Senators sponsored a resolution disapproving the sale. *N.Y. Times*, June 12, 1987, at A1, col. 1; see *Wash. Post*, June 15, 1987, at A1, col. 3.

[150] *N.Y. Times*, June 6, 1986, at 1, col. 6. Opponents of the sale noted, however, that the Executive Branch had reportedly scaled back the initial proposal because of concerns about congressional opposition, and then removed from the package the portable antiaircraft missile (known as the Stinger) to help win enough votes in the second round in the Senate. Id.

places that the President can sidestep Congress by certifying that "an emergency exists which requires [the sale or proposed export] in the national security interests of the United States."[151] No President has resorted to either of these override provisions, presumably preferring to try to work with Congress rather than go around it and thereby create a difficult political fight. In any case, the "report-and-wait" approach is only a limit on the President's ability to allow arms exports and does not restrict his sweeping powers to prevent them.

The highly controversial arms sales to Iran in 1985–6 stand as a fascinating example of the possible impact of the AECA. Since the Secretary of State has designated Iran as a country supporting terrorism,[152] the Act requires that the President first find that the sale is necessary for national security, and then report this finding to the Speaker of the House and the Senate Committee on Foreign Relations.[153] A 1986 amendment to the AECA, effective August 1986, similarly prohibits the export of arms to a country designated as supporting terrorism unless the President waives this prohibition for U.S. national interests and "submits to the Congress a report justifying that determination and describing the proposed export."[154] The Reagan Administration, however, failed to notify Congress of these arms sales until November 1986, after reports of the sales appeared in the press. This secretiveness seems to violate the reporting requirements of the AECA and possibly other export laws.[155]

Apparently the Administration believed that the sales could be justified as part of a covert intelligence activity, and thus be exempt from the

---

[151] 22 U.S.C. § 2776(b)(1) and (c)(2).

[152] 15 C.F.R. § 385.4(d)(1) (1987).

[153] 22 U.S.C. § 2753(f)(2) (1982 & Supp. III 1985). As discussed above at note 148, the President would also be required to report under the normal reporting requirements if the exports were of "significant" military equipment in excess of $14 million.

[154] Omnibus Diplomatic Security and Antiterrorism Act of 1986, Pub. L. No 99–399, § 509, 100 Stat. 853, 874 (codified at 22 U.S.C.A. § 2780 (West Supp. 1987)).

[155] Besides the AECA, the Export Administration Act requires the Executive Branch to notify certain congressional committees "at least 30 days before any license is approved for the export of goods or technology" above a designated amount to any country which the Secretary of State has determined supports international terrorism. 50 U.S.C. app. § 2405(j) (1982 and Supp. III 1985). From 1985 through August 27, 1986, the minimum amount was $7 million. This was lowered to $1 million in August 1986 by the 1986 Omnibus Act, supra note 154, § 509(b) (codified at 50 U.S.C.A. app. § 2405(j)(1) (West Supp. 1987)).
The U.S. Government reportedly was involved in one arms sale to Iran in October–November 1986. *Report of the President's Special Review Board* III–19 (1987) (hereinafter *Tower Commission Report*). The 500 TOW antitank missiles were worth more than $1 million, but there was no prior notification to Congress. Id. However, the applicability of the EAA to the Iranian arms sales might be questioned on the ground that a sale by the U.S. Government does not require an export license.

export laws.[156] Yet the key reporting statute for intelligence activities, section 501 of the National Security Act of 1947, requires in subsection (a) that certain members of Congress be kept "fully and currently informed of all intelligence activities."[157] If for some reason the required report is not given in advance, then subsection (b) directs that the "President shall fully inform the intelligence committee in a timely fashion."[158] Given the Reagan Administration's nondisclosure to Congress for more than fourteen months from the start of the operation, it seems clear that the Administration also failed to adhere to these reporting requirements.

Instead, President Reagan made a "finding" in January 1986. Noting that the arms sales to Iran were "important to the national security of the United States," he instructed his director of Central Intelligence not to report to Congress "due to . . . [the operation's] extreme sensitivity and security risks."[159] The Administration has not formally offered any more detailed legal rationale for its refusal to report.

When news of the arms sales became public, the resulting brouhaha led President Reagan to announce that he was instructing his staff to prepare an executive order that clarified his plans for future notification.

---

[156] See House Select Committee to Investigate Covert Arms Transactions with Iran and Senate Select Committee on Secret Military Assistance to Iran and the Nicaraguan Opposition, *Report of the Congressional Committees Investigating the Iran–Contra Affair*, H.R. Rept. 433, S. Rep. No. 216, 100th Cong., 1st Sess. 418. [hereinafter *Iran–Contra Report*]; see *Tower Commission Report*, supra note 155, at B-57 to B-67.

[157] 50 U.S.C. § 413(a) (1982). See also 22 U.S.C. § 2422 (1982) (funds expended by or on behalf of the CIA in foreign countries considered a "significant anticipated intelligence activity" under 50 U.S.C. § 413).

[158] 50 U.S.C. §413(b). The Senate report accompanying the 1980 amendments to the reporting requirements said about subsection (b): "The Senate Select Committee and the Executive branch and the intelligence agencies have come to an understanding that in rare extraordinary circumstances if the President withholds prior notice of covert operations, he is obliged to inform the two oversight committees in a timely fashion of the action and the reasons for withholding of such prior notice." S. Rept. No. 730, 96th Cong., 2d Sess. 12 (1980). What constituted a "rare extraordinary circumstance" was not defined.

The House and Senate Committees investigating the Iran–contra affair concluded that the congressional notification provisions of the National Security Act were abused by the delay in notifying. *Iran–Contra Report*, supra note 156, at 415–16. But see id. at 544–5 (minority report) (concluding that the "vague" language of section 501 allows the President to decide how long to wait before notifying Congress).

[159] *Tower Commission Report*, supra note 155, at B-60. Note, however, that no finding existed at the time of the U.S. sale of 504 TOW missiles and only a retroactive finding existed for the November 1986 sale of HAWK missiles. *Iran–Contra Report*, supra note 156, at 418. Also, Israel transferred HAWK and TOW missiles to Iran in 1985 that Israel had obtained from the United States under the AECA. The Reagan Administration failed to follow the required AECA procedures for allowing the Israeli transfer to Iran. 22 U.S.C. § 2753(a) (1982 & Supp. IV 1986); see *Iran–Contra Report*, supra at 418.

He stated that "in all but the most exceptional circumstances, timely notification to Congress under section 501(b)...will not be delayed beyond two working days of the initiation of a [covert] activity."[160]

Even with President Reagan's promised reforms, the controversy over the arms sales should at a minimum encourage Congress to tighten the statutory reporting requirements. One possible measure would be to mandate reports in advance of sales or within a specified time period. The requirements could even be backed by penalties for noncompliance. Congress might pass still other provisions to ensure that it is informed and has an opportunity to express its views.

D. THE COMPREHENSIVE ANTI-APARTHEID ACT OF 1986

Although the more sweeping provisions of the Comprehensive Anti-Apartheid Act of 1986 are against imports and private financial transactions, it added a few new limits on exports to South Africa.[161] Moreover, even those provisions that essentially codified existing export controls are noteworthy because they cannot be changed at the President's discretion. Subject to certain exceptions, the statute imposed controls on exports to South Africa of crude oil and petroleum products to all customers, on exports of most nuclear items or materials, and on exports of computers and items on the Munitions List to many South African Government agencies.

The prohibition on export of *crude oil* and *petroleum products* is new, not having been covered in previous regulations. The jurisdictional scope is potentially very broad since the limits apply to any item "subject to the jurisdiction of the United States or which is exported by a person subject to the jurisdiction of the United States."[162] Presumably drawing upon the 1985 amendments to the EAA, the provision includes an exception for exports "pursuant to a contract entered into before the date of enactment of this Act" (October 2, 1986). This contract sanctity protection, however, is even better than the EAA version, since there is no exception for "breach of the peace."[163]

---

[160] Letter from President Reagan to Senator David L. Boren, Chairman of the Senate Select Committee on Intelligence (Aug. 7, 1987), quoted in *N.Y. Times*, Aug. 8, 1987, at A5, col. 1; see *Wash. Post*, Aug. 8, 1987, at 1, col. 6. As of May 1988, a new Executive Order had not yet been signed.

[161] Pub. L. No. 94-440, 100 Stat. 1086 (codified at 22 U.S.C. §§ 5001–5116 (Supp. IV 1986)) [hereinafter the 1986 Act]. See the overview discussion of the law in Chapter 3, Section A, and then the analysis of its limits on imports in Chapter 5, Section B.1, and on private financial transactions in Chapter 6, Section A.

[162] 22 U.S.C. § 5071 (a).

[163] Id. § 5071(b); see earlier discussion in Section A.4.c.

Although new and theoretically broad, these limits on crude oil and petroleum products will not have a significant impact. The U.S. exports of these items to South Africa totaled only about $33 million in 1985.[164] South Africa can still buy its oil from many other sources, and it has made considerable strides in reducing its dependence on foreign oil. Nevertheless, after the unsuccessful experience with partial sanctions by the League of Nations against Italy and by the United Nations against Rhodesia, cutting off petroleum to South Africa has considerable symbolism.

The statute also prohibits exports of nuclear materials, sensitive technology, and other *nuclear items* that might have significance for nuclear explosive purposes. These limits are very similar to those President Reagan imposed in September 1985.[165] The statute does allow, however, for two possibly important exceptions not found in the Executive Order. There is an exception when the President determines that the "prohibitions would be seriously prejudicial to the achievement of [U.S.] nonproliferation objectives or would otherwise jeopardize the common defense and security of the United States."[166] Also, there is an exception if South Africa maintains IAEA safeguards on all its peaceful nuclear activities or becomes a party to the Nuclear Non-Proliferation Treaty.[167] The point of these exceptions is apparently to leave some flexibility for the President under the statute, since a law would likely take longer to change than an Executive Order.

The statute also limits exports of *computers*, software, and related goods and technology to a number of entities of the South African Government, including the military, other security forces, and any agency enforcing apartheid. These provisions are essentially identical to Reagan's order of September 1985.[168]

---

[164] U.S. Department of Commerce, 2 *U.S. Exports* 1091, Pub. FT455/1985 Dec. and Annual (1986).

[165] Compare 22 U.S.C. § 5057, with Exec. Order No. 12,532, § 1(c), 50 *Fed. Reg.* 36,861 (1985).

[166] 22 U.S.C. § 5057(b). The provision does include a sixty-day report-and-wait requirement whereby the President must give sixty days' advance notice to Congress.

[167] Id. § 5057(a). The Executive Order had a narrower exception, allowing "assistance for International Atomic Energy Agency safeguards or IAEA programs generally available to its member states." Exec. Order 12,532, § 1(c), supra note 165.

[168] Compare 22 U.S.C. § 5054, with Exec. Order 12,532, § 1(b), supra note 165. The Reagan order, in turn, simply tracked in large part the strict limits on sales to the South African police and military that were imposed by Congress in the 1985 amendments to the EAA. 50 U.S.C. app. § 2405. (Supp. III 1985). The Department of State reported that U.S. computer sales to South Africa fell from $199 million in 1984 to $126 million in 1985 and anticipated a further drop even before the 1986 law. Department of State, *Misconceptions About U.S. Policy Toward South Africa* 15 (1986).

The 1986 law prohibits the sale or export of *arms* and other items on the Munitions List. This limit also follows existing regulations closely. However, presumably again to give the President some flexibility, the law makes an explicit exception for "exports solely for commercial purposes" and not for use by the South African police or military.[169]

Overall, these export limits will not reduce substantially the recent level of U.S. exports to South Africa, which totaled about $1.2 billion in 1985,[170] because most of these controls were already in place under existing regulations. However, the controls are now codified and the restrictions on petroleum do have special symbolic significance.

E. GATT AND EXPORT CONTROLS

Many of the present or likely target countries for economic sanctions are not contracting parties[171] to the General Agreement on Tariffs and Trade (GATT).[172] For example, the Soviet Union, East Germany, Iran, and Libya are not members of GATT.[173] For GATT members,[174] however,

---

[169] 22 U.S.C. § 5067. The exception is hedged by a thirty-day report-and-wait requirement whereby the President must inform Congress in advance. Id. § 5068. For a discussion of the Munitions List and the Arms Export Control Act, see the previous section.

[170] U.S. Department of Commerce, supra note 164, at 1090. Exports in 1984 were almost $2.3 billion. IMF, *Direction of Trade Statistics: Yearbook 1986*, at 401 (1986). They were presumably higher in 1984 because the South African economy was in better shape and President Reagan had not imposed the controls under IEEPA.

[171] The capitalized term "Contracting Parties" is used in this book to refer to the parties to the GATT acting formally as a body. Otherwise, the references to individual or several contracting parties, or members, are lower case.

[172] General Agreement on Tariffs and Trade, Oct. 30, 1947, 61 Stat. pts. 5, 6, T.I.A.S. No. 1700, at 639, 55 U.N.T.S. 194 (1950) (original text). For the current version, see Contracting Parties to the General Agreement on Tariffs and Trade, 4 *Basic Instruments and Selected Documents* (1969) [hereinafter GATT]. See also *Documents Supplement* 1 to J. Jackson and W. Davey, *Legal Problems of International Economic Relations* (1986). GATT has never come formally into force, since the requisite minimum number of states has never accepted it "definitively." All nations that apply GATT do so provisionally under various protocols. J. Jackson, *World Trade and the Law of GATT* 60–1 (1969) (an excellent analysis of GATT) [hereinafter Jackson, *GATT*].

[173] GATT, *GATT Activities in 1984* 72 (1985). Some other nonmembers that are possible targets include North Korea and Vietnam (see discussion of IEEPA in Chapter 9, Section B), Bulgaria, and the People's Republic of China. Id.

[174] Certain countries that are likely targets of U.S. sanctions do belong to GATT, but the U.S. trade relationship with them is a special combination of working through the GATT framework and bilateral agreements. These countries include Czechoslovakia, Hungary, Romania, and Poland. Although the United States and these countries participate in many GATT activities, the United States does not now grant most favored nation (MFN) status to Romania (after July 1988) and Czechoslovakia, and

the President's authority to impose export controls should be considered in light of U.S. obligations under GATT. These obligations generally involve import controls, which are discussed in Chapter 5, Section C. Nevertheless, exports are mentioned in at least thirteen GATT clauses and are related to obligations in several others.[175]

Central to GATT is the principle of nondiscrimination among nations in trade relationships. The most significant GATT provisions regarding exports are the most favored nation (MFN) treatment obligation in article I and the ban on quantitative restrictions in article XI.

American export controls on goods and technology for foreign policy purposes obviously discriminate among nations and could potentially create problems in GATT. A careful reading of the GATT provisions and decisions, however, suggests that U.S. export controls either do not violate GATT or might be classified as technical violations.[176] This is primarily because the GATT exceptions here are "so broad and vague as to almost render [the GATT export] obligations meaningless."[177]

Most relevant are the security exceptions of article XXI. They provide that no contracting party may be prevented from taking any action "which it considers necessary for the protection of its essential security interests" that relate to fissionable materials, traffic in arms or "in other goods and materials ... for the purpose of supplying a military establishment," or "in time of war or other emergency in international relations."[178] These exceptions would seem to allow virtually all current U.S. national security controls under the EAA as well as all controls under the Atomic Energy Act and the Arms Export Control Act.[179]

Article XXI, however, does not seem to cover completely all past or current U.S. foreign policy controls, such as export controls against terrorism or human rights violations. Nevertheless, although some GATT experts are uncomfortable about the frequent use of these types of con-

---

grants it to Hungary under a special bilateral agreement. The United States withdrew its one-time MFN treatment under GATT from Czechoslovakia and Poland and recently reinstated MFN status for Poland, as discussed in Chapter 5 at notes 77–104, 139. The arrangements with Hungary and Romania are also discussed there. See generally M. Kostecki, *East–West Trade and the GATT System* (1978).

[175] Jackson, *GATT*, supra note 172, at 498.

[176] See id. at 497–506; Abbott, supra note 6, at 849–57 (who suggests the possibility of a technical violation).

[177] Jackson and Davey, supra note 172, at 888.

[178] GATT art. XXI. Also excepted are actions taken pursuant to a country's obligations under the UN charter for the maintenance of international peace and security.

[179] The provision about the UN charter in the preceding footnote would allow actions under the UN Participation Act, discussed in Chapter 8, and the phrase "other emergency" would appear to cover controls under the Trading with the Enemy Act and IEEPA, discussed in Chapter 9.

trols, it seems unlikely that there will be any significant challenge to these controls in GATT in the near future.[180]

The first case in which GATT considered export controls for foreign policy purposes was Czechoslovakia's complaint in 1949 against the U.S. practice of export licenses. Czechoslovakia argued that the licensing program was a violation of the MFN obligation under article I. The United States defended itself primarily on the grounds of article XXI. The Contracting Parties voted overwhelmingly for the United States, with Czechoslovakia casting the sole vote in favor of finding that the United States had failed to carry out its GATT obligations.[181]

The United States recently cited article XXI to justify President Reagan's decision in May 1985 to impose against Nicaragua a trade embargo that prohibited exports from the United States as well as Nicaraguan imports to it. As discussed more fully in Chapter 5, Nicaragua reacted by asking for a special session of the GATT Council. The Council did not act on a Nicaraguan demand that GATT "disapprove" of the U.S. embargo, but established a panel to examine the matter. The panel ruled in late 1986 that the United States was within its rights under article XXI, but it also reportedly concluded that the embargo calls into question the rationale behind the Article and was contrary to the basic aims of GATT.[182]

Other than these two cases, no export controls for foreign policy purposes appear to have been seriously challenged in GATT.[183]

[180] E.g., see Abbott, supra note 6, at 852–7; C. Bergsten, *Completing the GATT: Toward New International Rules to Govern Export Controls* 25–6 (1974).

[181] GATT Doc. CP. 3/SR.22, at 4–10 (1949). The United States also justified any discrimination on the basis of article XX, but particularly relied on the national security ground of article XXI. Id. at 8. The vote was 1 for finding a U.S. failure to carry out its obligations, 17 against, 3 abstentions, and 2 absent. Id. at 9. One commentator explained that the result was partly caused by the fact that the "infant GATT had neither the capacity nor the prestige to undertake a serious examination of U.S. cold war measures." R. Hudec, *World Trade and the Law of GATT* 68 (1975).

[182] See Chapter 5, at notes 148–53. The GATT Council, established in 1960, is composed of representatives of all contracting parties who want to participate. It has broad jurisdiction, including the consideration of matters requiring urgent attention between sessions of the Contracting Parties, supervision of the work of other GATT bodies, and preparation for the sessions of the Contracting Parties. The Council meets about once per month. "The ease with which it can be called, the availability of its members' representatives in Geneva, and the flexibility of its procedures render this institution very useful." Jackson, *GATT*, supra note 172, at 156.

[183] For example, the GATT took no action against the oil-exporting countries in the 1973 OPEC oil embargo against certain industrialized countries. See Bergsten, supra note 180, at 26. Abbott makes the point that, even though U.S. export controls get by in GATT, "the harm they may cause to the international trading system should be considered as a cost of their utilization." Abbott, supra note 6, at 853. However, since this book does not propose any significant increase in the use of export controls,

F. CONCLUSIONS

The 1985 amendments to the Export Administration Act were intended to limit somewhat the President's authority to control exports. In particular, the President does need to move more carefully in the future in imposing agricultural embargoes or terminating existing contracts. Generally, however, the President's discretion remains very broad, and he can stop almost all U.S. exports to a particular country. Moreover, his decisions are subject only to minimal administrative or judicial review.

it does not analyze further what expanded use of these controls would mean to GATT or the international trading system.

5

Imports to the United States

Import controls under U.S. laws differ markedly from export controls. First, while export controls are largely a post–World War II development and grant the President broad discretion under general guidelines, import controls and especially tariffs have always been subject to detailed congressional direction.[1] Second, export controls are designed primarily for foreign policy purposes (broadly defined to include national security), but import controls have been created for many reasons.

These reasons include the formerly important need to raise revenues from tariffs, the continuing interest in protecting infant and even established U.S. industries, and the desire to have a base from which to negotiate with other countries.[2] The objective of protecting industries and jobs is backed by powerful domestic constituencies that traditionally wield major clout with Congress. At the same time, classical economic theory and the experience of the Depression have created competing pressures on legislators to resist the use of import controls for purely protectionist purposes.[3]

The congressional suspicion of Executive Branch discretion over imports and the multiple reasons for import controls have led to myriad

---

[1] A. Lowenfeld, *Trade Controls for Political Ends* 9–10 (1983) [hereinafter Lowenfeld, *Trade Controls*]; see J. Jackson, "United States Law and Implementation of the Tokyo Round Results," in J. Jackson, J.-V. Louis, and M. Matsushita, *Implementing the Tokyo Round* 140–1, 177–8 (1984) [hereinafter Jackson, "Tokyo Round Implementation"] R. Baldwin, *The Political Economy of U.S. Import Policy* (1985). The second law passed by Congress was the Tariff Act of 1789, 1 Stat. 24 (July 4, 1789), which indicates the traditional importance of import laws. The first statute had established the oaths of office for members of Congress and other officers of the U.S. Government. A. Lowenfeld, *Public Controls on International Trade* 100 (1983) [hereinafter Lowenfeld, *Public Controls*].

[2] See Lowenfeld, *Public Controls*, supra note 1, at 99–142.

[3] Id.; I. Destler, *Making Foreign Economic Policy* 129–49 (1980); see generally I. Destler, *American Trade Politics: System Under Stress* (1986).

laws. Most are triggered not by foreign policy considerations, but by economic factors, such as injury to domestic industries, discriminatory pricing, or subsidies.

The few laws that involve foreign policy considerations generally relate to a particular country (such as South Africa or Libya), product (such as sugar), or policy issue (such as emigration). An exception is section 232 of the Trade Expansion Act of 1962, which gives the President limited discretion over some imports for "national security" reasons. Overall, unlike the President's discretion to restrict almost all exports, his authority to restrict imports for foreign policy reasons is very circumscribed.

The following analysis considers the relevant import laws by categorizing them as follows: (A) section 232; (B) other foreign policy controls (by country, product, or issue); and (C) economic-based controls. Since import controls can potentially violate U.S. obligations under the General Agreement on Tariffs and Trade (GATT), the analysis will also consider the impact on GATT.

A. SECTION 232 AND NATIONAL SECURITY: DOES IT COVER ONLY FOREIGN OIL?

Section 232 of the Trade Expansion Act of 1962 (19 U.S.C. § 1862) provides the President with his broadest authority to limit imports for foreign policy reasons. It permits him to "adjust the imports" of an article if it "is being imported into the United States in such quantities or under such circumstances as to threaten to impair the national security."[4]

The broad phrase "national security" is not defined in the statute. Nevertheless, the accompanying statutory language, the legislative history, the uses of the statute, and the sparse case law indicate that the purpose of section 232 is to limit imports of critical defense materials, especially in order to protect the domestic production base. A recent exception to this norm was President Reagan's 1982 embargo on oil imports from Libya, which was motivated mainly by broader foreign policy reasons.

The statutory language accompanying the "national security" criterion lists factors that the President "shall... give consideration to." These factors include the "domestic production needed for projected national

---

[4] Pub. L. No. 87-794, § 232(b), 76 Stat. 877, codified as amended at 19 U.S.C. § 1862(b)(1982). The section starts to operate when the Secretary of Commerce commences an investigation at his own initiative, upon the request of the head of any department or agency, or upon the application of an interested party. Within one year, the Secretary must report his findings and recommendations to the President, who "shall take such action, and for such time, as he deems necessary," including taking no action at all. Id.

defense requirements" and generally address the issue of whether the United States will have the "industries and the capacity . . . to meet national security requirements."[5]

The legislative history of section 232 further demonstrates that the statute was enacted to protect domestic industrial capacity for critical items. Section 7 of the Trade Agreements Act of 1955 — the predecessor of section 232(b) — initially provided that the President could "adjust the imports" of an article if it was "being imported into the United States in such quantities as to threaten to impair the national security."[6] The 1955 House Committee Report expressed concern over the nation's ability, in an emergency, to call upon essential industries, plant capacities, and skills. Special mention was made of industries producing synthetic organic chemicals, electrical machinery, and machine tools, as well as the U.S. capacity to produce coal, oil, lead, zinc, and a variety of other

---

[5] 19 U.S.C. § 1862(c). The criteria include "domestic production needed for projected national defense requirements, the capacity of domestic industries to meet such requirements, existing and anticipated availabilities of the human resources, products, raw materials, and other supplies and services essential to the national defense, the requirements of growth of such industries and such supplies and services including the investment, exploration, and development necessary to assure such growth, and the importation of goods in terms of their quantities, availabilities, character, and use as those affect such industries and the capacity of the United States to meet national security requirements." More general language follows. The President is told to take into consideration "the impact of foreign competition on the economic welfare of individual domestic industries; and any substantial unemployment, decrease in revenues of government, loss of skills or investment, or other serious effects resulting from the displacement of any domestic products by excessive imports shall be considered, without excluding other factors, in determining whether such weakening of our internal economy may impair the national security." Id.

[6] Trade Agreements Extension Act of 1955, ch. 169, § 7, 69 Stat. 166. Note that this is the same language as quoted above from Section 232(b), except that it lacks the phrase "or under such circumstances."

Section 7 amended the 1954 extension of the Trade Act, which provided only that there would be no trade agreement reducing the duty of an article if the reduction would threaten domestic production needed for projected national defense requirements. See H. Rep. 50, 84th Cong., 1st Sess. 21–31 (1955), reprinted in 1955 *U.S. Code Cong. & Admin. News* 2071, 2096–7 (minority views). A similar provision remains at 19 U.S.C. § 1862(a).

Responsibility for conducting the investigation and for advising the President about the need to adjust imports was assigned to the Director of the Office of Defense Mobilization under the 1955 and 1958 statutes. *Federal Energy Administration v. Algonquin SNG, Inc.,* 426 U.S. 548, 552 (1976). Under the 1962 statute, this responsibility shifted to the Director of the Office of Emergency Planning, where it remained until the Trade Act of 1979 abolished the office and transferred the advisory functions to the Secretary of the Treasury. In 1980, the advisory responsibility shifted again to the Secretary of Commerce, with whom it currently rests. Exec. Order No. 12,175, 44 *Fed. Reg.* 70,703 (Dec. 10, 1979); Reorganization Plan No. 3 of 1979, § 5(a)(1)(B), 93 Stat. 1381.

raw materials.[7] The Senate Report evinced similar concern, but it devoted special attention to increasing U.S. dependence on petroleum imports.[8] Rather than engaging in a potentially divisive debate over which commodities and products deserved protection under the umbrella of national security, the House and Senate adopted a generic provision that did not mention any specific articles.[9]

Congress amended section 7 when it enacted the Trade Agreements Extension Act of 1958.[10] The Act expanded the bases for import relief by also authorizing the President to act when a given article was being imported "under such circumstances" as to threaten to impair U.S. national security, and not just when the imports were "in such quantities" as to be a threat. Also added were the numerous factors, discussed earlier, that currently appear in section 232(c).[11] Although the amendments broadened the President's authority, they also better defined the situations in which he should act. The Senate Committee Report stated that the 1958 amendments were designed "to give the President unquestioned authority to limit imports which threaten to impair defense-essential industries."[12]

When Congress next reexamined the national security provision, it reenacted it without material change as section 232(b) of the Trade Expansion Act of 1962.[13] Congress again reenacted section 232(b) without material change when it passed the Trade Act of 1974.[14] No material changes in the statutory language have been made since.[15]

---

[7] H. Rep. No. 50, supra note 6 (minority views). The majority did not analyze the section.

[8] S. Rep. No. 232, 84th Cong., 1st Sess. 4 (1955), reprinted in 1955 *U.S. Code Cong. & Admin. News* 2071, 2103–4.

[9] See 101 *Cong. Rec.* 5298 (1955) (statement of Sen. Barkley); id. at 5297–8 (Sen. Flandors and Sen. Byrd). The Conference Report essentially recited the proposed amendment's language. Conf. Rep. No. 745, 84th Cong., 1st sess. (1955), reprinted in 1955 *U.S. Code Cong. & Admin. News* 2136, 2139–40. See also *Algonquin*, 426 U.S. at 562–7 (discussion of the legislative history of the 1955 provision).

[10] Pub. L. No. 85–686, 72 Stat. 678 (1958).

[11] Id.; see *Algonquin*, 426 U.S. at 568.

[12] S. Rep. No. 1838, 85th Cong., 2d Sess. 3614 (1958).

[13] Pub. L. No. 87–794, 76 Stat. 877 (1962). See *Algonquin*, 426 U.S. at 568–70.

[14] Pub. L. No. 93–618, 88 Stat. 1933 (1974). See *Algonquin*, 426 U.S. at 570.

[15] In 1980, Congress did add subsection (e) to 19 U.S.C. § 1862. It provided that any action by the President under section 232(b) could be terminated by a "disapproval resolution," defined as "a joint resolution by either House of Congress." Crude Oil Windfall Profit Tax Act of 1980, Pub. L. No. 96–223, § 402, 94 Stat. 229, 301 (1980). But this provision for a single-house legislative veto is presumably invalid today. See *Immigration and Naturalization Service v. Chadha*, 462 U.S. 919 (1983); see discussion in Chapter 9, Section D.2.

Amendments designed to facilitate use of section 232(b) passed both houses of Congress in 1987. A compromise version appeared in the 1988 trade bill, H.R.3, § 1501, which was vetoed by President Reagan. See supra note 59 in Chapter 2.

Imports to the United States

1. Applications before Libya

During the thirty-three-year history of section 232 and its predecessor statute, the President has used this authority sparingly to impose controls, and then only to restrict petroleum imports.[16]

In response to considerable political pressure,[17] President Reagan threatened to expand the use of section 232 to limit imports of machine tools. Manufacturing of machine tools is an important domestic industry that arguably falls within a narrow reading of the statute. After President Reagan announced in May 1986 that he would defer a formal decision under section 232 for six months, the United States reached voluntary restraint agreements with two major suppliers, Japan and Taiwan, but not with West Germany and Switzerland. Reagan then threatened in December 1986 to "take unilateral action" under U.S. law (presumably section 232) against these two countries if their exports of machine tools to the United States exceeded specified limits. The White House also promised retaliation against any other major foreign supplier undermining the President's program to strengthen the domestic industry.[18]

[16] To be sure, the President, his Cabinet officers, and private entities have formally requested that the possibility of import controls be investigated in other cases. Sixteen investigations, hardly a huge number, were conducted between 1964 and early 1985. Letter from Paula Stern, chairwoman of the International Trade Commission (ITC), to Sen. Lloyd M. Bensten 3 (Apr. 15, 1985) (discussing the import laws that authorize the President to initiate trade actions and their recent use) [hereinafter Stern letter]. In addition to petroleum, these investigations have included products such as watches, movements, and parts (1965); nuts, bolts, and large screws of iron or steel (1978), Stern letter, supra; glass-lined chemical processing equipment (1981), 46 Fed. Reg. 45,977 (1981); chromium, manganese, and silicon ferroalloys (1981), U.S. Import Weekly (BNA), No. 137, at A-1 (July 21, 1982); and machine tools, 7 U.S. Import Weekly (BNA) 753, 754 (Mar. 16, 1983).
In the ferroalloy investigation, press reports indicate that Commerce determined that there was injury to an industry critical to the national security. U.S. Import Weekly (BNA), No. 142, at 640 (Aug. 25, 1982). President Reagan initially sidestepped the Department's recommendation by ordering a stockpile upgrading program for ferromanganese and ferrochromium. See 8 U.S. Import Weekly (BNA) 879 (Sept. 14, 1983). He also ordered the ITC to conduct an investigation pursuant to section 406 of the Trade Act of 1974, discussed in Section B.5, this chapter, to determine whether market disruption was being caused by ferroalloy imports from communist countries. 9 U.S. Import Weekly (BNA) 345–6 (Nov. 30, 1983). Ultimately, President Reagan announced his determination that ferroalloy imports do not threaten national security, thus formally denying relief under Section 232. 9 U.S. Import Weekly (BNA) 1032 (May 23, 1984).
[17] For example, besides pressure from industry, Commerce reportedly recommended that substantial restraints on imports of machine tools be imposed under section 232. 2 Int'l Trade Rep. (BNA) 1050 (Aug. 21, 1985).
[18] 22 Weekly Comp. Pres. Doc. 1654 (Dec. 16, 1986); 3 Int'l Trade Rep. (BNA) 1537 (Dec. 24, 1986); see N.Y. Times, May 21, 1985, at D1, col. 4.

Relief was first granted in 1959 when President Eisenhower invoked the 1958 version of the provision. The Director of the Office of Defense Mobilization advised Eisenhower that "crude oil and the principal crude oil derivatives and products are being imported in such quantities and under such circumstances as to threaten to impair the national security." As a result, Eisenhower established the Mandatory Oil Import Program (MOIP), which imposed a system of quotas on imports of petroleum and petroleum products.[19]

Despite the quotas, domestic consumption of oil continued to increase faster than domestic production. President Kennedy, President Johnson, and President Nixon each reacted by amending the MOIP to raise the permissible quota levels.[20]

President Nixon radically amended the program in 1973, after a Cabinet task force found that the MOIP was not fulfilling its objectives. Acting pursuant to section 232(b), Nixon suspended existing tariffs on oil imports and provided for a gradual transition from the existing quota method to a system of gradually increasing fees for importers.[21] Nixon's program also encountered difficulties.[22] In January 1975, President Ford invoked section 232(b) to accelerate by several months an increase in the 1973 license fees to the maximum levels. Ford also imposed a supplemental fee of one dollar per barrel on all imported oil entering the United States on or after February 1. These supplemental fees were scheduled to rise promptly to two and then three dollars per barrel.[23]

Eight states, their governors, and other parties promptly started their unsuccessful challenge to these import fees in the *Algonquin* litigation, discussed next in Section A.2. Also, on February 19, 1975, Congress voted to suspend the President's powers under section 232(b) for ninety days and to negate any action taken after January 15 – that is, to stop

---

[19] See Proclamation No. 3279, 24 *Fed. Reg.* 12781 (1959). See *Algonquin*, 426 U.S. at 552.

[20] *Algonquin*, 426 U.S. at 552.

[21] Proclamation No. 4210, 3 C.F.R. 31–2 (1974); *Algonquin*, 426 U.S. at 553.

[22] On January 4, 1975, President Ford's Secretary of the Treasury initiated a section 232(b) investigation for imports of petroleum and petroleum products. *Algonquin*, 426 U.S. at 553. Section 232(b) directs the Secretary, "if it is appropriate . . . , [to] hold public hearings or otherwise afford interested parties an opportunity to present information and advice." 18 U.S.C. § 1862(b). Secretary Simon found, however, that such procedures would interfere with "national security interests" and were "inappropriate" in this case. As a result, the investigation proceeded without any public hearing or call for submissions from interested private parties. *Algonquin*, 426 U.S. at 554. On January 14, Simon reported to President Ford that "crude oil, principal crude oil derivatives and products, and related products derived from natural gas and coal tar are being imported into the United States in such quantities . . . and under such circumstances as to threaten to impair the national security." Id.

[23] Proclamation No. 4341, 3A C.F.R. 2 (1975).

Ford's program. On March 4, President Ford vetoed the bill but suspended imposition of the supplemental fees for two months. On May 27, 1975 – after deferring the increase a second time – Ford finally imposed the second dollar of the supplemental fee.[24]

The seizure in Iran of American hostages on November 4, 1979, triggered another use of section 232(b). The Carter Administration was concerned that rapidly deteriorating relations might prompt Iran to cut off, or threaten to cut off, its oil sales to the United States. Although Iran was an important supplier, the Administration determined that an Iranian embargo could be managed by increased conservation and by increased purchases from other sources.[25] To preempt the Iranians and deny them a propaganda victory, Carter invoked section 232(b) on November 12 to terminate all crude oil imports from Iran.[26] Although President Carter declared a national emergency two days later and froze billions of dollars of Iranian assets, he did not impose comprehensive import sanctions under IEEPA until April 1980.[27] In the meantime, the section 232 embargo on oil continued.[28]

---

[24] Proclamation No. 4377, 40 *Fed. Reg.* 23,429 (1975). President Ford later signed the Energy Policy and Conservation Act of 1975, Pub. L. No. 94-163, 89 Stat. 871 (codified at 42 U.S.C. § 6201–6422 (1982)). That Act was intended to encourage domestic oil production by gradually decontrolling the price of domestic crude oil. On January 3, 1976, indicating that the Act would serve "the purposes of the supplemental [oil import license] fee," Ford announced the elimination of the supplemental fees. Proclamation No. 4412, 3 C.F.R. 3 (1977). He did not, however, eliminate the fees originally imposed by Presidential Proclamation No. 4210, 3 C.F.R. 31 (1974).

[25] G. Sick, *All Fall Down* 227 (1985). (Sick was a key member of the National Security Council staff dealing with the Iranian hostage crisis during the Carter Administration.) The United States was importing an average of 700,000 barrels per day from Iran. Id. In contrast, the United States was importing only about 150,000 barrels per day from Libya at the time of President Reagan's March 1982 embargo. See later discussion at note 43.

[26] Proclamation No. 4702, 44 *Fed. Reg.* 65,581 (1979). Carter indicated that he was acting on the advice of his Secretaries of Treasury and Energy. Note that the whole procedure apparently took at most eight days. Carter declared, "[R]ecent developments...underscore the threat to our national security which results from our reliance on Iran as a source of crude oil." Id. One of Carter's purposes, however, was apparently to cut Iran off from a major source of revenue (i.e., the United States). Sick, supra, note 25. (Presumably, however, Iran would be able to sell its oil elsewhere at nearly comparable prices.) This revenue-denial objective is beyond the purposes underlying section 232. Carter's move apparently took the Iranians by surprise. They quickly announced a termination of oil exports to the United States, but they were too late to have any effect. Id.

[27] Exec. Order No. 12,221, 45 *Fed. Reg.* 26,685 (1980). Prohibited transactions included "the direct or indirect import from Iran into the United States of Iranian goods or services, other than materials imported for news publication or news broadcast dissemination." Id.

[28] Most of the sanctions against Iran, including the oil embargo, were rescinded on January 19, 1981. Exec. Order 12,282, 46 *Fed. Reg.*, 7925 (1981).

Carter's use of section 232 against Iran seems consistent with the congressional intent behind the statute. Iran was an important supplier of a critical commodity, and it had become decidedly unreliable. By invoking the statute, Carter was adjusting sources of supply. That section 232 was used to limit only oil imports, and not other imports, was further consistent with the narrow scope of the statute.

Carter also added his chapter to the saga of efforts by previous Presidents to curb consumption of imported oil by using section 232(b). He imposed a gasoline conservation fee on imports of crude oil and gasoline.[29] This effort ran afoul of the courts in *Independent Gasoline Marketers Council, Inc. v. Duncan.* Then Congress stopped the program.[30]

2. Judicial interpretations

Relevant judicial interpretation of section 232(b) is sparse. The leading case is *Federal Energy Administration v. Algonquin SNG, Inc.*, 426 U.S. 548 (1976). There, President Ford's sharp increase in the oil import fees in 1975 triggered a challenge to the Nixon–Ford license fee approach. The district court upheld the presidential action.[31] The U.S. Court of Appeals reversed, however, holding that the President's delegated authority is limited to adjusting the level of imports through direct mechanisms, such as quotas. The court found that license fees were indirect controls on imports beyond the scope of section 232(b).[32]

In a unanimous – though narrow – opinion, the Supreme Court reversed the Court of Appeals and upheld the license fees under section 232(b). The Court noted that all parties agreed that section 232(b) allowed import quotas, and it emphasized that the issue was whether the section allowed the use of license fees to adjust the level of imports.[33] The Court concluded that both the statutory language and the legislative history allowed the use of fees.[34]

The Court did not consider when section 232(b) can properly be in-

[29] Proclamation No. 4744, *Weekly Comp. Pres. Doc.* 592–3 (Apr. 7, 1980).

[30] See discussion in the next section.

[31] *Massachusetts v. Simon*, Civil No. 75-0129 (D.D.C., Feb. 21, 1975), reprinted at 518 F.2d 1064, 1066 (D.C. Cir. 1975).

[32] *Algonquin SNG, Inc. v. Federal Energy Administration*, 518 F.2d 1051, 1062 (D.C. Cir. 1975), reversed sub nom., *Federal Energy Administration v. Algonquin SNG, Inc.*, 426 U.S. 548 (1976). Judge Tamm wrote the majority opinion and was joined by Judge Levanthal. Judge Robb dissented. For an analysis of the opinion, see "Case Note," 89 *Harv. L. Rev.* 432 (1975).

[33] *Algonquin*, 426 U.S. at 551–2.

[34] The Court noted the statute's broad authorization to the President to "take such action...as he deems necessary." Nowhere does the language restrict the manner in which the President may adjust imports. Id. at 561. Similarly, the legislative history imposed no limits on the President's selection of methods. Id. at 562–70.

voked. It did not define "national security," observing only that it was a narrower criterion than "national interest." The Court noted that section 232(c) articulated some standards that guided the President's use of section 232(b), but it did not discuss them further.[35] Finally, the Court did not address whether there should be judicial review of the President's determination that a threat to "impair the national security" warranted steps to adjust the imports of an article.[36]

The Court did, however, emphasize that the President's authority under section 232(b) pertains chiefly to imports. The court concluded its opinion by noting: "Our holding today is a limited one. . . . [O]ur conclusion here . . . that the license fee is authorized by § 232(b) in no way compels the further conclusion that *any* action the President might take, as long as it has even a remote impact on imports, is also so authorized."[37]

This caveat on the scope of section 232 was heavily relied on by the district court in 1980 in *Independent Gasoline Marketers Council, Inc. v. Duncan*,[38] when it struck down President Carter's Petroleum Import Adjustment Program (PIAP). Established in 1979 pursuant to section 232(b), the PIAP imposed a license fee on imported crude oil and gasoline, but the primary purpose was conservation – to lower domestic gas consumption by raising the retail price of *all* gasoline by $.10 per gallon.[39] The court concluded that "[a]ny

[35] Id. at 569. The Court addressed these issues in comparing section 232 with an amendment proposed in 1962 that was deleted by the Conference Committee. The amendment would have given the President broad powers to impose import restrictions when he found it in the "national interest." It had no further criteria. Id. In contrast, the Court of Appeals gave greater attention to the issue of what comprises "national security." The majority opinion noted that "the number of articles potentially covered under the umbrella of 'national security' is great." 518 F.2d at 1056. The opinion later cautioned, "Neither the term 'national security' nor 'emergency' is a talisman, the thaumaturgic invocation of which should, *ipso facto*, suspend the normal checks and balances on each branch of Government." Id. at 1062.

[36] In other cases, district courts have opined that there should not be judicial review of the President's "national security" determination. In *Texas American Asphalt Corp. v. Walker*, 177 F. Supp. 315 (D. Tex. 1959), the court rejected a challenge to President Eisenhower's imposition of oil import controls under the 1958 version of section 232(b). The court said the President had essentially unlimited discretion to determine whether the controls are necessary to protect the national security. "The soundness of the President's judgment that the facts call for the application of his statutory authority to restrict oil imports is not subject to judicial review." Id. at 326 n. 11. In *Independent Gasoline Marketers Council, Inc. v. Duncan*, 494 F. Supp. 614 (D.D.C. 1980), the court struck down President Carter's particular fee arrangement but emphasized that it was not, and should not be, questioning his "national security" finding. Id. at 620.

[37] *Algonquin*, 426 U.S. at 571.

[38] 492 F. Supp. 614 (D.D.C. 1980).

[39] Through a reimbursement system, the cost of the fee on imported oil was to be borne by the distributors, and then by the consumers, of both domestic and imported

impact on imports will be indirect."[40] The Government appealed. However, Congress responded with legislation, passed over the President's veto, that specifically repealed the program with its politically unpopular effect of raising gasoline prices.[41]

3. Libyan sanctions

President Reagan's oil embargo against Colonel Qaddafi's Libya appears to have been the only use of section 232 with foreign policy goals that were broader than simply limiting imports of critical materials to protect the U.S. production base or to protect against cutoff by an important foreign supplier. Nominally, the ban was within the generally accepted confines of the statute. Reagan's proclamation in March 1982 noted "the threat to the national security posed by imports of petroleum continues.... [W]e no longer consider Libya to be a reliable supplier of United States energy needs, and...we must ensure that we are not vulnerable to Libyan action in this area."[42]

Imports of Libyan oil, however, then accounted for only about 3 percent of total U.S. energy imports.[43] The embargo was also in good measure a response to Libyan involvement in terrorist activities and efforts to promote instability in the Middle East and Africa. The presidential proclamation mildly observed that "Libyan policy and action supported by revenues from the sale of oil imported into the United States are inimical to U.S. national security."[44] Other formal and informal com-

---

gasoline. Id. at 616. The system was a complicated one. The amount of the import fee would float, and it would be determined by the effect of the fee on the retail price of gasoline. The initial cost of the fee would be borne by importers. However, an entitlement program would help reimburse the importers. PIAP also provided that all costs incurred from the conservation fee could be passed through the chain of distribution. Id.

[40] Id. at 618. The court reasoned, "Because of the displacement of the initial import fee onto both domestic and imported oil, and the nature of the fee itself, the PIAP could not act as a disincentive to reduce imports." Id. at 617. The court's analytical approach has been cogently criticized. H. Bruff, "Judicial Review and the President's Statutory Powers," 68 *Va. L. Rev.* 1, 54–5 (1982). After ruling out the use of section 232, the court considered whether the President had the inherent authority, independent of Congress, to impose a gasoline conservation fee. It concluded that he did not. Id. at 619–21.

[41] 126 *Cong. Rec.* 13,524 and 13,593 (1980).

[42] Proclamation No. 4907 (Mar. 10, 1982), 18 *Weekly Comp. Pres. Doc.* 280 (March 15, 1982).

[43] *Wash. Post*, Mar. 11, 1982, at A1, A19. Libyan imports had fallen to about one-fourth of their former peak. Even the lower imports at the then reduced prices, however, were equivalent to about $2 billion per year, or 25% of Libya's oil revenues at that time. Id.

[44] Proclamation No. 4907, 47 *Fed. Reg.* 10,507 (1982).

ments from the White House and State Department were more explicit about U.S. opposition to Qaddafi's aggressive activities. There were even reports of an apparent Libyan effort to kill many U.S. officials and their families by planting plastic explosives in stereo speakers at an American club in Sudan.[45]

President Reagan's comprehensive sanctions against Libya in January 1986 because of its support of terrorism, however, did not rely on section 232, even for the nearly total ban on imports. Rather, the President cited sections 504 and 505 of the 1985 foreign assistance act and IEEPA.[46] Possibly, the President did not cite section 232 because of these other ample and more appropriate statutory authorities.

In sum, although on the face of it the "national security" phrase in section 232 is broad, the accompanying statutory language, the legislative history, the uses of the section, and the sparse case law are more confining. Even in the Libyan case, the product involved (petroleum) was traditionally covered by section 232 and the supplier was potentially unreliable.

B. FOREIGN POLICY STATUTES LIMITED TO PARTICULAR COUNTRIES, PRODUCTS, OR ISSUES

Other U.S. laws exist that, for foreign policy reasons, either mandate import controls or allow the President the discretion to act against particular countries, or specific products, or for specific policy reasons.

1. The Comprehensive Anti-Apartheid Act of 1986

The 1986 law imposing wide-ranging sanctions against South Africa mandates a potpourri of import controls. In addition to codifying controls that President Reagan had ordered against krugerrands, nuclear items, and arms, the law included prohibitions against uranium, coal, iron, steel, textiles, agricultural products, sugar, and items from a South African "parastatal organization."[47]

---

[45] *Wash. Post*, supra note 43; Department of State Statement, Mar. 10, 1982, 82 *Dept. of State Bull.* 68 (June 1982). Section 232 has been invoked only one more time – to revoke in 1983 the long-standing oil import licensing system first established by President Eisenhower. Proclamation No. 5141, 48 *Fed. Reg.* 56,929 (1983).

[46] Exec. Order No. 12,543, 51 *Fed. Reg.* 875 (1986). Sections 504 and 505 are discussed later in Section B.2, this chapter, and IEEPA is discussed in Chapter 9.

[47] Pub. L. No. 99-440, 100 Stat. 1086 (1986) (codified at 22 U.S.C. §§ 5001–5116 (Supp. IV 1986)) [hereinafter 1986 Act], 22 U.S.C. §§ 5051 (krugerrands and other gold coins), 5052 (military articles), 5053 (products from parastatal organizations), 5057 (nuclear trade), 5059 (uranium, coal, and textiles), 5069 (agricultural products

The import control with probably the greatest impact on the South African economy was the continued ban against the krugerrand.[48] American imports of the gold coin had been about $600 million in 1984, approximately 50 percent of South Africa's krugerrand exports.[49]

Though the provisions codifying the import bans against arms and nuclear items limited the President's discretion, they had little economic significance. Imports of these items had been minuscule even before Reagan's order.

The prohibitions on new items seemed a pragmatic mixture of controls that might hurt South Africa economically and those that were designed to improve the chances of the bill's passage in Congress. Overall, it was estimated that these new prohibitions accounted for about $300–350 million of the $2.2 billion worth of U.S. imports from South Africa.[50] At least as important as their economic impact on South Africa, however, the bans against steel, textiles, and agricultural products appealed to powerful constituencies in the United States. They were added during the Senate floor debate in August 1986.[51]

and food), 5070 (iron and steel), and 5073 (sugar). A "parastatal organization" is defined, with a narrow exception, as a corporation or partnership owned or controlled or subsidized by the South African Government. Id. § 5053(b).

President Reagan had imposed import controls on gold krugerrands, nuclear items, and arms pursuant to IEEPA in 1985. Actually, krugerrands and nuclear items had been the subject of the conference bill that was on the verge of passing when President Reagan preempted it with his declaration of a national emergency and the imposition of IEPPA controls. See Chapter 9, Section C.

[48] 22 U.S.C. § 5051. Note that President Reagan had prohibited only the importation of krugerrands, but the 1986 Act also applies to "any other gold coin minted in South Africa or offered for sales by the Government of South Africa." The purpose of this additional provision was presumably to prevent the South Africans from minting a new coin. Not even this provision, however, applies to imports of gold from South Africa in forms other than coins, such as gold bars. It remains to be seen how much South Africa's total gold sales to the United States will be reduced by the ban on imports of gold coins.

[49] *Wash. Post*, Aug. 7, 1985, at A14, col. 3.

[50] *Wash. Post*, Oct. 3, 1986, at 1, col. 4.

[51] Compare the Act as passed with S. 2701 as reported to the Senate on August 6 by Sen. Lugar for the Committee on Foreign Relations. Indeed, S. 2701 as reported by the Committee had a provision for possible *future* measures against South Africa that included import bans on steel, textiles, and agricultural products. S. 2701, § 501. These future measures were added to the present prohibitions in the final law. 1986 Act, supra note 47, §§ 309, 319, 320, 22 U.S.C. §§ 5070, 5069, 5059. However, reflecting the hurried nature of the Senate debate on this bill, the final law also included bans on steel, textiles, and agricultural products as possible future measures. Section 501. This is obviously redundant. (After the Senate passed the amended bill, the House of Representatives passed it without change, and then both houses overrode the President's veto.) A new law was enacted a month later in November 1986 to clear up this and other problems in the Comprehensive Anti-Apartheid Act. Pub. L. No.

The 1986 law also contains the specific threat of the President recommending, and Congress approving, controls in the future on diamonds and strategic minerals.[52] However, even without counting these items, the import controls against South Africa are extensive. These prohibitions are also mandatory, leaving very little discretion to the President.

2. Other countries: Libya, terrorists, and Uganda

In 1985, Libya received the dubious honor of joining Cuba[53] as the only specific countries from which the President has broad discretion to prohibit imports.[54] Another 1985 provision authorizes the President to ban imports "from any country which supports terrorism or terrorist organizations or harbors terrorists or terrorist organizations."[55] These two provisions can trace their roots to the increasingly strong public reaction against terrorism, and countries like Libya that support it.[56]

Limited only by country, these provisions represent a potentially sem-

---

99-631, § 1(a)(26), 100 Stat. 3518 (1986) (codified at 22 U.S.C. §§ 5001–5116 (Supp. IV 1986)). See 22 U.S.C. § 5091(c) for the revised list of the additional measures that the President might recommend. The list does not include those items whose importation has already been prohibited.

[52] Id. § 5091(c).

[53] 19 U.S.C. § 2370(a)(1) (1982) (Cuba). The provision states, in pertinent part, that "the President is authorized to establish and maintain a total embargo upon all trade between the United States and Cuba." This statute was passed in 1961 when U.S. relations with Fidel Castro had soured. Pub. L. 87-195, pt. III, § 620, Sept. 4, 1961, 75 Stat. 444. The U.S. maintains today a comprehensive economic boycott of Cuba. However, the boycott is grounded primarily on the Trading with the Enemy Act, discussed in Chapter 9, Section B. See *Regan v. Wald*, 468 U.S. 222, 225 n.1 (1984).

[54] International Security and Development Cooperation Act of 1985, § 504(a), 22 U.S.C. § 2349aa-8(a) (Supp. III 1985). The provision reads, "Notwithstanding any other provision of law, the President may prohibit any article grown, produced, extracted, or manufactured in Libya from being imported into the United States." Subsection (b) of the statute contains similar authority regarding exports.

[55] Id. § 505, 22 U.S.C. § 2349aa-9. This provision requires that the President, "in every possible instance," consult with Congress before exercising the authority and then to report immediately afterward. He is also required to consult Congress while the authority is being used. Id. The House Conference report noted that the reporting requirement parallels the one found in IEEPA's section 204, 50 U.S.C. § 1703 (1982). H. Conf. Rep. No. 99-237, 99th Cong., 1st Sess. 124 (1985).

[56] No version of either provision appeared in the House and Senate bills as reported from their respective committees. However, versions of these and other antiterrorist provisions were added on the House and Senate floor and then worked out by the Conference Committee. H. Conf. Rep. No. 99-237, supra note 55, at 123–4; see 91 *Cong. Rec.* H5363 (daily ed. July 10, 1985) (statement of Rep. Gilman introducing his amendment).

inal step taken by Congress to authorize the use of broad import controls for foreign policy reasons in nonemergency situations. President Reagan was quick to invoke them. He cited both provisions as bases for his embargo of Libya in January 1986, although he also declared a national emergency and cited IEEPA. Then, in October 1987, President Reagan relied on the second provision to cut off almost all imports of Iranian goods and services.[57]

The only other recent resort to import controls in a similar situation occurred when Congress mandated (rather than authorized) the use of import as well as export controls against Idi Amin's Uganda. After Idi Amin's rise to power in 1971 and during the resulting reign of terror, the United States began imposing a series of sanctions, from closing the American embassy to terminating foreign assistance.[58] In 1975 imports from Uganda were not accorded duty-free treatment under the Generalized System of Preference.[59] Congress, however, felt that more should be done. As a major activity to target, for example, the United States imported in 1977 more than 33 percent of Uganda's total coffee exports (its major source of foreign exchange).[60] Over the objections of the Carter Administration, Congress imposed in October 1978 a mandatory ban on both imports from and exports to Uganda.[61]

A force of Ugandan exiles and Tanzanian soldiers invaded Uganda in January 1979 and by April occupied Kampala, the capital. Amin fled Uganda. Though there is some dispute over the effectiveness of the full

---

[57] For Libya, see Exec. Order 12,543, 51 *Fed. Reg.* 875 (1986). Sections 504 and 505 dealing with trade would not have been sufficient statutory support for some of the financial controls that President imposed. See id. and Exec. Order 12,544, 51 *Fed. Reg.* 1235 (1986) (freezing Libyan assets); see discussion on IEEPA in Chapter 9. For Iran, see Exec. Order 12,613, 51 *Fed. Reg.* 41, 940 (1987).

Congress seems inclined to resort more to statutory provisions like these, which allow the President to stop imports from (as well as exports to) specific countries, rather than pass provisions that give the President broad authority over imports. For example, the 1987 trade bill passed by the Senate had such provisions aimed at Iran and at other states in the Persian Gulf if they attack U.S. vessels, facilities, or personnel in the Persian Gulf region. Omnibus Trade and Competitiveness Act of 1987, H.R.3, 100th Cong., 1st Sess. (formerly S. 1420) (1987), §§ 963–66. The bill also authorized the President to prohibit the import or export of goods to Afghanistan, except for trade with the resistance groups there. Id. § 958.

[58] See K. Abbott, "Linking Trade to Political Goals: Foreign Policy Export Controls in the 1970s and 1980s," 65 *Minn. L. Rev.* 778–82 (1981); G. Hufbauer and J. Schott, *Economic Sanctions Reconsidered: History and Current Policy* 453–60 (1985); J. Miller, "When Sanctions Worked," 39 *Foreign Pol'y* 118 (1980).

[59] Exec. Order No. 11,888, 3A C.F.R. 207 (1975). See later discussion at notes 106–17 regarding the GSP.

[60] Abbott, supra note 58, at 780; Miller, supra note 58, at 121.

[61] Bretton Woods Agreement Amendments Act, Pub. L. No. 95-435, § 5(c)–(d), 92 Stat. 1051 (1978). (Section 5(c) was repealed in 1979. Section 5(d) was codified at 50 U.S.C. app. §2403, but expired in 1979.)

range of U.S. sanctions, they definitely hurt Uganda economically, helped undercut Amin's support, and were conducive to the invasion. The exact role of the import ban is even less certain. Even before October 1978, American companies had ceased buying Ugandan coffee. But they apparently did so because of growing congressional and other U.S. public pressure.[62]

3. Product specific: a strange mix

The President has various degrees of authority to limit the imports of a strange mix of products. Because nuclear goods and technology, arms, and other defense items are so important to national security and safety, the President has sweeping authority over their importation. This is similar to his discretion over exports of those items.[63]

Beyond that, import quotas or flat prohibitions on specific products can provide a basis for foreign policy sanctions. Import quota systems exist today on a wide range of commodities – from peanuts to cattle.[64] The quotas can apply globally or against specific countries, the latter having the greatest potential for sanctions use. Congress has either prescribed the quotas or authorized the President or an executive agency to set the quotas for a variety of purposes. These purposes are primarily economic – to protect U.S. agriculture or industry, to carry out trade agreements, to stabilize the U.S. balance of payments, or to provide temporary import relief. The statutes or history, however, seem to allow at least the quotas for sugar and beef to be used for foreign policy purposes.[65]

[62] See Hufbauer and Schott, supra note 58, at 456–9; Miller, supra note 58, at 121–9; Abbott, supra note 58, at 781–2.

[63] See discussion of the Atomic Energy Act and the Arms Export Control Act in Chapter 4, Sections B and C.

[64] See "Quotas and Restraints," in *Int'l Trade Rep. (BNA), U.S. Import Weekly Reference File* 43:0101 (1988). Tariff-rate quotas exist on such items as cattle, milk, and tuna fish. Absolute quotas under section 22 of the Agricultural Adjustment Act, 7 U.S.C. § 624 (1982), exist for, among others, certain dairy products, cotton, peanuts, and sugar. There are also quotas for items covered by trade agreements or international commodity agreements, such as sugar, coffee, and textiles. Id. at 43:0101–2.

[65] Id. This book does not purport to be an exhaustive study of the many complex quota systems. It highlights only the two commodities where the statutes or history indicate that the President has the most discretion to use quotas for foreign policy reasons.

Chile and copper provide another example of the use of tariffs or quotas on a particular product for foreign policy purposes. In 1966, the United States suspended by new statute the duty on Chilean copper for two years. It was part of a U.S. effort to support the regime of President Eduardo Frei, as well as to help roll back recent Chilean price increases. See D. Berteau, "The Harriman–Solomon Mission and the

The present provisions for *sugar quotas* are deceptive. The President is authorized to reduce or otherwise change these quotas in certain ways if he finds that the change "will give due consideration to the interests in the United States sugar market of domestic producers and materially affected contracting parties to the [GATT]."[66] This provision is ambiguous and does not specify foreign policy reasons.[67]

President Reagan nevertheless relied on this authority in 1983 to reduce sharply the sugar quota for Nicaragua and to reallocate it to three neighboring countries – Honduras, Costa Rica, and El Salvador.[68] An accompanying White House statement noted that this step was intended to "reduce the resources available to [Nicaragua] for financing its military buildup and its support for subversion and extremist violence in the region." At the same time, the reallocation would "significantly help" the three neighbors who were "experiencing enormous problems, caused in considerable part by Nicaraguan-supported subversion and extremist violence."[69] Reagan's use of the sugar quota was similar to prior uses of

1966 Chilean Copper Agreement," in *Economic Coercion and U.S. Foreign Policy* 173 (S. Weintraub ed.) (1982).

Another possible use of quotas as a sanction was suggested during the recent dispute with New Zealand over U.S. warships making port calls there without assurances that the vessels carried no nuclear weapons. At one point, U.S. officials said they were studying termination of the preferential treatment that New Zealand receives for imports of lamb and wool. *N.Y. Times*, Feb. 12, 1985, at A13, col. 1.

It should also be noted that the President is authorized to suspend any or all of a number of quotas for a particular country if that country has wrongfully nationalized or imposed discriminatory taxes or other laws on the property of U.S. citizens or corporations. 7 U.S.C. § 1158(c) (1982). The same statute includes a section authorizing a similar suspension if the President finds that a "national economic or other emergency exists with respect to sugar or liquid sugar." Id. § 1158(a).

[66] Headnote 2 of sched. 1 pt. 10, subpt. A, of the Tariff Schedules of the United States, 19 U.S.C. § 1202 (1985). A 1987 law imposed a specific prohibition on sugar imports from Panama, unless the President certifies that constitutional guarantees have been restored to the Panamanian people. 1988 continuing resolution, supra note 37 in Chapter 3, § 571.

[67] Cf. *United States Cane Sugar Refiners' Ass'n v. Block*, 683 F. 2d 399, 402 n. 5, 404 (C.C.P.A. 1982) (though private parties have standing to challenge his actions, the President has broad discretion under the statute).

[68] Proclamation No. 5104, 48 *Fed. Reg.* 44,057 (1983). The 1984 quota for Nicaragua was reduced to 6,000 short tons from the existing 58,000 tons. The existing quotas then for the other countries were 28,000 tons for Honduras, 42,000 tons for Costa Rica, and 72,800 tons for El Salvador. "Announcement of Revised United States Sugar Import Quotas for Nicaragua, Honduras, Costa Rica, and El Salvador," *Public Papers of President Ronald Reagan*, vol. I, at 685, 685–6 (1983) [hereinafter "Revised Sugar Import Quotas"].

[69] "Revised Sugar Import Quotas," supra note 68. The change would deny Nicaragua a foreign exchange benefit of about $14 million per year because of the high U.S. sugar price. Id. There apparently was no legal challenge in the U.S. courts to President Reagan's quota cutback. Nicaragua did challenge the move in the GATT. See discussion in Section C, this chapter.

the quota by President Eisenhower against both Cuba and the Dominican Republic, though Eisenhower had more explicit statutory authority for his sanctions.[70]

The President also has the authority to suspend a country's import quotas for most types of *meat*, when the "action is required by over-riding . . . national security interests."[71] "National security interests" are not defined and presumably are narrower than a criterion of foreign policy interests or national interests. In any case, it does not appear that the President has exercised this authority as an economic sanction.

A mandatory prohibition exists against the importation of seven *animal*

---

[70] In 1960, Eisenhower drastically reduced and then canceled the Cuban sugar quota that had been established under section 408 of the Sugar Act of 1948. Proclamation No. 3355, 25 *Fed. Reg.* 6414 (1960); Proclamation No. 3383, 25 *Fed. Reg.* 13,131 (1960). He acted pursuant to a specific 1960 law that allowed him to change the Cuban quota if he found the change to be "in the national interest." Sugar Act of 1948 – Amendments, Pub. L. No. 86-592, 74 Stat. 330 (1960), codified at 7 U.S.C. § 1158. The language invoked by Eisenhower was later amended and has since expired.

Rather than the statutory language specifying Cuba, the Eisenhower Administration had proposed an amendment to the 1948 Act that the President be delegated authority to reduce quotas of any country, other than the Philippines (whose quota was fixed by treaty), "when he found it necessary to do so in the national interest or to insure adequate supplies of sugar." Quoted in C. L. Brown-John, *Multilateral Sanctions in International Law: A Comparative Analysis* 221 (1975). The appropriate House committee rejected this broader language, and the President received only the authority for Cuba. Id. at 224. This became important shortly when President Eisenhower, as discussed below, wanted to limit the Dominican Republic's quota.

The cutback of the Cuban sugar quota led Congress to reallocate the quota to other countries, the Dominican Republic getting a revised quota that was nearly four times its 1959 sales to the United States. In a special message to Congress, Eisenhower requested legislation authorizing him to curtail the Dominican Republic's windfall because of Trujillo's flagrant violation of human rights and acts of aggression against Venezuela. "President's Message to Congress on Sugar Act Problems," 2 *U.S. Code Cong. & Admin. News* 1571 (1960).

Seven months later Eisenhower received statutory authority that the United States was not obligated to purchase sugar from any country "with which the United States is not in diplomatic relations." Publ. L. No. 87-15, 75 Stat. 40 (1961). (The United States had earlier broken diplomatic relations with the Dominican Republic.) See Brown-John, supra, at 203–5; Hufbauer and Schott, supra note 58, at 302–3. This step was part of a series of measures the United States and other OAS countries agreed to take. Id.

[71] 19 U.S.C. § 1202 (1982). The covered meats include beef, veal, sheep (except lamb), and goats. The statute provides for a global quota and then for country quotas. The President is allowed to suspend these quotas (and even to increase them). The statute also allows the President to act for "overriding economic . . . interests." Although it did not address the provision on national security interests, the Conference Report noted that the managers from both the House and Senate understood that "the overriding economic interests . . . include largely trade and balance-of-payment considerations." Conf. Rep. No. 1824, 88th Cong., 2d Sess. (1964), reprinted in 2 *U.S. Code Cong. & Admin. News* 3079 (1964).

skins – including ermine, fox, and mink – from the Soviet Union.[72] This was imposed in 1951 for foreign policy reasons – to protest Moscow's role in the Korean War. There have been efforts in recent years to lift the ban.[73] In the meantime, the restriction will continue to be known as the one against "the seven deadly skins."

4. Policy issues: emigration and others

The United States extends most favored nation (MFN) status to many countries, either through bilateral agreements or under the GATT. In addition, it extends special tariff benefits to some developing countries under the Generalized System of Preferences (GSP) and the Caribbean Basin Initiative (CBI).

For various policy reasons, U.S. laws provide the President with some discretion to extend these MFN, GSP, or CBI benefits to countries or to deny them to those countries now receiving these benefits. For example, because of the Soviet invasion of Afghanistan and the resulting puppet government there, President Reagan terminated MFN status to Afghanistan in 1986.[74]

---

[72] Headnote 4 of schedule 1, pt. 5, subpt. B of the U.S. Tariff Schedule, 19 U.S.C. § 1202 note (1985). The full list includes ermine, fox, kolinsky, marten, mink, muskrat, and weasel. Id. Why weasel, but not sable, is included is a question this book will leave for other researchers.

[73] A similar ban against furs from the People's Republic of China was repealed in 1983. Pub. L. No. 97-446, § 103, 96 Stat. 2329 (1983). In 1985 Commerce Secretary Baldridge urged Congress to end the ban against Soviet furs. *N.Y. Times*, May 30, 1985, at B6, col. 2. More recently, the 1988 trade bill passed by the House and Senate, but vetoed by President Reagan, would have repealed the ban. April 1988 Trade Bill, supra note 59 in Chapter 2, § 1722. This was in contrast to the 1987 Senate bill, which strongly urged continuation, noting the many unsubsidized fur farms that would be injured by Soviet imports. It ominously warned that the "United States fur deficit will rise." 1987 Senate Trade Bill, supra note 57, § 899B.

[74] Proclamation No. 5437, 51 *Fed. Reg.* 4287 (1986). The President's decision was very much encouraged by a law Congress had just passed. It granted the President authority to revoke Afghanistan's MFN status and required that he report to Congress if he had not done so within forty-five days of enactment of the bill. Pub. L. No. 99-190, §§ 118, 552, 99 Stat. 1314, 1319 (1985). Even without the statute, it would seem that the President had authority under the agreements with Afghanistan and under existing laws to revoke Afghanistan's MFN status. See 19 U.S.C. § 2434(c) (1982 & Supp. IV 1986); Letter from William Ball, Assistant Secretary of State for Legislative and Intergovernmental Affairs, to Senator Packwood, Chairman of the Senate Committee on Finance (July 22, 1985), in *MFN Status for Hungary, Romania, China, and Afghanistan: Hearing Before the Subcomm. on Int'l Trade of the Senate Comm. on Finance*, 99th Cong., 1st Sess. 263 (1985) [hereinafter *Hearing*]. The action was largely symbolic. In 1984, the United States imported $13 million in goods from Afghanistan, while exporting more than $7 million in goods to it. *Hearing*, supra, at 36 (prepared statement of Sen. D'Amato).

President Carter had withdrawn the country's GSP status in 1980.[75]

Discussed below are policy issues of current interest. These include the well-publicized issue of denying MFN status to countries with nonmarket economies that make emigration difficult, the recent U.S. denial of MFN status to Poland, and the various policy hurdles to extending GSP and CBI status.[76]

a. Opening the doors: emigration. Title IV of the Trade Act of 1974, as amended,[77] authorizes the President under certain circumstances to extend MFN trade treatment to a so-called nonmarket economy country that at the time of the Act was not already receiving this treatment from the United States. The MFN treatment is to be provided via a bilateral commercial agreement that includes a number of safeguards, such as allowing import restrictions for market disruption and protecting patents and copyrights.[78]

The statute reopened the possibility of MFN treatment to most communist countries. When the Cold War was especially chilly in 1951, Congress required the President to deny or suspend any country "dominated or controlled by" communism, except Yugoslavia, the benefits of lower tariffs negotiated through trade agreements. As a result, imports from these communist countries were made subject to the high rates of

[75] Exec. Order 12,204, 16 *Weekly Comp. Pres. Doc.* 549 (Mar. 31, 1980). As discussed at note 109, Carter was required to do this under the law because the country was communist.

[76] Another law worth noting is the mandatory prohibition on imports of all goods or articles mined, produced, or manufactured in whole or part by convicts or other forced labor. 19 U.S.C. § 1307 (1982). This statute has apparently been used only once, in 1951. Imports of Russian crabmeat were banned on the ground that it was produced by forced labor. At that time, American crabmeat packers, with some congressional support, were protesting that the Russians were dumping crabmeat in the United States at unfair prices. *N.Y. Times,* Nov. 8, 1983, at A3, col. 4.

The U.S. Commissioner of Customs attempted to resuscitate the statute in 1983 when he recommended to the Secretary of the Treasury, who is charged with implementing the law, that the United States bar the importation of some three dozen products from the Soviet Union because they were made with the help of forced labor. The Commissioner's letter came shortly after the Soviet downing of the Korean airliner. Id. Debate over whether there should be new resort to the statute has occurred sporadically since. See, e.g., *McKinney v. U.S. Dept. of Treasury,* 799 F.2d 1544 (Fed. Cir. 1986) (dismissing on ground of lack of standing a private action to enforce section 1307); section 1906 of the April 1988 Trade Bill, supra note 59 in Chapter 2, which requested the President to instruct the Secretary of the Treasury to enforce section 1307.

[77] Pub. L. No. 93-618, tit. IV, 88 Stat. 1978, 2056-66 (Jan. 3, 1975) (codified in scattered sections of 19 U.S.C.) [hereinafter 1974 Trade Act].

[78] See especially 19 U.S.C. § 2435 (1982).

the 1930 Smoot–Hawley Tariff.[79] As post–World War II agreements progressively lowered the MFN tariffs, the differential with the Smoot–Hawley rates widened, and imports from communist countries were increasingly disadvantaged.[80] (Poland, however, qualified specially for MFN treatment starting in 1960.)[81]

With the growth of détente after the first U.S.–Soviet summit in May 1972, the Nixon Administration sought to improve trade relations with the Soviet Union. The U.S.–Soviet Trade Agreement of 1972 was signed, its entry into force contingent on Congress agreeing to MFN status for the Soviet Union. Several factors – including Soviet restrictions on Jewish emigration and domestic U.S. politics – led to a tangled situation, however. Finally, well-publicized trilateral negotiations among the Soviets, the U.S. Executive Branch, and the Congress (especially Senator Jackson) resulted in title IV of the 1974 Trade Act.[82]

A key provision of the statute is that no nonmarket country is eligible to receive MFN treatment (or certain other benefits)[83] if the President determines that the country denies its "citizens the right or opportunity to emigrate," or imposes more than a nominal tax on emigration.[84] Under the Act, however, a nonmarket country can qualify for MFN treatment if the President determines that the country is not violating these statutory conditions.[85] Alternatively, the President can waive the conditions if he

---

[79] Trade Agreements Extension Act of 1951, ch. 141, § 5, 65 Stat. 72, 73 (1951). See Senate Committee on Finance, 93d Cong., 2d Sess., *Executive Branch GATT Studies* 12 (Comm. Print 1974).

[80] See Lowenfeld, *Trade Controls,* supra note 1, at 11–12.

[81] President Eisenhower terminated the 1951 suspension of Poland's MFN status in November 1960 after Poland and GATT entered into an agreement. Because of some later statutory requirements, President Johnson made a determination permitting the continuation of Poland's MFN treatment in March 1964. "Administration Reviewing Measures to Suspend Poland's MFN Tariff Treatment," 18 *U.S. Export Weekly (BNA),* No. 3, at 94, 95 (Oct. 19, 1982). Title IV of the 1974 Trade Act contained a grandfather clause exempting from the Act's coverage those nonmarket countries that already had MFN status. 1974 Trade Act § 401, 19 U.S.C. § 2431. President Reagan, however, suspended Poland's MFN status during 1982–7 as discussed in the next section.

[82] For excellent analyses of the events leading up to the 1974 Trade Act and the aftermath, see P. Stern, *Water's Edge: Domestic Politics and the Making of American Foreign Policy* (1979), and Lowenfeld, *Trade Controls,* supra note 1, at 166–90.

[83] These other benefits include participation in any U.S. program that "extends credits or credit guarantees or investment guarantees, directly or indirectly." 1974 Trade Act, § 402(a), 19 U.S.C. § 2432(a). It should be noted that there are other statutory provisions limiting the participation of the Soviet Union and other communist countries in certain of these programs. See Lowenfeld, *Trade Controls,* supra note 1, at 183–90.

[84] 1974 Trade Act, § 402(a), 19 U.S.C. § 2432(a).

[85] Id. § 402(a) and (b), 19 U.S.C. § 2432(a) and (b). The President is required to report this to Congress initially and then make semiannual reports. Id.

determines that waiver will substantially promote free emigration, and if he has received assurances to that effect. The waiver extends for twelve months only and then must be renewed.[86]

The publicity surrounding the trilateral negotiations was apparently more than the Soviets could accept. In January 1975 the Soviet Union notified the United States that it thought the Trade Act was contrary to the 1972 Trade Agreement that would have allowed it MFN status. The Soviets refused to put the trade agreement into force.[87]

Pursuant to the 1974 Act, however, Presidents have waived the emigration conditions and thus allowed MFN treatment for Romania starting in 1975 (through mid-1988),[88] for Hungary in 1978, [89] and for the People's Republic of China in 1979.[90] These waivers have been renewed regularly,[91] though not without occasional controversy.

The statute's conditions and the force of public attention on the emigration issue do seem to have encouraged Romania to relax its emigration restrictions, or at least to do so at crucial times when the waiver was initially granted or was being renewed.[92] For example, Romania

---

[86] Id. § 402(c) and (d), 19 U.S.C. § 2432(c) and (d). Note that section 402 operates "notwithstanding any other provision of law." Id. If the terms of section 402 are satisfied, sec. 404, 19 U.S.C. § 2434, allows the President to extend MFN treatment to a foreign country that enters into a bilateral commercial agreement as referred to in sec. 405, 19 U.S.C. § 2435. Section 405 allows commercial agreements for up to three years, subject to a variety of conditions. As discussed below, pursuant to these sections, the United States entered into commercial agreements with Romania in 1975, Hungary in 1978, and China in 1979.

Title IV also contains Sec. 406, 19 U.S.C. § 2436, which authorizes the President to limit imports from communist countries when there is "market disruption." See the discussion at notes 125–31, this chapter.

[87] See Stern, supra note 82, at 190; see also Lowenfeld, *Trade Controls,* supra note 1, at 177–8.

[88] Exec. Order No. 11,854, 3 C.F.R. 987 (1971–75). See note 96 infra.

[89] Exec. Order No. 12,051, 3 C.F.R. 173 (1979).

[90] Exec. Order No. 12,167, 3 C.F.R. 153 (1980).

[91] E.g., Determination Under Subsection 402(d)(5) of the Trade Act of 1974 – Continuation of Waiver Authority, No. 86-10, June 3, 1986, 51 *Fed. Reg.* 22,057 (1986) (Romania).

[92] See Hufbauer and Schott, supra note 58, at 517–22 (giving the statute significant credit for easing emigration restrictions in Romania). Emigration restrictions are not a problem with China, at least recently. As President Reagan noted in 1983, China "continued its open emigration policy.... The limiting factor on Chinese emigration remains less official constraint than the limited ability or willingness of this and other countries to receive large numbers of potential Chinese immigrants." *N.Y. Times,* June 4, 1983, at 24, col. 1.

On the other side of the coin, it must be asked whether passage of section 402, including the surrounding debate, also had its drawbacks. For example, if the 1972 U.S.–Soviet Trade Agreement had gone into force, would it have led to improved U.S.–Soviet trade and other relations that were in the U.S. interest, and would it possibly even have encouraged the higher levels of emigration that were prevailing in

allowed a substantial increase in emigrants in the second half of 1975 while Congress was reviewing the President's initial waiver of April 1975.[93] Then, in March 1983, President Reagan threatened to suspend Romania's waiver unless it rescinded a new "education tax" imposed on emigrants, which required them to pay the state a charge for the costs of their past education.[94] Romania agreed in May 1983 to suspend implementation of the tax.[95] Finally, since late 1985 there has been considerable outcry in the United States about Romania's emigration policies and its treatment of Protestant and labor groups. In what was described as an "exceptionally difficult" decision, the Reagan Administration nevertheless renewed Romania's waiver in June 1987. Reacting unfavorably to the continued pressure, Romania in February 1988 unilaterally renounced renewal of its MFN status, effective that July.[96]

Notwithstanding the waivers for the three countries, the President's discretion either to determine that the emigration objectives have been met or to waive them is limited.[97] Although the Executive Branch often

---

1972–74 versus the later drop-off? See Stern, supra note 82, at 197–202, 217–18. Also, do the annual renewals of the waivers create commercial uncertainty that hampers expanded U.S. trade with, say, Romania? Is any such cost worth the benefit of the annual review of the country's emigration policies?

[93] Note, "An Interim Analysis of the Effects of the Jackson–Vanik Amendment on Trade and Human Rights: The Romanian Example," 8 *L. & Pol'y Int'l Bus.* 193, 206–7 (1976).

[94] *Wash. Post*, Mar. 3, 1980, at A17, col. 3. Reagan Administration sources estimated then that withdrawal of the trade benefits would probably cost Romania about $200 million in sales to the United States. Id. at col. 4.

[95] *N.Y. Times*, May 19, 1983, at A3.

[96] For Romania's decision, see 5 *Int'l Trade Rep.* (BNA) 499 (April 6, 1988) and 286 (March 2, 1988). For the Reagan Administration decision see 4 *Int'l Trade Rep.* (BNA) 763 (June 10, 1987) (quoting a White House press release).

When Romania's waiver was renewed in June 1986, Assistant Secretary of State Rozanne L. Ridgway said the decision was a "tough call" because of "religious rights issues and the treatment of the Romanian people across a broad range of human-rights issues." *Wash. Post*, Aug. 2, 1986, at A11, col. 1. Although section 402(a) does focus on emigration policies, there is the introductory phrase: "To assure the continued dedication of the United States to fundamental human rights...." The section also provides that the President "may, at any time, terminate by Executive order any waiver granted...." No reasons are required.

[97] This is even after the several legislative veto provisions in title IV have presumably been invalidated. For example, any section 402 waiver after the first eighteen months of the law (enacted January 3, 1975) required approval by a concurrent resolution from both the Senate and House. Similarly, entry into a commercial agreement with a nonmarket country and the related extension of MFN treatment pursuant to sections 404 and 405 required approval by a concurrent resolution. These provisions were presumably invalidated by the *Chadha* case, discussed in Chapter 9, Section D.2. Without serious objection by Congress, the Executive Branch has treated these veto provisions as invalid and severable from the rest of the statute. *N.Y. Times*, Dec. 4,

engages in diplomatic discussions with representatives from these countries in which private assurances may be given by the other country, the statute requires that the President report his decisions to Congress. Moreover, many of the data on emigration involve relatively public, objective facts. Closely monitoring the situation are powerful political groups that have a strong interest in Jewish emigration or that are generally opposed to improved trade with communist countries.

b. The Polish ploy. President Reagan suspended Poland's MFN status from 1982 to 1987 for foreign policy reasons. The legal basis for the suspension was unique, however, and will probably remain so.

Poland had enjoyed MFN treatment since 1960 and was exempted from the emigration provisions of the 1974 Trade Act.[98] Starting in late 1981, however, the United States imposed a series of sanctions against Poland and the Soviet Union in response to the increasing repression in Poland, including efforts to suppress Solidarity.[99] In October 1982, as one of the last sanctions imposed, President Reagan suspended Poland's MFN status indefinitely.[100] Reagan said that Poland's official outlawing of Solidarity on October 8 left the United States no reason to "continue withholding action on its trade complaints against Poland."[101]

As the legal basis for his action, however, the President fell back to relying on breach of a trade agreement. He cited Poland's 1967 protocol of accession to the GATT, which required that it increase the total value of its imports from GATT Contracting Parties by 7 percent per year. Since 1978, Warsaw had failed to meet those commitments.[102] Administration spokesmen then pointed to the President's statutory authority

1985, at 1, col. 3; see T. Franck and C. Bob, "The Return of Humpty-Dumpty: Foreign Relations Law After the *Chadha* Case," 79 *Am. J. Int'l L.* 929–31 (1985) (regarding severability).

[98] See discussion above in notes 77–81.

[99] E.g., President Reagan's television address of December 23, 1981, 17 *Weekly Comp. of Pres. Doc.* 1406 (Dec. 28, 1981). The sanctions against Poland included suspending all U.S. official and guaranteed credits for Poland, suspending civil aviation privileges for LOT airline in the United States, suspending Polish fishing privileges in U.S. waters, and stopping issuance of some export licenses. "'Limited Steps' on Economic Sanctions for Poland Announced by Administration," 20 *U.S. Export Weekly (BNA)*, No. 6 (Nov. 8, 1983), at 208.

[100] Proclamation No. 4991, 47 *Fed. Reg.* 49,005 (1982).

[101] Id.; 7 *U.S. Import Weekly (BNA)* 161 (Nov. 3, 1982); 18 *U.S. Export Weekly (BNA)*, 130 (Oct. 26, 1982).

[102] Id. American officials estimated that about half of U.S.–Polish trade would be affected by the tariff actions, but the impact would vary among sections. Even before this action, U.S.–Polish trade had declined, Poland exporting slightly more than $100 million to the United States in the first half of 1982. 18 *U.S. Export Weekly (BNA)* 94, 95 (Oct. 19, 1982).

to proclaim increased duties or other import restrictions "as he deems necessary or appropriate" when the United States acts pursuant to a trade agreement to suspend or modify an obligation concerned with the trade of a foreign country.[103] Poland challenged the U.S. action unsuccessfully in the GATT.[104]

President Reagan revoked the suspension in February 1987. He said the reinstatement was a reward for Poland's release of political prisoners and other steps toward reconciliation with Solidarity members and the Catholic Church.[105]

c. Limiting the GSP and CBI. The President has considerable discretion to grant or withdraw for foreign policy reasons extensive tariff benefits to less developed countries (LDCs) under the GSP and the CBI. The *GSP program* eliminates duties on a wide range of articles imported into the United States from LDCs. Its primary purpose is to assist LDC economic development by promoting trade rather than aid. Under it, U.S. import duties for qualifying countries have been eliminated for about 3,000 product categories. In 1986 approximately $13.8 billion worth of these imports entered the United States, which amounted to slightly more than 3.5 percent of all U.S. imports.[106]

The President had designated 141 countries and dependent territories as eligible "beneficiary developing countries" under the GSP as of December 1987.[107] Subject to certain absolute and conditional limits, the

---

[103] Section 125(c) of the 1974 Trade Act, 19 U.S.C. § 2135(c) (1982).
[104] See discussion later at notes 165–7.
[105] See Proclamation No. 5610, 3 C.F.R. 5425 (1988); *N.Y. Times*, Feb. 20, 1987, at 1, col. 3.
[106] See *N.Y. Times*, Dec. 12, 1987, at D1, col. 1. In 1985 approximately $10.8 billion worth of imports entered under the GSP. Although this represented only slightly more than 4 percent of total U.S. imports, it accounted for nearly 15 percent of the dutiable imports from the GSP countries. Department of State, "Generalized System of Preferences," *Gist* (Feb. 1985).

In January 1988, President Reagan announced that Taiwan, Hong Kong, South Korea, and Singapore would be removed as of January 1989 from GSP status because "their recent improvements in competitiveness" indicated that they did not need the treatment. These four countries were responsible in 1986 for nearly $10 billion in duty-free imports into the United States, or more than 60 percent of all GSP-eligible imports. See 5 *Int'l Trade Rep. (BNA)* 133 (Feb. 3, 1988).

A system of tariff preferences for LDCs was discussed at the first UN Conference on Trade and Development in 1964. Authority for tariff preferences was added to the GATT in 1971. In 1976 the United States became the nineteenth developed country to implement a national GSP program. The Generalized System of Preferences Renewal Act of 1984 extended the U.S. program until July 1993. Publ. L. No. 98-573, tit. V, 98 Stat. 3018 (codified at 19 U.S.C. §§ 2461–5 (Supp. IV 1986)) [hereinafter GSP Renewal Act].

[107] *N.Y. Times*, supra note 106.

law provides the President with considerable discretion to decide which countries to designate.[108] The absolute limits include a prohibition against the designation of certain developed or communist countries, such as members of the European Economic Community (EEC), the Soviet Union, and Poland.[109] Another absolute limit exists against members of OPEC or other cartels that withhold supplies of vital commodities from international trade or raise the price of such commodities to unreasonable levels.[110]

There are several conditional limits on the President's authority to designate. The conditions include foreign policy ones against countries that expropriate or grant sanctuary to international terrorists.[111] The President, however, can still make the designation if he determines that it "will be in the national economic interest of the United States and reports such determination to the Congress."[112]

After a country is designated, the President has almost unlimited authority to withdraw, suspend, or limit the designation. The law requires him only to "consider" certain factors, which are essentially economic ones, and to report his decision to Congress.[113] When the President ends the designation, the country still qualifies for whatever tariff treatment

---

[108] 19 U.S.C. § 2462 (1982 & Supp. IV 1986). The section does require that the President notify Congress in advance of his intention to make such a designation and to notify Congress sixty days before he withdraws a designation. Id. § 2462(a)(1), (2).

[109] Id. § 2462(b). The 1984 amendments deleted Hungary from the list. GSP Renewal Act, supra note 106, at § 503(b)(1).

[110] 19 U.S.C. § 2462(b). Under an exemption no longer available, Indonesia, Venezuela, and Ecuador were designated as GSP beneficiaries in 1980 after each signed with the United States a bilateral, product-specific trade agreement as authorized by the Trade Agreements Act of 1979. "Generalized System of Preferences," supra note 106.

[111] 19 U.S.C. § 2462(b). The other conditions are primarily economic ones, against countries that (1) grant reverse preferences to other developed countries, (2) do not take adequate steps to prevent illegal drugs from entering the United States, (3) refuse to recognize as binding certain arbitral awards in favor of U.S. citizens or corporations, or (4) fail to take steps to afford internationally recognized worker rights to its labor force.

[112] Id.

[113] 19 U.S.C. § 2464(a); see H. Kaye, P. Plaia, and M. Hertzberg, 2 *International Trade Practice* § 40 (1985). The factors include the effect of designation on that country's economic development, the extent to which other developed countries have their own GSP programs, and the anticipated impact of the designation on U.S. producers of competitive products. Id. In *Florsheim Shoe Co., Division of Interco v. United States*, 744 F.2d 787, 792-97 (Fed. Cir. 1984), the U.S. Court of Appeals concluded that the President's decision was reviewable to determine whether it was within his delegated authority. The court emphasized, however, the President's broad discretion. "The President's findings of fact and the motivations for his actions are not subject to review." Id. at 795. *Accord, Sunburst Farms, Inc. v. United States*, 620 F. Supp. 735 (Ct. Int'l Trade 1985).

it received before – that is, MFN or the statutory Smoot–Hawley tariffs.[114]

Presidents have used their discretionary authority under the GSP for foreign policy reasons. In 1980, President Carter withdrew GSP status from Ethiopia because of its expropriation of U.S. investments.[115] Also, Carter designated Uganda as a beneficiary country, a status that had been denied it in 1975 because of Idi Amin's human rights policies.[116] More recently, President Reagan withdrew or suspended in 1987 the GSP eligibility of Chile, Romania, Nicaragua, and Paraguay because they were not taking steps to afford internationally recognized rights to workers in their countries.[117]

The *Caribbean Basin Initiative* of the Reagan Administration is an effort to assist economic development in the Caribbean Basin, including Central America, in a comprehensive way. The "centerpiece" of the program is the elimination of tariffs on most articles imported into the United States from beneficiary countries.[118]

The President's discretion to designate a country, or to suspend or withdraw its designation, is very similar to that of the GSP. The list of possible countries is, of course, more limited – confined to those in Central America or the Caribbean (with Cuba excluded). One difference is that the limit on communist countries is conditional rather than absolute.[119] As part of his Administration's sanctions against Panama, President Reagan denied "until further notice" Panama's designation under CBI (as well as GSP) in March 1988.[120]

Although the President's discretion under the GSP or CBI is considerable, the foreign policy impact is limited by the scope of the programs. Only certain developing countries can qualify, and tariff-free treatment applies only to certain goods. The President has, in short, a useful tool

---

[114] 19 U.S.C. § 2464(a). There are certain cases in which a country is supposed to have its designation withdrawn, in whole or in part. Complete withdrawal should occur when a country's per capita GNP exceeds a certain amount. Id. § 2464(f). Also, the President must withdraw eligibility on imports of a specific product from a beneficiary that exceed certain limits. Id. § 2464(c). See generally id. § 2464.

[115] Exec. Order 12,204, 16 *Weekly Comp. Pres. Doc.* 549 (Mar. 31, 1980). He also withdrew GSP status from Afghanistan, id., but he was required to do that under the law because the country was communist.

[116] Id.; Exec. Order 11,888, 3A C.F.R. 207 (1975).

[117] See 52 *Fed. Reg.* 389 and 49,137 (1987); 5 *Int'l Trade Rep.* 10 (Jan. 6, 1988).

[118] Department of State, "Caribbean Basin Initiative," *Gist* (Mar. 1987). See Caribbean Basin Economic Recovery Act, Pub. L. No. 98-87, 97 Stat. 384 (1983) (codified at 19 U.S.C. §§ 2701–6 (Supp. IV 1986)). Progress under CBI has been mixed. See *N.Y. Times*, Feb. 1, 1987, at F6, col. 1.

[119] See 19 U.S.C. § 2702.

[120] 53 *Fed. Reg.* 9850 (1988).

for imposing sanctions, but hardly a broad authority to prohibit or restrict all imports from a particular country.

5. Possible end runs with other economic-based statutes: a whiff of ammonia

Numerous other laws allow the President to restrict imports for economic reasons – such as injury to domestic industries, merchandise being sold for less than fair value, or illegal subsidies. However, except for unusual circumstances or for some limited discretion under section 301, none of these economic-based statutes provides the President with any notable authority to impose import sanctions for foreign policy reasons. None is a ready-to-use tool.

These statutes vary widely according to the type of economic criteria that allow presidential action, the precision of the criteria, and the administrative restrictions on the President. For present purposes, the statutes can be grouped roughly into two categories – those in which the International Trade Commission (ITC) has some jurisdiction and those in which it does not. The latter category allows more presidential discretion.

ITC participation is important because the Commission is an independent agency that has often differed from the President on trade matters. Helping to ensure this are the staggered, long terms of the commissioners and a requirement of political diversity. Established in 1916 as the U.S. Tariff Commission, the present ITC has six commissioners, who are appointed for staggered nine-year terms. The chairperson, who is generally responsible for administering the Commission, and the vice-chairperson are designated by the President for two-year terms. Succeeding chairpersons may not be of the same political party, and not more than three commissioners may be members of the same political party.[121]

a. Where ITC has jurisdiction. Most of the economic-based statutes give the ITC at least some jurisdiction. Their use for foreign policy sanctions is very unlikely and very chancy. This was demonstrated by the ammonia case, discussed below.

Probably least susceptible to foreign policy use are the otherwise often used statutes for dumping and countervailing duties. Both sets of statutes

---

[121] 19 U.S.C. §§ 1330–1 and 2231–2 (1982). If the six commissioners are equally divided (such as 3 to 3), the President can usually consider the determination by either group as the Commission's recommendation. See id. § 1330(d).

have relatively precise criteria, critical ITC participation, and other administrative requirements. Moreover, the relief the statutes offer is essentially limited to duties or other actions against the specific products being challenged, not against all imports from a country.[122]

Almost as tightly confined are statutes allowing import restraints as a result of "unfair methods of competition" or interference with U.S. agricultural programs. In these two cases, the triggering criteria are a little broader than those for dumping or countervailing duties. Otherwise, the statutes also provide for ITC participation and other administrative protections, and relief is also limited to the products involved.[123]

---

[122] *Dumping* is a type of international price discrimination. Under U.S. law, it is defined as foreign merchandise being sold in the United States "at less than its fair value," usually measured by comparing (with adjustments) the price in the United States with that in the home market at the same point in the production process. Such sales must cause or threaten "material injury" to a U.S. industry or materially retard its establishment. The primary relief is to impose an antidumping duty that reflects the difference by which the foreign market value exceeds the U.S. price. 19 U.S.C. § 1673 (1982 & Supp. IV 1986). (For definitions, see 19 U.S.C. §§ 1677, 1677a, and 1677b.) If the merchandise is not sold in the home market or if the sales there are relatively small, the foreign market value is determined by the price at which the merchandise is sold or offered for sale in third countries or on the basis of a "constructed value." Id. § 1673. The ITC is charged with making the essential determination regarding injury. 19 U.S.C. §§ 1673b and 1673d. Moreover, the dumping laws are replete with various procedural requirements, including hearings, before both the ITC and the Department of Commerce. See id. at §§ 1671–8.

As for *countervailing duties*, duties reflecting the net subsidy can be imposed on foreign merchandise if the foreign manufacture, production, or export of that merchandise is being subsidized, directly or indirectly. These duties are in addition to any other duties imposed. 19 U.S.C. §§ 1671 (1982 & Supp. IV 1986) (for most countries) and 1303 (for other countries). For most cases, there is a requirement of real or threatened injury similar to that under the dumping laws, and the ITC is charged with making this determination. This injury determination and ITC involvement are required for countries covered by section 1671 and for nondutiable imports from countries under section 1303. However, the ITC determination is not required for dutiable imports from countries covered by section 1303.

Both statutes include extensive procedural requirements. See 19 U.S.C. §§ 1671–1671h and § 1303. A major unifying provision of the two sections is that "subsidy" in section 1671 has the same meaning as the term "bounty or grant" in section 1303. 19 U.S.C. § 1677(5). Unfortunately, none of the terms is well defined in the statutes.

For detailed analysis of both the dumping and countervailing duty statutes, see "Dumping Duties" and "Countervailing Duties," in *Int'l Trade Rep. (BNA), U.S. Import Weekly Reference File*, 37:0101–0128 and 40:0001–0126 (1988); H. Kaye, P. Plaia, and M. Hertzberg, *1 International Trade Practice* (1985).

[123] Section 337 of the Tariff Act of 1930, as amended, declares unlawful "unfair methods of competition and unfair acts" in importing articles, when "the effect or tendency . . . is to destroy or substantially injure [a U.S.] industry, efficiently and economically operated, . . . or to prevent the establishment of such an industry, or to restrain or monopolize trade and commerce in the United States. . . . " 19 U.S.C. § 1337(a)(1982 & Supp. IV 1986). The remedy is usually the exclusion of the goods from the U.S. market. Id § 1337(d). For a general discussion of the statute, see "ITC

The section 201 escape clause does not require that there be dumping, subsidies, or other types of unfair competition. However, it does have a more demanding injury requirement – that the increased imports be "a substantial cause of serious injury" to the competing domestic industry or that they threaten such injury. The ITC is again the entity that must make the requisite injury determination before relief is allowed.[124]

Section 406 of the Trade Act of 1974 is the least demanding of the economic-based statutes where the ITC has some jurisdiction. It authorizes the President to impose import controls if the ITC determines that imports from a communist country are causing "market disruption."

Protective Action," in *Int'l Trade Rep.* (BNA), *U.S. Import Weekly Reference File*, 52:0101–0108 (1988); Kaye, Plaia and Hertzberg, supra note 122 at 4–1 to 12–34.

Though the terms "unfair methods of competition and unfair acts" are relatively broad, the statute was used before 1974 primarily for patent infringement cases. Even now, it is generally invoked for cases involving patents, trademarks, copyrights, and false and deceptive advertising. "ITC Protective Action," supra. Moreover, the ITC investigates the alleged violations and determines the appropriate relief, though the President has the authority to disapprove the ITC termination. 19 U.S.C. § 1337.

Section 22 of the Agricultural Adjustment Act allows the President to raise duties on or restrict imports of any articles that tend to render ineffective, or materially interfere with, a Department of Agriculture price support or other program. Although the criteria are broad, the statute and the possible relief under it are limited to certain commodities, and it is the ITC that does the investigation. 7 U.S.C. § 624 (1982 & Supp. IV 1986). The ITC makes its recommendation to the President, who then decides whether to act. The statute does permit the President to take emergency actions without awaiting the recommendations of the ITC; these actions are to continue pending the ITC report and recommendations. Id. As of April 15, 1984, the ITC had completed forty- seven investigations under this provision since 1939. The President had generally taken emergency action when he requested the investigation. Stern letter, supra note 16.

[124] Section 201 of the Trade Act of 1974, as amended, allows temporary relief if the ITC determines that "an article is being imported into the United States in such increased quantities as to be a substantial cause of serious injury, or the threat thereof, to the domestic industry producing an article like or directly competitive with the imported article." 19 U.S.C. § 2251(b)(1) (1982 & Supp IV 1986). If the Commission determines that the injury criteria are met, it recommends to the President appropriate import relief. Id. § 2251(d). The President can then accept, modify, or reject the ITC recommendation. Among the steps the President can choose are imposing or increasing tariffs, tariff-rate quotas, or quantitative restrictions. Id. § 2253(a). The President can also negotiate an orderly marketing agreement regarding the articles in question, or he can take a combination of these possible actions. Id. The President may also direct the Secretary of Labor or of Commerce to give expeditious consideration to petitions for adjustment assistance for workers, firms, and communities that are adversely affected by the import competition. Id. § 2252(a). As with the other statutes discussed above that involve the ITC, there are numerous procedural requirements for obtaining relief under the escape clause. See, e.g., id § 2251(c) (public hearing required).

The critical limit here on presidential discretion is, of course, the initial requirement that the ITC must determine that the economic injury criteria are met before it can recommend any relief. Without the ITC recommendation, the President cannot order relief. Moreover, even if relief is allowed, it is limited to the products involved.

This exists whenever imports of an article, "like or directly competitive" with a domestic article, are "increasing rapidly, either absolutely or relatively, so as to be a significant cause of material injury, or threat thereof, to such domestic industry."[125] Nevertheless, as President Carter was rudely reminded in 1980, ITC participation and even a relatively relaxed requirement for economic injury can sharply limit the President's discretion to use the statute.

The story began in 1979. Upon receipt of a petition, the ITC commenced an investigation into the possibility of market disruption caused by the importation of large quantities of ammonia from the Soviet Union. By a 3 to 2 vote in October 1979, the Commission found market disruption and recommended a three-year quota to the President.[126] Carter, however, reported that he was not persuaded by the ITC's determination and denied relief in early December because it was not in the "national economic interest."[127] Carter was apparently strongly influenced by his efforts to keep détente alive and to obtain the Senate's advice and consent to the SALT II Treaty.

Then, in late December, the Soviets invaded Afghanistan, killed the Afghan leader, and set up a client government. The President and the American public were understandably outraged. Carter imposed a partial embargo on agricultural and other exports. No one could effectively challenge that under the export laws.

Carter also decided that it was now appropriate to limit ammonia imports from the Soviet Union. The Soviets were the largest source of

[125] 19 U.S.C. § 2436 (1982). The legislative history and ITC decisions indicate that section 406 is less demanding than the section 201 escape clause. For example, section 406's injury requirement that increased imports be "a significant cause of material injury, or threat thereof" is less rigorous. See id. Section 201 requires the ITC to find that increased imports are "a *substantial* cause of *serious* injury, or threat thereof." Id § 2251(b)(1) (emphasis added). See ITC, "Anhydrous Ammonia from the U.S.S.R.; Report to the President," 45 *Fed. Reg.* 27,570, at 27,577 (1980) (dissenting opinion of Commissioners Bedell and Moore) [hereinafter ITC Ammonia Decision]; see S. Rep. No. 1298, 93d Cong., 2d Sess. 212 (1974).
The ITC regulations reflect this. To establish market disruption it is necessary to show only an idling of productive facilities, not a "significant idling"; the inability of a number of firms to operate at a reasonable level of profit, not a "significant" number; and unemployment, not "significant" unemployment. Compare 19 C.F.R. § 206.9(f) (1987) with § 206.14(f). See "Market Disruption by Communist Countries," in *Int'l Trade Rep. (BNA), U.S. Import Weekly Reference File*, 64:0101 (1988).
Another difference between the two sections is that section 406 authorizes the President to order temporary import relief while waiting for an ITC determination if he believes that emergency action is necessary. 19 U.S.C. § 2436(c). Section 201 has no such emergency provision.
[126] 44 *Fed. Reg.* 61,270 (1979).
[127] President Carter, "American Anhydrous Ammonia Industry," 15 *Weekly Comp. Pres. Doc.* 2221 (Dec. 11, 1979).

imported ammonia,[128] and ammonia constituted a major Soviet export to the United States. In January 1980, Carter asked the ITC to institute another section 406 investigation. Pending the ITC determination, he decided that there was an emergency, and he restricted imports of Soviet ammonia to 1 million short tons during the year beginning January 24.[129]

To the Administration's chagrin, the ITC determined in April 1980 that there was no market disruption. The 3 to 2 ITC decision turned on the economic injury criteria and a change in one member of the Commission.[130] This decision effectively ended legal efforts to limit the ammonia imports. It left the President in the strange position of stopping most American exports to the Soviet Union, but being unable to prevent imports without invoking emergency powers.[131]

b. No ITC jurisdiction. Section 301 of the Trade Act of 1974, expanded by the Trade and Tariff Act of 1984, is probably the most open-ended of the maze of import statutes tied to economic criteria and not providing some jurisdiction to the ITC. It authorizes the President to "take all appropriate and feasible actions within his power" (1) to enforce U.S. rights under any trade agreement or (2) to respond to any act by a foreign country that is inconsistent with a trade agreement or that is "unjustifiable, unreasonable, or discriminatory."[132] If the foreign country is vi-

---

[128] ITC Ammonia Decision, supra note 125, at 27,570–1.

[129] Proclamation No. 4714, 45 *Fed. Reg.* 3875 (1980). Carter noted that "[r]ecent events have altered the international economic conditions under which I made my determination that it was not in the national interest to impose import relief on anhydrous ammonia from the U.S.S.R." Id.

In the absence of a quota, Occidental Petroleum had expected to import about 1.5. million tons of the chemical in 1984. For a good discussion of the ammonia case and the contemporaneously successful effort to stop U.S. exports of phosphates, see Subcommittee on Europe and the Middle East of the House Committee on Foreign Affairs, 97th Cong., 1st Sess., *An Assessment of the Afghanistan Sanctions: Implications for Trade and Diplomacy in the 1980's,* 53–64 (Comm. Print 1981) (report prepared by the Congressional Reference Service).

[130] ITC Ammonia Decision, supra note 125. Michael Calhoun, a Carter appointee who voted against the President's petition, had replaced Commissioner Parker. The other Commissioners voted as they had in the earlier decision. Compare 44 *Fed. Reg.* 61,269 (1979) with ITC Ammonia Decision, supra note 125.

[131] The example suggests that the President often has the most foreign policy leverage under statutes requiring ITC review after the ITC has reported an affirmative finding recommending relief. As noted earlier, the President then has the power to accept the ITC finding, modify it, or reject it. He cannot be embarrassed by the ITC reversing him. In the ammonia case, Carter had his maximum leverage when the ITC recommended relief in October 1979.

[132] 19 U.S.C. § 2411(a) (1982 & Supp. IV 1986). Actually, the relevant sections include Sections 2411–16. Section 304 of the Trade and Tariff Act of 1984, Pub. L. No. 98-573, tit. III, 98 Stat. 3002, 3005, amended section 301 to provide for taking action in response to unfair foreign practices on investment, as well as goods and

olating a trade agreement or acting unfairly, the President has a wide range of options for relief. He can suspend or withdraw the benefits under the trade agreement, impose duties or other import restrictions on that country's goods, or deny foreign access to certain U.S. service sectors, such as communications.[133]

With the ITC not involved, the President has essentially complete discretion to act under section 301. He may initiate an action on his own.[134] Alternatively, interested persons can file a petition with the U.S. Trade Representative (USTR), a presidential appointee, who then decides whether to initiate an investigation. If the USTR concludes an investigation with an affirmative recommendation to the President, the President is then directed to "determine what action, if any, he will take."[135]

In spite of section 301's broad charter for retaliation, it would be difficult to justify most uses of this statute for economic sanctions for foreign policy purposes. First, the triggering criteria of a trade agreement violation or of "unjustifiable, unreasonable, or discriminatory" acts turn on the trade or investment practices of foreign countries, not on their military or other foreign policy activities. The economic nature of these criteria are made more explicit by the statutory definitions of the objectionable acts. For example, "discriminatory" includes any act "which denies national or most-favored-nation treatment to United States goods, services, or investment."[136]

Second, although referral of petitions to the USTR rather than the ITC should give the President more discretion, the USTR is involved primarily in trade and investment issues, not general foreign policy.

Third, the past use of section 301 has been limited to trade and investment issues. As of February 1987, the USTR had fifty-eight cases that were under investigation or had been terminated. A common complaint in those investigations was that foreign countries gave subsidies for exports to the United States or to third countries where the United States

---

services. See generally, "Presidential Retaliation," *Int'l Trade Rep. (BNA), U.S. Import Weekly Reference File* 49:0101–0107 (1987); B. Fisher and R. Steinhardt, "Section 301 of the Trade Act of 1974: Protection for U.S. Exporters of Goods, Services, and Capital," 14 *L. & Pol'y Int'l Bus.* 569 (1982). Another statute not requiring ITC involvement is 19 U.S.C. § 1303, covering subsidies on dutiable imports from certain countries. See earlier discussion at note 122.

[133] 19 U.S.C. § 2411(b), (c). Though the President would usually retaliate only against the offending foreign country, the statute authorizes him to act on a nondiscriminatory basis against countries other than the one that triggered the retaliation. Id. § 2411(a)(2). Thus, the President could raise the tariff on all imports on a given product. However, given the requirement of nondiscrimination, it is hard to imagine how the President might use this broader authority in cases of foreign policy sanctions.

[134] Id. § 2411(d)(1).

[135] Id. §§ 2412–16, 2412(d)(2).

[136] Id. § 2411(e).

sent competing exports. Other complaints concerned various import restrictions, such as restrictive quotas or excessive tariffs. There were also several cases challenging restrictions on access to foreign countries' service industries.[137]

One use of section 301 for the foreign policy purposes discussed in this book seems possible, however. The statutory standards, expanded in 1984 to include foreign practices on investment as well as goods and services, allow retaliation for expropriation of U.S. businesses. This would authorize a trade sanction to complement the possible cutoff of foreign assistance under the Hickenlooper amendment or the denial of special tariff treatment under the GSP.[138] Otherwise, section 301 usually does not provide appropriate authority for economic sanctions for foreign policy purposes.

C. RUNNING AFOUL OF THE GATT

Even though the GATT focuses primarily on imports, U.S. obligations under it have not been a serious problem so far when import controls have been employed for foreign policy purposes. First, many of the present (or likely) target countries of these sanctions are not GATT members. Examples are the Soviet Union, Iran, and Libya. Even for GATT members, some of those countries that are likely targets of U.S. sanctions have a trade relationship with the United States that is a special combination of working through the GATT framework and bilateral agreements. These countries today include Czechoslovakia, Hungary, Romania, and Poland.[139] Second, U.S. import controls for foreign policy reasons have been used on only a few occasions against the countries the United States trades with on a regular basis under GATT, and GATT includes broad exceptions that can often be invoked to justify such uses.[140]

---

[137] "Presidential Retaliation," supra note 132, at 49:0105, 49:0801–816 (1987).

[138] On Hickenlooper, see Chapter 3 at notes 40–6. On the GSP, see notes 106–16 in this chapter.

[139] For a recent list of the members of GATT, see GATT, *GATT Activities 1986*, at 92–3 (1987). As for special cases with GATT members, the United States grants MFN treatment to Hungary and Poland under special bilateral trade agreements, but does not grant it to Czechoslovakia or Romania. See earlier discussion at notes 77–82 and 88–105, this chapter; see also, e.g., GATT, 31st Supp. BISD 180 (1985) (protocol of accession of Hungary to GATT) and Proclamation No. 4560, 43 *Fed. Reg.* 15,125 (1978) (United States enters into trade agreement with Hungary); GATT, 30th Supp. BISD 194 (1984) (protocol of accession of Romania to GATT) and Proclamation No. 4369, 40 *Fed. Reg.* 18,389 (1975) (United States enters into trade agreement with Romania); GATT 24th Supp. BISD 139 (1979) (Poland's protocol of accession to GATT); see generally J. Jackson and W. Davey, *Legal Problems of International Economic Relations* 1183–7 (1986).

[140] A third reason is that the target countries for a variety of reasons sometimes

Since an expanded use of import controls could create problems under GATT, it is useful to analyze the justifications that have been or could be employed. Those most available under GATT are article XXI or XXV or resort to what might be termed "tacit exceptions."[141] There is also the special recent case of Poland. Justifications should also be viewed in the context of the problems encountered with GATT's dispute settlement process, which is sometimes slow and often offers inadequate relief.

The security exceptions of *article XXI* are broad. They include actions that a country "considers necessary for the protection of its essential security interests" relating to fissionable materials, arms or other goods that will help supply a military establishment, or wartime or international emergencies.[142]

Article XXI was first used to justify foreign policy sanctions in response to Czechoslovakia's challenge to the U.S. export licensing program in 1949. As discussed earlier, the Contracting Parties decisively voted

---

choose not to raise the sanctions in GATT. For example, South Africa has apparently not challenged the U.S. export controls against it or the recent U.S. ban on several imported goods. Possibly this is because South Africa realizes the weakness of its international standing on the question of apartheid.

Similarly, Rhodesia did not challenge the sanctions against it in the late 1960s and 1970s, possibly because the sanctions appear easily justified under the GATT exception in article XXI for UN obligations. See J. Jackson, *World Trade and the Law of GATT*, 751 (1969) [hereinafter Jackson, *GATT*]. Also, Cuba apparently did not challenge the U.S. trade embargo imposed in 1962, possibly because the United States invoked it under its national emergency powers.

[141] On first impression, the general exceptions in article XX might appear useful. However, the specific provisions would seem to cover only a few cases of foreign policy sanctions. For example, the provisions allowing measures "necessary to protect public morals" or "relating to the products of prison labour" might be stretched to cover human rights violations or racial discrimination.

[142] See discussion in Chapter 4 at notes 178–9. Article XXI reads:

Nothing in this Agreement shall be construed

(a) to require any contracting party to furnish any information the disclosure of which it considers contrary to its essential security interests; or

(b) to prevent any contracting party from taking any action which it considers necessary for the protection of its essential security interests

(i) relating to fissionable materials or the materials from which they are derived;

(ii) relating to the traffic in arms, ammunition and implements of war and to such traffic in other goods and materials as is carried on directly or indirectly for the purpose of supplying a military establishment;

(iii) taken in time of war or other emergency in international relations; or

(c) to prevent any contracting party from taking any action in pursuance of its obligations under the United Nations Charter for the maintenance of international peace and security.

against the challenge.[143] During the next thirty years, apparently only two sanctions cases arose formally in GATT in which the imposing country relied on article XXI. Neither case involved the United States, and neither led to a request that the Contracting Parties authorize suspension of concessions or other relief.[144] This paucity of cases could well reflect the lack of a requirement in article XXI for the country imposing the sanction to report its use of this exception, as well as target countries' recognition that a contracting party is allowed to define its own "essential security" exceptions.[145]

In 1982 article XXI was raised specifically in discussions of the suspension of imports from Argentina by the United Kingdom, the EEC, Australia, and Canada during the Falklands conflict. None of the countries imposing the sanction notified GATT. When Argentina protested the sanction at a GATT council meeting, the EEC argued that it imposed the restrictions on the basis of its inherent rights, of which article XXI was a reflection. The EEC added that its exercise of these rights constituted a general exception to the GATT, which required neither notification, justification, or approval, as confirmed by thirty-five years of implementation of the General Agreement. The Council chairperson noted that there were widely differing views as to whether the trade measures against Argentina violated GATT obligations, whether notifi-

---

[143] See discussion in Chapter 4 at note 181. "Contracting Parties" (capitalized) refers in this book to the parties to the GATT acting formally as a body. References to individual or several contracting parties or members are lower case.

[144] In 1954, Czechoslovakia complained about Peru's prohibition on imports from it. The ban was part of a Peruvian decree of 1953 that restricted trade with countries having centrally planned economies. The prohibition against Czechoslovakia was apparently lifted after consultations in GATT. Jackson, *GATT*, supra note 140, at 750, citing GATT Doc. 1/235 (1954), Doc. SR.9/27, at 10 (1955), but also noting GATT Doc. L/2844 (1967), where Peru announced that it had abrogated in 1967 its 1953 decree; R. Hudec, *The GATT Legal System and World Trade Diplomacy* 87, 285 (1975).

In 1961, Ghana announced during deliberations on Portuguese accession to GATT that it would ban all imports from Portugal under article XXI. Ghana said that its boycott was justified by its security interests, because the "situation in Angola [then a Portuguese colony] was a constant threat to the peace of the African continent and that any action which, by bringing pressure to bear on the Portuguese government, might lead to a lessening of this danger, was therefore justified." GATT Doc. SR.19/12, at 196 (1961). Ghana's interpretation of article XXI was surely a broad one. Ghana also said that it would invoke article XXXV to prevent the General Agreement from becoming effective between Ghana and Portugal if Portugal acceded to the GATT. Id.

[145] See Jackson, *GATT*, supra note 140, at 750. Other sanctions that could well have been raised in GATT and then defended on article XXI grounds, but were not raised at all, include the U.S. ban on trade with Cuba in 1962 and the UN trade embargo against Rhodesia. Id. at 751 (regarding Rhodesia case).

cation, justification, or approval was necessary, and whether the matter under consideration was within the competence of GATT.[146]

At the annual meeting of the Contracting Parties in November 1982, however, GATT's member states adopted a decision that increased the procedural requirements for using article XXI. A party invoking the article is required to inform the other members "to the fullest extent possible of trade measures taken under Article XXI." Also, the target country retains its full rights under the General Agreement, including recourse to the complaint procedures.[147]

In the most recent use of article XXI, the United States cited the article as a justification for its May 1, 1985, decision to impose a trade embargo against Nicaragua. Nicaragua reacted by asking for a special session of the GATT Council.[148] At the meeting on May 29, Nicaragua claimed that the embargo violated several GATT clauses, including the MFN and nondiscrimination provisions. In response, the U.S. delegate explicitly cited article XXI and said that the United States "sees no basis for GATT contracting parties to question, approve, or disapprove the judgment of each contracting party as to what is necessary to protect its national security interests." He added that "GATT is a trade organization and has no competence to make judgments on such matters."[149] The United States met with considerable criticism at the meeting from other members for using economic measures for political reasons. Nevertheless, the Council did not act on a Nicaraguan demand that GATT "condemn" the U.S. embargo. The Council president said that he would hold consultations with the two countries.[150]

Following the consultations, the Council agreed at its October meeting to establish a panel to investigate the matter. The United States noted its understanding that the panel could not examine or judge the validity of, or the motivation for, the U.S. use of article XXI:(b)(iii).[151] After even further consultations, the Council finally agreed in March 1986 on the terms of reference to be used by the panel.[152]

---

[146] GATT, *GATT Activities in 1982* 72–3 (1983).

[147] GATT Doc. L/5426 (1982); GATT Doc. SR.38/10, at 2–3 (1982). See also the "Understanding Regarding Notification, Consultation, Dispute Settlement, and Surveillance," 26 BISD 210 (1980).

[148] GATT Doc. L/5802 (1985). Incidentally, the United States informed GATT of the President's May 1 decision on May 9. GATT Doc. L/5803.

[149] 2 *Int'l Trade Rep. (BNA)* 765 (June 5, 1985).

[150] Id.; GATT Doc. L/5909, at 77–87 (1985).

[151] Id. at 90. The specific clause in the article refers to actions "taken in time of war or other emergency in international relations." See discussion below at notes 170–4 regarding use of panels in GATT dispute resolution.

[152] GATT Doc. C/M/196 (1986). The terms of reference were as follows: "To examine, in the light of the relevant GATT provisions, of the understanding reached

The panel reported its results to the Council in November 1986. It determined that the United States was within its rights in imposing the trade embargo but noted that the panel's terms of reference were limited by accepting as valid the U.S. motives for invoking article XXI. The panel further noted that the embargo raised questions about the rationale behind article XXI and indicated that, irrespective of the article, the U.S. embargo was contrary to the basic aims of GATT. The report is expected to lead to further discussions in GATT about the use of article XXI.[153]

Another possible ground for justifying U.S. import controls is paragraph 5 of article XXV. It allows the Contracting Parties in "exceptional circumstances not elsewhere provided in this Agreement" to "waive an obligation" imposed on an individual contracting party. This *waiver* requires a two-thirds vote of those voting.[154]

Neither the contracting party nor GATT has always specified the basis for some actions that might fall under this waiver. However, article XXV was possibly the basis for the Contracting Parties' approval of the U.S. suspension of MFN status to Czechoslovakia in 1952.

The United States had suspended MFN treatment to a number of communist East European countries in 1951, including Czechoslovakia, which was a GATT contracting party. The United States brought this to the attention of GATT and specifically asked for a waiver for both countries under paragraph 5 of article XXV. The U.S. delegate noted "the exceptional circumstance that the general relations between the United States and Czechoslovakia have now become so fundamentally altered that commercial policy undertakings between them are no longer meaningful."[155] After a lengthy debate in 1952, the Contracting Parties adopted a declaration stating "that the Governments of the United States and Czechoslovakia shall be free to suspend, each with respect to the

---

at the Council on 10 October 1985 that the Panel cannot examine or judge the validity of or motivation for the invocation of Article XXI:(b)(3) by the United States, of the relevant provisions of the Understanding Regarding Notification, Consultation, Dispute Settlement and Surveillance (BISD 26S/211–218), and of the agreed Dispute Settlement Procedures contained in the 1982 Ministerial Declaration (BISD 29S/13–16), the measures taken by the United States on 7 May 1985 and their trade effects in order to establish to what extent benefits accruing to Nicaragua under the General Agreement have been nullified or impaired, and to make such findings as will assist the CONTRACTING PARTIES in further action in this matter." Id.

[153] See GATT, *GATT Activities 1986*, at 58–9 (1987); 3 *Int'l Trade Rep. (BNA)* 1368 (1986) (report on dispute panel); see generally Note, "The Politics of Procedure: An Examination of the GATT Dispute Settlement Panel and the Article XXI Defense in the Context of the U.S. Embargo of Nicaragua," 19 *L. & Pol'y Int'l Bus.* 603 (1987).

[154] GATT art. XXV, para. 5. The two-thirds majority must also comprise more than half of the total members. Id.

[155] GATT Press Release 46 (1951), at 1.

other, the obligations of the General Agreement...." The declaration did not refer specifically to any GATT clause that authorized it.[156]

The declaration is sometimes viewed as a waiver.[157] However, some contracting parties did not wish to utilize the waiver authority. One delegate favored the nonspecific declaration because it only acknowledged the state of affairs and would not provide a precedent under the General Agreement, which "was a technical instrument to deal with technical trade problems."[158] As a result, the case could also be considered a "tacit exception" under GATT.

A *tacit exception* is one that cites no specific GATT exception, but allows a situation to continue because it involves broader political questions. An explicit claim for such an exception was the U.S. rationale for its cutoff of Nicaragua's sugar import quota in 1983. The United States explicitly declined to rely on any GATT clause.[159] Nicaragua complained to the GATT about the U.S. action, and a panel examined the matter. The panel report concluded that the U.S. action was not consistent with the obligations of nondiscrimination set forth in article XIII:2 and noted that the United States had not claimed any GATT exception.[160] The GATT Council adopted the panel's report in March 1984.[161]

The United States took no corrective action. Indeed, it later declined to give Nicaragua any share of an increase in the overall sugar quota. Nicaragua continued to pursue the matter of GATT Council meetings in 1984. The consistent U.S. response was that the U.S. actions had been taken for broader reasons than trade considerations, and ending the measures would require a resolution of the broader issues. At the same time, the United States did not object to Nicaragua's resort to the GATT dispute settlement process and even recognized that Nicaragua had certain rights under article XXIII (which include the possibility of Nicaragua withdrawing trade concessions).[162]

The U.S. position regarding Nicaragua's resort to GATT was consistent with the General Agreement, and it was eminently pragmatic. Article XXIII allows a contracting party to seek relief if it is being harmed by "the application by another contracting party of any measure, *whether*

---

[156] Jackson, *GATT*, supra note 140, at 750.

[157] See id.

[158] Id., citing GATT Doc. CP6/SR.13, at 4 (1951). At least one commentator has since argued that the best interpretation of this declaration is that the members recognized an accomplished fact "they were powerless to influence." Abbott, supra note 58, at 853.

[159] GATT Doc. L/5607, at 5–7 (1984).

[160] Id. at 6–7.

[161] GATT, *GATT Activities in 1984* 39 (1985).

[162] GATT Doc. C/M/178, at 27 (1984).

or not it conflicts with the provisions" of the Agreement.[163] Moreover, other contracting parties apparently supported Nicaragua's claim, as reflected in the Council's adoption of the panel's report. Finally, the worst that could happen to the United States was that the Contracting Parties would authorize Nicaragua to suspend concessions it had made to the United States or to suspend other obligations,[164] and the United States was clearly willing to absorb any retaliatory action by Nicaragua.

Less certain is the U.S. decision to avoid reliance on any GATT provision to justify its action. As noted earlier, the United States did cite article XXI as its justification for imposing the broader trade embargo against Nicaragua in 1985. These U.S. positions seem somewhat inconsistent. If the cutoff of the sugar quota did not have to be based on an explicit GATT exception, why should the more wide ranging trade embargo be tied to a GATT clause? It was probably easier to fit the embargo under article XXI because of the declaration of national emergency, but the underlying reasons for the 1983 and 1985 actions were much the same. Possibly, the panel report in the sugar case taught the United States that there was no benefit in failing to cite an exception as justification. It meant that a panel would find any violation of a GATT article unjustified and not consider possible exceptions, such as in article XXI.

The U.S. suspension of MFN treatment for Poland in 1982 was a special case. As noted earlier, the United States resorted there to an unusual legal ground for its action – relying on Poland's failure since 1978 to meet its import commitments under its 1967 protocol of accession to the GATT.[165] Poland challenged the U.S. action in the GATT Council and at the November 1982 meeting of the Contracting Parties, where the matter was discussed extensively.[166] The United States pointed to Poland's clear failure to satisfy its commitments. The U.S. delegate did not deny the importance of factors other than trade, but he said that these other factors were outside the purview of GATT.[167] The matter was effectively tabled in GATT when the Contracting Parties agreed only to pursue the matter further in the Council.

The effectiveness of any complaints in GATT against import (or export) sanctions is considerably affected by the GATT *dispute resolution machinery* – which is complicated, sometimes cumbersome, and often inadequate. The GATT articles contain more than thirty provisions re-

---

[163] GATT art. XXIII (emphasis added).
[164] See discussion below at notes 168–75 regarding the GATT dispute settlement machinery.
[165] The protocol required Poland to increase the total value of its imports from other GATT members by 7% a year. See discussion at notes 98–105, this chapter.
[166] GATT, *GATT Activities in 1982* 75 (1983).
[167] GATT Doc. C/M/162, at 6 (1982) (Nov. Council meeting).

lating to dispute settlement procedures.[168] Central to the process, especially for claims against foreign policy sanctions, are articles XXII and XXIII. Article XXII provides for consultation between parties "with respect to any matter affecting the operation of this Agreement." Article XXIII provides for mediation by the Contracting Parties and, if they authorize it, retaliation by the affected party by suspending "concessions or other obligations" under the General Agreement as may "be appropriate in the circumstances."[169] The GATT procedures were reassessed in the late 1970s during the Tokyo round of multilateral trade negotiations. In 1979, the Contracting Parties adopted an "Understanding Regarding Notification, Consultation, Dispute Settlement, and Surveillance," which helped standardize dispute settlement and formally recognized the use of panels.[170]

Unless an affected member seeks direct consideration in the Council,[171] the usual dispute settlement process now has five main stages:

1. A complaining party first attempts to settle the dispute through consultations and conciliation under articles XXII and XXIII.
2. If consultations fail, a complaining party can request that a panel be established. The decision to do so is made by a consensus that includes the disputing members.
3. The panel requests information from the parties and meets to consider the information and arguments. The panel writes a report of its analysis and conclusions. The report is first given to the disputing parties in the hope that they will reach a solution.
4. If a bilateral settlement is not reached, the panel's report is circulated and considered at a meeting of the GATT Council, which decides whether to adopt the report. The decision is made by a consensus

---

[168] ITC, *Review of the Effectiveness of Trade Dispute Settlement Under the GATT and the Tokyo Round Agreements* 1, ITC Pub. 1793 (Dec. 1985) [hereinafter ITC Review].

[169] See Jackson, *GATT*, supra note 140, at 181–3. In practice, only one dispute has resulted in suspension of concessions under article XXIII – a complaint by the Netherlands against the United States in the 1950s. Id. at 182, 185. There has been no suspension of "other obligations" under GATT. Nevertheless, Professor Jackson notes that "the language of ... article [XXIII] is broad and sweeping. The language itself is not limited just to 'compensating' redress but is broad enough to be used as the basis for serious sanctions. For instance, all concessions of all other contracting parties could be suspended vis-à-vis a notoriously offending contracting party – in effect, driving it out of GATT – if the CONTRACTING PARTIES determined this to be 'appropriate.' Likewise, lesser penalties, but still stronger than compensating redress, could be authorized for application by groups of contracting parties." Id. at 186–7.

[170] 26 BISD 210 (1980).

[171] E.g., as discussed above, Nicaragua requested a special Council meeting in reaction to the U.S. trade embargo against it in 1985.

that includes the disputing parties. The Council may adopt all or some of the panel's recommendations.

5. If the Council adopts the panel's findings, the charged party decides whether and how to comply. If the complaining party is not satisfied with these steps, it may raise the problem again with the Contracting Parties. As a last resort, under article XXIII:2 the complaining party may seek authorization to suspend "such concessions or other obligations under this Agreement as [the Contracting Parties] determine to be appropriate in the circumstances."[172]

Many have criticized the GATT procedures, charging that they are often cumbersome and ineffective.[173] One 1985 ITC study indicates, however, that the procedures usually operate within a reasonable time and that the GATT dispute settlement mechanisms have been adequate for managing all but the most contentious disputes.[174] The problem, of course, is that the difficult disputes often arise from the use of import (or other trade) controls for foreign policy purposes, such as the U.S. cutoff of the Nicaraguan sugar quota.

For an injured country, an even greater problem than the slow procedures is the relief available under GATT. As noted earlier, the Contracting Parties are likely at most to authorize the injured party under article XXIII to suspend the concessions it has granted the other country or suspend other obligations owed that country. This relief is limited, particularly when the country imposing the sanctions is willing to absorb some costs to carry out its foreign policy. The situation is especially unsatisfactory when the target country is much smaller than the country imposing the sanctions, because the small country's retaliation is unlikely to have any significant effect on the large country.[175] For example, even if Nicaragua had been authorized to suspend offsetting concessions to the United States after the U.S. action on the sugar quota, this retaliation would have had an infinitesimal impact on the United States. Indeed, the

---

[172] ITC Review, supra note 168, at vi–vii. The GATT dispute procedures are open only to the governments of members. However, section 301 (19 U.S.C. § 2411) establishes an explicit set of procedures for a private individual or entity to complain to the U.S. Government when he feels that a foreign government's actions are injuring him and are either unfair or in violation of international trade agreements such as GATT. (See earlier discussion of section 301 at notes 132–38, this chapter.) This could lead to U.S. Government actions. See "Tokyo Round Implementation," supra note 1, at 175.

[173] E.g., G. Putka, "GATT Knows Who the Trade Sinners Are, But It Doesn't Matter," *Wall St. J.*, Jan. 2, 1986, at 1, col. 6; see J. Jackson, "Governmental Disputes in International Trade Relations: A Proposal in the Context of GATT," 13 *J. World Trade L.* 4–8 (1979) [hereinafter Jackson, "Governmental Disputes"].

[174] ITC Review, supra note 168, at x.

[175] See Jackson, "Governmental Disputes," supra note 173, at 5.

United States itself later decided to cut off exports to, as well as imports from, Nicaragua.

In sum, the infrequent use of import sanctions against GATT members by the United States for foreign policy reasons has occasioned only rare disruptions of the GATT trading system. In the case of the Nicaraguan sugar quota, for example, the U.S. sanction generated a critical panel report, which was supported by GATT members, but its overall effect on the international trading system is at best marginal. More frequent U.S. resort to import sanctions could have a much more significant impact unless carefully controlled. The danger would be that increased U.S. use of trade sanctions for foreign policy purposes would lead others to follow suit. This would weaken the effort to move toward an open, nondiscriminatory trading system that produces important economic benefits for the United States and other countries.[176]

D. CONCLUSIONS

An increased use of import sanctions, however, is difficult under existing U.S. laws. The President has no general statutory authority to restrict imports for foreign policy reasons. His authority is scattered among several statutes that allow a mixed bag of limited actions – for example, restrictions on imports of critical defense materials, on imports of sugar, on imports from Libya or from other countries that support terrorists, or on imports from certain communist countries that deny their citizens the opportunity to emigrate freely.[177] This hodgepodge of existing laws restricts the President's discretion significantly and skews his decisions on the type of economic sanctions to employ.

[176] See, e.g., Abbott, supra note 58, at 856; Jackson, *GATT*, supra note 140, at 752.
[177] Although the Comprehensive Anti-Apartheid Act of 1986 imposed a variety of import controls, these were essentially targeted only against South Africa, and their scope was largely defined by the statute. The President was left with very little discretion.

6

Private financial transactions

A potentially important sanction is the regulation of financial transactions that U.S. banks or other private entities can have with foreigners. Indeed, financial sanctions are a major component of the U.S. measures against South Africa, and extensive financial controls were imposed against Iran in 1980 and Libya in 1986.

At present, however, the President's general authority over these financial transactions is very limited. For instance, if New York-based Citibank wants to loan money to the government or private entities in Chile, Iraq, or Poland, the President cannot stop that loan for foreign policy reasons, at least in the absence of a declared national emergency.[1]

This lack of control over private financial transactions is especially important today because international financial activity is growing dramatically and increasingly intersecting with foreign policy. For example, about $12 billion in Iranian assets was in the possession of U.S. banks and other entities here and abroad when the President acted to freeze these assets during the Iranian hostage crisis. Similarly, when Chase Manhattan and other U.S. banks decided, for a variety of reasons, not to roll over short-term loans to South Africa in mid-1985, it was partly responsible for that country's temporary closure of its stock exchange and its declaration of a four-month freeze on repayments of most foreign debts.[2] The decision also contributed to continuing financial pressures on South Africa.[3]

---

[1] In a national emergency situation, the President can restrict these financial transactions. See Chapter 9. For Panama, the Reagan Administration declared a national emergency in April 1988 to restrict some financial transactions. Id. at note 60. In March 1988, however, the U.S. Government initially denied the Noriega regime access to the Panamanian Government's deposits in U.S. banks when it certified that Eric Arturo Delvalle, the man deposed by General Noriega, was still the legitimate President of Panama. See *N.Y. Times*, Mar. 8, 1988, at A3, col. 1; 12 U.S.C. § 632 (1982).

[2] *Newsweek*, Sept. 9, 1985, at 30.

[3] 18 *Nat'l J.* at 1820, 1822 (1986); *Newsweek*, Jan. 27, 1986, at 36.

In the world of international finance, U.S. banks and other financial entities play a major role. For example, American banks reported claims against foreigners that exceeded $500 billion at the end of 1986, versus about $90 billion in 1977.[4]

The relative importance of U.S. credit varies by region and country. For example, in mid-1985, U.S. banks held only about 6 to 7 percent of the total debt owed by the Soviet Union and other East European countries to foreign banks.[5] In contrast, U.S. banks, traders, and other entities have provided a large amount of credit to a number of noncommunist countries in Latin America and Asia. For instance, as of mid-1986, U.S. banks' claims as a percentage of total foreign bank claims were 47 percent for Chile, 43 percent for Mexico, 33 percent for Guatemala, 24 percent for Taiwan, 26 percent for South Korea, and 17 percent for the Philippines.[6]

Although U.S. banks continue to be a major force in private international banking, their premier role of the 1960s and early 1970s has eroded considerably as Japanese and European banks have grown and become more active internationally.[7] One indicator of the shift has been a decline

---

[4] *Economic Report of the President* 369 (Feb. 1988) and 363 (Jan. 1987). Incidentally, international operations are important to U.S. banks. During 1979–83, these operations accounted for a big percentage of the earnings of the ten largest U.S. banks – the annual average ranging between 42 and 56%. K. Lissakers, "Bank Regulation and International Debt," in *Uncertain Future: Commercial Banks and the Third World* 45, 46–8 (R. Feinberg and V. Kalab eds. 1984).

[5] *Controls on the Export of Capital from the United States: Hearings on S. 812 Before the Senate Comm. on Banking, Housing, and Urban Affairs*, 99th Cong., 1st Sess. 139 (1985) (statement of David C. Mulford, Asst. Secretary of the Treasury). These percentages are confirmed by analyzing published data for the end of 1985, which provide total external bank claims and total U.S. bank claims for each country, though the data come from two different sources. Data for country totals are taken from Bank for International Settlements (BIS) and Organisation for Economic Co-operation and Development (OECD), *Statistics on External Indebtedness: Bank and Trade-Related Non-Bank External Claims on Individual Borrowing Countries and Territories at End-June 1984*, Table I at 5–7 (July 1986). Data for U.S. bank claims are from U.S. Department of Treasury, *Treasury Bulletin* 54 (Summer 1986). The BIS and Department of Treasury data indicate that U.S. banks at the end of 1985 held, e.g., only 0.9% of the total bank claims against the Soviet Union, 1.9% for Poland, and 10.3% for Hungary.

[6] See Table 1 in Chapter 2, at p. 26, and sources cited there.

[7] A 1988 report indicated that Tokyo had overtaken New York as a center for international lending and that Japanese banks had maintained their lead over U.S. banks in international assets. Japanese banks were estimated to have more than twice the international assets of U.S. banks as of September 1987, having passed the American banks in late 1985. French banks were third, West German banks were fourth, and British banks were fifth. *Wash. Post*, Feb. 10, 1988, at F1, col. 1, citing a February 1988 report by the Bank for International Settlements (BIS). This situation contrasts with the situation at the end of 1984, when the BIS estimated that U.S. banks accounted for the largest share (28%) of the assets in the international banking system, followed

in the number of American banks among the world's largest banks. At the end of 1985, the fifty largest commercial banks included twenty Japanese, seven U.S., and five German. Only one American bank was among the ten largest banks in the world in 1985 versus seven in 1970.[8] Size does have some influence on a bank's competitive position in the international marketplace.[9]

The statutory framework for controlling private financial transactions in which foreigners have an interest can best be analyzed by categorizing the transactions into three basic types: (1) deposits in U.S. banks, (2) loans related to trade, and (3) loans for investment or other purposes.

At present, no U.S. laws exist for controlling foreigners' deposits for foreign policy reasons in nonemergency situations, except for the special case of South Africa. As for trade financing, section 15 of the Export Administration Act provides the President with authority to restrict export financing, but not import financing or other financial transactions. Finally, the only example of regulation of foreign investment or other credit activities for foreign policy purposes are the 1986 sanctions against South Africa. Otherwise, the Johnson Act of 1934 and certain lending limits on individual borrowers provide the President with only a modicum of authority. He also has some informal, though modest, influence arising from the Executive Branch's general regulation of banks.

A. THE CREDIT PROVISIONS OF THE ANTI-APARTHEID ACT OF 1986

Among its many provisions, the 1986 Anti-Apartheid Act contained three major restrictions on private financial transactions. These provisions marked a sharp departure from previous congressional action, which had not given a leading role to limits on these financial transactions, focusing instead on government assistance programs, exports, imports, or U.S. votes in international financial institutions.

The first major restriction prohibited almost all loans by U.S. nationals to the South African Government or to any corporation or other entity owned or controlled by it.[10] "Loan" was defined broadly to include "any

by the Japanese (23.5%), French (9%), British (7%), and West Germans (6.5%). BIS, *The Nationality Structure of the International Banking Market and the Role of Interbank Operations* 4 (1985).

[8] "World's Top 500 Banks," *Am. Banker*, July 30, 1986, at 36.

[9] J. A. Spindler, *The Politics of International Credit* 5 (1984).

[10] 22 U.S.C. § 5055 (Supp. IV 1986). There was an exception for loans for education, housing, or humanitarian benefit that was non-discriminatory. Id. "[N]ational[s] of the United States" were essentially U.S. citizens and corporations or other entities organized under U.S. or state laws. Id. § 5001(5). As a result, the extraterritorial reach of this statute is limited. See discussion in Chapter 4, Section A.6.

transfer or extension of funds or credit on the basis of an obligation to repay." It did not include, however, "normal short-term trade financing, as by letters of credit" or "rescheduling of existing loans, if no new funds are thereby extended."[11]

Though important, this restriction essentially extended the prohibition imposed by President Reagan pursuant to IEEPA in September 1985. Indeed, banks were already voluntarily reducing their loans to the South African Government. According to one estimate, the value of loans from U.S. banks had dropped from nearly $5 billion in September 1984 to $3.4 billion in September 1985. The steepest drop came between June and September, when (as noted earlier) the banks declined to roll over their short-term loans. This led first to a drop of $500 million in loans and then to a South African moratorium on loan repayments.[12]

The Act's second restriction is new, but less important. It prohibits U.S. banks from holding a deposit account from the South African Government or from any entity owned or controlled by that Government. There is an exception for accounts authorized by the U.S. President for diplomatic or consular purposes.[13] In conjunction with the restriction on loans, this limit on deposits seems designed to make it difficult for the South African Government to do business in the United States.

Third, the Act prohibits U.S. nationals from making "any new investment" in South Africa, except in firms owned by black South Africans.[14] "New investment" is defined broadly to include "contributions of funds or other assets" and "extension[s] of credit." It does not encompass, however, "the reinvestment of profits generated by a controlled South African entity" into a South African entity or situations in which funds are needed to allow a controlled South African entity to operate "in an economically sound manner, without expanding its operations."[15]

This investment restriction is new and important. It is the first time in recent years that Congress has specifically prohibited investment in a particular country. Of course, in the two years before the law was passed, U.S. businesses had apparently stopped making new investments in South Africa and had even begun to divest. The data on this are confused by the sharp drop in the value of the South African rand against the dollar, which reduces on paper the value of U.S. investments. According to Department of Commerce figures, direct U.S. investment in South Africa was about $1.3 billion in 1985, down from $2.3 billion in 1982. Even

[11] Id. § 5001(3).
[12] Madison, supra note 3, at 1822.
[13] 22 U.S.C. § 5058. The section applies to "United States depository institution[s]," which includes all major U.S. banks. See 12 U.S.C. § 461(b)(1)(A) (1982).
[14] 22 U.S.C. § 5060.
[15] Id. § 5001(4). See also 51 *Fed. Reg.* 41,908 (1986) (implementing regulations).

after changes in the exchange rate are corrected for, this suggests that U.S. investment had declined.[16] Nevertheless, if South Africa somehow regained its financial stability and became attractive again to foreign investors, the statute would act as a bar against new investment.

These restrictions mandated against South Africa stand in sharp contrast to the limited authority that other statutes generally provide the President over private financial transactions.

B. STOP THOSE EXPORTS: SECTION 15 OF THE EAA

The President's primary statutory authority to control U.S. private credit is contained in section 15, which provides the following:

> The President and the Secretary [of Commerce] may issue such regulations as are necessary to carry out the provisions of this Act. Any such regulations issued to carry out the provisions of section 5(a), 6(a), 7(a) or 8(b) may apply to the *financing,* transporting, or other servicing of exports and the participation therein by any person.[17]

The language of section 15 strongly suggests that the section was designed to help implement export controls under EAA, and that it was not intended to be an independent authority to control international payments or other financial transactions.[18] In other words, the President is not authorized to impose a few export controls on goods and technology to Chile, and then prohibit all financing to that country under section 15.

Moreover, none of the other provisions of the EAA envisions general controls on financing.[19] Sections 5(a), 6(a), and 7(a) authorize the Pres-

---

[16] Madison, supra note 3, at 1822.

[17] 50 U.S.C. app. § 2414 (1982 & Supp. III 1985) (emphasis added).

[18] H. Moyer and L. Mabry, "Export Controls as Instruments of Foreign Policy: The History, Legal Issues, and Policy Lessons of Three Recent Cases," 15 *L. & Pol'y Int'l Bus.* 1, 107–8 (1983).

[19] The legislative history of the export laws indicate that they are not designed to authorize total embargoes of which export controls are only a part. Rather, the authority for peacetime comprehensive embargoes is now contained exclusively in IEEPA. In 1979, the House Foreign Affairs Committee stated:

> Export licenses are one of the devices employed in implementing economic embargoes against foreign nations.... Legal authority to impose total economic embargoes, however, is contained in specific provisions of law or exercised under general authorities other than those of the Export Administration Act.
>
> General authority for total economic embargoes is contained in the International Emergency Economic Powers Act....
>
> In H.R. 4034 [the House bill as reported by the relevant House Committee] the Committee makes explicit its intent that the Export Administration Act of 1969 does not constitute general authority to impose total economic embargoes and that any future embargoes be imposed

ident to prohibit or restrict the exportation "of any goods, technology, or other information" for defined national security, foreign policy, or short-supply reasons. (Section 16 of the Act defines "good" and "technology," but neither definition includes "international financing.")[20] Section 8(b) deals with the special case of the U.S. response to foreign boycotts.

The legislative history of section 15 similarly indicates the intent only to help the implementation of the EAA through regulation of financing and other ancillary activities.[21] The predecessor of section 15 was section 3(a) of the Export Control Act of 1949, which provided that "to the extent necessary to achieve effective enforcement of this Act, such rules and regulations [as the President may direct to control exports] may apply to the financing, transporting, and other servicing of exports and the participation therein by any person."[22] The Senate Report accompanying the 1949 Act explicitly explained that section 3(a) was designed to assist the enforcement of the Act and that "[n]o general regulatory power over banks or other persons involved in servicing exports is intended."[23]

This provision was reenacted in later versions of the export acts[24] until 1979, when the substantially rewritten EAA was passed. In adopting the new section 15, Congress split old section 3(a) into the two sentences

only by specific legislative authority or under the general provisions of [IEEPA]. [H. R. Rep. No. 200, 96th Cong., 1st Sess. 13–14 (1979)]

Although the Conference Committee dropped the specific provision that the House Committee was referring to, the Conference Report stated: "[T]he conferees agreed that, although certain authorities provided in this Act are used to help implement total U.S. economic embargoes . . . authority for such embargoes is contained exclusively in section 5(b) of the Trading with the Enemy Act and section 5(b) of [IEEPA]. The conferees . . . felt this was sufficiently clear that it was unnecessary to so provide in the act itself." H. R. Rep. No. 482, 96th Cong., 1st Sess. 46, reprinted in 1979 *U.S. Code Cong. & Admin. News* 1180, 1184.

[20] "Good" is defined as "any article, material, supply or manufactured product, including inspection and test equipment, and excluding technical data." "Technology" is defined as "the information and know how that can be used to design, produce, manufacture, utilize, or reconstruct goods, including computer software and technical data, but not the goods themselves." Section 16(3) and (4), 50 U.S.C. app. § 2415(3) and (4) (1982 & Supp. III 1985).

[21] Moyer and Mabry, supra note 18, at 106–8.

[22] Export Control Act, ch. 11, § 3(a), 63 Stat. 7 (1949).

[23] S. Rep. No. 31, 81st Cong., 1st Sess. 6 (1949). The Report also stated: "Additional powers, solely designed for enforcement, are included in section 3(a). These are intended to make clear the existence of enforcement authority to obtain, by regulations or otherwise, the aid and cooperation of persons connected with 'financing, transporting, and other servicing of exports,' in preventing and uncovering export control violations here and abroad." Id.

[24] See Senate Committee on Banking and Currency, Export Expansion and Regulation Act, S. Rep. No. 336, 91st Cong., 1st Sess. 18 (1969).

quoted earlier and dropped the phrase "to the extent necessary to achieve effective enforcement." The discussion in the House committee suggests that Congress did not intend to change the existing law.[25] Though section 15 was substantially expanded to include various administrative provisions in the 1985 Export Administration Act Amendments, these two sentences were not changed, nor were any other provisions added that suggest any changes in the President's authority over foreign financing.[26]

The 1980 Moscow Olympics

The only controversial use of section 15 occurred when President Carter moved to limit U.S. participation in the 1980 Moscow Olympics after the Soviet invasion of Afghanistan. On March 28, 1980, the President directed the Secretary of Commerce to issue regulations prohibiting the export of virtually all goods and technology, including such items as souvenirs and sporting equipment, that were associated with the Olympics. He also directed the prohibition of "payments or transactions which are in any way related to arrangements involving or requiring . . . exports, where such payments or transactions could provide financial support for such Games."[27] The Commerce Department regulations, issued the same day, included a prohibition against "any direct or indirect payment or transaction . . . for the benefit of . . . the Soviet Union . . . if such payment or transaction is consideration for any acquisition of commercial or proprietary rights concerning the 1980 Moscow Olympics and if the acquisition or exploitation of such rights involves the export of goods or technology to the Soviet Union by a person subject to the jurisdiction of the United States."[28]

The financial controls were designed primarily to prohibit the National Broadcasting Co. (NBC) from making further payments under its contract to broadcast the Olympics. The contract required NBC to pay $87 million. When the Administration imposed the controls, NBC had already transported the bulk of the necessary equipment to Moscow but still had three remaining payments totaling $20–26 million.[29]

[25] *Extension and Revision of the Export Administration Act of 1969: Hearings and Markup Before the Subcomm. on Int'l Economic Policy and Trade of the Comm. on Foreign Affairs*, 96th Cong., 1st sess. 810–11 (1979) (Apr. 27 discussion between Subcommittee Chairman, Mr. Bingham, and legislative counsel Strokoff).

[26] Sec. 116 of the 1985 Act, 50 U.S.C. § 2414 (Supp. III 1985).

[27] Memorandum on Prohibition of U.S. Transactions with Respect to the Olympic Games, 16 *Weekly Comp. Pres. Doc.* 559–60 (Mar. 28, 1960).

[28] *Fed. Reg.* 21,612, at 21,614 (1980). The regulations were issued pursuant to sections 6 and 15 of the EAA. Id. at 21,612. However, as discussed earlier, section 6 does not provide authority for the financial controls.

[29] Subcommittee on Europe and the Middle East of the House Committee on Foreign Affairs, 97th Cong., 1st Sess., *An Assessment of the Afghanistan Sanctions:*

The President's directive and the resulting regulations on financial transactions were explicitly tied to "involving or requiring...exports." Consequently, they were on their face consistent with the language and legislative history of section 15. Moreover, NBC still had to export some equipment. Two experts argue, however, that these NBC payments "were not directly related to U.S. exports. Rather, the monies to be paid by NBC were partial consideration for the contractual right to broadcast, a transaction that was clearly not a U.S. export within the meaning of the EAA."[30] NBC did not challenge the controls, however.[31]

Although the arguably broad use of section 15 for the Olympics may be a precedent, the section's clear statutory language and legislative history militate against attempts to use the section to restrict private credit that is not connected with controls on the export of goods and technology.[32]

C. THE JOHNSON DEBT DEFAULT ACT

The Johnson Act of 1934 provides a possible obstacle for extending private credit to some foreign governments. However, it is now mainly a trap for the unwary and gives the President no discretion, except for the prosecutorial discretion of deciding whether to go after violators.

The Act provides criminal penalties for "whomever, within the United States, purchases or sells the bonds, securities, or other obligations of any foreign government or political subdivision thereof...while such government [or] political subdivision...is in default in the payments of its obligations...to the United States [Government]."[33] This 1934 Act reflected congressional annoyance with the foreign governments that had defaulted on the payment of their World War I debts to the U.S. Government.[34]

Implications for Trade and Diplomacy in the 1980's, at 92–3 (Comm. Print 1981) (report prepared by the Congressional Reference Service) (1981) [hereinafter House Afghanistan Report].

[30] Moyer and Mabry, supra note 18, at 108 (footnote omitted). Moyer was General Counsel, Counsellor to the Secretary, and Deputy General Counsel of the U.S. Department of Commerce during the Carter Administration.

[31] This was probably because NBC was insured for about 90% of the costs. House Afghanistan Report, supra note 29, at 91; see Moyer and Mabry, supra note 18, at 40 n.238. Also, such a challenge probably would not have been good public relations, and there would have been a much smaller U.S. viewing audience given the lack of a U.S. team.

[32] Moyer and Mabry, supra note 18, at 108, share this conclusion.

[33] 18 U.S.C. §955 (1982) (as revised in 1948).

[34] C. T. Corse and B. Nichols, "United States Government Regulation of International Lending by American Banks," *International Financial Law* 105 (R. Rendall ed. 1980).

The scope of the Act is now quite narrow. To begin with, it applies only to foreign governments that are in default on debts owed to the U.S. Government.[35] The Act has also been riddled with several major exceptions. First, any countries that are members of both the World Bank and the International Monetary Fund are exempted from the Act.[36] Second, the U.S. Attorney General concluded that the Act does not apply to loans from foreign branches of U.S. banks,[37] a large loophole today since many U.S. banks have overseas branches. Third, the statute has been interpreted as not prohibiting trade financing (e.g., for exports), as distinct from general-purpose loans and the sale of foreign government obligations.[38]

For those occasional cases in which the statute might apply, its terms give no discretion to the President. His only role is to decide whether to enforce the statute.

D. FEDERAL LENDING LIMITS

Lending limits have been characteristic of U.S. banking for more than 100 years.[39] They are not helpful, however, as a vehicle for limiting foreign lending for foreign policy reasons. The limits are fixed and, like the Johnson Act, do not give the President any discretionary authority, except to determine whether there have been violations.[40]

The federal lending limits for national banks[41] provide that the total amount of loans and extensions of credit to a single person shall not exceed 15 percent of the bank's "unimpaired capital and unimpaired surplus." This limit can rise to 25 percent if the portion above 15 percent is fully secured.[42]

[35] See 18 U.S.C. § 955.

[36] Id.

[37] 39 Op. Att'y Gen. 398, 401–2 (1939) (the opinion relies heavily on the position in the statute of the phrase "within the United States"); see also Corse and Nichols, supra note 34.

[38] 42 Op. Att'y Gen. 357, 362 (1967) (Opinion of Att'y Gen. Ramsey Clark states that "the Johnson Act is not to be construed as prohibiting transactions by United States firms or banking institutions for the financing of export sales of particular goods or services. . . ."); 42 Op. Att'y Gen. 229 (1963) (Att'y Gen. Robert F. Kennedy).

[39] Corse and Nichols, supra note 34, at 105. See generally Note, "The Policies Behind Lending Limits: An Argument for a Uniform Country Exposure Ceiling," 99 Harv. L. Rev. 430 (1985).

[40] The applicable statute does give the Comptroller of the Currency, a presidential appointee, the authority to prescribe rules and regulations for carrying out the lending limits, including the authority to determine whether a loan to a person shall be attributed to another person in measuring the total amount of loans. 12 U.S.C. § 84 (1982). See discussion below regarding the means and purpose tests.

[41] As discussed at notes 47–48, some banks are state-chartered and are not national banks. However, state laws (e.g., in New York and California) impose similar limits in many cases on state-chartered banks. Corse and Nichols, supra note 34, at 107.

[42] 12 U.S.C. § 84(a)(1) (1982). These percentages were increased, but some loop-

The lending limit covers foreign as well as domestic borrowers. However, before 1979, the limits (even lower then) were unimportant since the banks and regulators treated different state enterprises and agencies in one country as different persons.[43] The Treasury's Comptroller of the Currency now combines loans to a foreign government and its agencies for purposes of the lending limit, unless the loans pass both a "means" test and a "purpose" test. The means test requires that the borrower have "resources or revenue of its own sufficient... over time to service its debt obligations." The purpose test requires that the purpose of the loan be "consistent with the purposes of the borrower's general business."[44] Consequently, loans to a state agency with an independent

holes eliminated, by the Garn–St. Germain Depository Institutions Act of 1982, Pub. L. No. 97–320, § 401, 96 Stat. 1508 (1982) (codified at 12 U.S.C. § 84). The limits are subject to ten statutory exceptions, id., but most of them are exceptions for loans secured by various types of collateral that international borrowers are not likely to possess. See Corse and Nichols, supra note 34, at 106. The phrase "unimpaired capital and unimpaired surplus" is not defined in the statute, but by regulations issued by the Comptroller of the Currency. 12 C.F.R. pt. 3 (1987). Part 3 provides extensive definitions of "capital" and "surplus." The regulations specifically eliminate any need to distinguish "impaired" from "unimpaired" capital and surplus. 12 C.F.R. § 3.100(a) and (d).

Preliminary research fails to indicate any careful, published calculations of what this lending limit means in practice for banks. The legislative history of the 1983 amendments to 12 U.S.C. § 84 provide some data. There, capital is defined as "the sum of a bank's preferred stock, common stock, surplus, undivided profits, and reserves for contingencies and other capital reserves." House Rep. No. 175, 98th Cong., 1st Sess. 36, reprinted in 1983 *U.S. Code Cong. & Admin. News* 1919. This definition is close to the regulatory one. According to this report, each bank's capital in June 1982 is set forth in the following tabulation, from which the 15% lending limit is easily derived:

Bank	Capital (millions of dollars)	Lending limit (millions of dollars)
Bank of America	4,119	617.9
Chase Manhattan	3,186	477.9
Citibank	5,141	771.2
Manufacturers Hanover	2,007	301.1
Morgan Guaranty	2,341	351.2

Based on these figures, Citibank could have loaned $771 million to a single borrower.

It appears, moreover, that many banks have significantly increased their capital since 1982. For example, Chase Manhattan apparently increased its capital 15% from 1984 to 1985, after an increase of 28% from 1983 to 1984. Chase Manhattan Corporation, *Annual Report 1985* (1986). With this, the lending limit per borrower would likewise increase proportionally.

[43] Lissakers, supra note 4, at 54.

[44] 12 C.F.R. § 32.5(d)(1)(i) and (ii) (1987).

source of revenue (e.g., a state oil or trading company) would be treated as a separate borrower. Loans to a state agency dependent on the central treasury would, however, be lumped with loans to the central government.

The lending limits and the means and purpose tests might have influenced certain banks' reduction in lending to some of the financially shaky developing countries.[45] Given the large lending still allowed under the statute, however, the effect seems minor.[46] Moreover, the limits do not provide any flexibility for use as an economic sanction for foreign policy purposes.

E. TWISTING ARMS

The U.S. system for regulating and supervising banks and other entities that provide private credit to foreigners is labyrinthine – including numerous federal agencies as well as state ones. Nevertheless, the extensive and intensive federal regulation appears to provide only limited opportunity for the President to influence the flow of private credit for foreign policy reasons.

For commercial banking organizations, the current federal system of regulation is divided among the Office of the Comptroller of the Currency (OCC), the Federal Reserve Board (FRB), the Federal Deposit Insurance Corporation (FDIC), the Securities and Exchange Commission (SEC), and the Justice Department, with a complex maze of interrelationships. The largest banks and normally the ones with the most international business are usually either banks with national charters or state-chartered banks that are members of the Federal Reserve System. The former are regulated by the OCC. The latter are regulated by both the FRB and their state regulator.[47]

Regulation of the banks is only one of the two layers of federal supervision over them. Well over half of all U.S. banks are now owned by

---

[45] Some U.S. banks were loaning heavily to one or more borrowers in a few foreign countries. Karen Lissakers calculated that the loan exposure of the nine largest U.S. banks in 1982–3 to borrowers in the twelve largest developing-country borrowers equaled 210% of their aggregate capital. Lissakers, supra note 4, at 52–3.

[46] See M. Cohen, "U.S. Regulation of Bank Lending to LDCs: Balancing Bank Overexposure and Credit Undersupply," 8 *Y.J. World Pub. Ord.* 200, 221 (1982); Lissakers, supra note 4, at 54–5.

[47] *Blueprint for Reform: The Report of the Task Group on Regulation of Financial Services* 18 (July 1984). State-chartered banks that are not members of the Federal Reserve System are regulated both by the FDIC (if they are federally insured) and by their state supervisory agency. Id. (The *Blueprint for Reform* is the report of an interagency group within the Federal Government, chaired by Vice President Bush. It made more than four dozen recommendations for reorganizing the federal financial regulatory system.)

holding companies, and federal controls exist for these companies. The Federal Reserve now regulates all U.S. bank holding companies, even if it is not responsible for regulating the banks themselves.[48]

For the international operations of U.S. banks, however, the federal regulatory system has until recently been more organizational superstructure than substance. These operations had been "subject to a minimum of regulation and, at best, spotty supervision."[49]

In the past, U.S. banking regulators were concerned primarily with the management of domestic savings and credit flows, the growth of the money supply, and the protection of domestic depositors, borrowers, and investors. The foreign operations of U.S. banks were considered largely irrelevant to these concerns. At the same time, regulators in Britain, West Germany, and other international banking centers typically focused only on those activities of foreign banks in their jurisdiction that involved the local currency and local depositors and borrowers. International lending in dollars, such as in the burgeoning Eurocurrency market, essentially went unregulated.[50] For example, in the early 1970s, only "a handful of [U.S.] government examiners, with one office in London, were assigned to go out and look at the books of the hundreds of foreign branches... and subsidiaries... of U.S. banks. They were, moreover, barred from many countries. And there were no uniform standards for measuring country exposure."[51]

Under pressure from Congress, changes began to be made in 1977 and reached a peak in 1983. In 1977, federal agencies required banks to report semiannually on their exposure on a country-by-country basis.[52] The next year, the three federal agencies supervising foreign lending – the OCC, the Federal Reserve, and the FDIC – adopted uniform examination standards.[53] In 1979, these three agencies set up the Interagency Country Exposure Review Committee (ICERC) so that they could work together to decide which countries should be classified as above-average risks. (Countries are now categorized as strong, moderately strong, weak, substandard, value-impaired, or loss.) Bank examiners were informed of the ratings and required to use them in their examination of a bank's international operations.[54]

---

[48] Id. at 20.

[49] Lissakers, supra note 4, at 48.

[50] Id. at 48–9.

[51] Id. at 51.

[52] Id.

[53] "A New Supervisory Approach to Foreign Lending," Federal Reserve Bank of New York, *Quarterly Review* 1 (Spring 1978), cited in Lissakers, supra note 4, at 68.

[54] B. Stokes, "Mystery Surrounds Agency, Decisions of Foreign Loan Review Committee," 17 *Nat'l J.* 2136–7 (1985); Lissakers, supra note 4 at 54, 59; Bench, "A

The growing crisis over international debt, particularly Mexico's, led to passage of the International Lending Supervision Act of 1983.[55] Among its many important provisions, the Act forced banks to disclose more information to the public about their foreign loans, including country risk reports to be made on a quarterly basis. The Act also authorized the regulators to require beefed-up capital and loan-loss reserves to strengthen banks against potential losses on foreign loans.[56] As a result, federal regulation of foreign lending is now more intense and more uniform.[57]

Does the present U.S. regulatory system, however, provide the President with any influence over the flow of private credit to a particular foreign country for foreign policy reasons? The President could try to operate in either of two ways: getting a country's category changed so that banks would be more hesitant to make loans to it or simply applying pressure on the banks to restrict their lending to that country regardless of its credit rating.

1. Changing a country's category

A change in a country's category could discourage new lending to the country. For example, if the ICERC switches loans to a country from the category of moderately strong or weak to that of substandard, banks are not required to take any special action, but the shift can hinder the country's borrowing prospects.[58] Even more significantly, if the ICERC rates loans to a country as "value-impaired," banks with such loans are

Framework and New Techniques for International Bank Supervision," presented at the IMF Central Banking Seminar, Washington, D.C., at 29–32 (June 28 to July 13, 1982) (available from the Office of the Comptroller, Washington, D.C.).

[55] Publ. L. No. 98–181, tit. IX, 97 Stat. 1278 (1983) (codified at 12 U.S.C. §§ 3901–12 (Supp. IV 1986)). See generally C. Lichtenstein, "The U.S. Response to the International Debt Crisis: The International Lending Supervision Act of 1983," 25 *Va. J. Int'l L.* 401, 419–26 (1985); C. Friesen, "The Regulation and Supervision of International Lending: Part I," 19 *Int'l L.* 1059, 1068–85 (1985).

[56] Lissakers, supra note 4, at 50–2.

[57] Moreover, there is growing international cooperation for international bank supervision, though it is still "in a primitive state." Lissakers, supra note 4, at 65. A major vehicle for this cooperation is the Basle Committee on Banking Regulation and Supervisory Practices created under the auspices of the Bank for International Settlements (BIS) in Basle, Switzerland. Id. at 62. In December 1987, the Committee issued a consultative paper with proposals for tying minimum bank capital requirements to asset risks. "Proposals for international convergence of capital measurement and capital standards" (Dec. 1987). The Federal Reserve Board issued draft guidelines to implement the proposals. Since the guidelines would limit the use of loan loss reserves as a component of capital, they are expected to force some large U.S. banks with Third World debt problems to build up their capital or shrink their assets. See *Wash. Post*, Jan. 28, 1988, et E1, col. 1.

[58] Stokes, supra note 54, at 2137.

required to set up special reserves, called Allocated Transfer Risk Reserves (ATRRs).[59] Generally, a reserve of 10 percent is required, and the value of the loan on the bank's books must be reduced by 10 percent. If the country is still not paying its debts four months later, the review committee usually requires an additional 15 percent allocation to the ATRR, and then further allocations.[60] The money that banks set aside has to come out of their current earnings, which hurts their quarterly reports and could reduce the price of their stocks.

The ICERC is not immune to presidential pressure. Its members are bank examiners from the Office of the Comptroller, the Federal Reserve Board, and the FDIC. Indeed, there is some concern in the banking community that the White House, through the Treasury or State Department, can influence the review committee's decisions.[61]

Critics have charged that the committee's handling of Peru's debts in June 1985 is an example of bending to political pressure. An economist with a major New York bank complained that "Peru's classification doesn't fit the review committee's own well-established criteria. [It] refrained from marking Peru down from substandard to value-impaired, although Peru was not working with the IMF and had not paid interest for a long time.... [T]he State Department lobbied to give them a chance."[62] Defenders of the committee have responded, however, that the committee must show some flexibility. Peru was scheduled to inaugurate a new, populist President one month after the committee's meeting, and a credit squeeze could have hurt his new administration.[63]

Whatever the merits of the Peru case, it would seem that the President's power to influence country classifications is at best very limited. First, the target country must in fact be somewhere near the substandard or value-impaired situation. A country that is regularly making payments on its debts seems relatively invulnerable to this tactic. Second, the discretion of the review committee and the regulatory agencies is generally confined by the detailed criteria for the various categories. For example, the 1983 Act requires the special reserves for impaired loans when there has been (1) "a protracted inability of public or private borrowers in a foreign country to make payments on their external indebtedness" or (2)

---

[59] 12 C.F.R. §§ 20.8(b)(2), 211.43(b)(2), 351.1(b)(2)(ii) (1987). See Friesen, supra note 55, at 1080.

[60] Stokes, supra note 54; Lissakers, supra note 4, at 59. During 1983–5, five countries – Bolivia, Nicaragua, Poland, Sudan, and Zaire – had their loans rated value-impaired, and none has worked its way out of the classification. Stokes, supra note 54.

[61] Stokes, supra note 54, at 2138.

[62] Quoted in id.

[63] Id. at 2138–9.

"no definite prospects exist for the orderly restoration of debt service."[64] Although the committee might declare other loans impaired, it realistically will feel constrained by the statutory criteria as well as by its other criteria and past precedent.

2. Pressuring the banks

The President might try directly or in various indirect ways to pressure the banks not to extend credit to a target country. For example, a bank that continued to make loans might encounter regulatory obstacles to opening new branches, difficulties in getting access to discount loans, or closer supervision of its loan portfolios.[65]

During the Polish debt crisis in early 1982, for instance, some U.S. officials wanted to pressure U.S. banks to declare Poland in default. (They would also have had the U.S. Government declare Poland in default on the loans that the Commodity Credit Corporation had assumed.)[66] After considerable debate and confusion, the Administration took no such action.[67]

In an analogous situation, the Executive Branch apparently tried to influence U.S. banks to continue and expand their loans to financially troubled developing countries in late 1982 and early 1983. According to one published account, the Federal Reserve informed commercial banks that they would not be criticized if they renewed or even increased by 7 percent their loans to Mexico. Conversely, banks failing to do this would find their Mexican loans coming under closer scrutiny by bank examiners.[68]

Such efforts, however, appear to constitute "an unusual, partial exception to the rule" that U.S. agencies do not instruct U.S. banks on foreign lending.[69] To be sure, some U.S. banks do appear to exhibit a sensitivity to U.S. foreign policy. This is often the case, though, for purely commercial reasons. For example, if the United States is strongly com-

---

[64] 12 U.S.C. § 3904 (Supp. IV 1986); see Stokes, supra note 54, at 2138–9; see Lissakers, supra note 4, at 59.

[65] See Cohen, supra note 46, at 215–16 n.89.

[66] See discussion in Chapter 3 at note 74.

[67] Spindler, supra note 9, at 198.

[68] N. Y. Times, Jan. 15, 1983, at 29, col. 1; see Spindler, supra note 9, at 197 n.38. According to another report, regional administrators of the Federal Reserve quietly pressured smaller banks to extend further credit to Mexico. Wash. Post, Mar. 16, 1984, at E11, col. 4. The State Department also encouraged large U.S. banks to continue to lend to financially troubled Yugoslavia at least once and possibly several times during 1982, though Treasury officials openly criticized this effort. Spindler, supra note 9, at 200.

[69] Spindler, supra note 9, at 200.

mitted to supporting a government (such as Egypt's or Mexico's in 1982–3), the banks are more comfortable about lending to that country because of the likelihood that the United States would be willing to devote additional resources to protecting the government if troubles arose.[70]

Some future effort by the President to press banks to restrict credit to a foreign country would likely encounter serious opposition and would, at best, be only partially successful. First, given the lack of clear statutory authority, the President and his Administration would have to expend considerable political capital and effort to ensure cooperation.[71] Second, though banks would have no legal obligation to cooperate with the President, they might well have a commercial interest in continuing to lend to a target country that was a good credit risk. Bank officers feel a duty to make profits.[72] Finally, the President would be operating against a long-standing tradition of an arm's-length relationship between the banks and the U.S. Government.[73] During interviews conducted by one expert in late 1982, senior bank executives at several of the largest banks "indicated a general unwillingness to cooperate with *any* attempt by the U.S. government to instruct them on where and when to lend internationally."[74]

F. CONCLUSIONS

The 1986 prohibitions against loans to the South African Government and new investment there, as well as the uses of financial sanctions under the national emergency powers, suggest some of the possibilities for utilizing financial controls as sanctions. Except for South Africa or national emergencies, however, the President's statutory authority over private financial transactions with foreigners is essentially limited to control over

---

[70] Id. at 201.

[71] Bankers are not necessarily neutral parties in the making of foreign policy decisions that have an impact on the international financial system. See D. Koschik, "Foreign Policy Motivated Credit Restrictions: Potential Bases of Authority and a Practical Analysis," 16 L. & Pol'y Int'l Bus. 539, 553 n.68 (1984). During the debate over whether to default Poland, e.g., several bankers spoke out against declaring default. See, e.g., *Polish Debt: Hearing Before the Senate Comm. on Banking, Housing and Urban Affairs*, 97th Cong., 2d Sess. 40–8 (1982) (testimony of John Petty, Pres., Marine Midland Bank, N.A., and President, Foreign Bondholders Protective Council).

[72] Spindler, supra note 9, at 196–201; Koschik, supra note 71, at 553–4. Note that the international operations of the ten largest U.S. banks accounted for more than 42% of their net earnings in each year from 1979 to 1983. Lissakers, supra note 4, at 46–48.

[73] Spindler, supra note 9, at 194–5.

[74] Id. at 201. In one of the interviews, on the analogous question of extending credit at the request of the Government, a high official at one of the largest banks stated, "If any senior officer of [our bank] got a call from a U.S. government official [urging us to make a loan], we would almost certainly do exactly the opposite." Id.

export financing. There is no similar statutory authority for financing imports, nor is there any substantial authority over general international lending or over the bank deposits or other assets of foreigners.

Whether the President should be given additional authority, however, raises difficult questions. As discussed in the final chapter, further powers should be given to the President cautiously and selectively.

7

International financial institutions

International financial institutions (IFIs), such as the International Monetary Fund (IMF) and the World Bank, control billions of dollars. Their decisions on what to do with those funds can often be critical to the survival or at least the good health of a country's government. On first impression, this makes them potentially very attractive to the United States as vehicles for imposing economic sanctions for foreign policy reasons. The United States, however, is very limited in its ability to use IFIs for economic sanctions. This is a result of the apolitical purposes of these institutions and their multilateral decision making concerning the extension of financial assistance.

The small influence that the U.S. Government has arises from its alliances with other countries and from informal persuasion, rather than from formal voting power. The one exception is the U.S. veto on loans from the relatively small Fund for Special Operations in the Inter-American Development Bank (IDB). Informal U.S. influence is also probably the most pronounced in the IDB.

The IFIs include the International Monetary Fund and the four multilateral development banks (MDBs): the World Bank Group,[1] the Inter-

---

[1] The World Bank Group consists of three institutions: the International Bank for Reconstruction and Development (IBRD or World Bank), the International Development Association (IDA), and the International Finance Corporation (IFC). National Advisory Council on International Monetary and Financial Policies, *International Finance* 16 (1987) (annual report to the President and the Congress for fiscal year 1986) [hereinafter *Int'l Finance FY 1986*].

The IBRD, presently composed of 149 member states, was formed in 1945 as a result of the Bretton Woods Agreements, which helped establish the structure of the postwar international economic system. J. Sanford, *U.S. Foreign Policy and Multilateral Development Banks* 3 (1982). IBRD operations consist primarily of loans at near-market interest rates to middle-income nations. Id. at 7. The IBRD finances its lending operations primarily by borrowing money in private capital markets, backed

American Development Bank, the Asian Development Bank (ADB), and the African Development Bank (AFDB). Although the purposes of the IMF and the MBDs differ, all have nonpolitical objectives.

The IMF is designed to promote international monetary cooperation and stability in foreign exchange. The IMF provides its 149 member countries with assistance only on balance-of-payments problems and does not extend development assistance.[2] Gross drawings on IMF resources during fiscal year 1984, for example, amounted to about $11.4 billion (or SDR 10.4 billion) by 86 member countries.[3]

In contrast, the purposes of the MDBs are to assist in the economic and social development of developing countries.[4] The World Bank makes

by guarantees by its member governments. *Int'l Finance FY 1986*, supra, at 16.

The IDA is the "soft loan" window of the World Bank Group. Formed in 1960 as an affiliate of the original World Bank, the IDA makes low-interest long-term loans to the world's poorest nations. Sanford, supra, at 7. IDA funds derive principally from member government contributions. *Int'l Finance FY 1986*, supra, at 17.

The IFC, established in 1956, encourages the growth of private enterprise in developing countries through equity investments and loans to local firms. Sanford, supra, at 7. It finances its operations through member government subscriptions and through borrowings in private capital markets. Department of State, *Gist*, Dec. 1985 (unpaginated) (providing basic data on World Bank Group).

In October 1985, the World Bank opened for signature a convention creating a new development institution, the Multilateral Investment Guarantee Agency (MIGA). It will encourage investment in developing countries by providing guarantees against noncommercial risks, by promoting improvements in the investment climates of the developing countries, and by engaging in various promotional activities. *Int'l Finance Fy 1986*, supra, at 18. See generally I. Shihata, "The Multilateral Investment Guarantee Agency," 20 *Int'l L. 485 (1986)*.

[2] A. Chandavarkar, *The International Monetary Fund: Its Financial Organization and Activities* 1 (IMF Pamphlet Series No. 42: 1984). This monograph provides a thorough analysis of the IMF. See also the IMF Articles of Agreement, art. I.

[3] *Int'l Finance FY 1984* 3 (1985) (annual report for fiscal year 1984) [hereinafter *Int'l Finance FY 1984*]. The SDR, or Special Drawing Rights, is an international reserve asset that was created by the IMF in 1970 to supplement existing reserve assets and provide a common unit of account. It serves as the IMF's principal unit of account. International Monetary Fund, *Annual Report 1986*, at 67–8 (1987); IMF, *The International Monetary Fund: An Introduction* 20 (April 1982) (pamphlet providing basic data; available from IMF headquarters in Washington, D.C.). The SDR's value is calculated daily as the sum of values in U.S. dollars, based on market exchange rates, of specified amounts of five currencies in a valuation "basket": the U.S. dollar, West German deutsche mark, French franc, Japanese yen, and British pound sterling. Chandavarkar, supra note 2, at 9. As of December 31, 1987, one SDR was approximately equal to $1.42. International Monetary Fund, *International Financial Statistics* 529 (May 1988).

[4] The Charter of the World Bank is typical of the MDBs. It provides that the purposes of the World Bank include "the encouragement of the development of productive facilities and resources in less developed countries." IBRD Articles of Agreement, art. I, sec. 1.

loans to assist the growth of developing countries around the world, and the other banks help countries in their particular regions. Each bank provides ordinary loans (at near-market rates of interest) and concessional loans (at reduced interest rates). Concessional loans are reserved for the poorest countries and sometimes for special projects.

The MDBs are the largest source of governmental development assistance to developing nations. In U.S. fiscal year 1986, the banks made loans and other financial commitments totaling about $23.1 billion – $17.5 billion from the World Bank Group,[5] $2.3 billion from the IDB,[6] $1.9 billion from the ADB,[7] and $1.3 billion from the AFDB.[8]

The charters of the IFIs specify their nonpolitical objective. The World Bank Charter, for example, provides that the Bank and its officers "shall not interfere in the political affairs of any member; nor shall they be influenced in their decisions by the political character of the member or members concerned. Only economic considerations shall be relevant to their decisions,..."[9]

[5] *Int'l Finance FY 1986*, supra note 1, at 16–18. The IBRD accounted for approximately 75% of the Group's commitments, making new loan commitments of about $13.2 billion. The IDA extended credit totaling about $3.1 billion, and the IFC provided loans and equity investments of $1.2 billion. Id. at 16.

James Baker, U.S. Secretary of the Treasury, proposed an even larger role for the World Bank in response to the debt crisis in the less developed countries. *N.Y. Times*, Feb. 25, 1986, at D1; B. Stokes, "Liberals and Conservatives Struggling Over the World Bank's Proper Role," 18 *Nat'l J.* 334, 335 (1986).

[6] *Int'l Finance FY 1986*, supra note 1, at 18. Of this amount, $2.3 billion consisted of loans on conventional terms from the IDB's ordinary capital (OC) and interregional capital (IRC) resources, and $157 million was composed of loans on concessional terms from the Fund for Special Operations. Id. A new IDB affiliate, the Inter-American Investment Corporation, was established in November 1984. Its purpose is to promote the expansion and modernization of private enterprise in developing member countries. The United States initially has 25.5% of the corporation's capital shares out of an initial paid-in capital stock of $200 million. Id. at 19.

[7] Id. at 19. Of this amount, $1.1 billion was composed of loans at near-market terms from the ADB's ordinary capital resources, and concessional loans from the Asian Development Fund accounted for $800 million. Id.

[8] Id. at 20. Of this amount, $873 million consisted of loans at near-market interest rates from the AFDB. Another $400 million consisted of loans at concessional rates from the African Development Fund. Id.

[9] IBRD Articles of Agreement, art. IV, sec. 10. Similar language appears in the Articles of Agreement of the IDA (art. V, sec. 6) and the IFC (art. III, sec. 9). The Rules and Regulations of the IMF also reflect a political orientation. Regulation N–8 prohibits staff members from engaging "in such political activity as ... is inconsistent with, or reflects adversely on, the independence and impartiality required by their position as international civil servants." The regulation was adopted on Sept. 25, 1946, and amended on June 22, 1979. 3 International Monetary Fund, *The International Monetary Fund 1972–1978* 472 (M. de Vries ed. 1985). The ADB Charter directs that "only economic considerations shall be relevant to its decisions and that such considerations shall be weighed impartially." Art. 36, sec. 2.

In addition, some IFI charters prohibit the institution from accepting contributions with strings attached.[10]

The IFIs have explicitly adhered to these charter provisions in some past decisions. For example, in 1965 the World Bank made loans to South Africa and Portugal, despite resolutions by the UN General Assembly calling upon the Bank and other entities to refrain from providing economic assistance to either country. In defending the loans, the Bank's general counsel specifically noted the Charter's prohibition of political activities by the Bank.[11]

The objectives of the IMF and development banks are generally consistent with U.S. policies of encouraging international monetary stability and development of the less developed countries.[12] Indeed, except for the AFDB – from which it was initially excluded[13] – the United States was a leader in establishing these international institutions and has actively participated in their operations.

Problems arise, however, when the United States seeks to use the IFIs for its own foreign policy purposes. For example, as illustrated in Section C, the United States has tried to cut off assistance to leftist governments or to governments that engage in gross violations of human rights. It has attempted to inject these foreign policy goals either as a result of an independent Executive Branch decision (as was primarily the case of Chile in 1970–73 and Nicaragua currently) or as a result of an Executive Branch decision encouraged by congressionally initiated legislation.

The U.S. legislation covers a wide range of activities by a recipient country. The strictest laws instruct the U.S. director of an IFI to oppose

[10] For example, the ADB Charter provides that "the Bank shall not accept loans or assistance that may in any way prejudice, limit, deflect or otherwise alter its purpose or function." Art. 36, sec. 2.

[11] 14 M. Whiteman, *Digest of International Law* 1004–8 (1970). The resolutions objected to South Africa's apartheid policies and to Portugal's colonial policies. Id.

[12] See, e.g., 22 U.S.C. §§ 286k (IMF and World Bank), 2169 (development assistance), and 2166 and 290h–1 (AFBD) (1982 & Supp. IV 1986); Department of Treasury, *United States Participation in the Multilateral Development Banks in the 1980s* 3–5 (1982).

[13] The African Development Bank, established in 1963, initially limited its membership to African countries. This exclusion, however, hindered the AFDB's ability to raise private capital, and in 1982 the Bank opened its membership to non-African countries. The United States became a member of the AFDB in February 1983. *Int'l Finance FY 1986*, supra note 1, at 20; S. Zamora, "Voting in International Economic Organizations," 74 *Am. J. Int'l L.* 566, 577 n.41 (1980) [hereinafter *Voting*]. In 1973 the AFDB established an affiliate, the African Development Fund (AFDF). The AFDF serves as the concessional lending window of the AFDB and makes soft loans only to the poorest African nations. The AFDF was open to non-African nations from its inception, but the United States delayed joining until November 1976. Sanford, supra note 1, at 53.

a loan or other assistance to the offending country. For example, certain laws instruct U.S. directors at the MDBs to oppose assistance if a country expropriates U.S. property without paying prompt, adequate, and effective compensation,[14] if it provides refuge to airplane hijackers, or if it engages in a pattern of gross violations of internationally recognized human rights.[15] There is an exception in the last two cases if the assistance is directed specifically to programs that serve the basic human needs of the citizens of the country.[16] Although the U.S. director at the IMF is not under such constraints with respect to expropriation or human rights issues, the law does require him to oppose IMF assistance to countries harboring terrorists, to communist dictatorships, and to countries practicing apartheid.[17]

The U.S. directors have frequently opposed loans on these grounds, though some critics argue that the laws should be invoked more often.[18] For example, Senator Kennedy and others contended in early 1986 that Chile was grossly violating human rights, which should trigger the statutory provision requiring U.S. directors to oppose loans to Chile in the World Bank and IDB.[19] The Reagan Administration, however, contended

[14] E.g., 22 U.S.C. §§ 284j (IDA), 283r (IFC), 285o (ADB), 283r (IDB) (1982 & Supp. IV 1986). The President may waive these provisions if the parties have submitted the dispute to international arbitration or if good-faith negotiations are underway.

[15] Id. § 262d (1982 & Supp. IV 1986). The human rights provision is popularly known as the Harkin amendment. The provision was last amended in 1983 to drop the word "consistent" from the phrase "consistent pattern of gross violations." This was done partly because of congressional concern that the Reagan Administration was less than energetic in having the U.S. Director oppose MBD loans on human rights grounds. See W. Curry and J. Royce, "Enforcing Human Rights: Congress and the Multilateral Banks," *Int'l Pol'y Rep.* 12–18 (Feb. 1985). In addition, there are laws requiring U.S. Directors to take other considerations into account, such as whether a country has exploded a nuclear device or is a party to the Nuclear Nonproliferation Treaty. E.g., 22 U.S.C. § 262d(b).

[16] 22 U.S.C. § 262d(f).

[17] Id. §§ 286e–11 (terrorists), 286aa (1982 & Supp. IV 1986) (communist dictatorships and apartheid). There are provisions for exceptions to 22 U.S.C. § 286aa if the Secretary of the Treasury certifies the existence of certain facts.

In February 1982 the IMF granted South Africa a $1.1 billion credit, which helped fuel efforts in the United States to pass section 286aa. It became law in November 1983. "A Victory over Apartheid," *Int'l Pol'y Rep.* 1 (Apr. 1984). Note that the provisions for the MDBs do not mention apartheid, presumably because South Africa is unlikely to seek development assistance and because the human rights provisions are broad enough to include apartheid.

[18] Curry and Royce, supra note 15, at 12–18.

[19] E.g., *Wash. Post*, July 30, 1986, at A10, col. 1. Section 262d is triggered by "a pattern of gross violations of internationally recognized human rights, such as torture or cruel, inhumane, or degrading treatment or punishment, prolonged detention without charges, or other flagrant denial to life, liberty, and the security of person." Section 262d(e) then provides, "In determining whether a country is in gross violation ..., the United States Government shall give consideration to the extent of cooperation

that the statute did not apply, although by mid-1986 it began having second thoughts.[20] The dispute points up the difficulty of forcing the Executive Branch to act against its wishes on the basis of general criteria.[21]

The United States can raise these foreign policy considerations through its formal votes and by lobbying other member countries and the institution's staff. The decision-making structures at the IMF, World Bank, and regional banks are all similar.

With respect to formal voting, each institution has a board of executive directors, which votes on requests for financial assistance and oversees other operations.[22] The United States and other large donors usually have their own executive directors on the board, whereas smaller countries share directors.[23]

Most decisions on loan requests, however, are made by the executive boards through informal consensus rather than through formal voting procedures.[24] This practice makes it difficult to discern behind-the-scenes maneuvering on loan requests, since records of informal meetings are usually confidential. As a result, it is often difficult to determine when political pressure by one country is instrumental in a loan request being approved, rejected, or never even receiving formal consideration.

A. VOTING SYSTEMS

The voting systems of the IMF and the World Bank Group are very similar. Voting power is primarily a function of relative economic strength of the member countries. Each member receives an equal, small allocation of basic votes, and the remaining votes are distributed according to assigned levels of contributions (or quotas).[25] Generally, a simple majority of the votes cast is sufficient to resolve a financial request by a member.[26]

The IMF–World Bank model strongly influenced the voting systems adopted by the regional development banks. Although there are some important differences, all the banks employ the approach of a basic vote plus weighted votes, the latter allocated according to the member's sub-

---

of such country in permitting an unimpeded investigation of alleged violations . . . by appropriate international organizations. . . . " Obviously, the statutory provisions leave considerable room for discretion by the Executive Branch.

[20] See discussion at notes 56–8, this chapter.
[21] See discussion concerning U.S. bilateral foreign assistance in Chapter 3.
[22] *Voting*, supra note 13, at 577.
[23] Sanford, supra note 1, at 8.
[24] Id.
[25] *Voting*, supra note 13, at 576–7.
[26] Id. at 595. In the IMF, however, a "special majority" of more than 50% or sometimes even unanimity is required on the most important decisions, such as changes in the charter. Id.

scription.[27] Formal votes on loan decisions in the regional banks generally require a majority.

One exception to the usual requirement of a simple majority is the two-thirds vote required by the IDB's Fund for Special Operation (FSO) – the IDB's concessional loan window.[28] IDB rules also provide that the voting power of the member with the largest number of shares cannot be less than 34.5 percent.[29] Since the United States is easily the largest shareholder, it exercises veto power over all FSO loans.[30] Indeed, the IDB Executive Board usually does not even consider a request for an FSO loan if the United States has indicated that it will oppose the loan.[31]

Otherwise, the United States lacks the unilateral voting clout to stop assistance from the regular fund of the IBD or from the IMF, World Bank, or other regional banks. Table 2 lists the voting percentages for the United States in these institutions. The U.S. percentages are far less than a majority in each case. Moreover, they have generally declined over time as the contributions of other countries have grown and the relative U.S. subscriptions have decreased.

B. ALLIANCES AND INFORMAL PERSUASION

As noted earlier, most decisions on loan requests are reached by informal consensus rather than by formal votes. American officials have emphasized this as a way of discounting the limited U.S. voting power and poor track record in winning formal votes. For example, Fred Bergsten, an Assistant Secretary of the Treasury during the Carter Administration, has testified that a substantial network of informal international consultations guide IFI procedures and that the results of these consultations

---

[27] Id. at 577–8. However, the percentage of total votes allocated as basic votes rather than as a function of contributions varies widely among these banks. Id. at 578.

[28] IDB Articles of Agreement, art. IV, sec. 9(b).

[29] Id. at art. VII, sec. 4(b).

[30] The United States held 34.5% of the capital stock as of Dec. 31, 1986. IDB, *Annual Report 1986*, at 126 (1987). See *Voting*, supra note 13, at 578. The Reagan Administration has been trying since 1986 to increase its voting power to the IDB, so that it could have veto power, or something close to it, over even regular IDB loans. The Latin American and Caribbean members were generally opposed to increased U.S. control. As of April 1988, the slightly watered-down U.S. position was still that objections by two of the four directors representing industrial donor countries – the United States, Canada, Japan, and Europe – could block a loan. This would have the effect of giving the United States and Canada a joint veto over new loans. *N.Y. Times*, April 17, 1988, at F3, col. 1; see *N.Y. Times*, March 24, 1987, at D1, col. 1; see discussion at note 41.

[31] Sanford, supra note 1, at 8.

Table 2. *U.S. voting power in IFIs*

Institution	Percentage[a]
International Monetary Fund (IMF)[b]	19.3
World Bank Group	
International Bank for Reconstruction and Development (IBRD)[c]	19.4
International Development Association (IDA)[d]	18.4
International Finance Corporation (IFC)[e]	27.6
Inter-American Development Bank (IDB)[f]	34.5
Asian Development Bank (ADB)[g]	13.9
African Development Bank (AFDB)[h]	5.5

[a]Percentages rounded to nearest tenth.
[b]IMF, *Annual Report 1986*, at 120 (Data as of April 30, 1986).
[c]World Bank, *The World Bank Annual Report 1987*, at 179 (1987) (data as of June 30, 1987).
[d]Id. at 195 (data as of June 30, 1987).
[e]International Finance Corp., *Annual Report 1986*, at 59 (1986) (data as of June 30, 1986).
[f]IDB, *Annual Report 1986*, at 126 (1987) (data as of Dec. 31, 1986). The percentage provided reflects combined subscriptions to capital stock. See id. U.S. subscriptions to the concessional Fund for Special Operations (FSO) during calendar year 1986 totaled $4.63 billion, or 55% of total FSO allocations for 1986. Id at 57.
[g]Asian Development Bank, *Annual Report 1984*, at 78 (1985) (data as of Dec. 31, 1984).
[h]National Advisory Council on International Monetary and Financial Policies, *International Finance* 294 (1987) (data as of Sept. 30, 1986). The U.S. voting share in the African Development Fund – the AFDB's concessional loan window – was 6.9% as of Dec. 31, 1984. U.S. Department of Treasury, "Contributions to the African Development Fund and Voting Power" (internal working document dated Feb. 26, 1985; available from author).

– not the formal voting record – are the proper measure of U.S. influence in the IFIs.[32]

C. CASE STUDIES

To evaluate the ability of the United States to translate its foreign policy considerations into actual influence over decision making within the IFIs, it is useful to examine several case studies, involving both specific countries and specific issues (human rights).

[32] Id. at 185, citing Bergsten testimony in *Foreign Assistance and Related Agencies Appropriations for 1979: Hearings Before the Subcomm. on Foreign Operations of the House Comm. on Appropriations*, 95th Cong., 2d Sess. 428–9 (1978).

International economic sanctions

1. Nicaragua

The Reagan Administration's opposition to IFI loans to the Sandinista regime in Nicaragua illustrates the limits of U.S. influence, particularly in formal voting. During fiscal years 1977–85, the United States voted against seven loans to Nicaragua but succeeded in blocking only one.[33] This isolated success came when Nicaragua requested a concessional loan from the IDB's FSO, where the United States possesses a unilateral veto. Each time the U.S. voted against a loan to Nicaragua, it cited "inadequate macroeconomic policies" as its reason for opposition. Political motives, however, were clearly behind the negative U.S. votes.[34]

[33] See the following publications of the National Advisory Council on International Monetary and Financial Policies: *International Finance* 124 (1978) (annual report to the President and the Congress for 1977) (table providing negative votes and abstentions by the United States in the IFIs from July 1, 1976, to June 30, 1977) [hereinafter *Int'l Finance FY 1977*]; *International Finance* 109 (1979) (annual report for fiscal year 1978) [hereinafter *Int'l Financial FY 1978*]; *International Financial* 103 (1980) (annual report for fiscal year 1979 ([hereinafter *Int'l Finance FY 1979*]; *International Finance* 107 (1981) (annual report for fiscal year 1980) [hereinafter *Int'l Finance Fy 1980*]; *International Finance 93 (1982)* (annual report for fiscal year 1981) [hereinafter *Int'l Finance Fy 1981*]; *International Finance* 89 (1983) (annual report for fiscal year 1982) [hereinafter cited as *Int'l Finance FY 1982*]; *International Finance* 85–6 (1984) (annual report for fiscal year 1983) [hereinafter *Int'l Finance FY 1983*]; *Int'l Finance FY 1984*, supra note 3, at 69; *International Finance* 183–97 (1986) (annual report for fiscal year 1985) [hereinafter *Int'l Finance FY 1985*]. See also U.S. Department of the Treasury, "U.S. Negative Votes and Abstentions in the MDBs for Economic and/ or Financial Reasons" (May 6, 1985) (internal memorandum; available from author) [hereinafter Treasury Dep't Memorandum]. Of the seven loan requests against which the United States voted, two pertained to the IBRD and five to the IDB.

In the one successful case, the United States blocked a $2.2 million loan from the IDB's FSO when a final vote was taken on June 29, 1983. Reportedly, all other forty-two members of the IDB voted for the loan, and the U.S. position generated severe criticism from other board members, including Britain and West Germany. *Wash. Post*, July 30, 1983, at D8, col. 1. Strangely, no record of this vote appears in either the annual report for FY 1983 published by the National Advisory Council or in a comprehensive internal Treasury Department memorandum listing all U.S. negative votes and abstentions in the MDBs from FY 1975 through the spring of 1985. See *Int'l Finance FY 1983*, supra, at 86, 192–3; Treasury Dept. Memorandum, supra, at 4.

[34] According to the nonprofit Center for International Policy (CIP) in Washington D.C., U.S. officials in January 1982 regarded as technically sound a Nicaraguan request for a $16 million loan from the IBRD for municipal development. CIP, "World Bank – Nicaragua," Aid Memo, Mar. 10, 1982, at 1. Secretary of State Alexander Haig ordered a negative vote, however. He reportedly overruled the U.S. Executive Director at the World Bank, the Treasury Department, and the Latin American Bureau at the State Department. Haig's intervention failed to stop the loan, however, since all other member countries voted to provide assistance to Managua. Id.

In a more recent negative U.S. vote, the IDB Executive Board nevertheless approved in September 1983 a $31 million loan to help rehabilitate Nicaragua's fishing industry. According to the CIP, the United States argued against the loan on the grounds that

The United States has had a modicum of success in stopping loans to Nicaragua by applying political pressure. Although it applied pressure on all the relevant IFIs to curtail lending to the Sandinista Government, it has concentrated on the IDB. In November 1981, for example, the United States reportedly worked with unidentified South American countries to force Nicaragua to withdraw its request for a $30 million fisheries loan.[35]

The Reagan Administration further increased its behind-the-scenes pressure in early 1985. The U.S. executive director apparently threatened to walk out of any executive board meeting that considered a loan to Nicaragua, thereby imperiling the IDB's entire loan decision-making process.[36] The threatened U.S. walkout was precipitated by executive board consideration of Nicaragua's request for a $59.8 million agricultural loan.[37] IDB management reportedly considered the loan to be technically sound. Ironically, Nicaragua had carefully excluded state cooperative farms from its loan proposal in order to make it more palatable to the United States.[38]

The threat issued by the U.S. director was followed by an unprecedented private letter from U.S. Secretary of State George Shultz to IDB President Mena urging the IDB not to approve the loan.[39] In the letter, Shultz argued that Nicaragua was not creditworthy and that approval of the loan would enable Nicaragua to step up "aggression" against neighboring IDB members. In addition, Shultz warned that Congress

Nicaragua lacked the fuel to power the boats and that Nicaragua planned to use the boats to smuggle arms into El Salvador. CIP, "A New Catch-22: How Reagan Argued Against Nicaragua," AID Memo, Jan. 10, 1984, at 1. There is some irony in the U.S. position since the Reagan Administration was supporting efforts by the Nicaraguan contras to sabotage government fuel supplies. Id.

[35] CIP, "International Banks Cut Off Nicaragua," AID Memo, May 11, 1982, at 6. This episode is also cited in Paul E. Sigmund, "Latin America: Change or Continuity?" 60 *Foreign Affairs: America and the World 1981*, at 640. It is unclear why Nicaragua withdrew the loan request, since the request came under the IDB's ordinary capital account and therefore was not vulnerable to a unilateral U.S. veto. This may have been an occasion in which by lobbying other members, the United States was able to fashion a majority of votes.

[36] CIP, "U.S. Threatens Bank Over Nicaraguan Loan," Aid Memo, Jan. 15, 1985, at 1. IDB rules require the presence of Executive Directors representing at least three-fourths of the Bank's voting stock in order for there to be a quorum of the Executive Board. Since the U.S. has approximately 35% of the voting shares, a U.S. walkout could freeze decision making on all pending loan requests. Id.

[37] Id. at 7. Managua had first requested the loan in June 1982, but a barrage of delays – probably attributable to U.S. arm twisting – prevented the request from reaching the Executive Board until late 1984. Id. at 6.

[38] Id. at 8.

[39] K. DeYoung, "Shultz Intervenes on Loan," *Wash. Post*, Mar. 8, 1985, at 1, 17. It is unclear why the story went unreported for so long, since the State Department had issued press guidance on the Shultz letter on February 12, 1985.

might respond by cutting appropriations for U.S. contributions to the IDB.[40]

In March 1986, the United States escalated the pressure with a proposal for sweeping changes in IDB lending policies. The proposal had some substantive content, seeking to condition the bank's loans on market-oriented policies, such as faster deregulation. Possibly even more important, the United States reportedly sought an effective veto on all lending and placement of more North Americans in key positions at the bank. The U.S. proposal met opposition from the Latin American representatives concerned about U.S. control. Negotiations among the interested parties continue.[41]

In the meantime, Nicaragua continued to seek the agricultural loan. In March 1986, it brought its repayments to the IDB up to date. In April, the President of the Nicaraguan Central Bank charged, "The bank has completely caved in to pressure from the American Administration.... It is ceasing to be an honest international lender and is becoming a political agency of the United States Government."[42] Nevertheless, Nicaragua has yet to receive the loan. Overall, apparently at least in part because of U.S. pressure, there has been a sharp drop-off of IDB lending to Nicaragua in recent years. After receiving $35.1 million from IDB in 1982 and $30.8 million in 1983, Nicaragua received no aid at all in 1984 and through February 1988.[43]

2. Ethiopia and South Yemen

The United States consistently opposed IFI loans to the Soviet-oriented Mengistu regime in Ethiopia between 1977 and 1986, primarily on the

---

[40] Unpublished draft of letter from U.S. Secretary of State George Shultz to IDB President Antonio Ortiz Mena, Jan. 30, 1985. Treasury Secretary James Baker also testified before Congress in May 1985 that the Reagan Administration "has conveyed forcefully to senior [IDB] management a strong belief that a loan to Nicaragua makes no sense in light of the current policy environment in that country...." *Treasury News*, May 16, 1985, at 4.

[41] *N.Y. Times*, Mar. 26, 1986, at D2, col. 5; see discussion above at note 30.

[42] *N.Y. Times*, Apr. 13, 1986, at 6, col. 1; CIP, "Inter-American Bank Mission to Nicaragua," AID Memo, May 7, 1986, at 1.

[43] See telephone interview with Joseph U. Hinshaw, Assoc. Deputy for External Relations Advisor, IDB (June 23, 1987); IDB, *Annual Report 1986*, at 88, 107, 146 (1987); *N.Y. Times*, Apr. 13, 1986, at A8, col. 1.

Nicaragua has also experienced a drought in assistance from the World Bank Group, receiving no aid since a $16 million IBRD loan in January 1982. Telephone interview with Antonio Pimenta-Neva, Public Affairs Office, World Bank (June 23, 1987). The reasons for the World Bank situation are not entirely clear. Presumably there has been U.S. pressure against Nicaragua. Recently, however, Nicaragua has been in arrears on loan repayments to the World Bank, which automatically disqualifies it from receiving new lending. Telephone interview with Mr. Pimenta-Neva, supra.

grounds of an expropriation dispute. (The dispute was resolved with a U.S.–Ethiopian compensation agreement in December 1985.)[44] Analysis of statistics compiled by the Treasury Department, however, shows that the United States lost on all thirty-five votes it either cast against Ethiopia or abstained on during fiscal years 1977–85.[45]

Similarly, citing human rights abuses, the United States has opposed IFI assistance to the People's Democratic Republic of Yemen (South Yemen) since early 1978. During fiscal years 1977–85, the United States voted against or abstained on twenty-one loans, all requested from the IDA. Each loan was nevertheless approved.[46]

3. Chile

Efforts by the United States to apply economic pressure on the leftist Allende regime in Chile during the early 1970s constitute one of the most controversial, and possibly effective, examples of targeting a country within the IFIs. In 1970, when Allende was elected the Chilean President, President Nixon privately called for U.S. actions to "make the [Chilean] economy scream."[47] He issued a secret National Security Memorandum

[44] Compensation Agreement between the Government of the United States of America and the Provisional Military Government of Socialist Ethiopia, Dec. 19, 1985, reprinted in 25 *Int'l Legal Materials* 56 (1986). See Chapter 2 at note 38.

[45] Compare negative U.S. votes and abstentions with IFI loan approvals as reported in *Int'l Finance FY 1977*, supra note 33, at 124, 145; *Int'l Finance FY 1978*, supra note 33, at 109, 135, 252; *Int'l Finance FY 1979*, supra note 33, at 103, 228; *Int'l Finance FY 1980*, supra note 33, at 107, 242; *Int'l Finance FY 1981*, supra note 33, at 93, 113–14; *Int'l Finance FY 1982*, supra note 33, at 89, 107–8, 200–1; *Int'l Finance FY 1983*, supra note 33, at 85–6, 102, 178–9; *Int'l Finance FY 1984*, supra note 3, at 69; and *Int'l Finance FY 1985*, supra note 33, at 196. Three of the thirty-five votes (all abstentions) were on human rights grounds. See *Int'l Finance FY 1977*, supra note 33, at 124 (IDA loan votes in May 1977); *Int'l Finance FY 1978*, supra note 33, at 109 (IDA loan vote in Apr. 1978).

[46] *Int'l Finance FY 1977*, supra note 33, at 124; *Int'l Finance FY 1978*, supra note 33, at 109, 202–3; *Int'l Finance FY 1979*, supra note 32, at 103, 188–9; *Int'l Finance FY 1980*, supra note 33, at 107, 198–9; *Int'l Finance FY 1981*, supra note 33, at 93, 168–9; *Int'l Finance FY 1982*, supra note 33 at 89, 160–2; *Int'l Finance FY 1983*, supra note 33, at 85, 142–3; *Int'l Finance FY 1984*, supra note 3, at 69; *Int'l Finance FY 1985*, supra note 33, at 185, 189. Although a strong case for human rights abuse almost certainly exists, South Yemen's close relations with the Soviet Union, East Germany, and Cuba have also been part of the U.S. motivation. This conclusion is supported by strong anti–South Yemen statements by the Reagan Administration during the period in which most of the negative U.S. votes were cast and by the fact that the Reagan Administration has not opposed loans to other countries whose governments also abused human rights but were not leftist, such as Paraguay (until 1985), Argentina (pre-Alfonsin), and Chile.

[47] *Intelligence Activities, Senate Resolution 21: Hearings Before the Senate Select Comm. to Study Governmental Operations with Respect to Intelligence Activities*, 94th Cong., 1st Sess., vol. 7, at 96 (Dec. 4–5, 1975). CIA Director Richard Helms

that called for, among other steps, pressure on IFIs to limit assistance to Chile.[48] The United States intensified its efforts after Chile nationalized U.S. copper interests without compensation in late 1971.[49]

Chile experienced a substantial decline in lending by the multilateral banks during the Allende period. The World Bank, previously a major lender to Chile, provided no new loans during the Allende period, although it continued to disburse funds from loans approved earlier.[50] The IDB provided two educational loans totaling $11.6 million two months after Allende's inauguration, but these were the last IDB loans to Chile during the Allende period.[51] Pending Chilean loan requests by the pre-Allende Administration were apparently pigeonholed by IDB management, and the Bank never acted on requests for two additional educational loans submitted by the Allende Government.[52] The IMF, however, extended two compensatory loans to Chile worth more than $80 million, although the Fund did not enter into any standby arrangements with the Allende Government.[53]

There is general agreement that U.S. pressure did influence the IDB to reduce sharply its lending to Chile.[54] The evidence is less certain that the

recorded Nixon's directive in his personal notes after a meeting with Nixon on September 15, 1970. Id.

[48] S. Hersh, *The Price of Power* 294–6 (1983); but see H. Kissinger, *White House Years* 680–3 (1979) (while acknowledging U.S. pressures, Kissinger concludes that Allende's own policies caused his downfall).

[49] See P. Sigmund, "The 'Invisible Blockade' and the Overthrow of Allende," 52 *Foreign Aff.* 322, 326, 330, 332 (1974). The Chilean expropriations led to passage in March 1972 of the Gonzalez amendment instructing U.S. directors to vote against MBD loans to countries that expropriate U.S. companies.

[50] Id. at 329.

[51] Id. at 327. The IDB also continued to disburse $54 million from earlier, pre-Allende loans between December 1970 and December 1972. Id., citing *Multinational Corporations and United States Foreign Policy: Hearings Before the Subcomm. on Inter-American Affairs of the Senate Comm. on Foreign Relations*, 93rd Cong., 1st Sess., 533 (1973).

[52] Sigmund, supra note 49, at 327.

[53] Id. at 329.

[54] E.g., Sanford, supra note 1, at 212; Sigmund, supra note 49, at 327, 338. Jonathan Sanford, an analyst with the Congressional Research Service, emphasizes that Chile received no new development credits from the IDB during almost the entire course of the Allende regime – a significant departure from the bank's normal lending patterns. No other member experienced as protracted a financial drought during this period, and several member countries received new loans despite inflationary problems comparable to (and in some cases worse than) those in Chile during Allende. Finally, Sanford argues that the IDB moved rapidly to approve new loans for Chile after Allende was overthrown.

Paul Sigmund, a Latin American expert at Princeton, is convinced that the IDB's total cutoff of new loans to Chile after the copper nationalization stemmed from U.S. pressure. He disputes, however, allegations that the IDB promptly approved $65 million worth of new loans to Chile after Allende was toppled.

United States succeeded in getting the World Bank to stop new loans.[55]

A second chapter in the Chile case has begun. Elliott Abrams, the Assistant Secretary of State for Inter-American Affairs, disclosed in July 1986 that the Reagan Administration was giving serious consideration to voting against IFI loans to Chile unless Chile significantly improved its human rights record.[56] Such signals of possible U.S. opposition apparently led Chile in August to ask the World Bank and IDB to postpone final considerations of its pending loans. The loan requests, which were expected to be voted on in September or October, were delayed until November.[57] The United States then abstained on the World Bank vote approving a $250 million loan to Chile.[58]

4. Human rights

Since the enactment of the Harkin amendment in 1975,[59] the United States has frequently used its vote in the MDBs to oppose loans to countries with poor records in human rights. For example, from January 1977 through September 1981, the United States voted "no" or abstained 118 times on human rights grounds.[60] However, all 118 loans were approved

---

[55] E.g., compare Sanford, supra note 1, at 211, with Sigmund, supra note 49, at 326–8, 338. Sigmund argues that the World Bank also completely subordinated its lending policies to U.S. interests. For example, Sigmund believes that the World Bank's indefinite postponement of Chile's request for an agricultural loan was "closely related" to U.S. anger over nationalization of U.S. copper interests. In Sigmund's view, the bleak economic outlook for Chile provided a convenient excuse for opposing loans to Chile on the grounds that it was no longer "creditworthy." Id. at 326.

Sanford concludes, however, that the World Bank has traditionally been sensitive to the macroeconomic performance of its borrower countries, and by late 1971 the Chilean economic outlook had become bleak, due largely to a sharp drop in the world price of copper. He also points out that the Bank sent seventeen missions to Chile to study possible projects during the Allende period, and that the Bank was preparing a small-loan restructuring package for Board consideration the week before Allende's death. These events, Sanford believes, indicated that the World Bank was acting independently rather than setting its lending policies according to the Nixon Administration's wishes.

[56] N.Y. Times, July 31, 1986, at 1, col. 1.

[57] CIP, "Chile Asks for Postponement of MDB Loans," AID Memo, Aug. 27, 1986, at 1.

[58] N.Y. Times, Nov. 21, 1986, at A3, col. 1. In December 1987, Congress took the initiative and passed a new law that the United States should oppose all loans to Chile from the MDBs, except for those loans for basic needs, until the Chilean Government has ended its gross abuse of internationally recognized human rights and has taken significant steps to restore democracy. Foreign Operations, Export Financing, and Related Programs Appropriations Act of 1988, § 551, Pub. L. No. 100–202 (1987). See also id. § 577 (general statement of U.S. policy toward Chile, with an emphasis on the need for the Chilean Government to return to democracy).

[59] 22 U.S.C. § 262d. See earlier discussion in this chapter at note 15.

[60] Sanford, supra note 1, at 203–4.

despite this opposition, and there is no indication that U.S. opposition caused any significant diminution in MDB lending to countries with questionable human rights records.[61]

There are several reasons for the ineffectiveness of negative U.S. votes on human rights grounds. First, as seen above, the United States lacks sufficient voting power in any of the MDBs to enforce its will, except in the IDB's FSO. There, the prospect of a U.S. veto has led IDB management to present loan proposals for countries with questionable human rights records as ordinary capital loans rather than as FSO loans.[62]

Second, U.S. credibility is eroded by inconsistencies in the U.S. position on human rights. As noted earlier, the statutory provision governing U.S. voting on human rights in the IFIs does not apply to one of the biggest IFIs – the IMF. Moreover, the United States often fails to match its adverse votes in the IFIs with parallel bilateral sanctions.[63]

D. CONCLUSIONS

The United States has, then, only limited ability to use the IFI's to impose economic sanctions for specific foreign policy reasons. This situation results from the nonpolitical purposes and charter provisions of the IFIs and from the limited U.S. voting power. Because U.S. influence is weak in terms of formal voting power, there is greater potential to operate informally through persuasion and coalition building.

The major exception to this is the IDB. Because of its voting power in the IDB's small FSO and its formal and informal strength in the entire institution, the United States has sometimes succeeded in using the IDB for economic coercion purposes. Moreover, the United States has had

[61] Id. One author concludes, however, that "while no loans were formally denied because of opposition from the United States, the Carter Administration policy served to deter loan applications [to MDBs] by Latin America's most repressive governments." L. Schoultz, *Human Rights and United States Policy Toward Latin America* 299 (1983). In 1977, for example, pressure from the Carter Administration over human rights abuses caused the withdrawal of several loan applications after the country seeking assistance became aware of U.S. opposition. Id. at 295. One withdrawal occurred when U.S. Treasury Secretary Blumenthal informed the El Salvador Government that the United States would oppose a $90 million World Bank loan for an electric power project. Id. In another case, Chile withdrew a request for a $14 million IDB loan to improve its health facilities. Id.

[62] CIP, "Enforcing Human Rights: Congress and the Multilateral Development Banks," *Int'l Pol'y Rep.* 9 (Feb. 1985).

[63] Id. at 20. Sanford, however, writes, "An arguable case can be made that Congress intended the law to be a means for requiring the United States to go on record condemning the human rights situation in the violator countries, not necessarily as a mechanism for diminishing MDB assistance to those nations." Sanford, supra note 1, at 204.

some influence on World Bank loans, when it adamantly targets a country and there is a plausible case against that country's economic policies. Chile in the 1970s and possibly Nicaragua today are the primary examples.

The prospects for the U.S. increasing its use of the IFIs are poor. First, in a period of domestic budgetary restraint, U.S. contributions to the IFIs are likely to decline marginally relative to those of other countries, rather than increase. As a result, U.S. voting power is likely to decline slightly in most IFIs. Second, given the supposedly apolitical nature of the IFIs, there is no reason to expect that member countries that are otherwise friendly to the United States are any more likely to go along with special U.S. foreign policy interests than in the past. This does not rule out, of course, the extreme situations or major crises in which other countries feel a need to work together.

8

Miscellaneous laws for nonemergencies

In addition to the U.S. laws that deal primarily with one type of economic activity, such as exports or private financial transactions,[1] there are laws that span several types of activity and that give the President some power to impose economic sanctions for foreign policy purposes. The two principal examples are the antiboycott laws and the UN Participation Act.[2]

[1] Some of the statutes discussed earlier do cover more than one type of activity. For example, the Export Administration Act can be used to regulate export financing as well as exports, the Arms Control Export Act regulates both the export and import of defense items, and the Atomic Energy Act provides for licensing of exports and imports of nuclear items.

[2] Another law that does not fit in the categories discussed above (such as exports and imports) is the 1987 provision that denies tax credits to U.S. companies for the taxes paid by their subsidiaries in South Africa. See Chapter 3, at note 11. See also I.R.C. § 901(j) (enacted in 1986 to deny foreign tax credits on income from certain countries, such as those supporting terrorism). Using the tax laws to impose sanctions for foreign policy purposes is relatively rare. Previously the major use of the tax laws for such purposes is the provision against the Arab boycott. See notes 20–7, this chapter.

One statute that is applicable on its face is 22 U.S.C. § 1732 (1982), dubbed the "Hostage Act" during the Iranian hostage litigation. It appears to have very limited viability. Passed in 1868, section 1732 provides that when a U.S. citizen has been unjustly deprived of liberty by a foreign government, "the President shall forthwith demand the release of such citizen, and if the release so demanded is unreasonably delayed or refused, the President shall use such means, not amounting to acts of war, as he may think necessary and proper to obtain or effectuate the release...."

In *Dames & Moore v. Regan*, the Court declined to conclude that the statute directly authorized the President to suspend the claims in U.S. courts. 453 U.S. 654, 678 (1981); see discussion in Chapter 9, Section D.3. Justice Rehnquist noted, inter alia, that Congress was concerned in 1868 with the practice of certain countries refusing to recognize the citizenship of naturalized Americans traveling abroad and repatriating them against their will. That situation was different from the Iranian case. Id. at 676.

Justice Rehnquist did group the Hostage Act with IEEPA as "highly relevant in the looser sense of indicating congressional acceptance of a broad scope for executive action in circumstances such as those presented in this case." Id. at 677. Nevertheless, the statute's age, legislative history, and rare use suggest that, whatever it is called,

Miscellaneous laws for nonemergencies

A. THE ANTIBOYCOTT LAWS: THE UNITED STATES STRIKES BACK

In reaction to the continuing Arab boycott of Israel, the United States has imposed major limits on U.S. business activities complying with or supporting any boycott that is not approved by the United States and that is directed against a friendly country. These U.S. antiboycott laws further a number of American foreign policy interests – opposing discrimination, protecting U.S. sovereignty, and maintaining close ties to Israel.

The antiboycott laws, however, are not an affirmative weapon, but rather a reactive one. Other countries must act before the laws are triggered. Given the reactive nature of the laws and their focus on only one situation, a detailed examination of the complicated, often subtle provisions of the laws is beyond the scope of this book. Nevertheless, the U.S. response to the Arab boycott requires a brief discussion.

Even before Israel was recognized as a state in 1948, the Arab League[3] had instituted a boycott of goods produced by Jews in Palestine. After the creation of Israel and the defeat of the Arab armies, the Arab League took steps to establish an expanded and more sophisticated boycott. A "Unified Law on the Boycott of Israel" was adopted by the League's Council in 1954 and enacted (with minor variations) by each of the twenty member states.[4]

The resulting boycott is far reaching (though only sporadically enforced). It is a primary boycott – prohibiting trade and other transactions

---

section 1732 should have little life left. A. Mikva and G. Neuman, "The Hostage Crisis and the 'Hostage Act,'" 49 *U. Chi. L. Rev.* 292, 353–4 (1982).

[3] The League of Arab States was formed in 1944–5 to strengthen relations among its members, to coordinate policies, and to maintain a general concern for Arab interests. Member states include Algeria, Bahrain, Egypt, Iraq, Jordan, Kuwait, Lebanon, Libya, Mauritania, Morocco, Oman, Qatar, Saudi Arabia, Somalia, Sudan, Syria, Tunisia, United Arab Emirates, and the two Republics of Yemen. In 1976, the Palestinian Liberation Organization was admitted to full voting status as the twenty-first member. After Egypt and Israel signed a formal peace treaty in 1979, the Arab League Council voted to suspend Egypt's membership in the League. A. Lowenfeld, *Trade Controls for Political Ends* 310–11 (1983) [hereinafter Lowenfeld, *Trade Controls*].

For careful discussions of the Arab boycott and the resulting U.S. legislation, see id. at 307–423; H. Fenton, "United States Antiboycott Laws: An Assessment of Their Impact Ten Years after Adoption," 10 *Hastings Int'l & Comp. L. Rev.* 211 (1987); Symposium, "The Arab Boycott and the International Response," 8 *Ga. J. Int'l & Comp. L.* 527 (1978); Note, "Analysis and Application of the Anti-Boycott Provisions of the Export Administration Amendments of 1977," 9 *L. & Pol'y Int'l Bus.* 915 (1977) [hereinafter "Analysis of the Anti-Boycott Provisions"].

[4] Lowenfeld, *Trade Controls*, supra note 3, at 314.

between the Arab countries and Israel.[5] It is also a secondary and tertiary boycott – prohibiting many transactions, for example, involving U.S. entities as a way of inducing them to stop dealing with Israel. Prohibited activities include having an office, branch, or assembly plant in Israel; acting as an agent for Israeli companies or as a primary importer of Israeli products; or using items produced by a company (which may be non-Israeli) that is on the blacklist.[6]

The principal device for carrying out the boycott is the use of blacklists. The League's Central Boycott Office maintains a master boycott list and recommends changes, but each country also maintains its own separate list. Countries vary in their acceptance and interpretation of resolutions from the Central Office. For example, some Arab League states adhere to the primary boycott, but they do not practice the secondary or tertiary boycotts.

Businesses known or believed to have engaged in a prohibited activity are placed on the blacklist, or they are warned that they will be unless they prove that they do not belong on it. Exceptions to the basic rules have arisen so as to protect the Arab economies. For example, major U.S. arms companies are not blacklisted, in spite of their sales to Israel, because the Arab countries also want the latest weaponry.[7]

American concern over the Arab boycott did not become an important national issue until the mid–1970s, when the oil-rich Arab states emerged as world economic powers. The principal U.S. response was the 1977 amendments to the Export Administration Act, which continue today. Special tax provisions are also noteworthy.[8]

---

[5] This includes trade in goods from third countries that have parts of Israeli origin.

[6] Lowenfeld, *Trade Controls*, supra note 3, at 314–19; "Analysis of the Anti-Boycott Provisions," supra note 3, at 919–21. The last activity is a tertiary, or extended secondary, boycott. It means that product X of U.S. firm A could be barred by the Arabs since it incorporates product Y of U.S. firm B that is on the blacklist. As a result, firm A would be under pressure not to deal with firm B.

[7] Special provisions have also been created for oil companies, airlines, hotels, and banks. See sources cited in note 6.

[8] Before the passage of the 1977 amendments, there was considerable discussion about use of the federal antitrust laws, and one lawsuit was even brought. In early 1976, the Department of Justice sued Bechtel Corporation, an international prime contracting firm with extensive projects in Arab countries. The complaint alleged that Bechtel and coconspirators implemented agreements to further the Arab boycott by refusing to deal with blacklisted persons as subcontractors in connection with projects in the Arab League countries and by requiring subcontractors to refuse to deal with blacklisted persons on these projects. Lowenfeld, *Trade Controls*, supra note 3, at 342–3. Bechtel later consented to a proposed judgment against it that imposed significant limits on its activities. Id. at DS 496–504. After the passage of the 1977 amendments to the EAA, Bechtel announced that it no longer consented to the proposed judgment. However, judgment was entered against it. *United States v. Bechtel*

Miscellaneous laws for nonemergencies

1. Section 8 of the EAA

A variety of efforts in 1976–7 to amend the EAA received a big boost when representatives of the Business Roundtable and of principal Jewish groups negotiated compromise language for pending legislation. Their agreement was adopted by the Senate and the House without change in 1977.[9]

The EAA antiboycott provisions are relatively brief, but they are backed by detailed regulations. First, the law applies to "United States persons," which is defined to include the controlled foreign subsidiaries of U.S. companies.[10] Second, it applies only to actions in the "interstate or foreign commerce of the United States."[11] Third, the Act covers actions taken with intent to comply with, further, or support a foreign boycott against "a country which is friendly to the United States" and which the United States is not itself boycotting.[12] Though phrased in general terms, this provision clearly covers the Arab boycott of Israel. The statute has apparently never been enforced against other boycotts, though the possibilities have been sparse. Conceivably, it could have been used against the trade and financial sanctions that Britain and Argentina imposed against each other during the Falklands crisis and the European Economic Community's limits on imports from Argentina.[13]

Corp., 1979 Trade Cas. (CCH) § 62,429 (N.D. Cal. 1979), aff'd, 648 F.2d 660 (9th Cir. 1981), cert. denied, 454 U.S. 1083 (1981).

The 1977 amendments to the EAA were generally perceived to supplant future uses of the antitrust laws. See, e.g., J. Johnstone and J. Paugh, "The Arab Boycott of Israel: The Role of United States Antitrust Laws in the Wake of the Export Administration Amendments of 1977," 8 *Ga. J. Int'l & Comp. L.* 661, 662 (1978). This was the view even though the statute specified that it did not "supersede or limit the operation of the antitrust . . . laws." 50 U.S.C. app. § 2407(a)(4) (1982). The U.S. Government has apparently brought no new antitrust lawsuits based on boycott activities since 1977. See Lowenfeld, *Trade Controls*, supra note 3, at 396 (reporting no suits through 1982).

[9] Export Administration Amendments of 1977, Pub. L. No. 95-52, tit. II, 91 Stat. 235 (codified in scattered sections of 50 U.S.C. app. (1982)). See especially section 2407. For a fascinating account of the legislative process see T. Franck and E. Weisband, *Foreign Policy by Congress* 200–9 (1979). As one of the private representatives commented, "In a little more than two weeks the Jewish organizations and the [Business] Roundtable had achieved something unique – agreement on legislative language enacted without change by the Congress." Id. at 207. A broad challenge to the antiboycott provisions based on First Amendment grounds was rejected in *Briggs & Stratton Corp. v. Baldridge*, 728 F.2d 915 (7th Cir. 1984), aff'g, 539 F. Supp. 1307 (E.D. Wisc. 1982).

[10] 50 U.S.C. app. § 2410 (1982).

[11] Id. § 2407. This phrase has been defined at some length in the regulations. 15 C.F.R. § 369.1(d) (1987).

[12] 50 U.S.C. § 2407.

[13] For details on the steps by other countries, see *N.Y. Times*, Apr. 9, 1982, at D1 (British freeze); *N.Y. Times*, Apr. 11, 1982, at A1 (EEC import restrictions); *Wash. Post*, June 6, 1982, at A1 (Argentina's sanctions). During the crisis, the United States

The EAA contains a series of prohibited activities and a series of exceptions. The end result allows U.S. persons to comply with a primary boycott with a few exceptions. This is an attempt not to interfere with other countries' rights to conduct a direct boycott against another country. The law, however, generally prohibits compliance with secondary boycotts. This reflects the U.S. opposition to discrimination and anti-competitive activity, and a determination to protect its sovereignty. Moreover, the provisions help support Israel, with which the United States has close ties.[14]

For example, subject to carefully limited exceptions, the EAA prohibits a U.S. entity from (1) refusing to do business with any Israeli business or national pursuant to an agreement with or a request from an Arab country, (2) refusing to employ or otherwise discriminating against any U.S. person on the basis of religion or national origin, (3) furnishing information about whether any person has had or proposes to have any business relationship with Israel, and (4) paying, confirming, or otherwise implementing a letter of credit that contains any of the prohibited conditions or requirements.[15]

These prohibitions are subject to certain exceptions designed to permit compliance with primary boycott practices and other legitimate interests of the Arab states. For example, these exceptions allow compliance with (1) requirements of an Arab country barring imports of Israeli goods or services, (2) requirements barring the use of Israeli carriers, or (3) certain requirements for import and shipping documents, such as information about country of origin and the name of the carrier.[16]

maintained diplomatic and other relations with Britain and Argentina. The United States imposed no sanctions against Britain, rather cooperating very fully with its efforts to regain the islands.

The United States did take a few minor steps from April 30, 1981, to July 12, 1982, against Argentina after efforts to mediate the dispute had failed. They included a ban on arms exports (which had already been limited by law to commitments entered into before September 30, 1978), suspending the disbursement of some Eximbank loans, and halting a possible Commodity Credit Corporation credit of $2 million. These actions were labeled "largely symbolic." *Wash. Post*, May 1, 1982, at D8; *N.Y. Times*, July 13, 1982, at A1; G. Hufbauer and J. Schott, *Economic Sanctions Reconsidered: History and Current Policy* 717–24 (1985). It is not clear whether these measures would qualify under the antiboycott provisions as "any form of boycott pursuant to United States law or regulation." Id. §2407(a). Even if they did, they were in effect only against Argentina and only for part of the period covered by the British sanctions. It would also be necessary to analyze how the British or Argentine sanctions required U.S. persons to act in ways prohibited under the EAA antiboycott provisions.

The Department of Commerce has announced that the EAA antiboycott regulations do not apply to foreign boycotts against South Africa. 52 *Fed. Reg.* 7, 284 (1987).

[14] See S. Marcuss,"The Antiboycott Law: The Regulation of International Business Behavior," 8 *Ga J. Int'l & Comp. L.* 559, 561 (1978).

[15] 50 U.S.C. app. § 2407(a)(1).

[16] Id. § 2407(a)(2).

Miscellaneous laws for nonemergencies

The implementing regulations are very important in fleshing out the relatively skeletal statutory provisions.[17] Nevertheless, the President's ability to affect the scope of the regulations is limited sharply by the continuing, intense interest of business groups and Jewish groups in the details of the regulations.[18] Similarly, the President's discretion over enforcement of the antiboycott laws and regulations is circumscribed by the same intense interest.[19]

2. The tax laws

Before the passage of the 1977 EAA amendments, opponents of the Arab boycott added provisions to the Tax Reform Act of 1976[20] that were designed to discourage "participat[ing] in or cooperat[ing] with" an international boycott.[21] Violation results in the taxpayer being denied or limited in the opportunity to (1) receive a credit against U.S. tax for income taxes paid foreign countries,[22] (2) defer U.S. taxes on earnings of a foreign subsidiary,[23] and (3) defer U.S. taxes on earnings from so-called foreign sales corporations.[24] These sanctions are applied to the extent of the taxpayer's income from a particular operation.[25] In addition, the statute contains extensive reporting obligations.

Although some commentators called for the repeal of these tax provisions after the 1977 EAA amendments,[26] the provisions continue in force. Moreover, it appears that they have resulted in a substantial loss of tax benefits to a number of corporations.[27]

---

[17] "Analysis of the Anti-Boycott Provisions," supra note 3, at 932; see Marcuss, supra note 14, at 559–60.

[18] Marcuss, supra note 14, at 559–60.

[19] See generally, e.g., the systematic reporting of the activities of U.S. business and the enforcement activities of the U.S. Government in *Boycott Report*, a publication issued nine times per year by the American Jewish Congress.

[20] Pub. L. No. 94-455, §§ 1061–4, 1066–7, 90 Stat. 1649, 1654 (codified in scattered sections of the I.R.C.). The provisions were popularly known as the Ribicoff amendment, after their Senate sponsor.

[21] I.R.C. § 908 (1986).

[22] Id.

[23] Id. § 952(a). See 52 *Fed. Reg.* 25,118 (1987) (U.S. Treasury Department guideline that the tax antiboycott provisions do not apply to participation in Commonwealth sanctions against South Africa, given U.S. sanctions).

[24] Id. § 995(b)(1)(D).

[25] Id. §§ 908, 952, 995, 999.

[26] E.g., C. Estes, "Federal Tax Consequences of International Boycotts," 8 *Ga. J. Int'l & Comp. L.* 685, 709 (1978).

[27] The U.S. Department of the Treasury issues its own analysis of the reports of U.S. taxpayers regarding their business activities in the thirteen Arab countries for which Treasury requires a report from the taxpayer. The taxpayer is required to calculate whether it has lost any tax benefits by reason of its participation or cooperation in the boycott.

An overall assessment of the effectiveness of the antiboycott laws is difficult to make. There is some evidence that at least certain Arab countries have relaxed their boycott practices in reaction to strong U.S. opposition.[28] Moreover, the sharp loss of business by U.S. firms that some opponents of the laws predicted[29] has apparently not come to pass. Indeed, partly because of the dramatic rise in oil revenues for Arab countries (a rise that has recently been reversed), U.S. firms have considerably expanded their business with Arab countries since 1977. Whether U.S. firms could have done even better is not clear.[30]

B. THE UN PARTICIPATION ACT: BUT FOR THE VETO

On its face, section 287c of the UN Participation Act of 1945 gives the President sweeping powers to impose the full range of economic sanctions. He may "regulate, or prohibit, in whole or in part, economic relations or . . . communication" between any foreign country or national and any one subject to U.S. jurisdiction.[31] A critical precondition, however, is that these powers are triggered only when they are mandated by the UN Security Council.

For 1978–9, of the 2,892 taxpayers reporting, 179 assessed themselves a loss of tax benefits of $11,329,000 in 1978 and $9,962,000 in 1979. U.S. Department of Treasury, *The Operation and Effect of the International Boycott Provisions of the Internal Revenue Code* 4 (1982), cited in Hufbauer and Schott, supra note 13, at 420, 422; and in "Treasury Report Reveals Widespread Boycott Compliance," *Boycott Rep.* 3 (July 1982). For 1980–2, the Treasury Department reported that tax credits of $19,600,000 were lost. *Boycott Rep.* (June 1985).

[28] See Fenton, supra note 3, at 276–8; H. Stanislawski, "The Impact of the Arab Economic Boycott of Israel on the United States and Canada" 25–26, in *The Utility of Economic Sanctions* (D. Leyton-Brown ed. 1985); Lowenfeld, *Trade Controls*, supra note 3, at 386–7.

[29] See H. Steiner, "Pressures and Principles – The Politics of the Antiboycott Legislation," 8 *Ga. J. Int'l & Comp. L.* 529, 540–6 (1978).

[30] See Fenton, supra note 3, at 276–87; Hufbauer and Schott, supra note 13, at 418–22; Lowenfeld, *Trade Controls*, supra note 3, at 386–7; "U.S. Anti-Boycott Laws Have Not Hurt U.S. Exports," *Boycott Rep.* 4 (Sept. 1986).

[31] 22 U.S.C. § 287c (1982) provides in pertinent part: "Notwithstanding the provisions of any other law, whenever the United States is called upon by the Security Council to apply measures which said Council has decided, pursuant to article 41 of said Charter, . . . the President may, to the extent necessary to apply such measures, . . . investigate, regulate, or prohibit, in whole or in part, economic relations or rail, sea, air, postal, telegraphic, radio, and other means of communication between any foreign country or any national thereof or any person therein and the United States or any person subject to the jurisdiction thereof, or involving any property subject to the jurisdiction of the United States." In 1945, the United States had become a member of the United Nations and had ratified the UN Charter as a treaty after advice and consent by the U.S. Senate.

The Security Council has broad powers under article 41 to call for the "complete or partial interruption of economic relations and...communication."[32] However, particularly in recent decades, the Security Council has had trouble mandating any action, usually because it has been hamstrung by the veto of one or more of its five permanent members.[33] In particular, the conflicting interests of the United States and the Soviet Union generally make it difficult to agree on unified action in international crises.

A recent example of the nearly ubiquitous veto is the Iranian hostage situation. Although President Carter had quickly declared a national emergency and invoked his IEEPA powers in November 1979, the United States hoped to use the UN Security Council to develop and generate support for multilateral sanctions against Iran. There was international repugnance at seizing diplomats as hostages. A proposed ban on most exports to Iran was negotiated by the United States with its allies and Third World countries, but the proposal was stymied by a Soviet veto in January 1980. Although some U.S. allies later imposed sanctions unilaterally against Iran, there was greater wariness because of the lack of "the protective shield of a U.N. vote."[34]

Section 287c has provided the President the authority to impose sanctions in two situations – against Rhodesia and South Africa. Rhodesia was the first case in which the Security Council explicitly used article 41. White Rhodesians had made a "unilateral declaration of independence" from Great Britain in 1965, and initial British efforts to resolve the dispute failed. In December 1966, the Security Council passed resolution 232

[32] UN Charter, art. 41. The Security Council may call for economic sanctions after determining the existence of a threat to the peace, a breach of the peace, or an act of aggression. Id. at art. 39. Before recommending action under article 41, the Security Council may ask the parties concerned to comply with "provisional measures that it deems necessary or desirable." Id. at art. 40. Article 41 does not include "the use of armed force." The Security Council can decide on that under article 42.

[33] The Security Council has fifteen members. Five are permanent – China, France, the Soviet Union, Great Britain, and the United States. UN Charter, art. 23. Decisions on nonprocedural matters require nine votes, including the concurring votes of the permanent members. Art. 27(3).

[34] R. Carswell and R. Davis, "The Economic and Financial Pressures: Freeze and Sanctions," in *American Hostages in Iran* 196–8 (P. Kreisberg ed. 1985).
As of February 1988, there was some hope for a Security Council resolution imposing an arms embargo against Iran because of Iran's refusal to accept a July 1987 Council resolution calling for a cease-fire in the seven-year-old war with Iraq. In December 1987 the fifteen Security Council members announced that they were ready to proceed with an embargo. Efforts to draft a resolution, however, were slowed by Soviet hesitation to support it. The Soviets apparently wanted further efforts at diplomacy and were chary of offending the Iranians. *Wash. Post*, Feb. 8, 1988, at A13, col. 1.

calling for selective mandatory sanctions.[35] That was followed by resolution 253 in 1968 calling for comprehensive sanctions.[36]

Relying on section 287c, President Johnson issued Executive Orders implementing the UN resolutions and controlling transactions with Rhodesia.[37] In 1971, Congress cut a hole in these U.S. sanctions by passing the so-called Byrd amendment, which allowed the importation of some strategic materials from Rhodesia.[38] The amendment was later repealed in 1977.[39] The U.S. sanctions were terminated in December 1979 when an arrangement was reached for majority rule in Rhodesia, soon to be called Zimbabwe.[40]

As for South Africa, in 1977 the Security Council called for an embargo on shipments of arms, munitions, and military equipment to or from that country.[41] The United States, however, had already taken the required actions pursuant to its arms export laws. Indeed, U.S. sanctions against South Africa have been more thoroughgoing than mandated by the Security Council resolutions.[42] Section 287c has been cited as authority only in addition to other statutes.[43]

[35] UN Doc. S/RES/232, 21(2) UN SCOR Supp. at 7–9 (1966). During 1965–79, Rhodesia was also called at various times Southern Rhodesia and Rhodesia-Zimbabwe. The state is now Zimbabwe. For an excellent account of this period, see Lowenfeld, *Trade Controls,* supra note 3, at 452–535.

[36] UN Doc. S/RES/253 23 UN SCOR at 5–7 (1968).

[37] E.g., Exec. Order No. 11,322, 32 *Fed. Reg.* 119 (1967) (implementing UN Res. 232); Exec. Order 11,419, 33 *Fed. Reg.* 10,837 (1968) (implementing UN Res. 253). Although the President could cut off exports to Rhodesia and its sugar quota under other nonemergency laws, further restrictions on imports had to be based on section 287c. Alternatively, the President might have used his powers under TWEA, relying on the national emergency left over from the Korean War. See discussion on emergency statutes in Chapter 9, Section A.

[38] Pub. L. No. 92-156, 85 Stat. 423 (1971) (codified at 50 U.S.C. § 98–98h (1972)). The statute was upheld in *Diggs v. Shultz,* 470 F.2d 461 (D.C. Cir.), cert. denied, 411 U.S. 931 (1972) (which concluded, inter alia, that a later statute is controlling in domestic U.S. law over an earlier treaty commitment).

[39] Pub. L. No. 95-12, 91 Stat. 22 (1977).

[40] Exec. Order 12,183, 44 *Fed. Reg.* 74,787 (1979). The UN ended its call for sanctions shortly afterward. *N.Y. Times,* Dec. 27, 1979, at 8, col. 4.

[41] S.C. Res. 418, 32 UN SCOR at 5, UN Doc. S/RES/418, S/INF/33 (1977). This followed an earlier call for a voluntary arms embargo. S.C. Res. 181, 18 UN SCOR at 7, UN Doc. S/RES/181, S/INF/18/Rev. 1 (1963). Later Security Council Resolutions include S.C. Res. 569 of July 1985.

[42] Note, however, that the United States and Great Britain vetoed in February 1987 a Security Council resolution that would have imposed further mandatory sanctions against South Africa. *N.Y. Times,* Feb 21, 1987, at 3, col. 1. These were similar to those approved by Congress over President Reagan's veto in the Comprehensive Anti-Apartheid Act of 1986, discussed supra, at notes 11–16 in Chapter 3.

[43] E.g., when President Reagan imposed new sanctions against South Africa in September 1986 (including sanctions against imports of arms from South Africa), he cited section 287c as one of the bases for his actions. See Exec. Order No. 12,252, 50 *Fed. Reg.* 36,861 (1985).

C. CONCLUSIONS

Although both the antiboycott laws and the UN Participation Act authorize the President to regulate a wide variety of economic activities, the situations that trigger the use of either set of statutes are very limited. The antiboycott laws operate only in reaction to other countries' boycotts, notably the Arab boycott against Israel. The UN Participation Act requires the increasingly elusive mandate from the UN Security Council.

9

Present laws for a declared national emergency

Faced with the great variation in his authority for imposing different types of economic sanctions under the nonemergency statutes, the President can as one option declare a national emergency and invoke his sweeping emergency powers. Consequently, any careful analysis of the U.S. laws for governing economic sanctions must examine the emergency laws as well as the nonemergency ones. A comprehensive analysis such as this supplies the basis for recommending major changes in both sets of laws.

If the President is going to impose economic sanctions during a declared national emergency, the statutory vehicle will almost certainly be the International Emergency Economic Powers Act (IEEPA).[1] It is designed to deal with "any unusual and extraordinary threat, which has its source in whole or substantial part outside the United States, to the [U.S.] national security, foreign policy, or economy."[2] If the President determines that such a threat exists, he can declare a national emergency under the National Emergencies Act (NEA).[3]

IEEPA then authorizes him to employ a wide range of economic sanctions, such as cutting off exports or imports or restricting private financial transactions.[4] Before exercising these authorities, the President is directed

---

[1] Pub. L. No. 95-223, tit. II, 91 Stat. 1626 (1977) (codified at 50 U.S.C. §§ 1701–6 (1982)).

[2] Id. § 1701 (1982).

[3] Id. The National Emergencies Act is Pub. L. No. 94–412, 90 Stat. 1255 (1976) (codified at 50 U.S.C. §§ 1601–51 (1982 & Supp. III 1985)). As discussed in Section D.2, this chapter, the termination provisions were amended in 1985.

[4] 50 U.S.C. §§ 1701–2. The key statutory language providing him with these authorities is at section 1702(a)(1):

[T]he President may ...
(A) investigate, regulate, or prohibit –
    (i) any transactions in foreign exchange,
    (ii) transfers of credit or payments between, by, through, or to any

184

"in every possible instance" to consult Congress. Moreover, if he does use IEEPA, he must immediately make a report to Congress explaining his actions.[5] The President can continue IEEPA sanctions until he decides to terminate the emergency, unless Congress acts to terminate it by joint resolution.[6]

IEEPA was passed in 1977 to replace the Trading with the Enemy Act (TWEA),[7] which had become "essentially an unlimited grant of authority for the President to exercise, at his discretion, broad powers in both the domestic and international arena, without congressional review."[8] TWEA is still applicable for wartime, and a grandfather provision keeps it as the statutory basis for peacetime controls against certain countries such as Cuba.

This chapter considers (A) the history of TWEA through 1977, (B) the continuing role of TWEA, (C) past and present uses of IEEPA, and (D) important current issues surrounding IEEPA. These issues concern the criteria and procedures for invoking IEEPA, the provisions for terminating a national emergency, and the substantive powers provided the President. As will be seen, IEEPA's procedural requirements make it an improvement over TWEA. Recent developments, however, suggest that IEEPA, too, has flaws – the criteria for invoking it are vague, Congress has very little to say about its use, and there is no effective way to terminate a use that becomes inappropriate as time passes.

The statute has become a favorite of President Reagan for imposing

> banking institution, to the extent that such transfers or payments involve any interest of any foreign country or a national thereof,
>   (iii) the importing or exporting of currency or securities; and
> (B) investigate, regulate, direct and compel, nullify, void, prevent or prohibit, any acquisition, holding, withholding, use, transfer, withdrawal, transportation, importation or exportation of, or dealing in, or exercising any right, power, or privilege with respect to, or transactions involving, any property in which any foreign country or a national thereof has any interest; by any person, or with respect to any property, subject to the jurisdiction of the United States.

The statute exempts from coverage (1) "any postal, telegraphic, telephonic, or other personal communication, which does not involve a transfer of anything of value" or (2) "donations . . . of articles, such as food, clothing, or medicine," unless the President makes certain determinations.

[5] Id. § 1703(a) and (b).

[6] Id. § 1622(a), (c), and (d).

[7] The current version of TWEA is found at 50 U.S.C. app. §§ 1–5 (1982). See the historical discussion in Section A, this chapter, citations to earlier versions.

[8] House Committee on International Relations, *Trading with the Enemy Act Reform Legislation*, H.R. Rep. No. 459, 95th Cong., 1st Sess. 7 (1977) [hereinafter House IEEPA Report]; see Senate Committee on Banking, Housing and Urban Affairs, *International Emergency Economic Powers Legislation*, S. Rep. 466, 95th Cong., 1st Sess. 2 (1977) [hereinafter Senate IEEPA Report].

sanctions. Finding "unusual and extraordinary" threats, he has invoked it in recent years against Nicaragua, South Africa, Libya, and Panama.

A. A BRIEF BUT COLORFUL HISTORY TO 1977

TWEA was passed in 1917 at the start of World War I in order to "define, regulate, and punish trading with the enemy." Section 5(b) gave the President broad powers over international financial transactions in wartime. The section then exempted "transactions to be executed wholly within the United States" and did not include a provision permitting use of the act during national emergencies.[9]

Nevertheless, confronted with a financial crisis in 1933, Franklin Roosevelt in his first official act as President cited section 5(b) to declare a national emergency and then ordered a bank holiday.[10] When Congress convened, it "approved and confirmed" the President's actions retroactively,[11] and amended section 5(b) to provide that its authorities could be used by the President when he declared a national emergency.[12] The sense of crisis is succinctly noted in a later Justice Department memorandum: "The legislative history of the Emergency Banking Act is short; only eight hours elapsed from the time the bill was introduced until it was signed into law. There were no committee reports. Indeed, the bill was not even in print at the time it was passed."[13]

The period after World War II witnessed several important uses of TWEA in peacetime. First, concerned with a balance-of-payments deficit in 1968, President Johnson imposed controls on the export of capital for foreign direct investment. Johnson cited section 5(b) and relied on Pres-

---

[9] TWEA, ch. 106, 40 Stat. 411 (1917). After World War I, a 1921 law that terminated certain wartime powers explicitly exempted TWEA because of the substantial amount of alien property still being administered by the Government. 41 Stat. 1359 (1921) (codified then at 50 U.S.C. § 33).

[10] Proclamation No. 2039, 48 Stat. 1689 (1933).

[11] Emergency Banking and Bank Conservation Act of 1933, ch. I, § 1, 48 Stat. 1, 1 (codified at 12 U.S.C. § 95b (1982)).

[12] Id. § 2, 48 Stat. 1–2 (codified as amended at 50 U.S.C. § 5(b) (1982)).

[13] Memorandum of the Department of Justice for the Special Committee on the Termination of the National Emergency, May 21, 1973, quoted in House IEEPA Report, supra note 8, at 4. The next major uses of TWEA occurred in relation to World War II. In 1940 and 1941 President Roosevelt issued several regulations freezing the U.S.-held assets of countries occupied by the Axis powers and then freezing the assets of the Axis countries themselves. In August 1941 the President ordered the imposition of consumer credit controls to help fight inflation. All these actions were later ratified by Congress. Id. at 5; see Staff of House Comm. on International Relations, 94th Cong., 2d Sess., *Trading with the Enemy: Legislative and Executive Documents Concerning Regulation of International Transactions in Time of Declared National Emergency* (Comm. Print 1976) [hereinafter House TWEA Documents].

ident Truman's declaration in 1950 of a national emergency because of
the Korean War, a declaration that had never been terminated.[14]

Second, also concerned with a balance-of-payments deficit, President
Nixon imposed a 10 percent surcharge on imports in August 1971. In
his proclamation, Nixon declared a national emergency but did not cite
section 5(b) among his statutory authorities for acting.[15] The surcharge
was terminated four months later[16] after the major industrial nations
reached an important agreement on currencies.[17] Nevertheless, importers
of Japanese zippers had brought suit challenging the surcharge.

A three-judge panel of the Customs Court found the surcharge invalid
because it was not within the President's authority under the existing
trade laws. The authority of section 5(b) to "regulate... importation"
was interpreted in a restrictive way not to include supplemental duties.[18]
The U.S. Court of Customs and Patent Appeals reversed, however. While
agreeing that the regular trade laws did not authorize the President's
acts,[19] the court found in an extensive opinion that Nixon had declared
a national emergency, that the surcharge was reasonably related to the
broad authorities of section 5(b), and that the surcharge was reasonably
related to the particular emergency.[20]

In a different context, TWEA was invoked to continue the Export
Administration Act (EAA) regulations when the Act lapsed on four occasions during the 1970s.[21]

Finally, TWEA was used to prohibit all, or most, trade and other
financial transactions with several countries that were in serious dis-
agreement with the United States. Always relying on the national emergency declared by President Truman for the Korean War, Presidents
imposed controls on China, North Korea, Cuba, Vietnam, and Cambodia
from the 1950s through the 1970s.[22] The extraterritorial scope of some

[14] Exec. Order No. 11,387, 3 C.F.R. 702 (1970). Legislation ended these controls
in 1974. House IEEPA Report, supra note 8, at 5.
[15] Proclamation No. 4074, 36 *Fed. Reg.* 15,724 (1971).
[16] Proclamation No. 4098, 36 *Fed. Reg.* 24,201 (1971).
[17] See *United States v. Yoshida International*, 526 F.2d 560, 568–9 (C.C.P.A. 1975).
[18] *Yoshida International v. United States*, 378 F. Supp. 1155 (Cust. Ct. 1974),
rev'd, 526 F.2d 560 (C.C.P.A. 1975).
[19] In 1974, however, Congress did pass a new law directing the President to impose
import surcharges or quotas when there was a balance-of-payments problem in certain
nonemergency situations. Trade Act of 1974, Pub. L. No. 93-618, § 2132, 88 Stat.
1978, 1987 (1975) (codified at 19 U.S.C. § 2132 (1982)).
[20] *Yoshida*, 526 F.2d at 572, 578–80.
[21] See House IEEPA Report, supra note 8, at 5; Note, "The International Emergency
Economic Powers Act: A Congressional Attempt to Control Presidential Emergency
Power," 96 *Harv. L.R.* 1102, 1105 n.14 (1983) [hereinafter Harvard IEEPA Note].
[22] See House IEEPA Report, supra note 8, at 5–6. Also during this period, TWEA

of these TWEA controls gave rise on occasion to vehement differences between the United States and its allies,[23] presaging the 1982 dispute over the U.S. pipeline controls under the EAA.[24]

By the early 1970s some of the questionable uses of TWEA and the President's growing predominance in foreign policy troubled many people in Congress and elsewhere. American foreign policy had usually been "achieved by a zealous patriotic rallying behind the Presidential colors" during the thirty years after World War II.[25] The increasingly imperial Presidency, however, came under heavy congressional fire in the wake of Vietnam and Watergate.

During 1972–7, Congress reasserted itself on a number of fronts, sparking a renaissance of congressional influence in the making of U.S. foreign policy. Most important and fundamental were procedural changes in the decision-making process. The War Powers Resolution was passed in 1973, and congressional oversight was increased over foreign assistance (on such issues as human rights), arms sales, the making of executive agreements, and the conduct of CIA operations. Congress also won some specific fights, such as a ban on CIA activity in Angola and the termination

was used to prohibit certain strategic trade with any communist country, including that by foreign subsidiaries of U.S. corporations. See id. at 6.

[23] For example, the TWEA controls against trading with the People's Republic of China extended in the early 1960s not only to U.S. citizens and corporations, but also to corporations that were "owned or controlled" by U.S. individuals or corporations. This led to a major diplomatic confrontation in the *Fruehauf* case. Fruehauf-France was a French corporation with its factory and employees in France. But it was 70% owned by Fruehauf, a U.S. corporation based in Detroit, and five of its eight directors were U.S. citizens. Fruehauf-France entered into a contract to provide truck trailers to another French corporation that was selling them to China. The U.S. Treasury Department contacted Fruehauf- Detroit and instructed it to direct Fruehauf-France to cancel the contract. Fruehauf-Detroit complied. However, a French court took the unusual step of appointing a temporary administrator for Fruehauf-France. He was charged with carrying out the contract, the wishes of the majority owner of the company notwithstanding. The U.S. Treasury declined to press the matter further, but the French had been outraged. See A. Lowenfeld, *Trade Controls for Political Ends* 91–105 (1983) [hereinafter, Lowenfeld, *Trade Controls*], which includes *Société Fruehauf Corp. v. Massardy* (Cour d'Appel, Paris 1965).

Similarly, several countries objected to the initially wide extraterritorial reach of the TWEA controls against Cuba. Canada was particularly upset because of the large number of U.S. subsidiaries in that country. See Lowenfeld, *Trade Controls*, supra, at 102.

[24] See discussion in Chapter 4 at notes 102–22 on the EAA, as well as note 58 in this chapter regarding a UK court ruling in 1987 against the extraterritorial reach of IEPPA controls. Note that, before 1977, the EAA did not provide authority for control over exports of non-U.S.-origin goods and technology by foreign subsidiaries of U.S. concerns.

[25] T. Franck and E. Weisband, *Foreign Policy by Congress* 3 (1979).

of military assistance and arms sales to Turkey after its invasion of Cyprus.[26]

Included in this congressional activity was an effort to review all of the President's emergency powers. In 1973, a Senate special committee initially began to study the possibility of terminating the much cited national emergency over Korea proclaimed by President Truman in 1950. The committee soon discovered that not one, but four national emergencies continued in effect. In addition to that over Korea, there was the 1933 one declared by President Roosevelt because of a financial crisis, a 1970 national emergency declared by President Nixon because of a Post Office strike, and Nixon's 1971 national emergency to deal with the balance of payments. The committee also discovered that "no inventory existed of the hundreds of statutes delegating powers to the President which were activated by these Presidential declarations."[27]

The committee's study led to passage in 1976 of the National Emergencies Act, which terminated all powers and authorities possessed by the President as a result of any past declaration of a national emergency.[28] (As discussed in Section C, the Act also provided new procedures for declaring, conducting, and terminating future emergencies.) Congress exempted from the Act's coverage, however, certain emergency power statutes then in use because of their importance to the continued functioning of the Government. The appropriate congressional committees were directed to determine within nine months what should be done with these statutes. Section 5(b) of TWEA was one of the exempted statutes.[29] Congress then proceeded the next year to amend TWEA to cover only wartime and existing declared emergencies. IEPPA was passed to handle new national emergencies.[30]

---

[26] For the War Powers Resolution, see Pub. L. No. 93-148, 87 Stat. 559 (1973) (codified at 50 U.S.C. §§1541–8 (1982)). On foreign assistance, see Chapter 3, Section B.1. On arms sales, see Chapter 4, Section C. Regarding executive agreements, see 1 U.S.C. § 112(b) (1982). On CIA oversight, see Resolution to Establish a Standing Committee of the Senate on Intelligence, and for Other Purposes, S. Res. 400, 94th Cong., 2d Sess., 122 *Cong. Rec.* 253 (1976). As for the CIA in Angola, see discussion of the Clark amendment in Chapter 3 at note 29. On Turkey, see Chapter 3 at note 33. An excellent discussion of this period is found in Franck and Weisband, supra note 25, especially at 61–3.

[27] House TWEA Documents, supra note 13, at iii (foreword by Cong. Bingham). The Senate Committee discovered the existence of approximately 470 permanent emergency statutes. S. Rep. No. 549, 93d Cong., 1st Sess. 17-46 (1973). See Note, "The National Emergency Dilemma: Balancing the Executive's Crisis Powers with the Need for Accountability," 52 *S. Cal. L. Rev.* 1453 (1979).

[28] 50 U.S.C. §§ 1601 and 1622.

[29] Id. § 1651.

[30] In doing so, Congress eliminated the exemption for TWEA under the National

B. TWEA IS STILL GOOD ENOUGH FOR
SOME SITUATIONS

The 1977 statute limited the President's power under TWEA to solely "[d]uring the time of war."[31] However, rather than requiring the President to declare a new national emergency in order to continue then existing TWEA sanctions, such as those against Cuba and Vietnam, Congress included a grandfather provision. It allows the President to continue to exercise "the authorities conferred upon [him] by section 5(b)... which were being exercised with respect to a country on July 1, 1977, as a result of a national emergency declared by the President before such date."[32] Consequently, economic sanctions today against Cuba, North Korea, Vietnam, and Cambodia are imposed pursuant to TWEA.[33]

Emergencies Act. Pub. L. 95-223, tit. I, § 101(a)(1), 91 Stat. 1625 (1977) (codified at 50 U.S.C. app. § 5 (1982)). See discussion of the amended TWEA and the new IEPPA in the next three sections. Note that the other congressional efforts in 1973–7 were clearly in some legislators' minds when addressing IEEPA. E.g., 123 *Cong. Rec.* 22,478 (1977) (statement of Rep. Leggett describing IEEPA as a means of counteracting "the flow of power over the past several decades from the legislative to the executive branch"); id. at 22,477 (Rep. Whalen describing IEEPA as "a necessary analog to the war powers legislation" that would "call the President to task before the Congress").

[31] 50 U.S.C. app. § 5(b) (1982). The prior language had read, "During the time of war or during any other period of national emergency declared by the President...."

[32] Pub. L. No. 95-223, § 101(b), 91 Stat. 1625 (1977), reprinted in 50 U.S.C. app. § 5 note (1982). The grandfather provision also allows the President to extend the exercise of these authorities on an annual basis. Id.; see, e.g., Extension of the Exercise of Certain Authorities Under the Trading with the Enemy Act, 52 *Fed. Reg.* 33,397 (1987). For an extended discussion of the grandfather provision, see *Regan v. Wald*, 468 U.S. 222 (1984).

[33] See 31 C.F.R. pts. 500, 515, 520 (1987); G. Boyd, "Reagan Acts to Tighten Trade Embargo of Cuba," *N.Y. Times*, Aug. 23, 1986, at 3, col. 3. The EAA is also used. China was another country subject to some TWEA controls in 1977. However, the President ended the use of section 5(b) against China in 1980 and cannot now resurrect them. See *Regan v. Wald*, 468 U.S. at 260–1. Other, narrower economic controls continue under TWEA because of the grandfather provision. These include prohibitions on persons within the United States being involved in the shipment of merchandise between a foreign country and most communist countries. 31 C.F.R. pt. 505. The general prohibition on these transactions is narrowed by other regulations that grant a general license for most cases. Another set of regulations that continue under TWEA deal with assets of certain countries, or nationals of those countries, that were wholly blocked during World War II. 31 C.F.R. pt. 520. They have no current importance in East–West trade. S. Sommerfield, "Treasury Regulation of Foreign Assets and Trade," in *A Lawyer's Guide to International Business Transactions* 278 (W. Surrey and D. Wallace eds. 1977). The regulations now apply to the World War II blocked assets of Estonia, the German Democratic Republic, Latvia, Lithuania, and their nationals. 31 C.F.R. § 520.101.

Note that the law that included IEEPA also amended the EAA to confer nonemergency authority under the EAA to control non-U.S.-origin exports by foreign subsid-

Present laws for a declared national emergency

A question did arise as to whether the scope of the specific controls existing in 1977 against one of these countries could be expanded under TWEA, or whether resort to IEEPA was needed. In 1984 in *Regan v. Wald*, the Supreme Court by a 5 to 4 vote effectively decided that reliance on TWEA was sufficient for new controls against the countries subject to the grandfathered controls.[34]

C. PAST AND PRESENT USES OF IEEPA

Except for the countries still covered by TWEA, IEEPA provides the statutory basis for economic sanctions for foreign policy reasons during a declared national emergency.[35] In the statute's history of about eleven years, Presidents have resorted to it seven times for six distinct purposes.[36] The pace has accelerated. President Reagan has invoked IEEPA sanctions four times since April 1985 – against Nicaragua, South Africa, Libya, and Panama.

IEEPA was first used in the Iranian hostage crisis. The American embassy had been seized on November 4, 1979, and U.S. diplomatic per-

---

iaries of U.S. concerns. Pub. L. No. 95-223, tit. III, 91 Stat. 1625 (1977); see Senate IEEPA Report, supra note 8, at 6.

[34] *Regan v. Wald* involved a challenge to controls on travel to Cuba that were considerably tightened in 1982. The controls could not be justified under IEEPA since President Reagan did not declare a new national emergency or comply with IEEPA's reporting requirements to Congress.

The issue under TWEA was whether the revised, more restrictive travel regulations were an exercise of an authority covered by the grandfather provision. In 1977 a general regulation prohibited all transactions involving property in which Cuba or Cuban nationals had any interest whatsoever, unless specifically authorized by the Secretary of the Treasury. However, another regulation permitted by a general license most travel-related transactions with Cuba and Cuban nationals – i.e., no specific approval was required from the Treasury Department. Nevertheless, writing for the majority, Justice Rehnquist reasoned that the existence of the general regulation meant that the "authority" being exercised in 1977 was to regulate all property transactions with Cuba, including travel-related transactions. *Regan v. Wald*, 468 U.S. 232–40. For a discussion of the decision, see "The Supreme Court, 1983 Term," 93 *Harv. L. Rev.* 87, 184–95 (1984); see generally "Are the U.S. Treasury's Assets Control Regulations a Fair and Effective Tool of U.S. Foreign Policy? The Case of Cuba," 1985 *Am. Soc'y Int'l L.* 169.

The regulations for the other countries still covered by TWEA also start with a general regulation prohibiting all transactions, unless specifically authorized. 31 C.F.R. § 500.201–5. Consequently, it would seem that any new controls against those countries would similarly be upheld under TWEA.

[35] When IEEPA has been invoked, Presidents have usually cited nonemergency statutes as well, but the regulations are then regularly issued pursuant to IEEPA. (See the following discussion of IEEPA uses.) This probably reflects the fewer procedural requirements and more sweeping powers under IEEPA.

[36] See discussion about another possible use – against the Soviet invasion of Afghanistan – at note 69, this chapter.

sonnel were being held hostage. Receiving reports that the Iranian Government was about to withdraw its billions of dollars on deposit in U.S. banks, President Carter declared a national emergency on November 14 and, pursuant to IEEPA, blocked the transfer of all property of the Iranian Government.[37] The order froze about $12 billion of Iranian funds in U.S. banks or in the possession of U.S. corporations, whether located in the United States or abroad.[38] The IEEPA controls were later expanded to cut off almost all trade with Iran. Also, except for that of journalists, travel was restricted by prohibiting any financial transactions within Iran by U.S. citizens.[39]

In 1981, President Carter and then President Reagan took a number of steps to implement the so-called Algiers Agreements that resulted in the release of the hostages and the termination of the U.S. sanctions. These included ordering the transfer of billions of dollars back to Iran or to trust funds,[40] as well as suspending claims against Iran that were pending in U.S. courts.[41] All the Iranian sanctions and the actions to end them were upheld in U.S. courts under IEEPA,[42] except that the Supreme Court in *Dames & Moore v. Regan* looked to additional authority to uphold the suspension of claims then pending in U.S. courts.[43]

The second use of IEEPA was to preserve the Export Administration Act regulations when that statute twice lapsed because of deadlocks within Congress.[44] When the EAA expired on October 14, 1983, President Reagan declared the first of two national emergencies to continue the existing EAA regulations.[45] On December 5, 1983, Congress reinstated and extended the EAA and then later reextended it through March

---

[37] 15 *Weekly Comp. Pres. Doc.* 2117 (Nov. 14, 1979); Exec. Order 12,170, 44 *Fed. Reg.* 65,729 (1979).

[38] R. Carswell and R. Davis, "Crafting the Financial Settlement," in *American Hostages in Iran* 201, 203–7 (P. Kreisberg ed. 1985).

[39] E.g., Exec. Order No. 12,205, 3 C.F.R. 248 (1981); Exec. Order No. 12,211, 3 C.F.R. 253 (1981). There were a number of presidential orders under IEEPA during the crisis. A detailed account of the events (including the use of sanctions) is chronicled in *American Hostages in Iran*, supra note 38, and G. Sick, *All Fall Down* (1985).

[40] E.g., Exec. Order No. 12,227, 3 C.F.R. 105 (1982).

[41] E.g., Exec. Order No. 12,294, 3 C.F.R. 139 (1982).

[42] *Dames & Moore v. Regan*, 453 U.S. 654, 675–90 (1981); see also *American International Group v. Islamic Republic of Iran*, 657 F.2d 430 (D.C. Cir. 1981).

[43] *Dames & Moore*, 453 U.S. at 675–90; see discussion in Section D.3, this chapter.

[44] As also discussed in Chapter 4 at note 64, the Export Administration Act Amendments of 1985, which extended the EAA of 1979, had a long and difficult birth in Congress.

[45] Exec. Order No. 12,444, 48 *Fed. Reg.* 48,215 (1983). The EAA was originally to expire on September 30, 1983, but on that day Congress extended the Act's life through October 14. See Pub. L. No. 98-108, 98th Cong., 1st Sess. (1983).

30, 1984.[46] The EAA then expired again, so President Reagan declared another national emergency and continued the existing EAA regulations.[47] That emergency finally ended when the Export Administration Act Amendments of 1985 became law on July 12. The EAA now is not due to expire until September 30, 1989.[48]

IEEPA's third application came on May 1, 1985, when President Reagan declared a national emergency and ordered a number of actions against Nicaragua. These included a ban on import of Nicaraguan goods; a ban on export of goods to Nicaragua, unless destined for the U.S.-backed contras; a prohibition on Nicaraguan air carriers flying to or from points in the United States; and a prohibition on Nicaraguan vessels entering U.S. ports.[49]

IEEPA sanctions against South Africa followed shortly after those against Nicaragua. On September 9, 1985, Reagan declared a national

---

[46] The December 5 reinstatement was through February 29, 1984, and can be found in Pub. L. No. 98-207, 98th Cong., 1st Sess. (1983). See also Exec. Order No. 12,451 (Dec. 20, 1983), 48 *Fed. Reg.* 56,563 (1983) (rescinding the presidential declaration of emergency in Exec. Order No. 12,444). Congress then extended the EAA until March 30, 1984. Pub. L. No. 98-222, 98th Cong., 2d Sess. (1984).

[47] Exec. Order No. 12,470, 49 *Fed. Reg.* 13099 (1984). On March 28, 1985, when the declared emergency had lasted for one year (and would have been automatically terminated), the President continued it and kept the regulations in effect under IEEPA. 50 *Fed. Reg.* 12,513 (1985).

[48] 50 U.S.C. app. § 2419 (Supp. III 1985). For a thorough discussion of the EAA of 1979 under IEEPA, see J. Harris and J. Bialos, "The Strange New World of United States Export Controls Under the International Emergency Economic Powers Act," 18 *Vand. J. Transnat'l L.* 71 (1985). See also *Nuclear Pacific, Inc. v. United States*, No. C84-49R (W.D. Wash. June 8, 1984) (EAA regulations upheld under IEPPA, though court allowed judicial review).

[49] Exec. Order 12,513 3 C.F.R. 342 (1986). See also the White House Statement and the President's Message to Congress, May 1, 1985, reprinted in 85 *Dept. of State Bull.* 74 (July 1985). The Nicaraguan Trade Control Regulations, which implement the President's decision, are at 50 *Fed. Reg.* 19,890 (1985). The White House statement noted that the United States would also notify Nicaragua of its intent to terminate its Treaty of Friendship, Commerce, and Navigation with Nicaragua.
Reagan's order relied primarily on IEEPA. Exec. Order 12,513, however, also cited 50 U.S.C. § 191 (1982). That statute authorizes the President to govern the movement of foreign-flag vessels in U.S. territorial waters "[w]henever the President finds that the security of the United States is endangered by reason of . . . disturbances or threatened disturbances of the international relations of the United States." See discussion of port visits in Chapter 3 at notes 94–7. The implementing regulations, however, cited only IEEPA. 50 *Fed. Reg.* 19,890 (1985). Neither the Executive Order nor the implementing regulations cited any statutory authority, other than IEEPA, for prohibiting flights of Nicaraguan air carriers, in spite of the considerable nonemergency statutory authority that exists. See discussion in Chapter 3 at notes 98–109. As for the ban on U.S. exports, since the export regulations were then based on IEEPA because of the lapse of the EAA, no citation to the EAA was appropriate.

emergency and imposed the new sanctions against South Africa in response to a growing public outcry and imminent passage of sanctions by Congress.[50] Though not comprehensive, the sanctions were many and varied, affecting U.S. government programs, exports, imports, and private financial transactions. They reflected the fact that partial sanctions were already in place against South Africa, as well as the provisions of the congressional bill.

As for government programs, the President proclaimed that all U.S. firms in South Africa should adhere to fair labor principles, also known as the Sullivan Principles.[51] Existing export restrictions were expanded to include (1) a ban on exports of computers and related goods and technology to the South African security forces or any other governmental entity enforcing apartheid and (2) a ban on all exports of goods or technology that might be used in a South African nuclear facility, with certain exceptions.[52]

The major import control was the prohibition on imports of South African krugerrands.[53] Also prohibited were imports of arms, ammunition, or military vehicles produced in South Africa.[54]

Finally, financial institutions in the United States were prohibited from directly or indirectly extending loans or other credits to the South African Government or related entities. Even before Reagan's action, several

---

[50] Exec. Order No. 12,532, 3 C.F.R. 387 (1986). See also the President's Remarks, Sept. 9, 1985, reprinted in 85 *Dept. of State Bull.* 1 (Oct. 1985).

[51] Exec. Order No. 12,532, § 2, supra note 50. To encourage adherence, the President directed that no U.S. government agency could intercede with any foreign government regarding the exports of any U.S. firm employing more than twenty-five individuals in South Africa if that U.S. employer did not adhere to the fair labor principles. Id. Reagan's order also contained benefits as well as sanctions. For example, Reagan directed the Secretary of State to increase the amount of funds allocated for scholarships and for legal assistance for disadvantaged South Africans. Exec. Order No. 12,532, § 8, supra note 50.

[52] Exec. Order No. 12,532, § 1, supra note 50. The implementing regulations are at 50 *Fed. Reg.* 47,363 (1985); which cite for authority both Exec. Order No. 12,532 (which had cited IEEPA and the EAA, among others) and section 6(n) of the EAA, as amended by the 1985 Act. 50 U.S.C. app. § 2405(n) (1982 & Supp. III 1985). The 1985 amendments essentially revoked three regulations written by the Reagan Administration that had narrowed the export controls against South Africa.

[53] In his initial order, Reagan directed that only the possibility of an import ban be studied. Exec. Order No. 12,532, § 5. However, on October 1, he ordered a ban, citing only IEEPA. Exec. Order No. 12,535, 3 C.F.R. 393 (1986). The President also directed the Secretary of the Treasury to study the feasibility of the United States minting and issuing gold coins. Exec. Order No. 12,532, § 5(b), supra note 50. This was apparently a way to offset the demand for the South African coins.

[54] Exec. Order No. 12,532, § 1(d), supra note 50. This essentially implemented an earlier UN resolution. The Executive Order cited not only IEEPA, but also the UN Participation Act, 22 U.S.C. § 287, discussed in Chapter 8 at notes 31–43. Imports of these items were already minimal.

major banks had decided not to extend new loans to the South African Government. This decision helped trigger a temporary financial crisis in South Africa in August–September 1985 and contributed to continuing financial pressures on the country.[55]

These sanctions against South Africa were effectively superseded by the more comprehensive sanctions passed by Congress in September 1986 over President Reagan's veto. The Reagan Administration then allowed the emergency to lapse in September 1987 when it came up for renewal.[56]

Libya was the target of the next use of IEEPA. In January 1986, Reagan declared a national emergency and imposed very comprehensive economic sanctions against Libya. He acted in the wake of terrorist attacks at the Rome and Vienna airports. These sanctions include a ban on almost all imports from Libya and exports to it, a prohibition on any new loans or other credits to Libya, financial controls that effectively prohibit most travel to Libya or living there, and a freeze on all Libyan property interests in the United States or under the control of any U.S. person, including overseas branches of U.S. entities.[57]

The Libyan sanctions are similar in scope to the 1979–81 sanctions against Iran or the continuing TWEA sanctions against Cuba, except for somewhat narrower claims of extraterritorial jurisdiction. Jurisdiction for the Libyan sanctions is generally extended only over "United States persons," which are defined to mean U.S. citizens, juridical persons organized under U.S. laws (e.g., corporations), and persons in the United States. While this encompasses overseas branches, it does not include foreign subsidiaries, affiliates, and licensees of U.S. companies.[58]

---

[55] Exec. Order No. 12,532, § 1, supra note 50. Concerning the earlier actions of private banks, see discussion at beginning of Chapter 6.

[56] For an analysis of the Comprehensive Anti-Apartheid Act of 1986, see Chapter 3, Section A, and other chapters of this book, depending on the type of sanction. The termination issue is discussed at notes 89–101, this chapter.

[57] Exec. Order 12,543, 12,544, 3 C.F.R. 181, 183 (1987). The first Executive Order, dealing with all the sanctions except the asset freeze, cites IEEPA; sects. 504 and 505 of the International Security and Development Cooperation Act of 1985, Pub. L. No. 99-83, 99 Stat. 190 (codified at 22 U.S.C. §§ 2349aa-8 and 9 (Supp. IV 1986)) [hereinafter foreign assistance act of 1985], discussed in Chapter 5 at notes 54–7; and sec. 1114 of the Federal Aviation Act of 1958, as amended, 49 U.S.C. § 1514 (1982 & Supp. III 1985), discussed in Chapter 3 at notes 106–11. The second Executive Order, which froze Libyan assets, cited only IEEPA. The principal implementing regulations are at 51 *Fed. Reg.* 1354, 2462 (1986); both specifically cite only IEEPA. For a discussion of the Libyan controls, including analyses of their effectiveness, see generally U.S. General Accounting Office, *International Trade: Libyan Sanctions* (1987); J. Bialos and K. Juster, "The Libyan Sanctions: A Rational Response to State-Sponsored Terrorism?" 4 *Va. J. Int'l L.* 799 (1986).

[58] See 31 C.F.R. § 550.308 (1987) (definition of "United States person"); Bialos and Juster, supra note 57, at 814–24; compare also with the pipeline sanctions under the EAA, discussed in Chapter 4, at notes 102–22.

Nevertheless, even this relatively "modest" extraterritorial sweep encountered a considerable challenge in fall 1987 when a trial court in the United Kingdom ruled that Bankers Trust Company, a U.S. corporation, was obligated to pay the Libyan Arab Foreign Bank $292.5 million in funds that the Libyan bank had deposited with Bankers Trust and that the U.S. bank claimed had been frozen by President Reagan's order of January 1986. About half of the money had been in the London branch of Bankers Trust and the other half was money that the bank had failed to transfer, as directed by the Libyan bank, to its London branch before the freeze. In reaching its decision, the trial court concluded that the law of the place (i.e., UK law) applied to accounts in the United Kingdom, even at the branch of a U.S. bank. Rather than appeal this unfavorable opinion, Bankers Trust paid the Libyan bank the $292.5 million, plus $28 million in interest. The U.S. Treasury Department granted the necessary license for Bankers Trust to make the payment to a Libyan entity.[59]

The most recent use of IEEPA was against Panama on April 8, 1988, as part of the escalating U.S. pressures against General Noriega. President Reagan invoked the law to prevent payments by U.S. individuals or corporations, whether located in the United States or in Panama, to the Noriega regime and also to help freeze Panamanian government assets that were in the United States.[60]

D. CURRENT ISSUES SURROUNDING IEEPA

IEEPA was, by all accounts, designed to grant the President limited emergency powers in peacetime. The principal concerns with TWEA during peacetime were that it granted such broad powers, that Presidents had used them for actions unrelated to the declared national emergency, and that there was no congressional review.[61]

With IEEPA, Congress tried to improve the situation by narrowing the President's authorities and subjecting them to "strict procedural limitations, including consultation with Congress, periodic reporting requirements, and provision for termination of states of emergency by Congress." At the same time, Congress recognized that the President's

---

[59] *Libyan Arab Foreign Bank v. Bankers Trust Co.*, Q.B. Comm'l Ct. (Sept. 2, 1987), reprinted in 26 *Int'l Legal Materials* 1600 (1987); Marcom, "Bankers Trust Cleared by U.S. to Repay Libya," *Wall St. J.*, Oct. 13, 1987, at 31, col. 1.

[60] 53 *Fed. Reg.* 12,134 (1988); see Chapter 3, at note 13.

[61] E.g., *Dames & Moore*, 453 U.S. at 672–3; House IEEPA Report, supra note 8, at 1–2, 9–11; see Senate IEEPA Report, supra note 8, at 1–6.

powers "should be sufficiently broad and flexible to enable [him] to respond as appropriate and necessary to unforeseen contingencies."[62]

After more than ten years, IEEPA is obviously alive and robust. However, IEEPA's legislative' history, its provisions, and its uses raise important questions. Especially worth analyzing are the criteria and procedures for invoking IEEPA, the provisions for terminating an emergency, and the substantive powers provided the President.

1. Are we falling victim to dubious national emergencies?

"[E]mergencies are by their nature rare and brief, and are not equated with normal, ongoing problems. . . . A state of national emergency should not be a normal state of affairs."[63] With that viewpoint motivating some of IEEPA's drafters, the statute contained several provisions that were designed in part to limit resort to IEEPA. First, in contrast to TWEA's failure to define "national emergency," IEEPA provides that its authorities are to be exercised for an "unusual and extraordinary threat, which has its source in whole or substantial part outside the United States, to the national security, foreign policy, or economy of the United States." Second, the President must declare a national emergency for that situation before using IEEPA's powers.[64] Third, he is to consult Congress "in every possible instance." Finally, he must report immediately to Congress on his reasons for invoking IEEPA and on the actions he has taken.[65]

In practice, however, these provisions create few roadblocks for the President. If he wants to use IEEPA even in minor disputes or to avoid an airing of issues in Congress, there is little in the statute to stop him. The criteria of an "unusual and extraordinary threat" are subject to many interpretations. Indeed, the statute elsewhere authorizes the President to issue regulations "prescribing definitions" under the statute![66] Moreover, declaring an emergency requires only a brief executive order, which often does little more than recite the statutory criteria as a litany.[67]

Consultation with Congress is only encouraged and not mandatory. Also, nothing requires that the consultation be extensive or designed to

---

[62] House IEEPA Report, supra note 8, at 10–11; see Harvard IEEPA Note, supra note 21, at 1106.

[63] House IEEPA Report, supra note 8, at 10.

[64] 50 U.S.C. § 1701.

[65] Id. at § 1703.

[66] Id. at § 1704.

[67] E.g., see Exec. Order 12,170, 43 *Fed. Reg.* 65,729 (1979) (declaring national emergency for situation with Iran).

influence policy. Although the report required for IEEPA's use does ensure some presidential rationale for the actions, the White House is accustomed to issuing statements and reports routinely. The reporting requirement thus is probably not an important deterrent on the President.

In reviewing the past uses of IEPPA, the early experience seems consistent with the purposes of the Act. The Iranian hostage crisis was a fast-developing situation that had significant impact on U.S. foreign policy. Quick action was needed to block the withdrawal of Iran's deposits from U.S. banks and to impose other sanctions.[68]

Indeed, it is hard to understand why the statute was not also invoked in response to the Soviet invasion of Afghanistan. Possibly, the Administration was being cautious about its use of IEEPA or thought that it already had sufficient statutory powers to impose sanctions against the Soviet Union.[69] However, as demonstrated by the ITC's rejection of efforts to restrict ammonia imports, the Administration was hampered at least by its lack of authority to impose import controls.

Reagan's initial use of IEEPA – to continue the export regulations

---

[68] See Staff of House Comm. on Banking, Finance and Urban Affairs, 97th Cong., 1st Sess., Iran: *The Financial Aspects of the Hostage Settlement Agreement* iii (Comm. Print No. 5, 1981) (letter of transmittal by Rep. St. Germain).

[69] The actual reasons for not invoking it do not appear to be given in the available literature. No emergency was declared when the invasion occurred in late December 1979, about seven weeks after President Carter declared the emergency for the Iranian hostage crisis. Instead, among other steps, Carter used his nonemergency powers to restrict exports to the Soviet Union (see Chapter 4, Section A.3) and to try to restrict ammonia imports (see Chapter 5, Section B.5). Whatever the initial reasons for not invoking IEEPA, one participant in the process observed that resorting to it months later would have been difficult when the Carter Administration was trying to boycott the Olympics. Since IEEPA was not used to take the wide-ranging initial steps, it would have seemed strange to invoke it to stop athletes from traveling to Moscow. This later hesitancy not to employ IEEPA partly explains the strained use of section 15 of the EAA to stop NBC's payments for the Moscow Olympics (see discussion in Chapter 6 at notes 26–32). Telephone interview with Joseph Onek, former Deputy Counsel to President Carter (Mar. 14, 1986).

It should be noted that in an executive order on April 17, 1980, Carter referred to "the added unusual and extraordinary threat to the national security, foreign policy and economy of the United States created by subsequent events in Iran and neighboring countries, including the Soviet invasion of Afghanistan, with respect to which I hereby declare a national emergency...." The only sanctions that Carter ordered, however, were additional ones against Iran. Further Prohibitions on Transactions with Iran, Exec. Order 12,211, 45 Fed. Reg. 26,665 (1980). At least one scholar has concluded that this constituted a declaration of national emergency for the Afghanistan situation. M. Malloy, "The Iran Crisis: Law Under Pressure," 15 *Wisc. Int'l L.J.* 15, 23 n.44 (1984). However, in neither the April Executive Order nor any other does it seem that the President invoked any emergency powers against the Soviets because of Afghanistan. To the contrary, he explicitly cited nonemergency statutes for his authority, including the controls on payments for Olympics.

when the EAA lapsed – also seems consistent with the intentions of the Act's drafters. TWEA had been employed to fill in during earlier lapses, Administration witnesses had mentioned this as one of IEEPA's possible uses during hearings on the proposed law, and the legislative history appears devoid of any objection to this future use.[70]

Resorting to IEEPA for Nicaragua, South Africa, and Libya, however, seems questionable. These uses suggest that the statute can and will be invoked whenever the President wants to draw on its great powers, whether or not there is a genuine emergency.

Invoking IEEPA against *Nicaragua* seems more a case of a President wanting to avoid a protracted and difficult struggle with Congress than a response to an "unusual and extraordinary threat." To be sure, President Reagan's message to Congress and other Administration statements did list some recent events, such as the visit of Nicaraguan President Ortega to Moscow, but none demonstrated a sudden deterioration in the Reagan Administration's long-festering relations with the Sandinista Government.[71]

The more obvious triggering event was the rejection by the U.S. House of Representatives of Reagan's proposal for assistance to the contras. Resort to IEPPA was part of a prolonged struggle between Congress (especially the House) and the Administration over U.S. policy in Central America. The Administration apparently decided to circumvent the normal legislative approach and invoke IEEPA to impose a trade embargo.

Although the President's action was seemingly a perversion of the statute's purpose, it triggered only sporadic questioning in Congress or elsewhere.[72] Probably the most visible criticism came from Garry Trudeau in his popular comic strip *Doonesbury*. In part, opponents of the Administration's policies found it harder to be critical of economic sanctions against the Sandinista Government than to oppose the idea of "covert aid" to the contras, who were using force to overturn a recognized government. The Reagan Administration, with considerable evidence, had painted the Sandinista Government's record on human rights and other matters most unfavorably. Indeed, within a few months, several legislators had even reconsidered their opposition to aiding the contras. In

---

[70] Note that the export laws were used primarily during the TWEA period for national security purposes. On IEEPA's legislative history, see Harris and Bialos, supra note 48, at 79.

[71] See Reagan's Message to Congress and the White House Statement, reprinted in 85 *Dept. of State Bull.* 74 (July 1985).

[72] E.g., *N.Y. Times*, May 8, 1985, at I7, col. 1; 131 *Cong. Rec.* H2,751 (daily ed. May 1, 1985) (statement of Rep. Bonker questioning whether the requisite emergency existed).

DOONESBURY / BY GARRY TRUDEAU

July 1985, the Administration went back to Congress and successfully reversed the earlier House vote. Congress authorized $27 million in financial support, though limited it to "humanitarian assistance."[73]

The use of IEEPA sanctions against *South Africa* was at least as questionable as it was in the Nicaraguan case, though for different reasons. Turmoil was growing in South Africa. As President Reagan reported to

[73] 1985 foreign assistance act, supra note 58, § 722(g).

Congress, "The recent declaration of a state of emergency in 36 magisterial districts by the Government of South Africa, the mass arrests and detentions, and the ensuing financial crisis are of direct concern to the foreign policy and economy of the United States."[74] It was not clear, however, why the threat was so "unusual and extraordinary" that it was necessary to declare a national emergency,[75] especially since legislation to impose sanctions was already far along in Congress. A conference bill had passed the House by an overwhelming margin and was expected to pass the Senate.[76]

Even the Reagan Administration's public statements suggest that its chief aim in employing IEEPA was to preempt Congress. This was partly because Reagan believed that the congressional sanctions went too far, suggesting that they somehow might "damage the economic well-being of millions of people in South and southern Africa."[77] But Reagan also must have hoped to garner political credit for acting against apartheid.[78] The political posturing becomes evident when one compares the Reagan sanctions with those then pending in Congress. The similarities far outnumbered the differences. All the important sanctions that Reagan imposed were also found in substantially similar form in the conference bill.[79]

The conference bill had only one major additional provision. If the President determined that South Africa had not made significant progress over the next twelve months in eliminating apartheid, he was to recommend which additional, designated sanctions should be imposed. Though some of the alternatives were major, there was also a catchall of "[o]ther economic or political sanctions."[80] Consequently, despite con-

---

[74] 21 *Weekly Comp. Pres. Doc.* 1055 (Sept. 9, 1985).

[75] The U.S. sanctions, such as the ban on U.S. bank loans to the South African Government, were not going to help the financial crisis and possibly would aggravate it. Senator Garn briefly questioned the existence of a genuine national emergency at a hearing on December 4, 1985, and encountered surprising agreement from David Mulford, Assistant Secretary of the Treasury. *Controls on the Export of Capital from the United States: Hearings on S. 812 Before the Senate Comm. on Banking, Housing, and Urban Affairs*, 99th Cong., 1st Sess. 145 (1985).

[76] See *Wash. Post*, Aug. 1, 1985, at A1, col. 6 (Senate–House conferees agreeing on conference bill). The House approved the conference bill on August 1 by a 380 to 48 margin. *Wash. Post*, Aug. 2, 1985, at A28, col. 5.

[77] President's Remarks, Sept. 9, 1985, 21 *Weekly Comp. Pres. Doc.* 1054 (Sept. 16, 1985).

[78] It also appeared unlikely that Reagan could have stopped the congressional legislation simply by opposing it. See *Wash. Post*, Sept. 10, 1985, at A11, col. 1.

[79] Compare the Reagan sanctions, detailed earlier, with the proposed Anti-Apartheid Act of 1985, found in Conference Report, H.R. Rep. No. 242, 99th Cong., 1st Sess. (1985); see *Wash. Post*, Sept. 10, 1985, at A10, col. 3.

[80] Anti-Apartheid Act of 1985, § 16(c)(3), supra note 79. The full list of alternatives was a ban on new commercial investment in South Africa; a denial of MFN status

siderable rhetoric on all sides about how this provision made the conference bill stronger than the Reagan sanctions,[81] the difference was more apparent than real. Reagan would have had the discretion to make the determination about progress, and then only after a one-year period. Moreover, the residual clause would have allowed him to recommend a very minor next step, if he so desired.

Questions can also be raised about the use of IEEPA against *Libya* on January 7, 1986. As with Nicaragua, U.S. relations with Libya had been fractious for years, and the United States had already imposed import limits on oil and passport restrictions under nonemergency statutes.[82]

The event that triggered the imposition of comprehensive IEEPA sanctions was Colonel Qaddafi's apparent support of the cold-blooded attacks at the Rome and Vienna airports in December 1985. In all, nineteen people, including five Americans, were killed. Outrageous as the attacks were,[83] it should still be asked whether there was sufficient justification to declare a national emergency.

President Reagan already had available particularly broad nonemergency authorities. Congress had added provisions to the 1985 foreign assistance bill authorizing the President to cut off all imports as well as exports from Libya.[84] IEEPA, however, did uniquely provide the President with power to freeze Libyan assets and to ban travel to or in Libya. Hundreds of millions of dollars in Libyan assets were apparently vulnerable to a freeze.[85] As for travel, the United States had earlier tried to limit travel to Libya by imposing a prohibition on the use of U.S. passports. Thousands of U.S. citizens, however, continued to journey to Libya

---

to South Africa; a ban on importation of coal, uranium ore, and uranium oxide from South Africa and Namibia; and other economic or political sanctions.

[81] E.g., see *N.Y. Times*, Sept. 12, 1985, at 1, col. 2; *N.Y. Times*, Sept. 11, 1985, at 10, col. 4; *Wash. Post*, Sept. 10, 1985, at A11, col. 1.

[82] See discussion in Chapter 5 at notes 42–5, regarding the limit on oil imports and in Chapter 3 at notes 114–6, regarding the limit on the use of U.S. passports.

[83] There was considerable evidence of Libyan complicity. See Department of State Report on Libya Under Qaddafi, reprinted in *N.Y. Times*, Jan. 9, 1986, at A6, col. 1. Some Europeans questioned the evidence, however, even suggesting that the attackers had been trained in Syria or Syrian-held territory. This position might be explained by the reluctance among Europeans to join the U.S. sanctions. *N.Y. Times*, Jan. 19, 1986, at 10, col. 3; *N.Y. Times*, Jan. 12, 1986, at E1, col. 1.

[84] See discussion in Chapter 5 at notes 54–7. Possibly, there was some concern that the use of nonemergency statutes would require adhering to the new "contract sanctity" provisions in the Export Administration Act Amendments of 1985, discussed in Chapter 4 at notes 76–86. However, the sweeping provisions in the 1985 foreign assistance act that authorized a trade embargo against Libya were passed after the 1985 Act, and they specifically applied "[n]otwithstanding any other provision of law." 22 U.S.C. § 2349aa–8 (Supp. IV 1986).

[85] *N.Y. Times*, Jan. 12, 1986, at E1, col. 1; see UK bank case discussed in notes 59–60, above.

without using their passports. Under IEEPA, all financial transactions related to travel, including purchases of transportation, lodging, and meals, could be and were prohibited. This effectively prohibited travel to or in Libya.[86]

Given the American public's outrage toward Libya, the President could have gone to Congress and obtained special nonemergency laws authorizing the asset freeze and travel ban. This Executive Branch–Congressional effort would have highlighted the shared national attitude toward Libya. This normal legislative approach, however, would have taken a little more time and would have required the President to share center stage.

In sum, recent experience with IEEPA raises concerns about its possible casual use for dubious national emergencies.[87]

It is unlikely that the courts will step in to limit resort to IEEPA. They will analyze the specific measures taken in a national emergency to ascertain whether they are authorized under IEEPA. There is, however, nearly complete judicial deference to the President's determination that a national emergency exists. Considering President Nixon's import surcharge, the court in *Yoshida* observed that "courts will not normally review the essentially political questions surrounding the declaration or continuance of a national emergency."[88]

If limits are to be imposed on resort to IEEPA's broad authorities, the ball is definitely back with Congress. Alternatively, one must ignore the omens in recent history and rely on the future exercise of self-discipline by Presidents.

2. Will it ever end?

IEEPA's drafters envisioned the statute's use for national emergencies that were "rare and brief" and not for "normal, ongoing problems."[89]

---

[86] *N.Y. Times*, Jan. 31, 1986, at A8, col. 3; Jan. 9, 1986, at A8, col. 4.

[87] As discussed earlier, this is not what Congress intended in 1977. The drafters were probably more optimistic about the effectiveness of the consultation provision. However, that provision apparently has not had much effect on Presidential decision making under IEEPA, the War Powers Resolution, or other acts that included it. See Franck and Weisband, supra note 25, at 71–6 (experience with War Powers Resolution).

The drafters definitely saw the concurrent resolution provision for terminating emergencies as an important safeguard against IEEPA's casual use. House IEEPA Report, supra note 8, at 11. As discussed below at notes 92–6, these hopes were quashed by the *Chadha* decision.

[88] *Yoshida International*, 526 F.2d at 579, 581 n.32; *Sardino v. Federal Reserve Bank*, 361 F.2d 106, 109 (2d Cir.), cert. denied, 385 U.S. 898 (1966); *Beacon Products Corp. v. Reagan*, 633 F. Supp. 1191, 1194–5 (D. Mass. 1986), aff'd, 814 F.2d 1 (1st Cir. 1987).

[89] House IEEPA Report, supra note 8, at 10. A related, and major, concern of the

IEEPA and the National Emergencies Act include three methods for terminating a national emergency and thereby limiting the duration of the emergency powers.

Two are housekeeping provisions to ensure that a declared national emergency does not needlessly continue. First, the President can unilaterally terminate the emergency.[90] Second, the emergency will automatically terminate in one year unless the President renews it. Renewal is easy, however, because the President need only publish a notice in the *Federal Register* and notify Congress.[91]

The third and critical provision would have terminated the national emergency when Congress passed a concurrent resolution. Though Congress was unlikely to so challenge the President, particularly in the heat of a crisis, the possibility of its use might have provided Congress with substantial leverage to influence Executive Branch policy making. This would have been especially true in cases where the crisis had cooled but the use of emergency powers continued.[92]

In 1983, however, the Supreme Court in *Immigration and Naturalization Service v. Chadha* invalidated a provision allowing either house of Congress to "veto" INS decisions and compel the Executive Branch to reinstitute deportation proceedings.[93] The reasoning of the majority opinion by six Justices, echoed in later rulings by the Court, suggested strongly that IEEPA's provision for a two-house concurrent resolution is also invalid.[94]

---

drafters was the use under TWEA of a declared and continuing national emergency as the basis for actions on an entirely different event. For example, the emergency declared by Truman in 1950 during the Korean War had been used as the basis for Johnson's imposition of controls on foreign investment in 1964, long after the war had ended. Senate IEEPA Report, supra note 8, at 2; House IEEPA Report, supra note 8, at 5, 7. Consequently, IEEPA required that the President declare a national emergency with respect to the particular threat and that the IEEPA powers be exercised only for the purpose of dealing with that threat. 50 U.S.C. § 1701. In practice, the problem of unrelated use of IEEPA powers has not arisen, nor is it likely to. The President can easily declare a new national emergency with respect to any problem for which he wants to use IEEPA authorities. See Harvard IEEPA Note, supra 21, at 1114–16.

[90] 50 U.S.C. § 1622(a).

[91] Id. §1622 (d).

[92] See Franck and Weisband, supra note 25, at 80; but see Harvard IEEPA note, supra note 25, at 1118. A proposed House version of IEEPA would also have given Congress a legislative veto by concurrent resolution within thirty days after each IEEPA regulation was reported to it. Senate IEEPA Report, supra note 8 at 2.

[93] 462 U.S. 919 (1983). Chief Justice Burger wrote the majority opinion. Justice Powell concurred on a limited ground. Justice Rehnquist and White dissented.

[94] Id.; see *Consumer Energy Council of America v. Federal Energy Regulatory Comm'n*, 673 F.2d 425, 470–8 (D.C. Cir. 1982), aff'd, 463 U.S. 1216 (1983); *Consumers Union of the United States v. Federal Trade Comm'n*, 691 F.2d 575 (D.C. Cir. 1982), aff'd, 463 U.S. 1216 (1983) (decisions striking down one-house and two-

Congress consequently amended the provision to provide instead for termination by a joint resolution.[95] The practical effect, however, of this amendment is that a declared national emergency may now continue at the President's pleasure. Since the President can veto a joint resolution, Congress would need a very unlikely two-thirds vote of both houses to stop an emergency that the President wants continued.[96]

Unending national emergencies have not yet become a serious problem under IEEPA. The emergencies to extend the export regulations were ended when Congress passed new export legislation. Also, the Reagan Administration allowed the national emergency against South Africa to lapse in September 1987 when it did not renew the one-year emergency. The steps that Reagan had ordered pursuant to this emergency, however, had essentially been duplicated, and even broadened, by the nonemergency Comprehensive Anti-Apartheid Act of 1986.[97] Somewhat discouragingly, the emergency over Iran continues after more than eight years, though the sanctions have been cut back sharply to encompass mainly the continuing efforts to resolve disputed claims before the Claims Tribunal at the Hague.[98]

house legislative vetoes). The literature on *Chadha* is extensive. See, e.g., T. Franck and C. Bob, "The Return of Humpty-Dumpty: Foreign Relations Law After the Chadha Case," 79 *Am. J. Int'l L.* 912, 923–5 (1985); S. Breyer, "The Legislative Veto After Chadha," 72 *Geo. L.J.* 785 (1984); G. Spann, "Spinning the Legislative Veto," 72 *Geo. L.J.* 813 (1984).

The invalid provision did seem clearly severable from the rest of IEEPA. The statute had a severability clause. Pub. L. No. 95-223, § 208, 91 Stat. 1625, 1629 (1977) (codified at 50 U.S.C. § 1701 note (1982)). Moreover, it was added specifically because of congressional concerns about the constitutionality of the legislative veto provision. *Beacon Products*, supra note 88, 633 F. Supp. at 1196–8; see Senate IEEPA Report, supra note 8 at 2, 7; see *Chadha*, 462 U.S. at 931–4; see also Franck and Bob, supra, at 929–31. Cf. *Alaska Airlines v. Brock*, 107 S. Ct. 1476 (1987).

[95] Pub. L. No. 99-93, tit. VIII, § 801, 99 Stat. 407, 448 (1985) (codified at 50 U.S.C. § 1622 (Supp. III 1985)). The amendment reflected the limited choices that Congress has to react to *Chadha*. See the sources cited in note 94 and the discussion of possible changes in IEEPA in Chapter 12, section C.4.

[96] In contrast, the concurrent resolution required only a majority vote in both houses. If Congress did succeed in terminating a national emergency, the President could conceivably declare a new emergency. However, not only would this be politically difficult for the President, but Congress could protect against this situation by appropriately amending IEEPA or the National Emergencies Act when it terminated the disputed emergency.

[97] President Reagan had extended the emergency for a second year on September 4, 1986, 51 *Fed. Reg.* 31,925, shortly before Congress passed the new sanctions legislation on October 2. The Administration did not take affirmative steps to terminate the emergency after the Act was passed, but let it lapse eleven months later.

[98] The emergency was renewed again on November 10, 1987. 52 *Fed. Reg.* 43,549 (1987). See 51 *Fed. Reg.* 37,568 (1986) (control regulations). The controls on imports and exports were ended. 46 *Fed. Reg.* 7925 (1981).

As one hopeful sign, President Reagan relied on new nonemergency powers, rather

There are even more telltale warning signs. The national emergencies against Nicaragua and Libya threaten to become "a normal state of affairs."[99] Both national emergencies have been routinely extended each year.[100] Even though the Reagan Administration obtained $100 million in assistance for the Nicaraguan contras in 1986, it apparently made no effort then to obtain statutory authority to impose nonemergency import controls against Nicaragua. Similarly, in the case of Libya, the Administration is not seeking nonemergency powers to continue the freeze on assets or the travel ban.

It is not only the Reagan Administration that has been contributing to the problem. No sustained opposition has arisen in Congress calling on the Executive Branch to seek nonemergency authority for the continuing sanctions. The long-term danger of these national emergencies is that this country will "grow used to them as the fittings of ordinary existence."[101]

3. What can't he do?

There is very little that the President cannot clearly do under IEEPA when imposing economic sanctions. Explicitly included among IEEPA's sweeping powers is the authority to "regulate . . . or prohibit, any . . . importation or exportation . . . in which any foreign country or a national thereof has any interest." The President is also given the power to freeze foreign-owned assets and to prohibit new financial transactions, such as loans, to the foreign country or its nationals. Furthermore, through comprehensive restrictions on financial transactions, the President can very effectively ban travel to or in another country.[102]

The President's broad powers exist in spite of efforts by IEEPA's authors to limit them relative to the TWEA powers. IEEPA was understood *not* to include (1) the power to "vest," that is, to take title to foreign property; (2) the power to regulate purely domestic transactions; (3) the power to regulate gold or bullion; and (4) the power to seize records.[103] Moreover, IEEPA explicitly does not authorize the President to interfere

---

than IEEPA, to impose a new embargo on imports from Iran in October 1987. See Chapter 5 at note 57. The resort to new legislation was easy since the statute only imposed lenient requirements for consultation and reporting. Id. at notes 54–7.

[99] House IEEPA Report, supra note 8, at 10.

[100] 53 *Fed. Reg.* 15,011 (Apr. 1988) (Nicaragua); 52 *Fed. Reg.* 47,891 (Dec. 1987) (Libya).

[101] *Bauer v. United States*, 244 F.2d 794, 797 (9th Cir. 1957) (dicta), quoted in *Yoshida*, 526 F.2d at 581.

[102] See 50 U.S.C. § 1702, quoted at start of this chapter, and the Libyan regulations, discussed at notes 57–60, 82–6.

[103] House IEEPA Report, supra note 8, at 15.

with the international flow of mail and other communications.[104] None of these omitted powers seems vital to a President for use as an economic sanction.[105]

Omission of the vesting power does not seem significant in light of the President's other powers over foreign-owned property, including the power to "direct and compel" its "transfer, withdrawal . . . or exportation."[106] In *Dames & Moore*, the Supreme Court found these sufficient to uphold the President's order nullifying certain attachments against the $12 billion in frozen Iranian assets, and then transferring the assets back to Iran and to other parties.[107]

---

[104] 50 U.S.C. § 1702(b). Similarly, there is an explicit provision that IEEPA does not give the President authority to regulate certain donations of food, clothing, and medicine. Id.

[105] As for domestic transactions, IEEPA limits most of its authorities "to the extent that such transfers or payments involve any interest of any foreign country or a national thereof." Id. at § 1702(a). This qualification was intended to withhold from the President the use of emergency powers under IEEPA to regulate "purely domestic" transactions during peacetime. House IEEPA Report, supra note 8, at 4–5, 15. It is unlikely, however, that economic sanctions against a foreign country would require any such regulation of domestic transactions, such as consumer credit. Moreover, the President would still have considerable latitude over domestic transactions, given the potential broad scope of the phrase "any interest" in IEEPA and the existence of various banking statutes for emergencies. See Harvard IEEPA Note, supra note 21, at 1110–11.

The authority to regulate gold or bullion has clearly lost most of its significance in a day when the dollar is not tied to the gold standard. Moreover, during the IEEPA drafting, the Executive Branch thought the omission of the authority was merely "technical" because, through another statute, the President had lost his authority to prohibit U.S. citizens from holding gold. Id. at 1107 n.29.

Omitting the President's power to seize records appears to be a limitation without substance. IEEPA still authorizes the President to require the keeping of records and their production. 50 U.S.C. § 1702(a)(2).

[106] Id. § 1702(a)(1).

[107] "Although it is true that IEEPA does not give the President the power to 'vest' or to take title to the assets, it does not follow that the President is not authorized under . . . IEEPA . . . to otherwise permanently dispose of the assets in the manner done here." 453 U.S. at 672 n.5.

Some have argued that the Court's decision essentially gives the President the power to vest. E.g., L. Marks and J. Grabow, "The President's Foreign Economic Powers After *Dames & Moore v. Regan*: Legislation by Acquiescence, 68 *Cornell L. Rev.* 68, 79–80 (1982); Harvard IEEPA Note, supra note 21, at 1109–10. However, the transfer was done subject to the agreements with Iran, which originally had title to the property, and the United States did not keep title in any of the assets. Indeed, during the crisis, the U.S. policy makers understood that IEEPA did not give the President the authority to take title to the property. They even considered introducing special legislation to give him that authority, but President Carter decided that "given the enormous breadth of his existing powers, it would be unwise to seek this additional authority." R. Carswell and R. Davis, "The Economic and Financial Pressures: Freeze and Sanctions," in *American Hostages in Iran* 173, 199–200 (P. Kreisberg ed. 1985); cf. J. Hoffman, "The Banker's Channel," in id. at 235, 245.

The Court did conclude, however, that IEEPA did not specifically provide the President the authority to suspend the lawsuits of U.S. citizens pending in American courts.[108] As discussed in the next chapter, however, the Court concluded that Congress had acquiesced in the President's action. In any event, except in the Iranian case or other claims settlement situations, this power to suspend lawsuits has not been important for the effective functioning of economic sanctions.

E. CONCLUSIONS

With the possible exceptions of vesting title or suspending lawsuits, the powers that IEEPA does not provide the President are few and marginal. Given the authorities that IEEPA does provide, the President need not be concerned with inadequate statutory power for imposing economic sanctions in a declared national emergency. Indeed, the consensus of a number of foreign policy experts is that the existing legal authorities are adequate and proper.[109] And there is no persuasive evidence that the President's authorities in real emergencies are excessive.

The relevant issue is the danger of casual resort to these sweeping powers in the future. Today, there are no effective limits on the President invoking IEEPA for dubious national emergencies, and no effective way to terminate the statute's use if the use becomes inappropriate with the passage of time. As Justice Jackson warned in his famous opinion in *Youngstown Sheet & Tube Co.*, "We may say that power to legislate for emergencies belongs in the hands of Congress, but only Congress itself can prevent power from slipping through its fingers."[110]

[108] 453 U.S. at 675. Courts will also review, of course, the application of the emergency powers. *Real v. Simon*, 510 F.2d 557, 564 (5th Cir. 1975) (setting aside as an arbitrary action an application of the TWEA regulations against Cuba).

[109] "Those involved in making and implementing the Carter Administration's policies [in the Iranian hostage crisis] felt that in general the legal authorities in existence during the crisis were adequate and proper." A. Ribicoff, "Lessons and Conclusions," in *American Hostages in Iran*, supra note 107, at 374, 380. A footnote to this conclusion added, "This view was also shared by the diverse participants in the Council [on Foreign Relations] study group, who considered this issue at length." Id. at 380 n. 5.

[110] *Youngstown Sheet & Tube Co. v. Sawyer*, 343 U.S. 579, 654 (1952) (Jackson, J., concurring).

IO

Possible powers of the President beyond the statutes

Can the President impose economic sanctions with measures that exceed the authorities granted him in the U.S. statutes? The discussion thus far has intentionally not addressed this issue. With the exception of President Carter's suspension of lawsuits in the Iranian hostage case, almost every recent use of economic sanctions appears to have been clearly based on the President's nonemergency or emergency powers under the statutes.[1]

Indeed, during a crisis, U.S. policy makers are very sensitive about what authorities the President has and does not have. They are likely to try to avoid the use of sanctions that might lead to unnecessary litigation or even embarrassment in the courts.[2] For example, in the Iran case, officials were aware that IEEPA did not authorize vesting title of the frozen assets and consequently the President avoided taking that step.[3]

Nevertheless, the question of the President's extrastatutory powers can arise in a sanctions episode, and thus a brief analysis is appropriate. The central conclusion is that the President should tread cautiously and follow the existing laws. Otherwise, he risks successful challenge to any steps taken beyond his statutory powers, though the outcome will depend on the circumstances and is by no means certain.

The Constitution gives both the President and Congress substantial powers in foreign affairs. Article II provides the President with "executive Power," designates him the "Commander in Chief," gives him the "Power, by and with the Advice and Consent of the Senate, to make Treaties," and authorizes him to appoint and receive ambassadors. Es-

---

[1] Note, however, that some of President Roosevelt's peacetime uses of TWEA were ratified only later by Congress. See discussion in Chapter 9 at notes 10–13.

[2] See R. Carswell and R. Davis, "The Economic and Financial Pressures: Freeze and Sanctions," in *American Hostages in Iran* 173, 185–8 (P. Kreisberg ed. 1985); W. Christopher, "Introduction," in id. at 5; A. Ribicoff, "Lessons and Conclusions," in id. at 380–1.

[3] See discussion in Chapter 9, at note 107.

pecially during the first seventy years of this century, with two World Wars, the Depression, and the Cold War, Presidents came to play an increasingly important role in U.S. foreign affairs.[4]

Even with the recent renaissance of congressional involvement in foreign policy, the major role that the Constitution assigns Congress is often forgotten. The Constitution provides Congress plenary authority over foreign commerce and over the government purse – having the powers to "regulate Commerce with foreign Nations" and to "lay and collect Taxes, Duties, Imposts,"[5] along with the stricture that "No Money shall be drawn from the Treasury, but in Consequence of Appropriations made by Law."[6]

These provisions have traditionally given Congress the dominant role in international economic affairs. Congress has then delegated much of this economic authority to the President through a wide variety of laws, many of which have been discussed in previous chapters. Sometimes this delegation is very broad, as with IEEPA.

Listing these powers of Congress and the President leaves unanswered the question of whether the President's explicit constitutional powers or some inherent powers authorize him to impose economic sanctions on his own – that is, to employ sanctions that are not based on authority provided by Congress.

The question was muddied by the Supreme Court's opinion in *United States v. Curtiss-Wright Export Corp.*, 299 U.S. 304 (1936). There the Supreme Court upheld a congressional delegation of power authorizing the President to declare illegal certain arms exports.[7] Although the result can be interpreted on the relatively narrow ground of a valid congressional delegation of power, the opinion included sweeping dicta that the President has a foreign affairs power "which does not require as a basis for its exercise an act of Congress" and might even arise from outside the Constitution.[8]

---

[4] See discussion in Chapter 9, at notes 25–30.

[5] U.S. Constitution, art. I, § 8.

[6] Id. § 9, cl. 7. Congress also has substantial powers in the case of foreign hostilities, including "To declare War, . . . To raise and support Armies, . . . To provide and maintain a Navy . . . [and] To make Rules for the Government and Regulation of the land and naval Forces." Id. § 8.

[7] President Roosevelt was trying to stop arms exports to Bolivia, which was then engaged in an armed conflict. Congress had authorized him in a broad joint resolution to punish anyone who illegally sold arms to Bolivia. Id. at 311–14.

[8] Id. at 319–20, 315–18. For example, Justice Sutherland wrote: "[T]he investment of the federal government with powers of external sovereignty did not depend upon the affirmative grants of the Constitution. The powers to declare and wage war, to conclude peace, to make treaties, to maintain diplomatic relations with other sovereignties, if they had never been mentioned in the Constitution, would have vested in the federal government as necessary concomitants of nationality." Id. at 318. "[W]e

Possible extrastatutory powers of the President

Curtiss-Wright's dicta was substantially trimmed by the decision in *Youngstown Sheet & Tube Co. v. Sawyer*, 343 U.S. 579 (1952). There the Court rejected the President's sweeping claims of executive power to seize and operate most of the nation's steel mills during a strike in the midst of the Korean War.[9] In an often cited concurring opinion, Justice Jackson provided a three-pronged test to assess the President's authority to act in a given case. First, "[w]hen the President acts pursuant to an express or implied authorization from Congress, his authority is at its maximum, for it includes all that he possesses in his own right plus all that Congress can delegate."[10] In this case, the President's act is "supported by the strongest of presumptions and the widest latitude of judicial interpretation."[11]

Second, "[w]hen the President acts in absence of either a congressional grant or denial of authority, he can only rely upon his own independent powers." He enters a "zone of twilight in which he and Congress may have concurrent authority, or in which its distribution is uncertain."[12] In this situation, the Court noted twenty-five years later in *Dames & Moore*, "the analysis becomes more complicated, and the validity of the President's action ... hinges on a consideration of all the circumstances which might shed light on the views of the Legislative Branch ..., including 'congressional inertia, indifference or quiescence.' "[13]

Finally, Justice Jackson wrote, when the President acts contrary to the will of Congress, "his power is at the lowest ebb." The Court can sustain his actions "only by disabling the Congress from acting upon the subject."[14]

are here dealing not alone with an authority vested in the President by an exertion of legislative power, but with such an authority plus the very delicate, plenary and exclusive power of the President as the sole organ of the federal government in the field of international relations – a power which does not require as a basis for its exercise an act of Congress...." Id. at 319–20.

There is extensive secondary literature on the *Curtiss-Wright* decision, often critical of the broad sweep of Justice Sutherland's majority opinion. See, e.g., C. Lofgren, "*United States v. Curtiss-Wright Corporation:* An Historical Reassessment," 83 *Yale L.J.* 1 (1973); L. Henkin, *Foreign Affairs and the Constitution* 19–26 (1972).

[9] The President's order was based not on any specific statutory authority, but generally on all the powers vested in the President by the Constitution and laws of the United States. Id. at 582–5.

[10] Id. at 635 (footnote omitted). Justice Jackson put the *Curtiss-Wright* decision in this category. Id. at n.2.

[11] Id. at 637.

[12] Id.

[13] *Dames & Moore*, 453 U.S. at 668–9, quoting *Youngstown*, 343 U.S. at 637 (Jackson, J., concurring).

[14] *Youngstown*, 343 U.S. at 637–8 (footnote omitted). The literature on *Youngstown* is vast. See, e.g., M. Marcus, *Truman and the Steel Seizure Case: The Limits*

Jackson's categories were found "analytically useful" by the Court in *Dames & Moore*.[15] In examining the President's suspension of certain claims pending in U.S. courts, the Court concluded that this action was not specifically authorized by IEEPA.[16] The Court went on to determine, however, that IEEPA and the so-called Hostage Act[17] indicated congressional acceptance of a broad scope of presidential action in the circumstances of the Iranian crisis.[18] Moreover, there existed a history of congressional acquiesence toward Presidents entering international agreements to settle outstanding claims with another country.[19] Justice Rehnquist concluded: "Past practice does not, by itself, create power, but 'long-continued practice, known to and acquiesced in by Congress, would raise a presumption that the [action] had been [taken] in pursuance of its consent.' Such practice is present here and such a presumption is also appropriate. In light of the fact that Congress may be considered to have consented to the President's action in suspending claims, we cannot say that action exceeded the President's powers."[20]

Some commentators have criticized the opinion in *Dames & Moore* for its ease in finding congressional acquiescence,[21] thus pushing the

of Presidential Power (1977); T. Kauper, "The Steel Seizure Case: Congress, the President, and the Supreme Court," 51 *Mich. L. Rev.* 141 (1952).

[15] 453 U.S. at 669. Writing for the majority, Justice Rehnquist went on to note, however, that "Justice Jackson himself recognized that his three categories represented 'a somewhat over-simplified grouping,' 343 U.S., at 635, and it is doubtless the case that executive action in any particular instance falls, not neatly in one of three pigeonholes, but rather at some point along a spectrum running from explicit congressional authorization to explicit congressional prohibition." Id. The Court upheld President Carter's ordering the transfer of Iranian assets and nullifying attachments against them because they were based on specific authorization from Congress in IEEPA. 453 U.S. at 674–5.

[16] Id. at 675.

[17] 22 U.S.C. § 1732 (1982). See discussion in Chapter 8 at note 2.

[18] 453 U.S. at 677.

[19] Id. at 678–8.

[20] Id. at 686 (quoting *United States v. Midwest Oil Co.*, 236 U.S. 459, 474 (1915)) [citation omitted]. The Court later noted that its conclusion was "buttressed by the fact that the means chosen by the President to settle the claims of American nationals provided an alternative forum, the Claims Tribunal, which is capable of providing meaningful relief." Id. at 686–7. "Just as importantly, Congress has not disapproved of the action taken here." Id. at 687.

[21] E.g., L. Tribe, *Constitutional Choices* 38–40 (1985); L. Marks and J. Grabow, "The President's Foreign Economic Powers After *Dames & Moore v. Reagan*: Legislation by Acquiescence," 68 *Cornell L. Rev.* 68, 101–3 (1982); see Note, "The International Emergency Economic Powers Act: A Congressional Attempt to Control Presidential Emergency Power," 96 *Harv. L. Rev.* 1102, 1113–14 (1983); but see H. Bruff, "Judicial Review and the President's Statutory Powers," 68 *Va. L. Rev.* 1, 36 (1982). Also, the Court may have greatly eased access to the U.S. Court of Claims by persons injured by the President's foreign policy actions. See P. Trimble, "Foreign

President's suspension of claims toward Jackson's easy to uphold first category.[22] The Court is accused of implicitly creating "a presumption of legislative acquiescence in executive agreements, absent specific congressional disapproval."[23]

Whether or not *Dames & Moore* requires more evidence of congressional acquiescence than simply a lack of specific disapproval is not, however, a critical issue. Congress has, in fact, expressed fairly clearly its views about almost all the major types of controls that a President might employ.

Looking first at the nonemergency situation, Congress has legislated extensively about *bilateral government programs*, including foreign assistance. Most of this legislation is grounded on Congress's undoubted authority over government spending, which has few limitations.[24] Congress, however, has delegated broad discretion to the President over these programs, so that he can impose almost any sanction he wishes.[25] Given this discretion and because this book makes no major recommendations for changing the President's authority over these programs,[26] further analysis of the possibility of extrastatutory steps by the President is unnecessary.

As for *exports*, Congress has passed a series of statutes that define when the President may impose controls. The Export Administration Act and other statutes are both comprehensive and specific enough to demonstrate clearly that Congress intended to occupy the area of export regulation. This legislation, moreover, is grounded in Congress's plenary power over foreign commerce.

Although the export laws generally give the President broad discretion, specific procedures are established (e.g., regarding consultation with Congress or foreign availability), and he is explicitly limited in a few ways (e.g., the new EAA provisions regarding contract sanctity and agricultural embargoes). If the President were to act contrary to one of the few limits

---

Policy Frustrated – *Dames & Moore*, Claims Court Jurisdiction and a New Raid on the Treasury," 84 *Colum. L. Rev.* 317 (1984).

[22] Although the Court's analysis puts the President's action very near the first category, the Court never specifically placed it in any category. 453 U.S. at 669. Indeed, in its conclusions, the Court also draws upon Justice Frankfurter's concurring opinion in *Youngstown*. Id. at 678.

[23] Marks and Grabow, supra note 21, at 103.

[24] See T. Franck and C. Bob, "The Return of Humpty-Dumpty: Foreign Relations Law After the Chadha Case," 79 *Am. J. Int'l L.* 944–8 (1985); but see D. Wallace, Jr., "The President's Exclusive Foreign Affairs Power Over Foreign Aid," 1970 *Duke L. J.* 293, 302–5.

[25] See discussion in Chapter 3, Section B.

[26] See discussion in Chapter 12, Section A.

on his discretion or if he were to operate outside the statutory procedures, his power would be at "its lowest ebb." Given Congress's recognized authority over foreign commerce, the courts might well not uphold his act.[27]

As for *imports*, Congress has also legislated in a comprehensive and specific way and created an extensive regulatory system. The commerce power similarly applies here. Indeed, Congress historically has been more involved in controlling imports than exports.[28] Congress has not given the President anything approaching the same discretion to control imports for foreign policy reasons. When Congress thought the President needed more power to limit imports from countries that supported terrorists, it passed specific legislation in the summer of 1985.[29] Moreover, bills giving the President greater authority in nonemergency situations have been considered and not passed.[30] In contrast, Congress has given the President sweeping powers over imports in emergency situations. The clear implication of all this is that the courts might preclude the President from limiting imports in nonemergency situations in ways not authorized under the statutes.

The sparse case law provides some support for this conclusion. In *Yoshida*, the lower court and the appellate court agreed that President Nixon's imposition in 1971 of a 10 percent surcharge on imports was not authorized by any nonemergency statute. The courts said that the surcharge would have been held invalid, except for the existence of a national emergency and the President's TWEA powers.[31] And in *United States v. Guy Capps, Inc.*, the Fourth Circuit Court of Appeals held that the President did not have the authority to enter into an executive agreement with Canada that limited the importation of certain types of potatoes, because the agreement did not comply with the procedures that Congress had specified by statute. Congress had occupied the field.[32]

The courts, however, are likely to be very hesitant to restrict the President in this area. In *Guy Capps*, for example, the Supreme Court affirmed on nonconstitutional grounds and the majority of the Court consciously

---

[27] See discussion below regarding imports.

[28] See the beginning of Chapter 5. The Supreme Court, nevertheless, is receptive to broad delegations of import authority to the President. E.g., *FEA v. Algonquin SNG, Inc.*, 426 U.S. 548 (1976).

[29] See Chapter 5 at notes 53–7.

[30] E.g., see the discussion of S. 979 in Chapter 12 at note 79.

[31] *United States v. Yoshida International*, 526 F.2d 560, 578–80 (C.C.P.A. 1975). See discussion in Chapter 9 at notes 15–20.

[32] "Imports from a foreign country are foreign commerce subject to regulation ... by Congress alone. The executive may not bypass congressional limitations regulating such commerce by entering into an agreement with the foreign country...." 204 F.2d 655, 660 (4th Cir. 1953), aff'd on other grounds, 348 U.S. 296 (1955).

avoided the constitutional issue.[33] Indeed, the courts might resort to a variety of approaches to uphold the President's action. For example, they might find that the action is not so mandatory or formal that it conflicts with legislatively defined limits.[34] Or they might interpret a statute narrowly so that the actions of the President or of one of his appointees are held not to conflict.[35] Alternatively, the courts could interpret a statute broadly to find that it provides the necessary authorization for some or all of the President's actions.[36] Finally, as discussed later, the courts might avoid the substantive issues by deciding that the case is not justiciable.

Professors John Jackson and William Davey have concluded:

> The courts have generally treated the President kindly when interpreting his statutory powers. Since 1945, the U.S. Supreme Court has never found the President to have exceeded his powers in the area of international economic relations (but only a few cases of this type have been considered by the Supreme Court). The Executive Branch has not fared as well in the lower federal courts, but... that is usually because the contested action involved application by lower ranking government officials of specific statutory standards established by Congress in a detailed regulatory scheme such as the antidumping legislation, as opposed to the exercise by the President or his officers of a more discretionary power.[37]

The situation with *private financial transactions* is similar to that with imports. Congress has passed considerable legislation regarding the operations of financial entities and has created an extensive financial regulatory system. Again, Congress relied primarily on its commerce power.

The President has only very limited authority to restrict private financial transactions for foreign policy reasons, however, and this is apparently what Congress intended. Congress has considered bills that would have

---

[33] 348 U.S. 296 (1955) (upheld the directed verdict of the district court that the Government failed to present sufficient evidence to establish a breach of contract); see B. Schwartz, *Super Chief: Earl Warren and His Supreme Court – A Judicial Biography* 165–6 (1983).

[34] See e.g., *Consumers Union of the United States v. Kissinger*, 506 F.2d 136, 142–44 (D.C. Cir. 1974), cert. denied, 421 U.S. 1004 (1975).

[35] E.g., see *Japan Whaling Ass'n v. American Cetacean Soc'y*, 106 S. Ct. 2860 (1986) (the five-Justice majority arguably gave an artificially narrow reading to the statute and the legislative history); cf. *United States Cane Sugar Refiners' Ass'n v. Block*, 544 F. Supp. 883, 893–95 (Ct. Int'l Trade 1982) (interpreting statutes and an executive agreement not to conflict).

[36] E.g., *Dames & Moore*, 453 U.S. 654 (1981), discussed in Chapter 9, Section D.3. However, at some point, a court might find a presidential action that relies on a broad reading of a statute is not authorized under the statute. E.g., *Real v. Simon*, 510 F.2d 557, 564 (5th Cir. 1975) (setting aside as an arbitrary action an application of the TWEA regulations against Cuba).

[37] J. Jackson and W. Davey, *Legal Problems of International Economic Relations: Cases, Materials and Text* 132–3 (1986); see case excerpts in id. at 132–42.

given the President greater authority but has not passed them.[38] In contrast, Congress has given the President broad authority over these financial transactions in emergency situations under IEEPA.

International financial institutions raise different issues. Congress has passed considerable legislation concerning U.S. participation in the international financial institutions and concerning financial contributions to them. Much of this is based squarely on Congress's control over the purse.

The President's limited authority here, however, is less a result of the legislation than of the multilateral character of the IFIs. No branch of the U.S. Government has much voice. Since the limits on U.S. authority cannot be easily changed and since this book concludes that little can usefully be done to change the situation,[39] further consideration of possible extrastatutory steps by the President regarding IFIs is unnecessary.

When there is a *declared national emergency*, the existence of an emergency is not by itself decisive in assessing a President's action. The Court in *Dames & Moore* considered the existence of an emergency one of the "circumstances" to be used in determining whether there was congressional acquiescence to the President's need to act.[40]

A declared national emergency does allow use of the sweeping powers of IEEPA, which far exceed what the President is authorized to do in the absence of an emergency. For example, the availability of emergency powers under TWEA, the predecessor of IEEPA, was decisive in *Yoshida*.[41] And IEEPA's powers were clearly important in *Dames & Moore* in upholding the President's actions. Although the Court recognized that the President might be able to take a step that is not explicitly authorized under the statutes, the Court supported this with a history of congressional acquiescence.

In either nonemergency or emergency situations, then, the President

---

[38] See discussion of S. 812 in Chapter 12 at note 94. Also, Senator Heinz and Senator Proxmire introduced a bill (S. 502) in 1983 that would have given the Federal Reserve Board the authority to set limits on the amount of credit individual banks could extend to public and private borrowers in one country. M. Wines, "Banks Taking the Heat for Near-Panic of '82," 15 *Nat'l J.*, 601, 606 (Mar. 19, 1983).

[39] See Chapter 12, Section A.

[40] 453 U.S. at 677. One view is that emergencies do not create extraconstitutional powers. *Ex parte Milligan*, 71 U.S. (4 Wall.) 2, 120–1 (1866); *Home Bldg. & Loan Ass'n v. Blaisdell*, 290 U.S. 398, 425–6 (1934); *Wilson v. New*, 243 U.S. 332, 347–8 (1917). But cf. *Korematsu v. United States*, 323 U.S. 214, 223–4 (1944) (wartime exclusion of all persons of Japanese ancestry from selected West Coast areas); *Hirabayashi v. United States*, 320 U.S. 81 (1943).

[41] Also, cf. *Regan v. Wald*, 468 U.S. 222, 225 n.1, 230 (1984) (upholding regulations that effectively limited travel to Cuba; TWEA was the basis, and nonemergency statutes did not appear sufficient). As discussed in Chapter 9, Section D.3, IEEPA includes almost all of TWEA's authorities and probably all the important ones.

must follow the existing statutory framework or step very cautiously. Given the extensive congressional legislative activity in the international economic area and Congress's constitutional powers over foreign commerce and the purse, it is hard to find extrastatutory steps of any significance the President might want to take that would not potentially run afoul of the courts.

Problems of justiciability

This raises a related question of whether the courts will review the President's actions. The courts often decline to decide matters of foreign policy, especially those that might involve separation-of-power issues between the President and Congress. Courts will avoid the substantive issues by ruling, for example, that the case raises a political question[42] or is otherwise not justiciable.[43]

Although obtaining judicial review can be a problem, it is often not an insurmountable one. Some statutes, particularly in the import area, specifically provide for judicial review.[44] The courts have also reviewed presidential decisions under other laws, such as TWEA and IEEPA.[45] There are even possibilities for judicial review under the EAA, though that law sharply limits review of many Executive Branch decisions. In addition, a defendant in a criminal prosecution under EAA can raise statutory questions before the court.[46] Courts will also entertain claims that the Executive Branch is operating outside the scope of the statute.[47]

---

[42] See *Goldwater v. Carter*, 444 U.S. 996, 1002 (1979) (order granting certiorari, vacating lower court ruling, and remanding with directions to dismiss the complaint; challenge by several members of Congress to President Carter's termination of a security treaty with Taiwan; concurring opinion by Rehnquist, J., joined by three other Justices, viewing the matter as a political question); cf. *Baker v. Carr*, 369 U.S. 186 (1962). But cf. *Japan Whaling Ass'n*, supra note 35, at 106 S. Ct. at 2862. See generally G. Stone, L. Seidman, C. Sunstein, and M. Tushnet, *Constitutional Law* 101–11 (1986).

[43] See *Goldwater*, 444 U.S. at 997–8 (opinion by Blackmun, J., finding the issue not yet ripe for judicial review); see Franck and Bob, supra note 24, at 953–7.

[44] See discussion in Chapter 5.

[45] The obvious cases are *Yoshida* and *Dames & Moore*. See also *Nuclear Pacific, Inc. v. U.S. Dep't. of Commerce*, No. C84–49R, slip op. at 3–14 (W.D. Wash. June 8, 1984) (order denying defendants' motion to dismiss) (review of export regulations under IEEPA).

[46] See Chapter 4, Section A.5.

[47] See *Yoshida* and *Japan Whaling Ass'n*. One approach to increase the possibility of judicial review is for Congress to legislate to compel justiciability in certain circumstances. See Franck and Bob, supra note 24, at 944–6. For example, the Hickenlooper amendment, 22 U.S.C. § 2370(e)(2) (1982), specifically directs the courts to decide suits about foreign expropriation of U.S. assets "on the merits giving effect to the principles of international law." Because of the problems of statutory interpretation

In short, a President is well advised to stay within the statutory framework when he imposes economic sanctions. This conclusion reemphasizes the need to take a hard look at the U.S. laws, and to make necessary changes.

and the difficulty of obtaining judicial review, this book's recommendations are drawn with an eye toward keeping Congress involved (e.g., through sunset provisions) and toward ensuring that restrictions on the President are clear and easily measured (e.g., allowing compensation if existing contracts are terminated). See recommendations in Chapter 12.

11

Looking to the allies

The haphazard U.S. laws for imposing economic sanctions appear to differ from those of several major industrial allies. Unlike the U.S. President, the Chief Executives in the United Kingdom, Germany, and Japan have broad authority to control imports and private financial transactions as well as exports. This greater across-the-board authority is especially noteworthy because the other countries are parliamentary democracies, so the Chief Executives should be better able to push new laws through their legislatures during a foreign policy dispute or minor crisis. In the United States, one or more houses of Congress is often controlled by the opposition party, which might balk at or at least slow a legislative initiative from the President.

A host of reasons – from historical and cultural ones to existing institutional arrangements – help explain the differences. However, there is no comprehensive comparative study of the countries' laws for sanctions, and this book surely does not claim to be one.

Nevertheless, a few observations should underscore the possibility of the United States adopting different approaches in its legal system.[1] These observations focus on the United Kingdom, Germany, the European Community, and Japan.[2] The European Community is relevant because

---

[1] Such observations might also encourage further, much needed comparative study. An excellent example of what can be done is the comparative analysis of U.S., European Economic Community, and Japanese law on the related issue of implementing the trade agreements reached in the 1970s at GATT's Tokyo round of negotiations. J. Jackson, J. V. Louis, and M. Matsushita, *Implementing the Tokyo Round* (1984) [hereinafter Jackson, *Implementing*]. Another excellent, though limited, example is the comparison of West German and U.S. laws for economic sanctions in W. Hein, "Economic Embargoes and Individual Rights Under German Law," 15 *L. & Pol'y Int'l Bus.* 401 (1983).

[2] Looking briefly at yet another U.S. ally – Australia – it appears that the Prime Minister of that country has broad powers to prohibit imports as well as exports under the Customs Law of 1901. Australia in the past has imposed economic sanctions

its laws can constrain what its individual members want to do unilaterally. Among the questions addressed here are the relative difficulty of imposing import and private credit controls versus export controls, the protections accorded individual businessmen, and the relations between other countries' governments and their private international banks.

A. THE UNITED KINGDOM

Executive authority to impose economic sanctions for foreign policy reasons is quite broad in the United Kingdom.[3] Three statutes appear central to the British Cabinet's ability to impose sanctions without further legislation. The first applies to imports and exports of goods, and the other two to financial transactions.

The Import, Export and Customs Powers (Defence) Act of 1939 grants the Secretary of State broad authority to prohibit the export or import of any good for any reason.[4] Although designed as a temporary wartime measure, it remains in active use today.[5] In sanctions episodes, the statute was used as part of the effort to ban exports to Iran in 1980 and to ban trade with Southern Rhodesia in 1965.[6]

against Rhodesia, Iran, the Soviet Union, North Vietnam, France, Argentina, and South Africa. The sanctity of existing contracts usually seems to be respected, the controls applying only to future transactions. G. Herndon, "Import and Export Controls as Economic Sanctions: A Comparison of the American and Australian Approaches" (1986) (unpublished paper on file at Georgetown University Law Center).

[3] Ian Fagelson, an English solicitor at the Warner Cranston firm in London, was very helpful with his voluntary research on the legal questions regarding the United Kingdom. Letter from Ian B. Fagelson to Arthur T. Downey (Sept. 25, 1986) (copy on file at Georgetown University Law Center) [hereinafter the Fagelson letter].

[4] The Import, Export and Customs Powers (Defence) Act, 1939, 2 and 3 Geo. 6, ch. 69 [hereinafter Import, Export Act]. Section 1(1) provides in pertinent part, "The Board of Trade may by order make such provisions as the Board think expedient for prohibiting or regulating...the importation into, or exportation from, the United Kingdom...of all goods or goods of any specified description." See C. Schmitthoff, *The Export Trade: A Manual of Law and Practice* 305 (1950).

[5] Import, Export Act, supra note 4, at § 9(3). The Act today provides the legal authority for British import and export licensing requirements. See Import of Goods (Control) Order, Stat. Inst. No. 23 (1954) (prohibiting the importation of all goods into the United Kingdom except those licensed); Export of Goods (Control) Order, Stat. Inst. No. 849 (1985) (prohibiting the export from the United Kingdom of certain goods unless they are licensed). The latter order also controls the export of strategic goods and technology to Communist countries. Id. at arts. iv, vii.

The statute was recently upheld against a challenge as to whether it authorized the Secretary of State to impose Commonwealth import preferences protecting the Caribbean producers and shippers of bananas. *R. v. the Secretary of State for Trade ex parte Chris International Foods Ltd.* 1983 T.L.R. 528 (Q.B.) The Court noted that the Secretary of State's powers under section 1, quoted earlier, were not "unfettered," but had to be exercised "reasonably and not arbitrarily." Id.

[6] See discussion at notes 11, 12 about use of country-specific legislation.

The Exchange Control Law of 1947 gives the Treasury broad power to restrict or prohibit transactions in foreign exchange.[7] The law apparently has been used only once to help impose economic sanctions – for two months in 1979 to continue controls against Southern Rhodesia when controls against other countries were lifted.[8]

The other payments-control statute, the Emergency Laws, is limited as far as it concerns financial transactions to those the Treasury feels are "to the detriment of the economic position of the United Kingdom."[9] It was used, however, to freeze all Argentine assets in British banks during the Falklands crisis in 1982 and to prohibit the transfer of gold and other securities to Southern Rhodesia in 1965.[10]

Although the British Cabinet has this broad permanent statutory authority, it often seeks specific authority from Parliament to respond to a particular crisis. This was done against Iran and Southern Rhodesia, but not Argentina.[11] The country-specific legislation might have been requested partly to clarify ambiguities in the general laws, but the request also appears to be a vehicle for obtaining a demonstration of domestic political support.[12]

---

[7] Exchange Control Act, 1947, 10 and 11 Geo. 6, ch. 14.

[8] All exchange controls, except those regarding Southern Rhodesia, were abolished in October 1979. See Stat. Inst. Nos. 1331–7 (1979). The Southern Rhodesia controls were finally lifted in December with the issuance of a general exemption. The Exchange Control (General Exemption) Order, Stat. Inst. No. 1660 (1979). See also The Control of Gold and Treasury Bills (Southern Rhodesia) (Revocation) Directions, Stat. Inst. No. 1661 (1979). The last item lifted exchange bans ordered under the Emergency Laws (Re-Enactment and Repeals) Act, 1964, ch. 60 [hereinafter Emergency Laws].

[9] Emergency Laws, supra note 8, at § 2(1).

[10] For Argentina, Control of Gold, Securities, Payments and Credits (Argentine Republic), Stat. Inst. No. 512 (1982), revoked by Stat. Inst. No. 1926 (1982). See J. Amine, "Economic Sanctions: Falkland Islands (Malvinas)," 23 *Harv. Int'l L.J.* 404, 405 n.2 (1983). For Southern Rhodesia, Control of Gold and Treasury Bills (Southern Rhodesia) Directions, Stat. Inst. No. 1939 (1965), revoked by Stat. Inst. No. 1661 (1979).

[11] For Iran, the British Cabinet seemed reluctant to use general statutory authority to impose sanctions without a specific mandate from Parliament. Orders issued under the Import, Export Act reached only as far as those authorized by the Iran (Temporary Powers) Act, 1980, ch. 28. For Southern Rhodesia, orders under the Import, Export Act were issued in conjunction with those issued under the United Nations Act, 1946, 9 & 10 Geo. 6, ch. 45, § 1, and the Southern Rhodesia Act, 1965, ch. 76. Together, they effectively banned all exports from the United Kingdom to Rhodesia and 95% of all imports, including oil. G. Hufbauer and J. Schott, *Economic Sanctions Reconsidered: History and Current Policy* 409–10 (1985).

[12] Another statute appears to grant the Cabinet power to impose sanctions, although it has not been used as such. Under the Trading with the Enemy Act, 1939, 2 & 3 Geo. 6, ch. 89, the Secretary of State may label any country an "enemy," rendering impermissible trade with that country. This could be used to cut off all commercial transactions with that country.

Ian Fagelson writes: "It is generally believed that the Crown has, by virtue of

The Cabinet has additional authority to impose sanctions by virtue of British participation in multilateral organizations. Under the United Nations Act, the UK Government may do whatever is necessary to implement Security Council regulations.[13] Under the European Communities Act, the Cabinet has the power to implement European Community legislation.[14]

As a result of all these statutes, the British Prime Minister and Cabinet seem able to impose thoroughgoing controls over exports, imports, and private financial transactions for foreign policy reasons.

B. WEST GERMANY

West Germany has a relatively simple legal framework for foreign commerce, and one that differs from the U.S. approach. The basic German law is the Aussenwirtschaftsgesetz of 1961, the Statute of Foreign Commerce.[15] Though relatively short, it governs all international commercial transactions by German residents, including exports, imports, payments, and capital movements.[16] As a result, many of the provisions apply across all these transactions.[17] To the extent that the German Executive has the authority to impose sanctions, his authority is similar to exports, imports, or private credit transactions – a situation that is quite different from the haphazard situation with U.S. laws.

its prerogative, considerable non-statutory powers to regulate the movement of goods and persons into and from the country and to take other actions necessary to procure the safety of the Realm. However the precise ambit of the Royal prerogative is unclear. Accordingly, in modern times it has been thought necessary to enact legislation specifically conferring certain powers on the Crown." Fagelson letter, supra note 3, at 1.

[13] UN Act, supra note 10, § 1.

[14] European Communities Act, 1972, ch. 68, § 2(2), (4). See discussion in Section C, this chapter, about the European Community.

[15] Aussenwirtschaftsgesetz (AWG), 1961 Bundesgesetzblatt (BGBI) I 481 (W. Ger., as amended, 1980 BGB1 I 1905), cited in Hein, supra note 1, at 403–4.

[16] Section 1(1) of the Statute defines foreign commerce as "the exchange of goods, services, capital, payments and other economic valuables with foreign economic areas as well as the exchange of foreign economic valuables and gold if carried out by residents." AWG § 1(1), 1961 BGB1 I 482 (W. Ger.), quoted in Hein, supra note 1, at 404.

[17] Hein, supra note 1, at 422 ("one Statute establishing a uniform standard for the restriction of different forms of foreign commerce"). In addition to its direct statutory authority over private credit, the German Government has developed a variety of effective instruments for influencing the international behavior of German banks. An example was the Government's successful prodding of banks to extend a DM 1.2 billion (or more than $600 million) loan to Poland during 1980. The Government did this by combining the use of export credit guarantees with persuasion. J. A. Spindler, *The Politics of International Credit* 28–34 (1984) [hereinafter Spindler, *Politics*].

While providing similar power over different economic activities, the German statute does provide a number of protections for businesses that are not found in existing U.S. laws, particularly U.S. export laws. A critical principle expressed in the statute is that the freedom to engage in commerce is an individual right.[18] This principle dramatically changed the legal situation that existed before 1961. The former statute, left over from the occupation, in principle prohibited foreign commerce, and any exception required a government license.[19]

Although the German Executive is authorized to restrict foreign commerce by regulation, the controls must be imposed in specific ways for specific purposes.[20] An important constraint is that German courts "look more closely into foreign commerce actions than do U.S. courts."[21] Possibly even more important, existing contracts are exempted from sanctions as much as possible, and sanctions affecting existing contracts or the withdrawal of existing licenses "would generally require compensation."[22]

C. THE EUROPEAN COMMUNITY

The European Community[23] can both limit the ability of its members, such as the United Kingdom and Germany, to impose unilateral sanctions and impose sanctions itself against nonmember countries.

---

[18] The AWG's first provision states, "Foreign commerce is free in principle." AWG § 1(1), 1961 BGBl I 482 (W. Ger.), quoted in Hein, supra note 1, at 404 n.14.

[19] Hein, supra note 1, at 404–5. The theory of present U.S. export laws is closer to the former German laws than the present ones. In the United States, exportation is a privilege, not a right. See Chapter 4 at note 5.

[20] The authority is premised primarily upon the existence of a threat to national security, international peace, foreign policy, or the national economy. Hein, supra note 1, at 405.

[21] Id. at 423; also 406, 418–19.

[22] Id. at 423; also 415–22.

[23] The European Community is technically three communities, established by separate treaties: the European Economic Community (EEC), the European Coal and Steel Community (ECSC), and the European Atomic Energy Community (Euratom). Present members of the Community include Belgium, Denmark, the Federal Republic of Germany, France, Greece, Ireland, Italy, Luxembourg, Netherlands, Portugal, Spain, and the United Kingdom.

There has been increasing integration of the three Communities. For example, in 1965, a single Council and Commission were established. Treaty Establishing a Single Council and a Single Commission of the European Communities (Merger Treaty). In 1986, the Conference of the Representatives of the Governments of the Member States adopted a Single European Act, which included treaty modifications concerning foreign policy coordination as well as community institutions, monetary cooperation, research and technology, environmental protection, and social policy. (It can be found in the European Community *Bulletin*, Suppl. (Feb. 1986) and 25 *Int'l Legal Materials*

As for limiting the ability of its twelve members, the European Community laws are particularly restrictive about imposing sanctions *between* Member States. The Treaty of Rome of the European Economic Community (EEC) prohibits export or import controls between the Member States, as well as restrictions on private credit flows for foreign policy reasons.[24]

Although further analysis is needed, it appears that the European Community can also limit the flexibility of its members in taking action against third countries. Consistent with the primary focus of the Treaty of Rome, the use of import controls is most restricted.

A Member State might still be allowed to impose import controls against a third country – such as the United Kingdom banning, say, the importation of diamonds from South Africa.[25] However, the effectiveness of such a measure is severely undercut by the fact that the United Kingdom could not prohibit the importation of diamonds from South Africa by way of another European Community Member State. The prohibition on import controls against another Community member applies both to products originating in that country and to products coming from third countries that have cleared customs in a Member State.[26] The possibilities of indirect trade thus make any unilateral import control relatively ineffective, depending on the costs of transshipment (which, incidentally, would be small for diamonds).

503 (May 1986).) It came into effect in July 1987, after being approved by the twelve Member States.

For an excellent discussion of the Community's legal framework for trade, see J. V. Louis, "The European Economic Community and the Implementation of the GATT Tokyo Round Results," in Jackson, *Implementing*, supra note 1, at 21.

[24] Treaty of Rome, arts. 9, 10 (free movement of goods – customs duties), 30–6 (elimination of quantitative restrictions), and 67–73 (movement of capital). The provisions reflect the original intent of the Member States to integrate their economies.

Member States have, however, imposed certain monetary controls in times of domestic economic difficulties. For example, the Mitterrand Government in France in 1983 limited the amount of currency a French citizen could take out of the country, including currency taken to a Member State. Articles 104 through 109 of the EEC Treaty do allow a Member State to implement certain actions when "seriously threatened with difficulties as regards its balance of payments." Art. 108. However, the Community's legal limits on a Member State's actions are not always clear. See generally E. Stein, P. Hay, and M. Waelbroeck, *European Community Law and Institutions in Perspective* (1976 and Supp. 1985), including pp. 200–8 of the Supplement.

[25] See Fagelson letter, supra note 3, at 3.

[26] Treaty of Rome, art. 9(2). Article 10(1) provides, "Products coming from a third country shall be considered to be in free circulation in a Member State if the import formalities have been complied with and any customs duties or charges having equivalent effect which are payable have been levied in that Member State. . . . "

The European Community laws probably do not prohibit unilateral controls over exports to a third country or over private credit transactions with entities there. Some questions might be raised, however, under Treaty provisions regarding the "common commercial policy" and under other provisions regarding consultation among the Member States.[27]

Though the focus of this book is on a country's legal system for imposing sanctions, it is interesting that, beyond limiting the ability of its Member States to implement sanctions, the European Community can *impose sanctions itself.* The Community has clear authority to restrict imports in many situations and some apparent authority over exports and private credit. For example, it has decided in favor of sanctions in the past against Rhodesia, Iran, the Soviet Union, Argentina, and South Africa.[28]

In outlining the Community's authority, it is important to appreciate how the Community usually proceeds in determining whether to impose economic sanctions. The initial discussions among the Foreign Ministers usually focus on the steps to be taken and also on choosing "between a true Community approach or a perhaps coordinated but separate implementation" of measures.[29] The exact legal bases appear to be delineated later, and are sometimes left vague even in the Community documents.[30] This approach partly reflects the evolving growth of a supranational organization.

[27] See Treaty of Rome, arts. 110–16 (common commercial policy) and 224 (consultation), discussed below. See also title III (cooperation in foreign policy) of the Single European Act, supra note 23. The European Community is seen by many as a political institution that does not have a clear legal framework for all its actions. See generally Stein, Hay, and Waelbroeck, supra note 24.

[28] See discussion below about some of the past uses. See also, e.g., P. Kuyper, "Community Sanctions against Argentina: Lawfulness Under Community and International Law," in *Essays in European Integration* 141 (D. O'Keefe and H. Schermers eds. 1982); 29 *O.J. Eur. Comm.* (No. L 268) 1 (1986); 29 *O.J. Eur. Comm.* (No. L 305) 11, 45 (1986).

[29] Kuyper, supra note 28, at 144. See, for example, the coordinated but separate measures taken by the Member States against Syria in 1986–7, discussed below at note 32.

[30] See, e.g., the import ban discussed below on certain South African iron and steel products. Note further that the Council and the Commission can choose among the legal vehicles they use to implement a measure. The choice between, say, issuing a regulation or a directive has a substantive impact on the way a measure is implemented in the Member States. Article 189 provides for regulations, directives, decisions, recommendations, and opinions. It reads:

A regulation shall have general application. It shall be binding in its entirety and directly applicable to all Member States.
A directive shall be binding, as to the result to be achieved, upon each

A review of the Community's legal authorities and past uses of sanctions indicates that it has a strong basis for imposing import controls. Most often used is article 113 of the Treaty of Rome, which provides for "implementing the common commercial policy."[31]

When proposed sanctions do not fall under the common commercial policy, the Member States can still consult one another pursuant to article 224 and decide to implement sanctions individually.[32] Article 223 pro-

Member State to which it is addressed, but shall leave to the national authorities the choice of form and methods.

A decision shall be binding in its entirety upon those to whom it is addressed.

Recommendations and opinions shall have no binding force.

[31] Article 113(1) states that "the common commercial policy shall be based on uniform principles, particularly in regard to changes in tariff rates, the conclusion of tariff and trade agreements, the achievement of uniformity in measures of liberalization, export policy and measures to protect trade such as those to be taken in case of dumping and subsidies." The full scope of the EEC's broad powers under article 113 remains "undetermined and controversial" because the term "common commercial policy" is not defined in the Treaty of Rome. J. Schwarze, "Towards a European Foreign Policy: Legal Aspects," in *Towards a European Foreign Policy 69*, 71 (J. K. de Vree, P. Coffey, and R. H. Lauwaars eds. 1987).

[32] Kuyper notes the "Council's traditional theory that the goal of the measure concerned determines whether it falls under the common commercial policy or not." Kuyper, supra note 28, at 143; see Schwarze, supra note 31, at 72. For example, Kuyper concludes that, because of Community concerns that the trade sanctions called for by the United Nations against Rhodesia in 1966 and 1968 were "primarily of a political and security nature," and therefore not within the Community's competence as delineated in article 2 of the Treaty of Rome, the Community declined to rely on article 113, but chose article 224 instead to impose them. Kuyper, supra note 28, at 143. Kuyper, however, believes that the process leading to the decision to impose sanctions under article 113 can also be viewed as part of the article 224 framework of consultation. Id. at 148. Article 224 provides: "Member States shall consult each other with a view to taking together the steps needed to prevent the functioning of the common market being affected by measures which a Member State may be called upon to take in the event of serious internal disturbances affecting the maintenance of law and order, in the event of war or serious international tension constituting a threat of war, or in order to carry out obligations it has accepted for the purpose of maintaining peace and international security."

This "political cooperation mechanism" was invoked by the United Kingdom after a Syrian national was convicted in London of plotting to blow up an Israeli airliner. See *N.Y. Times*, Mar. 31, 1987, at A10, col. 1; *Financial Times*, Dec. 8, 1986, at A4. The process resulted in the implementation of sanctions against Syria, including a ban on new arms sales; the suspension of high-level visits to and from Syria; a review of the activities of Syrian diplomatic and consular missions in the Member States; and a tightening of security precautions around the Syrian national airline. *Europe: Political Day*, No. 4427, at 3 (Nov. 11–12, 1986). Although Greece refused to implicate directly the Syrian Government in the terrorist attack, it agreed with these sanctions and noted that it had implemented them on a de facto basis even before they were adopted by the other eleven foreign ministers in the Community. In mid–1987 the ban on high-level visits to Syria was suspended. *Wash. Post*, Sept. 7, 1987, at A24, col. 1.

vides a specific basis for sanctions involving "trade in arms, munitions and war material." Article 235 provides a residual basis for action – allowing the Council to take "appropriate measures" if action by the Community is necessary to attain one of the Community's objectives and the EEC Treaty has not provided the necessary powers.[33]

Recent sanctions illustrate the approach used by the Community. In March 1982, the Community reduced certain imports from the Soviet Union in protest over events in Poland. The action was taken by a regulation pursuant to article 113.[34]

About the same time, Argentina seized the Falkland Islands. In addition to military force, the British reacted with thoroughgoing sanctions, including a freeze on Argentine assets. The other European Community countries resorted primarily to import sanctions. The European Community Council unanimously decided in April 1982 to impose a temporary import ban, through a regulation based on article 113.[35] Though there were some loopholes in the ban that diminished its immediate impact,[36] the EEC decision and the basis for it were correctly viewed as an important precedent for future crises.[37]

Then, in 1986, after unsuccessfully encouraging South Africa to take certain ameliorative steps, the European Community's Foreign Ministers agreed on several measures, including a ban on imports of gold coins, iron, and steel, to protest South Africa's apartheid system. The regulation

---

[33] Article 235 provides: "If action by the Community should prove necessary to attain, in the course of the operation of the common market, one of the objectives of the Community and this Treaty has not provided the necessary powers, the Council shall, acting unanimously on a proposal from the Commission and after consulting the Assembly, take the appropriate measures."

In a major article, Professor Jürgen Schwarze analyzes the EEC's external activities within the alternative framework of the European Political Cooperation (EPC). Schwarze, supra note 31. He describes the EPA as an "extra-Community consultative mechanism in the area of foreign relations.... [Despite] various organizational and institutional links to the Community, legally speaking, the EPC is a strictly intergovernmental cooperation mechanism and thus stands outside the Community's legal system." Id. at 75. Schwarze adds: "The European foreign policy of today is conducted with two different legal systems [EEC Treaty and EPC]. Although there are fundamental legal differences in theory and nature it is often difficult to define the different foreign policy matters in practice. There are many links and overlappings to be noticed. Under the present legal system a clear distinction especially between foreign commercial policy matters of the Treaty (Art. 113) and European foreign political affairs of the EPC, often seems to be impossible." Id. at 78–9.

[34] Reg. (EEC) No. 596/82 in 25 *O.J. Eur. Comm.* (No. L 72) 15 (1982). See Kuyper, supra note 28, at 141.

[35] See 25 *O.J. Eur. Comm.* (No. L 102) 1 (1982).

[36] For example, the embargo exempted contracts concluded before the April 16 effective date of the EEC decision. Id.

[37] See, e.g., Hein, supra note 1, at 408–9; Kuyper, supra note 28, at 147–51.

prohibiting imports of gold coins was pursuant to article 113.[38] South African iron and steel products were banned by a Council Decision under the European Coal and Steel Community (ECSC) Treaty, rather than under article 113 of the EEC Treaty, because it is the ECSC Treaty that governs Community competence over such products.[39]

Although the Community has not made extensive use of export controls for foreign policy purposes, it does appear to have some power to impose them. In 1980, the Community imposed an embargo on the sale of arms to Iran, to be implemented individually by each Member State pursuant to article 223 of the EEC Treaty.[40] As noted earlier, article 223 is narrow, dealing with national security issues such as "trade in arms, munitions and war material." Nevertheless, a case might be made that commercial policy specifically includes "export policy" given the language in EEC article 110, and hence article 113 is also available for export controls. Furthermore, articles 224 and 235 are not specifically limited to import controls.

Similarly, the Commission might have some power to impose controls over private credit. In addition to articles 224 and 235, articles 67 through 73 give the Community considerable authority over capital movements.

In the case of South Africa, the European Community Council implemented a ban on new direct investment there.[41] This could be viewed as a control on the export of capital or as a limit on capital movements. The directive specifically cited article 235, discussed above. Moreover, in the memo from the Commission to the Council proposing the directive, the definition of "new direct investment" is based on an earlier directive implementing article 67, which deals with capital movements.[42] This blending of articles 235 and 67 makes the South African directive a possible precedent for future export controls or credit controls.[43]

---

[38] Council Reg. (EEC) No. 3302/86 of Oct. 27, 1986 in 29 *O.J. Eur. Comm.* (No. L 305) 11 (1986). The regulation exempted "import documents issued and contracts concluded before the entry into force of this Regulation."

[39] Article 71 of the ECSC Treaty reserves to Member States the authority to determine much of their own commercial policy for coal and steel products. Article 113 of the EEC Treaty has not absorbed this reservation. See Louis, supra note 23, at 38. Council Decision 86/459/ECSC is at 29 *O.J. Eur. Comm.* (No. L 268) 1 (1986). No specific article of the ESCS Treaty was cited. As with the regulation on gold coins, there is a contract sanctity provision. The ban will affect imports that have been worth about $424 million per year. 3 *Int'l Trade Rep. (BNA)* 1123, 1124 (Sept. 17, 1986).

[40] Kuyper, supra note 28, at 145.

[41] Council Decision 86/517/EEC at 29 *O.J. Eur. Comm.* (No. L 305) 45 (1986).

[42] See Proposal for a Council Directive Suspending New Direct Investment in the Republic of South Africa by Residents of the Community, COM(86) 522 final, Sept. 24, 1986, at 2.

[43] Since capital movements are differentiated in the Treaty of Rome (articles 67–

D. JAPAN

Although Japan has been hesitant to impose economic sanctions for foreign policy purposes,[44] the Government is able to resort to sanctions when they are deemed necessary. The Government lacks the extensive, explicit statutory powers found in the United Kingdom or West Germany, particularly over exports. However, the Japanese Government has relied on its economic control legislation as the basis for its authority and on "administrative guidance" as the primary basis for implementation. This guidance encompasses a range of measures by which the various ministries are able to influence voluntary compliance by private entities.[45]

Two statutes are central to ministerial authority to control foreign transactions. First, the Foreign Exchange and Foreign Trade Control Law (FECL)[46] permits the relevant ministry to restrict or prohibit transactions involving the import or export of goods or involving foreign exchange or investment.

Although the statute gives Japanese ministries broad discretion, its objectives are economic.[47] Moreover, the statute even recognizes a freedom to export. Article 47 provides, "Export of goods from Japan shall be permitted with the minimum restrictions thereon consistent with the purpose of this Law."[48] Indeed, in a rare judicial challenge to ministerial authority, the Tokyo District Court in 1969 held that Japanese enforcement of export controls pursuant to the CoCom agreement with its allies[49] was outside the scope of the FECL and unlawfully intruded on the con-

---

73), it would seem that the directive would be a better precedent for future controls on capital.

[44] This hesitancy reflects Japan's dependence on international trade and its post–World War II policy of avoiding diplomatic disputes.

[45] See later discussion regarding administrative guidance. On the Japanese legal system for foreign trade and credit, see generally the excellent chapter by Professor Mitsuo Matsushita, "Japan and the Implementation of the Tokyo Round Results," in Jackson, *Implementing*, supra note 1, at 77, 89–97 [hereinafter Matsushita, "Japan"]; A. Smith, "The Japanese Foreign Exchange and Foreign Trade Control Law and Administrative Guidance: The Labyrinth and the Castle," 16 *L. & Pol'y Int'l Bus.* 417 (1984).

[46] *Gaikokukawase oyobi gaikokuboeki kanri ho*, as amended, Law No. 228 of 1949.

[47] Article 1 provides: "This Law has as its objective the sound development of the national economy together with the balance of international payments and currency stabilization, taking as its basic tenet the liberalization of foreign exchange, foreign trade, and other foreign transactions, based on the minimum restrictions necessary for the control or regulation of foreign transactions, to further the normal development of foreign transactions." Quoted in Matsushita, "Japan," supra note 45, at 134 n.42.

[48] Id. at 90.

[49] See Chapter 4 at note 13 on CoCom.

stitutional right to export.[50] This case and the law's recognition of a citizen's freedom to export suggest that the Government's power to control exports may be more limited than its power to control imports.[51]

Second, the Export and Import Transactions Law[52] gives the Ministry of International Trade and Industry (MITI) authority to set export prices and quantities in certain cases where there are private export agreements, and to issue import orders in certain situations. MITI is thus given the power to operate when private agreements produce results that might be harmful to the Japanese economy.[53]

Restrictions in the FECL and Transactions Law to using the laws for economic purposes do not, however, prevent the Government from controlling exports, imports, and private credit for noneconomic foreign policy reasons. Even the plaintiffs in the CoCom case were denied recovery because they failed to prove that MITI imposed the controls maliciously or negligently.[54] Moreover, the 1969 case is the only "successful" legal challenge to MITI's attempts to control foreign trade for foreign policy reasons, and Japan continues to participate with its allies in CoCom.

The Government is able to use economic sanctions in large part because many of MITI's controls are imposed through administrative guidance, rather than by the invocation of specific legal authority. In Japan, administrative guidance, often informal, is a primary means of government regulation.[55] The area of foreign trade regulation is no different. For example, MITI has used administrative guidance to gain Japanese exporters' compliance with voluntary restraint agreements made with the United States. In such cases, MITI threatened to invoke its authority under the Transactions Law to fix prices and quantities, but it was able to achieve compliance without doing so.[56]

Japanese ministries have also used administrative guidance to expand their authority under the FECL. For example, under the statute, most foreign commercial transactions do not require prior ministerial approval, but do require prior notification to the "relevant" ministry. The

---

[50] See Matsushita, "Japan," supra note 45, at 91; M. Matsushita,"Export Control and Export Cartels in Japan," 20 *Harv. Int'l L.J.* 103, 106–8 (1979), citing *Pekin-Shanhai Nihon Kogyo Tenrankai v. Nihon*, 20 Gyosei Reishu 842 (Tokyo Dist. Ct. 1969).

[51] Matsushita, "Japan," supra note 45 at 94–5.

[52] *Yushutsunyu torihiki ho*, as amended, Law No. 299 of 1952.

[53] Id. at arts. 28 (exports), 7–2(1), and 30(1) (imports); see Matsushita, "Japan," supra note 45, at 92–3, 96.

[54] Matsushita, "Japan," supra note 45, at 91–2.

[55] Smith, supra note 45, at 420.

[56] Matsushita, "Japan," supra note 45, at 93–4.

ministries have designated the Bank of Japan (BOJ) as the governmental entity to receive the notification documents and to determine which ministry has jurisdiction over the transaction. As a result, a party must often consult the BOJ even before submitting any documents. In addition, if the relevant ministry objects to the proposed transaction as initially submitted by a party, it may "informally decline to formally accept" a party's documentation. In this way, ministries may express their disapproval and negotiate with a party, avoiding the need to prohibit an unfavored action officially.[57]

A party has incentives to heed administrative guidance from the ministries, whose favor the party is likely to need later. Ministries have been known to retaliate against uncooperative companies in unrelated areas.[58] Thus, well before the party has submitted documents or the ministry has taken official action, an informal approval process is underway, and the legal steps that follow are usually pro forma.[59]

Utilizing its statutory authority and administrative guidance, Japan has shown itself capable of imposing economic sanctions for foreign policy reasons. For example, despite its extensive economic ties with Iran, Japan took some mild steps against that country in 1979 during the hostage crisis. Japan agreed not to buy Iranian oil on the spot market and to hold its total imports of Iranian oil to prehostage levels.[60] Then, in response to the Soviet invasion of Afghanistan, Japan in 1980 restricted

[57] Smith, supra note 45, at 427–32.

[58] Id. at 426.

[59] Id. at 431–2. As an example of the result, in the area of private credit, Japan appears to coordinate its foreign policy closely with its large private banks. This reflects both an extension of the domestic economic and political relationships in Japan and the importance to it of international trade and finance. Spindler, *Politics*, supra note 17, at 114–34; J. Spindler, "The Growing Entanglement of International Banking and Foreign Policy," 8 *TransAtl. Persp.* 3, 4 (May 1983).

There are also specific government incentive programs. For example, MITI administers and underwrites export insurance covering many commercial and political risks. These include essentially all risks incurred by Japanese banks as a result of a foreign buyer's default. Noncommercial considerations regularly affect decisions on the allocation of insurance. During the early 1980s, MITI insurance covered more than 40% of all Japanese exports. In contrast, the guarantee and insurance programs of the U.S. Eximbank were equivalent to roughly 3% of U.S. exports for 1981. Spindler, *Politics*, supra note 17, at 122–3.

Possibly even more important, the continuing and frequent administrative guidance by the Japanese Government "has given the government a highly effective means of informally influencing Japanese banks' overseas business behavior." Id. at 134.

[60] Yoshitu, "Iran and Afghanistan in Japanese Perspective," 21 *Asian Surv.* 501 (May 1981). Japan did refuse to give up the Iran–Japan Petrochemical Company, a $2 billion capital investment for Japan that was 85% complete in 1980, and did not place any controls on its banks, which helped Iran circumvent the U.S. freeze on Iranian assets. Id.

credit to the Soviet Union and the export of capital machinery and high technology.[61]

In short, although comparisons among countries and their legal systems should always be undertaken with caution, the preceding observations reinforce the conclusion that present U.S. laws are not necessarily the only, or even the best, approach to imposing economic sanctions for foreign policy purposes.

[61] Japan also boycotted the Moscow Olympics and limited the exchange of trade personnel. H. Kerns, "An Outfall in the East," 117 *Far E. Econ. Rev.*, July 23, 1986, at 43. As a result of Japan's economic sanctions, it slipped from its status as the Soviets' No. 2 noncommunist trading partner (after West Germany) to No. 5. Business pressures led Japan to ease its sanctions gradually. Id. In December 1981, when President Reagan called for more sanctions against the Soviet Union because of Poland, Japan limited itself to largely symbolic gestures, such as canceling some trade meetings between Soviet and Japanese officials. Japan opposed the U.S. export prohibitions on oil and gas equipment and technology, which threatened to delay a major Japanese–Soviet oil and gas project. Id.; see Chapter 4, Section A.6.

12

Planning for the future

"If it ain't broke, then don't fix it," goes one down-home aphorism. Serious problems do exist, however, with the U.S. laws for imposing economic sanctions for foreign policy reasons. The analyses in the preceding chapters provide a foundation for recommending what should be done. Several important conclusions emerged, including the following:

1. Although measuring effectiveness is fraught with difficulty and controversy, there is persuasive historical evidence that sanctions can sometimes be an effective tool for achieving foreign policy objectives. In more than sixty cases since 1945 in which the United States has resorted to economic sanctions, they have arguably been successful more than one-third of the time.

This success rate has varied with the objective sought. Especially effective have been sanctions designed to destabilize a country, which have succeeded in an estimated ten out of fifteen efforts (or 67 percent). Examples include the toppling of Haiti's Duvalier in 1986, Uganda's Idi Amin in 1979, and Chile's Allende in 1973. Effective about 40 percent of the time have been U.S. sanctions with more narrow policy goals (e.g., against expropriation, or to limit the spread of nuclear weapons, or against terrorism or abuses of human rights). Examples include the measures taken to encourage Ethiopia to compensate U.S. companies for expropriation and U.S. efforts in 1975–7 to discourage South Korea and Taiwan from reprocessing spent nuclear fuel (a possible step toward developing nuclear weapons).

Indeed, even if sanctions might not be effective in accomplishing a foreign policy objective, they might still be used to give the President the appearance of "doing something." Faced with immediate political and diplomatic pressures to act, the President will often find that sanctions represent more concrete action than do diplomatic measures, and they are usually more acceptable to many constituencies and less costly than

233

the use of force. In short, at least the occasional use of economic sanctions has become inevitable.[1]

2. The choices among possible types of economic sanctions should not only encompass cutbacks in bilateral government programs or controls on exports. Rather, each use of sanctions should be based on a careful analysis of the vulnerabilities of the target country and the relative costs to the United States of alternative sanctions.

Controls on imports or private financial transactions might sometimes be advisable as part of a sanctions package, and they might even be the most effective and least costly measures. Indeed, one comprehensive empirical study concluded that import controls have been the most successful sanctions and that various financial controls have also been effective at times.[2] For example, increased U.S. duties on sugar imports from the Dominican Republic helped destabilize the Trujillo regime in 1961–2,[3] and U.S. threats to deny MFN status to imports from Romania encouraged Romania to relax emigration restrictions for several years.[4] The freeze on $12 billion of Iran's assets probably had the greatest impact of all the comprehensive U.S. sanctions against Iran during 1979–81.[5]

A preliminary analysis of the trade and credit situation of potential target countries indicates several cases in which a country would be at least as vulnerable to U.S. import and possibly credit controls as it would be to U.S. export controls. For example, the United States imports about 39 percent of all of South Korea's foreign sales, while its exports total only about 20 percent of South Korea's foreign purchases. American banks also provide about 26 percent of that country's private foreign credit. Other examples include Chile, Guatemala, Honduras, the Philippines, and Taiwan.[6]

Moreover, although calculating the domestic costs of various sanctions is difficult and inexact, import and financial controls might cost the United States less than export controls. For example, export sanctions directly cause lost sales for U.S. business and lost jobs for U.S. workers,

[1] See discussion in Chapter 2, Sections A and B.1.

[2] It also concluded that "financial controls are marginally more successful than export controls." G. Hufbauer and J. Schott, *Economic Sanctions Reconsidered: History and Current Policy* 89 (1985). However, its category of financial controls included bilateral government programs, private financial transactions, and international financial institutions. The study did not separately analyze the relative effectiveness of these three activities.

[3] Id. at 302–7.

[4] See Chapter 5 at notes 92–96.

[5] W. Christopher, "Introduction," in *American Hostages in Iran* 24 (P. Kreisberg ed. 1985); R. Carswell and R. Davis, "Crafting the Financial Settlement," in id. at 231–4 [hereinafter Carswell and Davis, "Crafting the Financial Settlement"].

[6] See Table 1 and discussion in Chapter 2, at notes 68–75.

and they raise longer-term questions about the reliability of U.S. suppliers. In contrast, import controls generally mean few, if any, lost jobs or sales in the United States in the short term, though there can be higher costs to purchasers and harmful long-term effects on productivity.[7]

3. The present U.S. laws for imposing economic sanctions for foreign policy reasons are haphazard. Most of the statutes were passed primarily for other purposes and without any serious consideration of the best legal regime for economic sanctions. Accordingly, there are dramatic variations in the amount of presidential authority in the five types of activity that sanctions restrict – bilateral government programs, exports, imports, private financial transactions, and lending by the international financial institutions.

Passing new, specific legislation in a timely fashion when a dispute or minor crisis arises is often difficult or even impossible. Consequently, the existing legal regime can lead to two undesirable results. First, it can skew the President's decisions in a nonemergency situation toward sanctions that may not be as effective as, or that may have more negative repercussions on the U.S. economy than, other options. Second, it encourages the President to resort to declarations of dubious national emergencies, which open the door to nearly unlimited economic power that Congress cannot effectively review or terminate.

As for the first result, existing laws can strongly influence the President's choice of which sanctions to employ when there is no declared national emergency – whether he wants to protest Soviet actions, to try to destabilize an unfriendly government, or to express displeasure with a country's policies toward human rights or terrorism. These laws partly explain why the United States frequently resorts to measures that are easy to impose, such as cutbacks in government programs or new export controls,[8] and why it less frequently employs limits on imports or private financial transactions.

A classic example is the U.S. reaction to the Soviet invasion of Afghanistan in late 1979. The United States terminated or restricted several government programs, such as Soviet fishing rights in U.S. waters and Aeroflot airline service to this country. Exports were sharply limited, particularly agricultural products and high-technology goods. The only effort to limit imports, however, was President Carter's abortive attempt to restrict imports of Soviet ammonia, an attempt that ran afoul of the International Trade Commission.[9] Private financial transactions were untouched, except for those related to exports.[10]

---

[7] See Chapter 2, at notes 76–81.
[8] See list in Hufbauer and Schott, supra note 1, at 70–7.
[9] See Chapter 5 at notes 125–30.
[10] See Chapter 6 at notes 27–32. Included in these export-related controls was the

As the second undesirable result, the haphazard legal regime for economic sanctions creates incentives for the President to declare a national emergency in order to employ the sweeping powers of IEEPA in dubious circumstances or to continue their use after the crisis has passed. For example, serious questions can be raised about President Reagan's resort to IEEPA for his recent actions against Nicaragua, South Africa, and Libya. Even if one believes that the President legitimately needed to use IEPPA powers to react quickly to each of these "unusual or extraordinary" threats, it is still unclear why he should continue to use IEEPA month after month against Nicaragua and Libya, rather than seek the appropriate nonemergency powers from Congress. Should the United States really come to accept national emergencies "as the fittings of ordinary existence"?[11]

The present U.S. legal system for economic sanctions is obviously not the only possible legal framework. The recent amendments in the laws, such as the export laws, suggest further useful steps. Moreover, even the preliminary analysis of the laws of major U.S. allies indicates other approaches.[12]

A. THRESHOLD CONSIDERATIONS

Anyone attempting to develop a better legal regime for imposing economic sanctions encounters two important threshold considerations. First, because the variety of possible sanctions involves myriad issues, there is no quick fix. Rather, once the principal problems associated with the present system have been identified, it is important to flesh out alternatives for improving the system.

In doing so, *it seems most productive to concentrate on three of the five broad activities for economic sanctions – exports, imports, and private financial transactions.* Changes in the remaining two categories, bilateral government programs and the U.S. role in international financial institutions (IFIs), are either less imperative or much more difficult to achieve.

In the area of government programs, the President now has nearly complete discretion to act. Giving him more discretion would add little to his authority. Taking some discretion away, however, does not seem advisable. These government programs are arguably the activity the Pres-

---

arguably broad use of the EAA to stop financial payments to the Soviets in connection with the Moscow Olympics.

[11] *Bauer v. United States*, 244 F.2d 794, 797 (9th Cir. 1957)(dicta), quoted in *United States v. Yoshida Int'l, Inc.*, 526 F.2d 560, 581n.32 (C.C.P.A. 1975). See the discussion of IEEPA in Chapter 9, Section C.

[12] See Chapter 11.

ident as Chief Executive should most control. Also, it is not clear how reducing the President's discretion would improve the use of sanctions or achieve some other worthwhile objective. Finally, as Congress has already discovered in its attempts to condition foreign assistance, limiting the President's discretion here is a very difficult task.[13]

As for the IFIs, asserting more U.S. control would be very difficult, given their charters and international character. The International Monetary Fund is designed to promote exchange, while the World Bank and the regional development banks seek to assist the economic and social development of developing countries. Their charters specify the IFIs' nonpolitical nature and often contain prohibitions against weighing political considerations.[14]

United States efforts to politicize the IFIs further would probably not only fail, but also weaken their effectiveness generally. Given the continuing serious problems of Third World debt and international financial stability, now does not seem to be the time to create further difficulties for these institutions.

A second threshold consideration is that the many laws regulating exports, imports, and private financial transactions almost always have purposes other than imposing sanctions. Indeed, although the export laws are created primarily for foreign policy purposes (in the broad sense that includes national security), nearly all the laws regulating imports and private financial transactions have other important purposes.

The import laws are designed, among other reasons, to protect American businesses and workers and to provide a negotiating basis for persuading other countries to reduce their trade barriers.[15] Likewise, the laws regulating private financial transactions with foreigners are designed to help ensure the solvency of banks and other financial entities, to protect depositors and borrowers, and to provide for the safe and efficient functioning of the U.S. and the international financial systems.[16]

A thorough analysis of all these other purposes and priorities of the laws is well beyond the scope of this study. *The most reasonable and efficient approach is a carefully tailored one – to consider alternatives that are intended to affect only the President's authority to impose economic sanctions for foreign policy purposes.* This requires considering how to give the President the authority to impose a sanction, such as

[13] See Chapter 3, Section B.1.
[14] See Chapter 7.
[15] See Chapter 5 at notes 1–3.
[16] See Chapter 6 at notes 47–57.

import controls, while specifically limiting that authority to its use for foreign policy purposes.

B. THE BROAD ALTERNATIVES: A MAJOR RESTRUCTURING

Given the problems of the present system and the two preceding considerations, what might a better legal regime entail? Three broad alternatives seem possible in nonemergency situations: (1) reducing the President's discretion to impose export controls so that it is more in line with his authority over import controls and private financial transactions, (2) increasing the President's discretion over import controls and private financial transactions to bring it more into line with his present authority over export controls, or (3) reducing the President's discretion over exports and increasing it over imports and financial transactions, so that his discretion over all three activities is roughly at some middle ground. Chart 2 depicts these three alternatives.

As discussed later, increasing the President's authority over some types of financial transactions (non-trade-related general loans and foreigners' bank deposits) ventures into relatively uncharted territory. The recommendations in that area are consequently more tentative than with imports.

All three alternatives are intended to narrow the disparity between the President's sweeping authority over exports versus his limited discretion over imports and private financial transactions. This would minimize the bias that the legal regime presently imposes upon his choice among alternative sanctions for foreign policy purposes.[17] The alternatives differ, however, in their approach to the means of reducing the disparities. Alternative 1 would allow the President only limited discretion, similar to his present authority over imports and private financial transactions. Alternative 2 would allow the President great discretion, similar to his present authority over exports. Alternative 3 would find a middle ground. To facilitate the process of choosing among the alternatives, each must be examined further.

Alternative 1. This alternative would require substantial amendments to the export laws in order to reduce sharply the President's power to impose controls.[18] The result would be very limited presidential authority over

---

[17] As discussed earlier, the impact of each alternative would be limited as much as possible to the effect on presidential authority to impose sanctions for foreign policy purposes and would not contribute to or detract from other purposes.

[18] See Table 3, at p. 244.

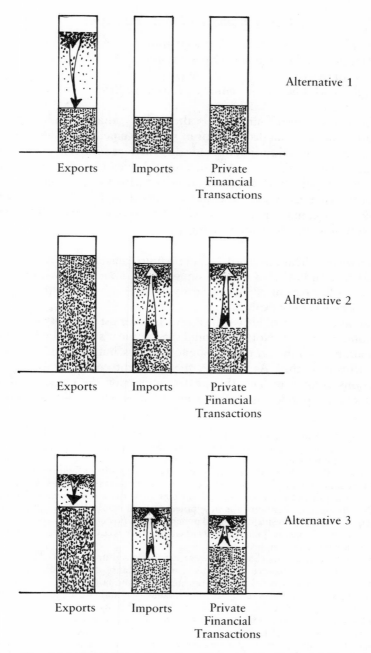

Chart 2. Alternatives. These three alternatives seek to narrow the disparity between the President's broad authority over exports and his limited discretion over imports and private financial transactions. As discussed in this section, however, the alternatives differ in their approach to reducing the disparities.

exports, imports, or private financial transactions in the absence of a declared national emergency. On first impression, this alternative would be very attractive to the U.S. Chamber of Commerce, exporters, unions, and others who believe in removing Executive Branch obstacles to U.S. sales abroad.

The glaring shortcoming of this alternative is that it would aggravate the problem of casual declarations of national emergencies and resort to IEEPA. As discussed earlier, not only do sanctions sometimes serve useful purposes, but Presidents appear determined to employ them as a tool of U.S. foreign policy. Making key economic activities difficult to control under nonemergency powers is likely to drive the President to his easily invoked, sweeping emergency powers. This problem makes the alternative even less attractive than the present system.[19]

Alternative 2. This alternative would require substantial increases in the President's authority to control imports and financial transactions for foreign policy reasons.[20] His authority would be similar to the extensive control he has over exports.

This alternative would give the President the most flexibility in selecting economic sanctions. Not only would the President's authority be roughly comparable over the various economic activities, but he would have broad authority in each.[21] As a result, the President could choose a set of sanctions tailored to have the greatest impact on the target country at the most acceptable cost to the United States. He would also feel less

---

[19] Another drawback of this alternative is that the President would be especially likely to oppose any efforts to limit the use of IEEPA, since IEEPA would become even more important to him.

[20] See Table 3. The new authority over imports and private financial transactions might be conceptualized as new "mini-emergency" powers for the President in minor foreign policy disputes or crises. Indeed, the new authority might be enacted in a mini-IEEPA. For special situations, the new powers would be available to fill in some of the gap between the President's limited nonemergency powers and his sweeping emergency powers. (Professor John Schmertz at Georgetown was very helpful in developing this "mini-emergency" approach.)

The discussion in this chapter, however, is expressed in terms of changes in the existing import and finance laws. This is partly because the preceding analysis of existing laws was structured in terms of those laws, and not along a new conceptual approach. Moreover, it would be difficult to define the criteria for a "mini-emergency," and the concept of such a state is strained somewhat by the existence under the nonemergency statutes of the President's broad authority over exports. Finally, given the strong jurisdictional sensitivities of congressional committees, it seems advisable to view the specific recommendations below as changes in or additions to the existing laws over imports and private financial transactions, rather than trying to mobilize a special effort such as was required to pass IEEPA.

[21] As discussed in Section A, he would also continue to have broad authority over bilateral government programs.

need to declare a national emergency and invoke IEEPA, since he would have so much nonemergency authority.[22]

Although alternative 2 has much to commend it, there are problems. First, it is difficult to make changes in the import and financial laws that affect only the President's authority to impose sanctions for foreign policy purposes. There is always room for some abuse of the legislative intent. For example, how assuredly can one provide the President with new import authority and not have him, say in an election year, restrict imports of televisions from Taiwan because of its alleged violations of human rights, or even shoes from Italy because it allegedly is not tough enough on terrorists? It would be tempting for the President to circumvent the extensive procedural and substantive protections in the present economic-based import laws.[23] The more new authority the President is given, the greater the room for abuse.

Second, even assuming that the new laws are written as tightly as possible, will alternative 2's new authorities make the use of economic sanctions so easy that it becomes excessive?[24] All economic sanctions have costs — whether to exporters, importers and consumers, bankers, or the international economic system. The full costs, such as lost markets for agricultural products or foreigners moving their bank deposits elsewhere to avoid a future freeze order, often take time to appear. If sanctions can be imposed more easily, the short-term political or foreign policy benefits might greatly expand their use, even though a longer-term assessment of their full costs would argue against many of the uses.[25]

Alternative 3. This alternative takes a middle ground. It would require a substantial increase in the President's authority to control imports and financial transactions but not as much as would alternative 2. At the same time, it would reduce the President's control over exports.[26]

This alternative would give the President great flexibility in selecting

---

[22] As discussed in Section C, this chapter, the new nonemergency authority should be carefully hedged with provisions regarding its invocation, its termination, and the role of Congress. Consequently, unless IEEPA is also amended, the President would still have considerable incentive to resort to IEEPA's essentially unconstrained grant of authority.

[23] See discussion of these statutes in Chapter 5 at notes 121–38. Although there would be restrictions on the new nonemergency powers (see Section C), the procedural and substantive requirements are unlikely to be as extensive and demanding as those now found in many of the economic-based import laws.

[24] Some would say that the present use of sanctions is already excessive and that the proposed new authorities would aggravate the problem.

[25] On costs, see Chapter 2 at notes 76–81.

[26] See Table 3.

controls over exports, imports, or private financial transactions. Since he would have considerable authority in each area, his decision would not be biased by the laws. Moreover, although there would be some constraints on his authority, he still could impose a wide range of sanctions. This alternative would reduce somewhat the President's incentives to invoke the sweeping powers of IEEPA since he would have more non-emergency authority than before, although the effect would depend on exactly how much authority the President were given.

The increased authorities would bring the same problems (of potential abuse and excessive use of sanctions) that accompany alternative 2, but they would not be as severe since the President would have less authority.

Choosing among the alternatives. Both alternatives 2 and 3 are preferable to the present system for the reasons discussed above. Alternative 1 is not preferable because it would lead to much more frequent use of IEEPA.

Alternative 3 is better than alternative 2.[27] Both alternatives recognize the logic of increasing the President's control over imports and private financial transactions and bringing his authority more in line with his power over exports. Alternative 3, however, also recognizes that the President's nearly unlimited control over exports would probably be unnecessary for foreign policy reasons once he had the other weapons in his arsenal. If the President could also impose import and financial controls, he would not need to rely so heavily on export controls.

Alternative 3 would also correct the inconsistency that today gives the President unfettered power over exports in spite of the pressing need for the United States to encourage export trade.[28] Limiting his control over exports might help reduce any excessive use of export controls and help signal a U.S. commitment to becoming a more reliable supplier.[29]

One positive side effect of adopting alternative 3, or even 2, would be

---

[27] The choice between alternatives 2 and 3 is close because much hangs on how effectively and carefully the laws can be amended to give the President greater authority over imports and financial transactions, and (in the case of alternative 3) less authority over exports.

[28] The U.S. merchandise trade deficit (i.e., the excess of imports over exports) was a record $171.2 billion in 1987, nearly 10% larger than the $156.2 gap in 1986, according to the Department of Commerce. 5 *Int'l Trade Rep. (BNA)* 198 (Feb. 17, 1988). The 1987 deficit began to show improvement in November and December 1987, largely because of the decline in the value of the dollar. Id. at 198–9. The improvement was continuing through March 1988. *N.Y. Times*, May 18, 1988, at A1, col. 6.

[29] See discussion in Chapter 2 at notes 76–7.

a strengthening of the case for amending IEEPA as well. If the President had a better package of authorities for imposing sanctions without having to declare a national emergency, there would be less need to use IEEPA. Moreover, unless IEEPA is amended to make its casual use more difficult, the President can nullify any qualifications on new nonemergency powers by continuing to resort to IEEPA.

The next section elaborates more detailed recommendations for changes in the President's authority to impose economic sanctions under nonemergency laws or pursuant to IEEPA. (These proposals are briefly sketched in Table 3.)[30]

C. SPECIFIC RECOMMENDATIONS

The loss of the legislative veto was a blow to congressional efforts to control presidential discretion in a carefully tailored way.[31] Nevertheless, a wide variety of legislative tools are still available for trimming the President's authority over exports and for expanding it over imports and private financial transactions, as well as for improving IEEPA.

A list of these tools would include provisions that specify what type of consultation would be required and when, flatly prohibit certain actions, redefine the criteria for imposing controls, provide for administrative and judicial review, and establish time limits tying the date when controls will become effective or when they will lapse to congressional approval by joint resolution.[32] The legislative reaction to the 1980 grain embargo suggests two additional tools – provisions for contract sanctity and compensation to the injured business. Finally, as discussed below

---

[30] Given the present haphazard U.S. laws for employing economic sanctions, the recommendations below do not require a precise overall model of the relationship between the President and Congress. Instead, these recommendations, which impose more rationality on the presently great disparities in the President's authority, can be supported by people with widely varying conceptions of the role of Congress in foreign affairs.

Nevertheless, I will note my belief that Congress should be in a constructive partnership with the President on foreign affairs, with the President taking the lead role (i.e., the general partner) and Congress playing an important supporting role. See generally W. Christopher, "Ceasefire Between the Branches: A Compact in Foreign Affairs," 60 *Foreign Aff.* 989, 998 (1982) (calling for a new "compact" between the two branches "based on mutually reinforcing commitments and mutually accepted restraints"); T. Franck and E. Weisband, *Foreign Policy by Congress* 61 (1979) (supporting a "system of *policy codetermination*"). This partnership approach is fully consistent with the Constitution. See the discussion in Chapter 10.

[31] See discussion of the *Chadha* case in Chapter 9 at notes 93–5.

[32] For a thorough, excellent study of many possible legislative approaches, see T. Franck and C. Bob, "The Return of Humpty-Dumpty: Foreign Relations Law After the *Chadha* Case," 79 *Am. J. Int'l L.* 912, 933–59 (1985).

Table 3. *A new regime*

I. President's nonemergency powers
  A. Exports: Broad powers retained, with some trimming
    1. Criteria, consultation, and reporting requirements retained
    2. Contract sanctity expanded, with compensation for existing contracts and licenses
    3. Sunset provision expanded
    4. Use of extraterritorial jurisdiction discouraged
  B. Imports: Broad powers granted
    1. Criteria, consultation, and reporting requirements enacted
    2. Sunset provision included
    3. Contract sanctity respected, with compensation for existing contracts
    4. (Possibly) linkage provisions:
      a. To controls on most imports
      b. To controls on government programs or other sanctions
    5. Adherence to GATT encouraged
  C. Private financial transactions:
    1. Trade financing: Broad authority granted, same as for "exports" and "imports" above
    2. General lending: Power to stop lending granted (probably limited to foreign governments)
      a. Criteria, consultation, and reporting requirements enacted
      b. Contract sanctity respected, with compensation if old loans terminated
      c. Sunset provision included
      d. Extraterritorial jurisdiction discouraged, and jurisdiction over U.S. persons only
    3. Foreigners' bank deposits and other assets: (Possibly) power to freeze; same provisions as for "General lending" above
II. President's emergency powers
  Applies to exports, imports, and private financial transactions: Sweeping authority retained, but ability to declare and continue emergency trimmed
    1. Tougher criteria and mandatory consultation requirements enacted; reporting requirements retained
    2. Sunset provision included
    3. Contract sanctity provisions the same as for nonemergency powers
    4. Use of extraterritorial jurisdiction discouraged

for imports and financial credit, "linkages" of various types might be required. For example, an import control could not be imposed unless other controls – on different products or even of a different type (such as an export control) – were also imposed.

Making lists is easy. It is more demanding to develop the most appropriate and effective measures for providing the President with the desired authority to impose sanctions for foreign policy reasons, while limiting the possibilities for misuse of that authority.

1. Trimming the President's authority over exports

Changes in the export laws should be at most evolutionary, rather than revolutionary. Indeed, recent amendments to the Export Administration Act provide an excellent starting point.

a. Expanding the contract sanctity provision. The contract sanctity provision of the EAA now prohibits the President from imposing foreign policy controls on the export of goods or technology for which there are existing contracts or validated licenses. The President may waive this prohibition if he certifies that there is a serious "breach of peace," and that prohibiting or curtailing the contracts or licenses would help remedy it.[33]

This contract sanctity provision should be expanded to apply to national security controls as well as foreign policy controls.[34] Extending the coverage closes an obvious loophole. As illustrated by President Carter's questionable declaration in 1980 that the Soviet grain embargo was imposed for national security as well as foreign policy reasons, the dividing line between these two types of EAA controls can easily be bridged.[35] Moreover, this expanded coverage will not tie the President's hands in dealing with sensitive national security matters since he can determine when a waiver is necessary.

Retaining a waiver provision would allow the President to act decisively, rather than to have the controls' impact diluted by numerous exceptions for continuing business relationships under existing contracts and licenses.

Nevertheless, the injured exporter should be compensated when the President invokes the waiver provision to terminate existing contracts and licenses.[36] And adding a cost to the President's action might also help deter casual resort to the waiver provision.

---

[33] See Chapter 4 at notes 80–6. As noted there, the phrase "breach of peace" is vague and subject to conflicting interpretations. For purposes of the recommendations here, however, the critical issue is whether the President uses the waiver to terminate existing contracts or licenses.

[34] As discussed in Chapter 4 at note 33, the EAA distinguishes between "national security" and "foreign policy" controls. However, unless this book is specifically addressing those controls in the EEA, the phrase "foreign policy" is used broadly to include national security considerations.

[35] See Chapter 4, Section A.3.

[36] West Germany generally allows compensation if the Government terminates existing contracts or licenses. See Chapter 11 at notes 18–22.

This cost would usually be small, however. First, it would be incurred only when the President instituted export controls and decreed that existing contracts and licenses were somehow limited or terminated. Potential contracts or pending license applications would provide no basis for relief. Second, most export controls for foreign policy purposes are levied against countries to which the United States does not export a great amount – such as Nicaragua and Libya. Even against the Soviet Union, U.S. exports are generally less than $3 billion per year.[37] Moreover, only *part* of a year's total exports would be covered at one time by existing contracts or licenses. Finally, consistent with accepted measures of damages, the exporter would be under an obligation to mitigate its damages by, for example, attempting to sell the goods elsewhere.

Although the costs would likely be small, compensation may be a useful deterrent since it seems difficult to provide other significant safeguards against dubious use of the provision. (Other legislative steps that could be useful include drafting the criteria for waiver as strictly as possible and requiring consultation with Congress and with exporters, but these measures would probably not be as helpful as the compensation provision.)[38]

Compensation would also reimburse exporters caught in the vagaries of international politics. Today, exporters themselves can assume the risk, and try to pass the costs on to their other customers or absorb the loss with resulting lower profits.[39] Exporters can also purchase insurance

[37] In 1981 (before the sanctions), U.S. exports were $184 million to Nicaragua and $813 million to Libya. Exports to the Soviet Union totaled $3.6 billion in 1979 (before the grain embargo) and were still $2.6 billion in 1982 and $1.5 billion in 1987. Exports to South Africa totaled $2.3 billion in 1984 and $1.3 billion in 1987. In contrast, U.S. exports in 1987 were $60 billion to Canada, $28 billion to Japan, and $15 billion to the United Kingdom. Total U.S. exports in 1987 were $253 billion. IMF, *Direction of Trade Statistics: Yearbook 1987*, at 404–6 (1987) and U.S. Dep't of Commerce, 68 *Survey* of *Current Business* 5–16–7 (March 1988).

[38] See earlier analysis of the limited utility of consultation and reporting provisions (e.g., Chapter 4, at notes 68–75) and of judicial review (Chapter 10 at notes 42–7). The mandatory consultation requirements, however, do raise a question whether compensation should be required for curtailing contracts entered into during the consultation period. (A similar question would arise for revoking licenses issued during the consultations, though the U.S. Government would presumably defer license decisions during this period.) The President should be able to declare at the start of consultations that, if sanctions were imposed, no compensation would be allowed for new contracts and licenses after that date. This would provide notice to exporters and would protect the United States from last-minute efforts to create claims against it.

[39] The present U.S. laws generally excuse the seller from performing under a contract when new government regulations make delivery impracticable. Hence, each party bears its own costs and loses any expected profits. U.C.C. § 2–615 and comments 4 and 10; accord, UN Convention on Contracts for the International Sale of Goods, art. 79, UN Doc. A/Conf. 97/18 (1980), reprinted in 19 *Int'l Legal Materials*. 668,

that covers cancellation of existing export licenses from the Foreign Credit Insurance Association (FCIA) or from other private insurers. This insurance, however, can be expensive and sometimes difficult to obtain, especially when the exporter is shipping to likely target countries such as the Soviet Union, South Africa, or Chile. The insurance companies are also aware of the risks.[40]

Whether the exporter insures or not, it faces the higher costs arising from the risk that the President will terminate or curtail its contracts for U.S. foreign policy reasons. This arguably is not a risk the exporter should have to bear, particularly since this country is trying to encourage com-

---

689–90 (1980). (There are also defenses in U.S. courts under the act of state doctrine and the Foreign Sovereignty Immunity Act of 1976, but it is not clear how they apply in the usual case in which the U.S. Government revokes an export license.) Foreign courts, however, have refused on occasion to allow U.S. export regulations to excuse a corporation in their countries from performing under a contract when the local law was found controlling. See *Sensor* case in Chapter 4 at notes 119–21; see also the recent UK case regarding U.S. controls under IEEPA, Chapter 9 at notes 59–60.

[40] FCIA is a private-sector group of about fifty insurance companies that offers export insurance in conjunction with the U.S. Export–Import Bank. FCIA has a wide range of export insurance programs, insuring exports worth about $36 billion during FYs 1981–5. FCIA, "America's Untapped Resource" (1986) (brochure on file with author); see generally A. Holden, "Export Credit Insurance and the FCIA," 14 *U.C.C. L.J.* 140 (1981); Eximbank, "A Map of Eximbank Programs" (undated brochure on file with author). For discussion of Eximbank, see Chapter 3 at notes 57–67.

An exporter can purchase political-risk insurance from FCIA that includes insurance against cancellation or nonrenewal of an export license. (It does not include denial of the license application, even if done for foreign policy reasons.) This insurance, which must usually be purchased with commercial-risk insurance, costs from 0.7 to 1.5% of the value of the exports for comprehensive coverage of many shipments to various countries by the exporter. Single-transaction coverage is also available but is usually more expensive. The insurance normally begins from the time of shipment. Preshipment coverage is available at an additional cost. Since the loss from revocation of an export license could often come before shipment, availability of this coverage could be important.

The cost of the insurance varies because of several factors, including the country to which the goods are being shipped. Risky countries mean higher rates, higher deductible amounts, a lower percentage of value covered (e.g., 100 or 90%), and other conditions. For some countries, insurance is not available because of the risk. In addition, FCIA is bound by Eximbank's political guidelines. Telephone interview with Robert L. Chapman, FCIA Assistant Vice President (Oct. 29, 1986). As a result, FCIA recently was not offering political-risk insurance for exports to Peru, Poland, Somali, the Soviet Union, and Zaire, among other countries. Insurance for exports to many other countries was heavily conditioned. Id.; see also FCIA, Country Limitation Schedule, Mar. 1, 1986, and supplements through July 17, 1986 (on file with author).

Outside the FCIA, private insurance companies do offer policies that include revocation of export licenses. Though the policies are not limited by the Eximbank guidelines, they are subject to varying rates and many conditions. For example, through National Union Fire Insurance Co., AIG Political Risk Inc. was offering in 1986 a political-risk policy, but it apparently has a minimum premium of $50,000. (See AIG documents on file with author.)

panies to increase their exports. The U.S. Government is taking action against the target country, and the exporter is caught in the fray.

Admittedly, private parties often bear the costs of government actions that adversely affect them, whether the actions are changes in trade policies, the tax laws, or zoning laws. Only in limited areas do the parties have a claim to just compensation under the fifth amendment of the U.S. Constitution.[41] And termination of export licenses and existing contracts to export are not constitutionally protected.[42]

Compensation provisions are not without precedent, however, The U.S. Government has on occasion provided by statute for compensation to people injured by its acts or by developments in the foreign trade area. Most analogous is the 1981 law that requires the Secretary of Agriculture to compensate farmers for an agricultural embargo against a major foreign purchasing country, whether imposed under the EAA for foreign policy or national security reasons. The compensation provision is generous since it assumes that producers of the embargoed commodities could qualify for prices equivalent to 100 percent of parity.[43]

Similarly, the trade adjustment assistance program has contained various compensation provisions over the years for businesses, workers, and communities adversely affected by increased imports. The original provision in the 1962 law required a link between the injury and tariff concessions by the U.S. Government, though such a link no longer need be demonstrated.[44] During its history, this adjustment assistance program has been much broader in scope and more expensive than the recommendation here for compensation.

The details of this compensation proposal need refinement. It would

---

[41] "[N]or shall private property be taken for public use, without just compensation." U.S. Constitution, amend. V, last clause. See generally, G. Stone, L. Seidman, C. Sunstein, and M. Tushnet, *Constitutional Law* 1445–65 (1986).

[42] See Chapter 4 at note 5 about exporting being a privilege rather than a right. See generally P. Trimble, "Foreign Policy Frustrated – *Dames & Moore*, Claims Court Jurisdiction, and a New Raid on the Treasury," 84 *Colum. L. Rev.* 317 (1984); A. Brownstein, "The Takings Clause and the Iranian Claims Settlement," 29 UCLA *L. Rev.* 984 (1982). The Trimble article raises some difficult policy questions about allowing compensation for takings in foreign affairs cases.

[43] See Chapter 4, at note 61.

[44] The original law was part of the Trade Expansion Act of 1962, Pub. L. No. 87–794, § 201, 76 Stat. 872. More recent versions were at 19 U.S.C. § 1801 et seq. The Trade Adjustment Assistance Reform and Extension Act of 1986 further extended adjustment assistance for workers and firms until September 30, 1991. Pub. L. No. 99–272, 110 Stat. 300, 304 (codified at 19 U.S.C. §§ 2291, 2297–8, 2345 (Supp. IV 1986)). See generally, "Adjustment Assistance," *Int'l Trade Rep.* (BNA), U.S. *Import Weekly Reference File*, 61:0101–09 (1987); R. Lawrence and R. Litan, *Saving Free Trade: A Pragmatic Approach* 51–62, 112–22 (1986); G. Hufbauer and H. Rosen, *Trade Policy for Troubled Industries* (1986).

seem that the party in the United States who held the existing contract or license should be the party compensated, provided, of course, that it could demonstrate losses. Although further analysis would be useful, compensation would probably not be provided to persons in the United States who were not direct parties to the license or contract, such as suppliers to the exporter. They too might be hurt by the export controls since the exporter would not make additional purchases from them to complete the contract. There would, however, be difficult evidentiary problems as additional parties were added. For example, who would the exporter actually have bought from? At what price?[45]

Even if the proposal does not cover these other parties, the U.S. Government could still decide to compensate them in special situations. For example, when President Carter cut back sharply on grain exports to the Soviet Union in 1980, his Administration took a number of steps to prop up agricultural prices beyond buying up existing export contracts. These steps included financial incentives to encourage the accumulation of larger grain reserves by farmers, increased government purchases of certain commodities, and diplomatic efforts and financial incentives to promote exports to other countries.[46]

Compensation almost certainly should not be provided to the foreign purchaser. This would be contrary to the purpose of the sanction and the invocation of the waiver clause, which is to put economic pressure on the target country.[47]

[45] Cf. *Illinois Brick Co. v. Illinois*, 431 U.S. 720 (1977) (limiting the parties able to recover in an antitrust price-fixing case).

[46] Subcommittee on Europe and the Middle East of the House Committee on Foreign Affairs, 97th Cong., 1st Sess., *An Assessment of the Afghanistan Sanctions: Implications for Trade and Diplomacy in the 1980's*, at 25–35 (Comm. Print 1981) (report prepared by the Congressional Reference Service) [hereinafter House Afghanistan Report]. The purpose was to try to offset the losses to farmers for sales to the Soviet Union that were not yet under contract and now were prevented by the embargo.

[47] It would also be politically difficult for the President to justify payments to parties in the country against which he was imposing sanctions. Even if the injured foreign party were an innocent middleman in a third country, compensation would also seem administratively and politically difficult.

Another administrative issue is the source of the monies for the compensation. They could come from general tax revenues or from a special fund created by fees of one sort or another. Though further analysis would again be useful, general revenues would seem to be the advisable source, just as these revenues would be the source if the 1981 agricultural embargo provision were triggered and just as these revenues are used for the trade adjustment assistance program. If a special fund were created, presumably the fees would be on exporters. This would, however, make them shoulder the costs of the U.S. Government's sanctions for foreign policy purposes, though the costs would be spread over a large number of export transactions.

Other administrative questions include: What department or agency should administer the law? What substantive rules and procedures should apply? What rights should the party have to administrative and judicial review? Definitive answers to all

b. Enlarging the sunset provision. If the President imposes a major export embargo against a country, he should be required to obtain congressional approval to continue the embargo beyond a short period. The 1985 Act already prohibits the President from imposing export controls on any agricultural commodity for more than sixty days, unless Congress enacts a joint resolution authorizing the action.[48]

This proposed "sunset" provision could usefully apply to any major embargo against a country.[49] Congressional review after, say, six months[50] would require the President to justify this dramatic and major act of a trade embargo. Given political realities, Congress would probably go along with him, but the review provision would stimulate greater discussion of the issues and require Congress to take a position.

The sunset provision might also require Congress to renew the embargo every year or six months. This would further ensure that Congress and the President had consciously addressed the need to continue the embargo.[51]

Despite its benefits, the sunset provision should not apply to any export control, but only to major embargoes. Congress cannot be expected to act every time the President adds or modifies an export control. This would be a burden on Congress and would unnecessarily hamper the President.[52]

---

these issues are beyond the scope of this book. However, many analogies and lessons can be found here, especially in the discussion of the EAA in Chapter 4.

[48] An exception is provided if the controls are part of a cutoff of all exports to that country. See Chapter 4 at notes 65–6.

[49] Carefully defining "major embargo" is important. For example, it might be defined as controls over exports that amounted to say, 80% of the U.S. exports to that country in the preceding twelve months. Otherwise, the President could stop all exports, except for one or two minor items, and argue that the sunset provision did not apply because the embargo was not major.

[50] Six months would probably give Congress adequate time to study the reason for the embargo and initial developments under it. This was the period established for initial review (and regular follow-up reviews) by the now invalid legislative veto under the National Emergencies Act and IEEPA. 50 U.S.C. § 1622 (1982). See Chapter 9, at notes 90–2.

Sixty days is another possibility. It is the period now for a major agricultural embargo, as well as the period (with a possible thirty-day extension) permitted under the War Powers Resolution, discussed below. However, sixty days seems a very short period for Congress to evaluate an embargo, especially since an embargo will probably not be as visible, nor as urgent, as the deployment of U.S. combat forces into hostilities or into situations where imminent involvement in hostilities is likely.

[51] The legislative veto provision in the National Emergencies Act and IEEPA had also provided for a regular six-month review. 50 U.S.C. § 1622.

[52] An alternative to the sunset provision would be a "report-and-wait" requirement whereby the President would have to inform Congress a designated period in advance before he imposed a major export embargo. Such provisions now exist for different circumstances in the EAA and the regulations for the Arms Export Control Act. For

A sunset provision has worked in a constructive way with the War Powers Resolution.[53] There, the President is required to "terminate any use of United States Armed Forces" if he does not obtain congressional approval within sixty, or possibly ninety, days after introducing the forces "into hostilities or into situations where imminent involvement in hostilities is clearly indicated by the circumstances."[54] The deployment of U.S. Marines to Lebanon in 1982–4 illustrates its use.

When the Marines began suffering casualties from hostile fire in August 1983, many in Congress argued that the sixty-day period had started running.[55] Facing a congressional vote, both the Executive Branch and Congress engaged in a more intense public discussion of U.S. policy in Lebanon and the need for the Marines. President Reagan, for example, made several major public statements. The result was a congressional joint resolution, signed by the President on October 12, 1983, in which Congress authorized the continued presence of the Marines in Lebanon for another eighteen months.[56]

The benefits of this process were soon demonstrated by the tragic events of October 23, when a suicide attack destroyed the Marine barracks and

example, the Executive Branch must notify three congressional committees "at least 30 days before any license is approved for the export of goods or technology valued at more than $1,000,000 to any country" that the Secretary of State has determined, among other things, supports international terrorism. 50 U.S.C. app. § 2405(j) (1982 & West 1987). Also, current federal regulations now treat a former legislative veto provision of the Arms Export Control Act as a thirty-day report-and-wait requirement. 22 C.F.R. § 23.10(e) (1987). See, for example, the discussion in Chapter 4 at notes 143–60.

This alternative seems considerably less attractive than the proposed sunset provision. In a minor dispute or crisis, it would hamper decisive action by the President. Reporting to Congress and then waiting delays the President's action and gives the target country (as well as Congress) advance notice of what he might eventually do. The country can then take appropriate countermeasures.

[53] 50 U.S.C. § 1541–8 (1982 & Supp. III 1985).

[54] Id. § 1544. The President can certify that the additional thirty days are needed in certain situations. Id. § 1544(b).

[55] The vague language of the War Powers Resolution regarding "hostilities" has led to frequent confusion over when the time period begins to run, i.e., when have U.S. forces been introduced into the requisite situation? In the case of Lebanon, the Executive Branch continued to maintain that the period had not started, even though Marines were being killed by sniper fire. President Reagan reiterated this claim when he signed the joint resolution discussed below. *N.Y. Times*, Oct. 13, 1983, at A7, col. 1. Similarly, the Reagan Administration has refused to say that the Resolution's time period has begun to run in the continuing crisis in the Persian Gulf where Iran and Iraq have been attacking ships. C. Madison, "A Reflagged Policy," 19 *Nat'l J.* 2036 (1987); *Wash. Post*, Sept. 19, 1987, at A3, col. 1.

A sunset provision for the export laws would *not* have the same ambiguity over the starting point because it would commence on the specific date the formal controls began.

[56] Pub. L. No. 98-119, 97 Stat. 805 (1983).

killed 240 Marines. The disaster was much less divisive between the President and Congress, and throughout the nation, than it might have been. The sunset provision had led to the creation, through negotiation and public debate, of a more acceptable policy and of a greater national consensus.[57]

c. Reining in extraterritoriality. Although the need for flexibility argues for retaining in the statutes the potentially sweeping extraterritorial reach of export controls,[58] experience teaches that resort to broad claims of extraterritorial jurisdiction be sharply circumscribed. Moreover, granting the President increased authority to impose other types of sanctions, such as import controls, would presumably reduce his reliance on expansive export controls.

Judicious use of extraterritoriality can be effective. In the analogous case of IEEPA financial controls against Iran, extending the freeze to U.S. banks abroad accounted for nearly one-half of the $12 billion in frozen assets[59] and met only muted foreign criticism.[60] In contrast, as dramatized by the Reagan Administration's efforts to stop the Soviet gas pipeline, broad claims of extraterritoriality can be decidedly counterproductive where the major U.S. allies do not share the U.S. position on the underlying issue.[61]

Part of the problem appears to stem from the lack of institutional memory in a new administration. For example, many of the decision makers in the Reagan Administration apparently had little sense of what they were getting into with the pipeline controls. They were probably unaware of the earlier brouhahas with U.S. allies over TWEA controls

---

[57] Cf. L. Aspin, "Congress versus the Defense Department," in *The Tethered Presidency* 259–60 (T. Franck ed. 1981) (predicting this effect before the Lebanon crisis). Public debate over the Lebanon disaster was also muted by the U.S. invasion of Grenada, which began two days later on October 25.

While sunset provisions have begun to appear in other statutes concerning foreign policy, none have apparently come into play in any important way in U.S. actions. The EAA provision on agricultural embargoes has not been triggered. And the Reagan Administration apparently did not consider the August 1986 amendment to the Arms Export Control Act applicable to its arms sales to Iran in October–November 1986. See discussion in Chapter 4 at notes 154–5.

[58] See Chapter 4, Section A.6.

[59] Carswell and Davis, "Crafting the Financial Settlement," supra note 5, at 205, 233 ("[t]hat extraterritorial reach provided the real leverage").

[60] See R. Carswell and R. Davis, "The Economic and Financial Pressures: Freeze and Sanctions" 177–99, in *American Hostages in Iran*, supra note 5 [hereinafter Carswell and Davis, "Economic and Financial Pressures"]. This was in large part because of the general international outrage at the seizure of diplomatic personnel. Id.

[61] See Chapter 4, at notes 102–22.

regarding China and Cuba.[62] When the Administration later imposed sanctions against Nicaragua, South Africa, and Libya, the extraterritorial reach of the regulations was more limited.[63] Presumably the pipeline experience partly accounted for this.

Despite extensive discussion of the extraterritoriality issue in the cases and scholarly literature,[64] no simple solutions present themselves for discouraging its use, while simultaneously preserving flexibility. This probably helps explain why Congress did not amend the jurisdictional provisions in the 1985 Act, event though the pipeline fiasco was still a vivid memory.

A call for consistent application of international law principles raises as many questions as it resolves, since the theories for jurisdiction are hardly consistent or precise.[65] If acted on, another recommendation that U.S. courts consider certain general matters, such as the interests of the foreign state or the likelihood of retaliation, might provide some guidance in deciding lawsuits under the U.S. antitrust or other laws that involve the interests of other nations.[66] However, since export controls can be so sweeping and have such immediate impact, an important objective of any recommendation must be to influence the President's initial decision on the scope of the controls, not await some long-delayed court decision.

At least one step would be an improvement: The use of extraterritorial sanctions should be discouraged, especially in their broadest applications, by first requiring the President to make certain findings before he imposes these controls, and then by allowing disgruntled private parties to bring administrative challenges.[67] This approach is similar to the EAA's "for-

---

[62] See Chapter 9, at note 23.

[63] For example, the export controls against Nicaragua and Libya were limited to exports from the United States. 3 C.F.R. §§ 540.204–.208 (Nicaragua); 550.201–207 (Libya) (1987). The freeze of Libyan assets included those in overseas branches of U.S. banks and other entities. Id. § 550.206. See the earlier discussion in Chapter 9 at notes 59–60 regarding the decision by a UK court that found the Libyan controls to be overreaching.

[64] See sources cited in Chapter 4, Section A.6, and Chapter 9, Section A.

[65] See, e.g., S. Marcuss and E. Richard, "Extraterritorial Jurisdiction in United States Trade Law: The Need for a Consistent Theory," 20 *Colum. J. Transnat'l L.* 439, 446–7 (1981).

[66] See, e.g., *Restatement (Third) of the Foreign Relations Law of the United States* § 403 (1987) [hereinafter the Restatement]; K. Feinberg, "Economic Coercion and Economic Sanctions: The Expansion of United States Extraterritorial Jurisdiction," 30 *Am. U.L. Rev.* 323, 343–4 (1981).

[67] For example, particularly questionable in the pipeline case were the unique assertions of jurisdiction to (1) the exports of foreign subsidiaries of U.S. firms of goods and technology that were of wholly foreign origin and (2) exports by independent foreign companies of foreign-origin products whose only link to the United States was a licensing agreement. In the future, the President might be required to

eign availability" provisions, which were toughened in the 1985 amendments to help ensure better evaluation of the potential effectiveness of controls in light of the foreign availability of goods the President wants to control.[68]

Other changes in the export laws that could impose major limits on the President's present authority are, of course, possible.[69] This book, however, does not recommend further limits. Among other reasons, major changes would simply encourage the President to use IEEPA more frequently.

The President's authority can be trimmed sufficiently by the changes recommended here – expanding the contract sanctity provision and even including a limited right to compensation, adding a sunset provision requiring congressional approval of a comprehensive export embargo, and discouraging frequent claims of extraterritorial jurisdiction.

2. Giving the President broad authority over imports

The *best* opportunity to improve the U.S. legal regime for imposing sanctions with foreign policy goals is to expand substantially the President's power over imports. Although the President now has only meager authority in this area, the United States already has considerable experience with other import controls, such as those for antidumping and foreign subsidies.[70]

make special findings for jurisdiction to extend beyond U.S. territory and U.S. nationals (wherever located). The President might also be directed to give due regard to the legitimate interests of foreign governments and the jurisdictional principles of international law. See, e.g., section 403 of the Restatement, supra note 66.

[68] See 50 U.S.C. app. §§ 2404(f), 2405(h) (1982 & Supp. III 1985); 15 C.F.R. § 391 (1987). See also discussion in Chapter 4, Section A.4.b. Further efforts to limit the use of extraterritoriality should be actively considered. For example, the Executive Branch or Congress might create a commission to develop further concrete proposals. Although the creation of commissions is often a tactic for avoiding concrete action, it is important with regard to the perplexing question of extraterritorial jurisdiction to begin developing a consensus among policy makers about the issues and specific proposals. Professor Abbott has suggested several steps (including a U.S. commission and international negotiations) and possible substantive approaches in a comprehensive, thoughtful article: "Defining the Extraterritorial Reach of American Export Controls: Congress as Catalyst," 17 *Cornell Int'l L.J.* 79 (1984).

[69] Some of the most thoroughgoing ones include greatly expanding the right of administrative and judicial review over the imposition of controls and individual licensing decisions, and eliminating the President's power to impose foreign policy (though not national security) controls. See J. Murphy and A. Downey, "National Security, Foreign Policy and Individual Rights: The Quandary of United States Export Controls," 30 *Int'l & Comp. L.Q.* 822 (1981); K. Abbott, "Linking Trade to Political Goals: Foreign Policy Export Controls in the 1970s and 1980s," 65 *Minn. L. Rev.* 873, 873–89 (1981).

[70] See analysis of economic-based import laws in Chapter 5 at notes 121–38.

The most constructive way to proceed, however, is not to build on the 1985 additions to the President's authority over imports from Libya or countries supporting terrorists. Those provisions are far too open-ended. The Libyan provision contains no limitations whatsoever on the President's authority, reflecting the low congressional regard for that country and the relatively small economic cost to the United States of imposing sanctions against it. The terrorism provision requires the President only to consult Congress in advance "in every possible instance" and to report any sanctions immediately.[71]

Expanding section 232 of the Trade Expansion Act of 1962 is also inadvisable because the statute would require a complete revision. The language regarding "national security," the legislative history, and the actual uses of the law are too confining to suit the purposes discussed here.[72]

The best approach is to draft carefully a new statute that incorporates a number of provisions designed to protect against hasty use of the new authority and against use for reasons other than foreign policy. The EAA, as amended in 1985, can provide many useful analogies.

An import control act should, of course, have *detailed criteria* defining when the restrictions are to be imposed. Similar to the EAA provisions for foreign policy controls, there should also be requirements for *mandatory prior consultation* with Congress and for some consultation with affected U.S. industries, consumer groups, and other countries. Moreover, the President should be required to *report fully* to Congress whenever he uses his new authority. Such provisions, however, are only the first step.[73]

There should also be a provision for *contract sanctity* similar to the recommendation made earlier for the export laws. The provision should cover all import controls for foreign policy reasons and should compensate the importer when the President certifies that he must order the breach of existing contracts.

The new law should also contain a *sunset provision*, whereby Congress must approve any major import ban within, say, six months. As discussed earlier, such a provision would require the President to justify his action and would ensure that both the Executive Branch and Congress give serious consideration to the policy at issue.

The contract sanctity and sunset provisions should help put a damper on inappropriate uses of the President's new authority over import con-

---

[71] See Chapter 5, at notes 53–7.
[72] See Chapter 5, at notes 4–46.
[73] See Chapter 4, at notes 68–75. Before the 1985 amendments to the EAA, provisions such as these were not a very effective check on a determined President. Although the amendments tightened the criteria and consultation requirements, their impact is still uncertain and probably limited. Id.

trols. A sunset provision, however, would probably check the President less effectively than would the similar provision for export controls. In recent years, Congress has been more willing than the President to encourage import controls, in contrast to its frequent questioning of export sanctions. This can be explained largely by the short-term benefits of import restrictions for U.S. businesses and workers versus the immediate injury that export controls inflict.[74]

Pressures to use the new law for protectionist purposes would surely arise, however. For example, the U.S. steel industry might become "very concerned" about human rights violations in Taiwan and South Korea, and call for a ban on steel imports from those countries. Though it would have a tougher case to make, the shoe industry might use Italy's refusal to extradite terrorists as grounds for seeking a stop to Italian shoe imports.

The potential harm of these pressures should not be overestimated. First, to the extent that there is some factual basis for the pressures (e.g., actual human rights violations in South Korea), they arguably help further important U.S. foreign policy interests. Second, even if the pressures lead to the imposition of import controls largely for protectionist reasons, the restrictions are likely to apply to only one or a few countries.[75] Alternative foreign suppliers would usually be available to help minimize any additional costs to importers and consumers. For example, stopping steel imports from South Korea and Taiwan would only reduce slightly total U.S. steel imports, and the decrease might well be offset by increased imports from other countries that are not likely targets of economic sanctions.[76]

---

[74] For example, there is substantial support in Congress for various forms of protectionist import legislation, but the export controls on grain and pipeline equipment to the Soviets generated considerable outcry.

[75] Passage of the Comprehensive Anti-Apartheid Act of 1986 apparently reflected a mix of pressures. The primary motivation for the Act was certainly opposition to apartheid in South Africa. However, some of the import provisions that were added on the Senate floor and presumably helped the bill gain supporters appear to have been added partly as the result of pressure by special-interest groups seeking to help domestic industries. The import bans added were those on steel, textiles, and agricultural products. See Chapter 5 at notes 50–1.

[76] To the extent that there are alternative suppliers, the domestic U.S. industries would have less incentive in the first place to seek the imposition of economic sanctions on a particular country or countries.

Note that the U.S. relations with its principal suppliers are such that imposing economic sanctions on them for (noneconomic) foreign policy reasons seems unlikely. The principal suppliers in 1987 were, in descending order of value, Japan, Canada, West Germany, Mexico, and the United Kingdom. See sources cited in note 37 supra. The most likely exception to this would probably be Mexico. Of course, the United States might be dependent on a very few countries for a certain item, such as a particular mineral. There is, however, usually more than one foreign supplier, and steps such as maintaining strategic reserves are possible. See generally, Office of Tech-

Nevertheless, additional steps might be taken to minimize the impact of protectionist pressures on decisions to impose controls for foreign policy reasons. Two provisions that have no analogues in the export laws should be seriously considered – one requiring "linkage" and another encouraging some consistency with GATT.[77]

As for *linkage*, a proposal meriting further study would require any import control to be linked to other import controls on at least several other goods from the target country. Such linkage would ensure that the United States' concern was with that country's policies, and not just, say, with its exports of steel or shoes. Requiring controls on several items that compete with U.S. industry at once is reasonable in a genuine policy dispute, and it would not inappropriately limit the President's new discretion. The broad controls would also give greater visibility to the President's action both in the target country and at home, thus increasing the need for a persuasive foreign policy rationale.[78]

Another possible, but even more problematic proposal for linkage would require that import controls be imposed only in conjunction with other types of economic sanctions – that is, controls on government programs, exports, or private financial transactions. This requirement would also give the President's actions broader impact in both the target country and the United States, thus creating a greater need for justification.[79]

nology Assessment, *Strategic Materials: Technologies to Reduce U.S. Import Vulnerability* (1985).

[77] Unlike export controls, there is no recommendation here regarding extraterritoriality. It is not a problem with import controls, because they limit imports into U.S. territory and hence have the strong jurisdictional basis of territoriality. It is worth noting, however, that import controls can have far-reaching influences on transactions abroad. For example, as part of the continuing U.S. embargo against Cuba under TWEA, there are regulations and specific certification procedures to ensure that imports from a third country (such as France) do not contain nickel from Cuba as one of their components. 31 C.F.R. § 515.536 (1987).

[78] Some potential problems do require that this proposal be studied further. For one thing, there is the problem of defining how many imported items must be affected. If the target country shipped only four major products to the United States, how would one prevent a situation from occurring in which the President would ban one of the important products (say, steel or shoes) plus twelve other items that either were not imported or were imported in minuscule quantities? Presumably this problem could be solved if the President were required to impose similar controls on, say, three of the four largest imports from the target country the previous year.

If a good working definition succeeded in making the President ban several of the country's important imports, the effect might be to increase protectionist pressures by encouraging the different U.S. industries affected to join together to lobby for the controls. However, requiring controls on several items might encourage more organized consumer opposition to the controls.

[79] A provision authorizing import controls when linked to export controls was considered in Congress in 1983–4. It was approved by the Senate, but not the House.

The purpose would again be to blunt protectionist efforts. Pressures for new import controls would be countered by pressures from other groups that opposed controls on exports or private financial transactions. However, the linkage provision would encourage efforts for export controls from industries, such as steel and shoes, that have previously sought only import controls and that would not be hurt by export controls since they produce primarily for the U.S. domestic market.[80]

A possible compromise would allow import controls only if there were also a cutback in U.S. government bilateral programs, and not link the controls to new export or private credit controls. Restricting government programs suggests that there was a genuine foreign policy dispute between the two countries. It would also avoid creating new pressures for export or credit controls.[81]

From another standpoint, any required linkage among various types

In April 1983, Senator Heinz and Senator Garn introduced a bill (S. 979) to amend the EAA, which would have allowed the President to impose import controls whenever he imposed export controls under the EAA's foreign policy section. See sec. 6, 50 U.S.C. app. § 2406. S. 979 was reported favorably out of the Senate Committee on Banking, Housing, and Urban Affairs. The Committee report explained, "Not only will the authority to control imports from countries that are the targets of foreign policy controls widen the President's options, it could also lessen the burden on American exporters, who have heretofore been asked to pay the entire price of foreign policy action in this area." The report went on to caution, "It is the intention of the Committee that such import controls be applied only against the target of the foreign policy controls and not against friendly nations whose cooperation might be necessary to ensure the effectiveness of the controls." *The Export Administration Act Amendments of 1983*, S. Rep. No. 170, 98th Cong., 1st Sess. 13 (1983).

The import control provision was opposed by the majority of the Senate Finance Committee and by the Reagan Administration. 130 *Cong. Rec.* S1712–13 (daily ed. Feb. 27, 1984) (Sen. Danforth). The principal objections were that the controls would be inconsistent with GATT, and that protectionist pressures would increase the use of economic sanctions, including the required initial export controls. Id. at S1712–13; see also id. at S1714–15 (Sen. Dole). The provision was amended on the Senate floor to require that the sanctions be imposed only if the President "determines and reports to the Congress, in advance of imposition of such controls, that such controls are consistent with the international obligations of the United States, including the [GATT]." Id. at 1715–16. In that form, it was passed by the Senate as part of S. 979 on March 1, 1984. 130 *Cong. Rec.* S2143 (daily ed. Mar. 1, 1984).

The House declined to include such a provision in its proposed EAA amendments in 1984. The Senate provision was dropped in conference, partly in exchange for the provision allowing the use of import sanctions against persons who violated the EAA national security controls. Telephone interview with Wayne Abernathy, an economist on the staff of the Senate Committee on Banking, Housing, and Urban Affairs (Mar. 12, 1986); see Chapter 4 at notes 89–90.

[80] See 130 *Cong. Rec.* S1714–15 (daily ed. Feb. 27, 1984) (Sens. Danforth and Dole).

[81] However, it would encourage the hypothetical steel and shoe industries to alter their tactics and lobby for cutbacks in government programs to certain countries, such as economic assistance to South Korea.

of controls would reduce the President's discretion.[82] The purpose of giving the President new authority to limit imports and private financial transactions is to provide him with more flexibility in choosing the best sanctions. Thus, the value of linkage in discouraging protectionism must be weighed against the possible loss of flexibility.

The clash of the new import sanctions with the GATT requirements of MFN treatment and nondiscrimination is a serious potential problem. As a result, the new statute should include a *provision at least encouraging the President to ensure that any new import controls be consistent with GATT.*

Though serious, the GATT problem is not insurmountable. As detailed earlier, many of the present (or potential) target countries for import sanctions – such as the Soviet Union, Iran, Libya, and Guatemala – are not GATT members. Moreover, some East European GATT members have trade relationships with the United States that limit U.S. obligations to them under GATT. Finally, some future import controls against GATT countries could well fit within the broad security exceptions of article XXI.[83]

Assuming that the other provisions of the new import statute would encourage the judicious use of these controls, the approach of "encouraging" the President to follow GATT is preferable to "requiring adherence." First, given the broad GATT provisions, it is not always clear at the outset whether an import restriction violates GATT, and there is no mechanism for obtaining a quick declaratory judgment. Second, if the President thinks the foreign policy issue is compelling, he should have the discretion to take steps that might violate the General Agreement, with the understanding that the other country could pursue its claims in GATT and obtain the allowed relief.[84] To help offset any potential negative impact the new U.S. law might have, the United States should

---

[82] Another conceivable type of linkage would be to require that import controls could be imposed only if there were multilateral sanctions – i.e., if other countries were also using economic sanctions against the target country. This approach, however, not only introduces a major new requirement, but seems inadvisable. First, there are major problems in defining what other country or countries should be involved and what sanctions the other(s) would have to impose. Second, and even more serious, this could create obstacles for prompt, decisive steps by the President. He might have to delay the imposition of sanctions until he found the necessary multilateral cooperation. Word of his plans could well leak out, allowing the target country to take countermeasures. Finally, the President might want to take action that primarily protected U.S. national interests. There should not be a requirement that he has to get another country, with different national interests, to agree to use sanctions also.

[83] See Chapter 5 at notes 142–53.

[84] For example, the United States acknowledged that Nicaragua could pursue its claims in GATT in response to the U.S. cutoff of the Nicaraguan sugar quota in 1983. See Chapter 5 at note 162.

probably accompany the law with other efforts to strengthen GATT and the international trading system generally.[85]

Finally, to help ensure presidential adherence to the letter and spirit of the new import law, its provisions – such as the criteria for invoking the act and the possible requirements for linkage – must be as precise as possible.[86] Bright statutory guidelines clearly influence the presidential decision-making process.[87] And, as proposed above, the law should include congressional review in a sunset provision, and it should award compensation if existing contracts or licenses are terminated.[88]

The new import law, then, should give the President major new authority, but it should also include provisions designed to guarantee that the authority is used appropriately.

3. Giving the President authority over private financial transactions: exploring virgin territory

The President should also be provided considerably increased authority over private financial transactions in order to impose economic sanctions in nonemergency situations. Delegating this authority to the President in

---

[85] Probably the most important step the United States could take would be to participate constructively in GATT's new Uruguay Round of trade negotiations. The United States got off to a promising start at the GATT meeting in Punta del Este in September 1986. In addition, the United States might promote an idea of Professor Jackson's that is very relevant to the proposed new import law. Jackson suggests that uses of article XXI be subject to review by a GATT working party, which may report its views. This would supplement the present procedures whereby the affected party can complain under article XXIII. J. Jackson, *World Trade and the Law of GATT*, 752 (1969). This approach would encourage better definition of article XXI's security exceptions.

[86] The proposals mentioned so far for a new import law do not include specific provisions for some general administrative or judicial review – and intentionally so. For example, since the purposes underlying the export licensing system do not apply here, it would be foolish and costly to add that licensing system to the regulation of imports. Similarly, the roles of the ITC and Department of Commerce under other import laws – making determinations of injury, unfair pricing, and the like – are not relevant to noneconomic foreign policy questions. For a dramatic example of economic determinations conflicting with broader foreign policy issues, see the ITC role in the Soviet ammonia case, Chapter 5 at notes 126–30.

[87] See Chapter 10 at notes 2–3 about the Executive Branch being careful to adopt measures that are authorized by statute and least likely to generate troublesome litigation.

[88] Judicial review is also available for claims that the President's actions are outside the scope of the statute or unconstitutional. Though courts are unlikely to uphold these claims except in extreme cases, the possibility that they might nevertheless do so provides another check on the Executive Branch. See Chapter 10, especially notes 42–7.

a constructive way can be difficult, however, depending on the type of financial transaction involved.

Regulating financial transactions is often hard because money is very fungible and easily transferable. Millions of dollars can be moved among several banks by wire in a few moments. Money cannot be traced as easily as, say, the export of a large computer. These problems are accentuated by the relatively limited experience of the United States in regulating private international financial transactions for foreign policy reasons. Further compounding the difficulties is the paucity of empirical research and technical analysis of the potential problems.

The types of financial transactions that might be regulated can be divided roughly into three categories, which differ considerably in their susceptibility to effective controls: (a) international trade financing, (b) general financing, and (c) foreign deposits in U.S. financial entities.

a. International trade financing. This is the easiest type of financial transaction for the President to control, and the most appropriate. International trade financing includes loans by a U.S. exporter or importer to a foreign seller or buyer; a U.S bank's letters of credit, acceptances, or similar direct financing arrangements to assist an international trade deal; or other loans by a U.S. bank that are related to the trade.

Since this financing is directly related to exports or imports, it is usually easy to identify. Moreover, the United States has had considerable experience with controls over export financing, unlike some other financial areas. The antiboycott laws have also generated extensive regulations about letters of credit and other bankers' trade documents.[89] This experience suggests that future controls over export or import financing can be effective.

In addition, it seems reasonable to have provisions for financing that are essentially similar to those for controls on the underlying export or import transaction. Indeed, the EAA already empowers the President to regulate export "financing," authority that was used broadly to limit U.S. business participation in the 1980 Moscow Olympics. This export authority should be continued. Similarly, the new import law should have a provision authorizing the President to regulate import financing.[90]

b. General international financing. This category includes general loans from U.S. banks and other financial entities to foreign governments or

---

[89] See 15 C.F.R. pt. 369 (1987), especially § 369.2(f).
[90] See Chapter 6 at notes 17–32. The authority should, of course, be subject to any of the changes in the export laws that were recommended above – such as strengthening contract sanctity and adding a sunset provision.

foreign entities. For example, Citibank or a syndicate of U.S. banks might loan several hundred million dollars to Chile to help it deal with a balance-of-payments problem, or to a private Chilean company to build an industrial complex.

Attempts to control this financing present serious problems of effectiveness and enforcement because of the fungibility of money and its rapid movement among banks. How effective, for example, would a prohibition on loans to Chile be? Instead of the prohibited loan, a U.S. bank might in good faith make an interbank loan to a Japanese, Swiss, or Panamanian bank. The next day that foreign bank might make a loan to Chile, at a slightly higher rate of interest to include that bank's costs and profit, thereby undercutting the U.S. restriction.

American banks are a major force in private international banking, even though their premier role of the 1960s and 1970s has eroded considerably as Japanese and European banks have grown and expanded their international activities. Moreover, the relative importance of U.S. credit varies by region, U.S. banks being particularly important in certain countries in Latin America and Asia.[91]

Cutting off general loans from U.S. banks would force a foreign borrower to search elsewhere for loans. The borrower might encounter some delays in finding another lender and might have to pay a slightly higher interest rate. These difficulties would vary from country to country, depending on which other banks were accustomed to doing business in a particular nation. The difficulties do not seem severe, however, with the possible exception of marginal borrowers who have a special relationship with one or more U.S banks.

Recent events in South Africa provide an important example, though possibly an unusual one, of the effective use of financial sanctions. The decisions in August–September 1985 by some private banks in the United States and elsewhere not to roll over short-term loans to South Africa triggered a financial crisis there. The decisions were made partly because bankers had become concerned about the country's long-term prospects and were wary of appearing to support apartheid. The financial pressures were continued by President Reagan's 1985 ban on new bank loans to the South African Government and then by the 1986 Comprehensive Anti-Apartheid Act, which codified Reagan's ban and added a prohibition on new private investment in South Africa.[92]

---

[91] See Chapter 6 at notes 4–9 and Table 1 in Chapter 2, Section B.3. Incidentally, U.S. banks are strong in Chile, U.S. banks' claims accounting for 47% of total foreign bank claims.

[92] See Chapter 6 at notes 2–3. Neither the President's action nor the 1986 Act appear to have been preceded by careful analysis of the effectiveness of the prohibition

Planning for the future

The South African experience, together with the possibility of formal or informal cooperation with U.S. allies, suggests that the President should have the authority to prohibit new general lending for foreign policy reasons. Given lingering questions about effectiveness and enforcement, however, further analysis would be useful.[93]

If new authority is provided, it should be carefully circumscribed.[94]

on loans. The Administration released no study, and no detailed analysis of this sanction appears in the legislative history.

[93] An alternative approach is to continue with the present arrangement, whereby the President has authority over general international lending only through special, ad hoc legislation (such as with South Africa) or by declaring a national emergency and using his IEEPA powers.

[94] It could be included either in a new law or in an amendment to the export laws under the assumption that this would be authority over the export of capital. An amendment to the EAA was the approach taken by Senator Garn and Senator Proxmire in 1985 when they introduced a bill (S. 812) to give the President the authority to limit financial transactions to any "controlled country." (These countries are the communist countries, including China but excluding Yugoslavia.) Under this bill, the President would be able to prohibit or regulate the export or transfer of money or other financial assets, including loans and the extension of credit, to the government of any controlled country. The capital controls would not be subject to the various safeguards for imposing other export restrictions found in the sections for national security or foreign policy controls – such as criteria for using the controls, consultation requirements, and foreign availability. Moreover, it would be applicable only to controlled countries and not to, say, South Korea or Chile. S. 812, 99th Cong., 1st Sess. (1985). Senator Garn stated that the bill was designed to begin a discussion about the advisability of capital controls and that he was willing to consider possible changes. *Controls on the Export of Capital from the United States: Hearings on S. 812 Before the Senate Comm. on Banking, Housing, and Urban Affairs*, 99th Cong., 1st Sess. 158–59, 201, 203 (1985) [hereinafter *1985 Hearings on S.812*].

Though some witnesses supported the bill or at least important aspects of it in 1985, bankers and the AFL–CIO opposed the bill as drafted. Id. at 93–114 (prepared statement of William McDonough, Executive Vice President and Chief Financial Officer of the First Chicago Corporation); 193–203 (AFL–CIO official Henry B. Schechter). The bill apparently occasioned a sharp split in the Reagan Administration. *N.Y. Times*, Dec. 3, 1985, at D27, col. 3. President Reagan decided to oppose the bill. *1985 Hearings on S. 812*, supra, at 133–4 (testimony of David C. Mulford, Asst. Secretary of the Treasury). The principal objections of the bill's opponents were that it would threaten to disrupt U.S. nonstrategic trade with the Eastern Bloc, including grain sales; it could lead to retaliation by other countries; and credit controls would not be effective because U.S. loans were a small percentage of Western credit to communist countries and because it was difficult to enforce general limits on international lending. Id. at 134–6 (Mulford), 193–203 (Schechter), and 93–114 (McDonough). There was no further action on the bill before the 99th Congress adjourned in 1986.

In March 1987, a nearly identical bill (S. 786) was introduced in the 100th Congress, with some additional provisions. The President's proposed new authority over exports of capital would be extended to countries supporting international terrorism as well as controlled countries. The bill would also bar controlled countries from ownership or control of federally insured banks. S. 786, 100 Cong., 1st Sess. (1987). In August 1987, a bill essentially identical to S. 786 was introduced in the House, with some

The President should be authorized to stop or regulate, for foreign policy reasons, any loans or other extensions of credit to another country. One way to confine this authority over general international lending might be to restrict the power over lending to a foreign government and its controlled entities, rather than extending it to independent private entities as well.

There is a danger that private entities would attempt to circumvent a ban against lending to a foreign government, by borrowing on behalf of that government.[95] The size of the loans, however, would make them relatively easy to detect and thus would impose an effective ceiling on this tactic. Also, restricting the President's authority to control loans to government entities reduces the threat that private foreign borrowers will perceive in the new law. They will not be as worried that the United States will limit their borrowing from U.S. banks in a foreign policy dispute.[96]

The authority to restrict foreign borrowing should be further limited by measures similar to those suggested for the new import bill – tough criteria for resort to the authority, mandatory consultation with Congress and suggested consultation with the U.S. banking industry and U.S. allies, and detailed reporting provisions. Most importantly, there should be a sunset provision that requires congressional approval for major new controls.

Also recommended is a contract sanctity clause to protect existing

added provisions requiring federally insured banks to report publicly their loans and investments in controlled countries. H.R. 3095, 100th Cong., 1st Sess. (1987); see 4 *Int'l Trade Rep. (BNA)* 978 (Aug. 5, 1987).

The addition of the antiterrorism provisions were obviously an effort to expand the coverage of the proposed new law, as well as an apparent means to broaden the domestic political support. Nevertheless, Congress had taken no significant action on either of the 1987 bills as of May 1988.

[95] Authority over loans to private entities is another way to limit U.S. foreign investment in the target country. This limitation, however, would have a less direct effect on the target government than stopping loans to the government itself. Also, specific legislation should be required, as with the 1986 anti-apartheid law.

[96] The IEEPA lending prohibitions against Iran, South Africa, and Libya applied only to loans to those Governments, though the President could have made them broader.

The President's authority might also be limited to new lending rather than encompassing existing loans. This approach was taken with South Africa and Libya. It avoids issues of contract sanctity. Moreover, if the loan has already been made to the foreigner, the only transaction remaining is probably repayment, which should not be discouraged.

A problem arises if the President also freezes foreign deposits (discussed next). The foreign lender then will have trouble continuing to make payments on its loan – not only might some of its assets in the United States be frozen, but the lender will not be inclined to send more funds here. In the 1979–81 Iran hostage case, the outstanding loans went into default.

loans, unless the President certifies that a "breach of peace" requires termination. To limit abuse, the U.S. Government should be required to compensate the U.S. financial institutions whose loans are terminated.[97]

The extraterritoriality provision should surely be more limited than the one proposed for exports. The President should be allowed to claim jurisdiction only over persons and entities within U.S. territory and over U.S. nationals abroad. This would not cover foreign subsidiaries or independent foreign companies, even if they had some contractual relationship with a U.S. company. The authorized jurisdiction would still permit the President to control lending by U.S. banks, including their overseas branches. Such extraterritorial reach was very helpful in the Iranian crisis and is now being used against Libya. There appear to be no reasons, however, for authorizing broader jurisdictional claims. And a lack of additional authority could help prevent potential abuse.[98]

c. Foreign deposits. The IEEPA controls used in the Iranian crisis and against Libya demonstrate that foreign deposits in U.S. banks – here or in branches abroad – can be effectively frozen, as can foreigners' funds held by U.S. corporations. The actions against Iran and Libya were carried out promptly, although not without some difficulties and with considerable uncertainty about the amount of funds that were frozen.[99]

Whether the President should be given this authority to freeze foreigners' deposits and other funds in the possession of U.S. entities in nonemergency situations is a close question. On the one hand, the asset freeze does appear to have been among the most important of the Iranian sanctions. Earlier freezes under TWEA also appear to have been effective.[100] On the other hand, concern about future freezes can deter foreign

[97] If monies for the loan have already been paid out to the foreigner before the control is imposed, the sanctions as applied would be meaningless. The payout might not have occurred, however, possibly because of a staggered schedule. A new control could prevent completion of the payout and thus create problems under the loan contract. If this occurs, as with the exporter or importer, the bank should be compensated for its damages, as an exporter or importer is compensated for damages caused by sanctions. In any case, the new control should not be written so as to prevent foreigners from repaying their loans. Letting foreigners off the hook is contrary to the purpose of the sanction.

[98] Foreign countries are especially sensitive to U.S. efforts to claim jurisdiction over local banks or other financial entities in their territory, viewing it as a special challenge to their sovereignty. Carswell and Davis, "Economic Financial Pressures," supra note 60, at 178. See also *Libyan Arab Foreign Bank v. Bankers Trust Co.*, 26 *Int'l Legal Materials* 1600 (Q.B. Comm'l Ct., Sept. 2, 1987). For a discussion of this recent UK case on the Libyan sanctions, see Chapter 9 at notes 59–60.

[99] Carswell and Davis, supra note 60, at 177–92, 201–7; see Chapter 9, Section C. As for Libya, the extraterritorial reach of the controls was successfully challenged in the United Kingdom. See Chapter 9 at notes 59–60.

[100] See Chapter 9, Section A.

governments or private foreign entities from depositing funds in U.S. banks, here or abroad, if they fear that these funds might become the target of a freeze. Thus, these banks might not only lose deposits but, more important, may lose customer relationships that generate other business.[101]

The precise cost of past freezes is difficult to measure. After a careful study, one expert concluded that "little harm seems to have come from the [Iranian freeze], owing primarily to its limited application and duration."[102] He then warned, however: "Over the longer term, ... should Washington be seen as developing an addiction to asset freezes after all ... – significant diversification into other countries' institutions and currencies could yet occur, and that could indeed be costly for the competitiveness of American banks."[103]

If the President is given new authority to freeze assets, its use should be restricted in the same way as the new authority over general international lending.[104] Similar provisions should apply – including tough criteria for invoking the authority, consultation and reporting requirements, a sunset provision, limits on extraterritorial jurisdiction, and a contract sanctity provision.

As for contract sanctity, the President would presumably invoke the waiver clause and regulate existing deposits. Just as U.S. exporters or importers would be covered by contract sanctity provisions discussed earlier, U.S. banks should be allowed compensation for provable damages that a freeze causes to existing business relationships. These damages would presumably be very small, since they would only be incidental to the freeze on deposits. The actual deposits would be those of foreign entities, who would not be compensated because that would be contrary to the purpose of the sanction and the use of the waiver clause, which is to put economic pressure on the target country.[105]

---

[101] See Carswell and Davis, "Crafting the Financial Statement," supra note 5, at 234.

[102] B. Cohen, *In Whose Interest? International Banking and American Foreign Policy* 169 (1986). After the Iranian freeze order, Arab countries moved some of their deposits out of American banks during 1980–1, but they increased their holdings of U.S. government and corporate securities. And in 1982–3, the growth of Arab deposits in U.S. banks resumed. Id. at 170. See R. Carswell, "Sanctions and the Iranian Experience," 60 *Foreign Aff.* 247, 263 (Winter 1981–2).

[103] Cohen, supra note 103, at 171.

[104] As with the discussion about possible controls on general lending, the alternative might be not to pass general legislation, but to require that there be special, ad hoc legislation or resort to IEEPA.

[105] Existing deposits would obviously be the principal funds frozen. It is unlikely that the foreigners who are the target of a freeze will deposit additional assets in U.S. banks once there is a freeze.

For a discussion of contract sanctity, see this chapter at notes 33–47. Also, for the

In short, in the absence of a declared national emergency, the President should receive new authority to limit import financing as well as export financing. In addition, there are arguments for providing him carefully crafted new authority to regulate general international lending by U.S. financial institutions and possibly to freeze foreigners' assets in the possession of U.S. entities.

4. *Making IEEPA less than an everyday occurrence*

If the changes recommended for nonemergency statutes are adopted in any substantial way, the already strong case for amending IEEPA would become even more compelling. Expanding the President's authority and making it more balanced for nonemergency situations would give the President less genuine need to resort to the sweeping emergency powers of IEEPA. Nevertheless, the President might be encouraged by short-term considerations to use IEEPA to avoid some of the restrictions proposed here to limit the abuse of nonemergency powers, such as contract sanctity and the sunset provision.

The key problems are to limit the ease of initial resort to IEEPA in minor foreign policy disputes and to prevent its continued use after a crisis has passed.[106]

The most important recommendation is to add a *sunset provision* to IEEPA. Congress should have to approve, by joint resolution, the declaration of a national emergency and the use of emergency powers after a certain period of time, and then at regular intervals. As the Lebanon experience under the War Powers Resolution demonstrates, a sunset provision can play a constructive role in building consensus in U.S. policy and in ensuring a congressional voice in the policy-making process.[107] The sunset provision can be viewed as a substitute, albeit an imperfect one,[108] for the now defunct legislative veto provision in the National Emergencies Act and IEEPA.

---

recent UK court case regarding the U.S. freeze on Libyan deposits, see Chapter 9 at notes 59–60. The relief ordered in that case was essentially the $292.5 million that was in the frozen Libyan accounts, plus interest. Additional damages had been expected to total only about $2 million. See *Wall St. J.*, Oct. 13, 1987, at 31, col. 1.

[106] See discussion in Chapter 9, Section D.

[107] See discussion at notes 48–57, this chapter.

[108] From the viewpoint of Congress, the legislative veto was a better tool because it left discretion in Congress as to whether there would be an actual vote on the concurrent resolution challenging the President's decision. Congress could avoid voting and simply allow the emergency to continue. Note that Congress generally prefers procedural devices that allow it to avoid up-or-down substantive votes. See Aspin, supra note 57, at 252–63.

The sunset provision, however, requires Congress to vote if it wants to approve the

The initial time period for the sunset provision could be six months, as was the initial period prescribed by the legislative veto provision. This should give Congress ample time to ascertain how the President is handling a crisis and whether he is appropriately consulting Congress and seeking legislation. Alternatively, the time period could be sixty to ninety days, similar to the War Powers Resolution and the agricultural embargo provision of the amended EAA. This shorter period, however, might place unreasonable demands on the decision-making processes in Congress.

The regular renewal periods should probably be six months or one year. The National Emergencies Act and IEEPA had provided for votes on concurrent resolutions at six-month intervals.

The exact lengths of the initial period and renewal periods will obviously influence how quickly and how often Congress reviews the President's decision, and they could well affect the pace of the President's actions. More important than the exact time periods, however, is that the President will recognize that his authority will be subject to congressional review in all but the shortest emergencies. Consequently, the President will presumably be more careful to consult Congress from the beginning and to develop policies that reflect a national consensus.

Further amendments to IEEPA can be recommended, but they are less important than a sunset provision. The second most important step is adding *contract sanctity provisions*. As with export or import controls in a nonemergency situation, existing trade contracts and export licenses should be honored unless there is a "breach of the peace" that requires their immediate termination. In that case, the injured exporter or importer in the United States should be compensated by the U.S. Government.

There should also be a contract sanctity provision regarding private financial transactions. IEEPA's present authorities allow the President to prohibit trade financing and general lending agreements and to freeze foreigners' deposits. For such financial controls, the same contract sanctity provisions proposed for the nonemergency laws should apply.

Contract sanctity provisions are not inappropriate for emergencies. All other considerations should not be discarded just because the President declares a national emergency. The rationales supporting the contract sanctity clause in the export laws – trying to improve the reputation of Americans as reliable business partners and protecting U.S. entities from sudden losses – are also valid in the emergency context. Furthermore, providing compensation when the President curtails or terminates exist-

President's action, thus going on record. Congress could end the emergency by not voting (as well as by voting against the resolution), but the effect of ending the President's emergency would be a very visible challenge by Congress, even if there were no vote.

ing contracts or licenses pursuant to the waiver clause should help deter casual resort to the waiver clause.[109]

The contract sanctity provision should be added to IEEPA for another reason as well. Failure to do so would encourage the President to resort to IEEPA as a way of avoiding the clause in the nonemergency laws.[110] IEEPA should not be an easy way out.

Also, rather than simply directing the President to consult Congress "in every possible instance," IEEPA can be amended to make *consultation mandatory* and to detail its scope. Of course, consultation, particularly of an extensive sort, might be difficult in a fast-breaking crisis. However, IEEPA deals with economic powers, not with use of the military. The President should at least be able to get the advice of a few congressional leaders before he uses these powers.[111]

The vague *criteria* for invoking IEEPA – "any unusual and extraordinary threat" – could be made more precise. The criteria could explicitly

---

[109] See discussion at notes 33–47, this chapter.

[110] Though the wisdom of President Reagan's uses of IEEPA against South Africa and Libya were questioned in Chapter 9, Sections C and D, Reagan does not appear to have resorted to IEEPA in order to circumvent the new contract sanctity clause in the Export Administration Act Amendments of July 1985. As for Libya, the 1985 foreign assistance act, effective in August 1985 after the EAA amendments, gave the President sweeping nonemergency powers over imports and exports (without any contract sanctity clause). South Africa is a more difficult question. The regulations implementing the September 1985 sanctions were issued by the Commerce Department and cited the EAA. The Reagan Administration, then, would seem to have accepted the possible applicability of the contract sanctity clause rather than avoiding it through sole reliance on IEEPA. However, other provisions in the 1985 EAA amendments reimposed the expanded export controls on computers. Pub. L. No. 99–64, § 108, 99 Stat. 120 (1985), amending 50 U.S.C. app. § 2405 (Supp. III 1985). Presumably the Administration would argue that this frees it from the requirements of the contract sanctity provision. (The author is unaware of any private party making claims under the EAA's contract sanctity clause as a result of the South African sanctions.)

[111] For example, in the Iranian situation, when Iran tried surreptitiously to withdraw its deposits from U.S. banks and a speedy U.S. response was needed, there were nevertheless some consultations with congressional leaders before President Carter declared a national emergency and froze assets. Carswell and Davis, "Economic and Financial Pressures," supra note 60, at 176; see A. Ribicoff, "Lessons and Conclusions," in *American Hostages in Iran*, supra note 5, at 374, 382–4.

The principal purpose of any consultation requirement is to ensure that the President has carefully considered his actions and that he realizes the long-term benefits of obtaining the advice of congressional leaders. See T. Franck and E. Weisband, *Foreign Policy by Congress* 75–7 (1979). It should be noted, however, that consultation provisions, such as with the War Powers Resolution, have proved to be of only limited use. Id. at 71–6. The recent failures by Reagan Administration officials to abide by various consultation provisions during the 1985–6 arms sales to Iran raise further questions about the provisions. See Chapter 4 at notes 152–60. As discussed above, a sunset provision should increase considerably the President's incentive to consult with Congress. See notes 48–57, this chapter.

define emergencies as "rare and brief" and state that use of IEEPA should be "terminated as soon as the threat has receded or as soon as necessary special legislation can be passed by Congress." Such statutory language would put the President on more notice not to use IEEPA casually. Precise language, however, is difficult to draft, since the statute was intended to cover a wide range of genuine emergencies and to afford the President considerable latitude in dealing with them.

Even if more precise language could be added, enforcement would remain a problem. As noted earlier, courts are very hesitant to question a presidential decision concerning the existence of a national emergency.[112] The real constraint on the President is Congress. If there is a sunset provision that requires a congressional vote for the controls to continue, the precise statutory language could be important in the debate over whether to extend the President's emergency powers.

These recommendations outlined above are designed to deal with IEEPA's principal defects by reducing the chances that the President will casually resort to the Act's powers or continue to rely on them after a crisis has passed. Steps could also be taken to deal with excessive and counterproductive claims of *extraterritorial jurisdiction* under IEEPA. The measures discussed for nonemergency laws – such as actual limits on the President's jurisdictional authority over general international lending and freezing assets – should also be adopted here. These measures are not only reasonable, but applying them to IEEPA will discourage its use as a way of evading the restrictions in the nonemergency laws.

In short, the need to amend IEEPA cannot be ignored. Addition of a sunset provision is the most important first step.

D. CONCLUSIONS

Economic sanctions for foreign policy purposes are here to stay. Indeed, for various reasons – many good – the use of these sanctions has increased, and no slackening is in sight.

It is important to begin considering possible sanctions and the underlying U.S. laws in a comprehensive fashion, rather than to look at only a few possible vehicles for sanctions, such as U.S. foreign assistance or exports. Comprehensive analysis of existing U.S. laws reveals a haphazard situation. These laws can skew the President's choice of sanctions or encourage him to resort offhandedly to his sweeping emergency powers.

The present legal "framework" is obviously not the only possible arrangement, and U.S. national interests can be better served. Recent

[112] See Chapter 9 at note 88. But also see the suggestion for improving the possibility of judicial review at note 47 in Chapter 10.

changes in the U.S. laws as well as a preliminary analysis of the laws of major allies suggest some alternative approaches. Most compelling is the need to correct the present disparity between the President's broad non-emergency authority over exports and his very narrow authority over imports and private financial transactions. The President's powers over the latter two activities should be substantially increased, while his authority to stop exports should be trimmed.

These changes will require a careful mix of statutory provisions to avoid encouraging excessive use of sanctions. Especially difficult is the problem of how to provide the President new authority over certain private financial transactions. Nevertheless, substantial improvements can be made by hedging any new presidential authority with restrictions such as sunset provisions and contract sanctity clauses.

These changes should be undertaken with an eye toward reducing the President's incentives to invoke emergency powers. Indeed, his ability to use IEEPA should be cut back.

Whatever one thinks of the United States employing economic sanctions, they are an unavoidable reality. Now is the time to bring order and wisdom to the underlying U.S. laws.

Selected bibliography

Abascal, Ralph S., and John R. Kramer. "Presidential Impoundment Part I: Historical Genesis and Constitutional Framework." 62 *Georgetown Law Journal* 1549–1618 (1974).
"Presidential Impoundment Part II: Judicial and Legislative Responses." 63 *Georgetown Law Journal* 149–85 (1974).
Abbott, Kenneth B. "Coercion and Communication: Frameworks for Evaluation of Economic Sanctions." 19 *New York University Journal of International Law and Politics* 781–802 (1987).
"Defining the Extraterritorial Reach of American Export Controls: Congress as Catalyst." 17 *Cornell International Law Journal* 79–158 (1984).
"Economic Sanctions and International Terrorism." 20 *Vanderbilt Journal of Transnational Law* 289–325 (1987).
"Linking Trade to Political Goals: Foreign Policy Export Controls in the 1970s and 1980s." 65 *Minnesota Law Review* 739–889 (1981).
Acheson, Dean. *Present at the Creation: My Years in the State Department*. New York: Norton, 1969.
Allison, Graham T. *Essence of Decision: Explaining the Cuban Missile Crisis*. Boston: Little, Brown, 1971.
American Hostages in Iran (Paul H. Kreisberg, ed.). New Haven, Conn.: Yale University Press, 1985.
American Law Institute. *Restatement (Third) of Foreign Relations Law of the United States*. Philadelphia, Pa., 1987.
Aspin, Les. "Congress versus the Defense Department." In *The Tethered Presidency* (Thomas M. Franck, ed.). New York: New York University Press, 1981.
Assessing the Effect of Technology Transfer on U.S./Western Security: A Defense Perspective. Washington, D.C.: Office of the Undersecretary of Defense for Policy, Feb. 1985.
Ayubi, Shaheen, Richard E. Bissell, Nana Amu-Brafin Korash, and Laurie A. Lerner. *Economic Sanctions in U.S. Policy*. Philadelphia, Pa.: Foreign Policy Research Institute, 1982.
Baldwin, David A. *Economic Statecraft*. Princeton, N.J.: Princeton University Press, 1985.
Baldwin, Robert E. *The Political Economy of U.S. Import Policy*. Cambridge, Mass.: MIT Press, 1985.

Selected bibliography

Ball, George. "The Coming Crisis in Israeli–American Relations." 58 *Foreign Affairs* 231–56 (Winter 1979–80).

Bank for International Settlements and Organization for Economic Co-operation and Development. *Statistics on External Indebtedness: Bank and Trade-Related Non-Bank External Claims on Individual Borrowing Countries and Territories at End-June 1986.* Paris and Basle, Jan. 1987.

The Nationality Structure of the International Banking Market and the Role of Interbank Operations. Basle: Bank for International Settlements, 1985.

Bergsten, C. Fred. *Completing the GATT: Toward New International Rules to Govern Export Controls.* Washington, D.C.: British North-American Research Association, 1974.

Berman, Harold J., and John R. Garson. "United States Export Controls – Past, Present, and Future." 67 *Columbia Law Review* 791–890 (1967).

Bettauer, Ronald J. "The Nuclear Non-Proliferation Act of 1978." 10 *Law and Policy in International Business* 1105–80 (1978).

Bialos, Jeffrey, and Juster, Kenneth. "The Libyan Sanctions: Rational Response to State-sponsored Terrorism?" 4 *Virginia Journal of International Law* 799–855 (1986).

Bingham, Jonathan B., and Victor C. Johnson. "A Rational Approach to Export Controls." 57 *Foreign Affairs* 894–920 (1979).

Blechman, Barry M., and Stephen S. Kaplan, *Force Without War.* Washington, D.C.: Brookings Institution, 1978.

Blueprint for Reform: The Report of the Task Group on Regulation of Financial Services. Washington, D.C.: U.S. Government Printing Office, July 1984.

Boycotts and Peace: A Report by the Committee on Economic Sanctions (Clark Evans, ed.). New York: Harper Bros., 1932.

Breyer, Stephen. "The Legislative Veto After *Chadha*." 72 *Georgetown Law Journal* 785–818 (1984).

Brown-John, C. Lloyd. *Multilateral Sanctions in International Law: A Comparative Analysis.* New York: Praeger, 1975.

Brownstein, Alan E. "The Takings Clause and the Iranian Claims Settlement." 29 *UCLA Law Review* 984–1075 (1982).

Brzezinski, Zbigniew. *Power and Principle.* New York: Farrar, Straus & Giroux, 1985.

Burand, Deborah K. "Civil Strife Coverage of Overseas Investment: The Emerging Role of OPIC." 34 *Federation of Insurance Counselors* 391–420 (1984).

Bureau of National Affairs. *International Trade Reporter.* Washington, D.C., 1985.

Carswell, Robert. "Economic Sanctions and the Iranian Experience." 60 *Foreign Affairs* 247–65 (Winter 1981–2).

Carswell, Robert, and Richard J. Davis. "The Economic and Financial Pressures: Freeze and Sanctions." In *American Hostages in Iran* (Paul H. Kreisberg, ed.). New Haven, Conn.: Yale University Press, 1985.

"Crafting the Financial Settlement." In *American Hostages in Iran* (Paul H. Kreisberg, ed.). New Haven, Conn.: Yale University Press, 1985.

Chandavarkar, Anand G. *The International Monetary Fund: Its Financial Organization and Activities*, IMF Pamphlet Series No. 42. Washington, D.C.: International Monetary Fund, 1984.

Christopher, Warren. "Ceasefire Between the Branches: A Compact in Foreign Affairs." 60 *Foreign Affairs* 989–1005 (1982).

Selected bibliography

Diplomacy: The Neglected Imperative (1981).

"Introduction." In *American Hostages in Iran* (Paul H. Kreisberg, ed.). New Haven, Conn.: Yale University Press, 1985.

Cohen, Benjamin J. *In Whose Interest? International Banking and American Foreign Policy.* New Haven, Conn.: Yale University Press, 1986.

Cohen, Marc R. "U.S. Regulation of Bank Lending to LDCs: Balancing Bank Overexposure and Credit Undersupply." 8 *Yale Journal of World Public Order* 200–35 (1982).

Cohen, Stephen B. "Conditioning U.S. Security Assistance on Human Rights Practices." 76 *American Journal of International Law* 246–79 (1982).

Committee on Banking, Housing and Urban Affairs, *International Emergency Economic Powers Legislation,* S. Rep. 466, 95th Cong., 1st Sess. Washington, D.C.: U.S. Government Printing Office, 1977.

Committee on International Relations, *Trading with the Enemy Act Reform Legislation,* H.R. Rep. No. 459, 95th Cong., 1st Sess. Washington, D.C.: U.S. Government Printing Office, 1977.

Congress, the Presidency and American Foreign Policy (John Spanier and Joseph Nogee eds.). Elmsford, N.Y.: Pergamon, 1981.

Controls on the Export of Capital from the United States: Hearings on S. 812 Before the Senate Comm. on Banking, Housing, and Urban Affairs, 99th Cong., 1st Sess. Washington, D.C.: U.S. Government Printing Office, 1985.

Corse, C. Thorne, and Bruce W. Nichols. "United States Government Regulation of International Lending by American Banks." From *International Financial Law* (Robert S. Rendall ed.). London: Euromoney Publications, 1980.

Dam, Kenneth W. *The GATT: Law and International Economic Organization.* University of Chicago Press, 1970.

Danaher, Kevin. *The Political Economy of U.S. Policy Toward South Africa.* Boulder, Colo.: Westview Press, 1985.

Destler, I. M. *Making Foreign Economic Policy.* Washington, D.C.: Brookings Institution, 1980.

American Trade Politics: System under Stress. Washington, D.C.: Institute for International Economics, 1986.

Domke, Michael. *Trading with the Enemy in World War II.* New York: Central Book, 1943.

Doxey, Margaret P. *International Sanctions in Contemporary Perspective.* New York: St. Martin's Press, 1987.

Economic Coercion and U.S. Foreign Policy: Implications of Case Studies from the Johnson Administration (Sidney Weintraub, ed.). Boulder, Colo.: Westview Press, 1982.

Economic Report of the President. Washington, D.C.: U.S. Government Printing Office, 1988.

Ellings, Richard J. *Embargoes and World Power.* Boulder, Colo.: Westview Press, 1985.

Estes, Carl, II. "Federal Tax Consequences of International Boycotts." 8 *Georgia Journal of International & Comparative Law* 685–709 (1978).

Farer, Tom J. "Political and Economic Coercion in Contemporary International Law." 79 *American Journal of International Law* 405–13 (1985).

Farley, Philip J., Stephen S. Kaplan, and William H. Lewis. *Arms Across the Sea.* Washington, D.C.: Brookings Institution, 1978.

Feinberg, Kenneth R. "Economic Coercion and Economic Sanctions: The Ex-

Selected bibliography

pansion of United States Extraterritorial Jurisdiction." 30 *American University Law Review* 323–48 (1981).

Feis, Herbert. *Three International Episodes: Seen from E.A.:* New York: Norton, 1966.

The Road to Pearl Harbor. Princeton, N.J.: Princeton University Press, 1950.

Feldman, Mark B., and David Colson. "The Maritime Boundaries of the United States." 75 *American Journal of International Law* 729–63 (1981).

Fenton, Howard. "State and Local Anti-Apartheid Laws: Misplaced Response to a Flawed National Policy on South Africa." 19 *New York University Journal of International Law and Policy* 883 (1987).

"United States Antiboycott Laws: An Assessment of Their Impact Ten Years after Adoption." 10 *Hastings International and Comparative Law Review* 211–87 (1987).

Fisher, Bart S., and Ralph G. Steinhardt III. "Section 301 of the Trade Act of 1974: Protection for U.S. Exporters of Goods, Services, and Capital." 14 *Law and Policy in International Business* 569–690 (1982).

Franck, Thomas M., and Clifford A. Bob. "The Return of Humpty-Dumpty: Foreign Relations Law After the *Chadha* Case." 79 *American Journal of International Law* 912–60 (1985).

Franck, Thomas M., and Edward Weisband. *Foreign Policy by Congress.* New York: Oxford University Press, 1979.

Friesen, Connie M. "The Regulation and Supervision of International Lending: Part I." 19 *International Lawyer* 1059–1117 (1985).

GATT, *GATT Activities in 1982–6.* Geneva: General Agreement on Tariffs and Trade, 1983–7.

General Accounting Office, *Export Controls: Assessment of Commerce Department's Foreign Report to Congress.* Washington, D.C.: U.S. General Accounting Office, 1986.

Gustafson, Thane. *Selling the Russians the Rope? Soviet Technology Policy and U.S. Export Controls.* Santa Monica, Calif.: Rand Corporation, 1981.

Harris, Joel B., and Jeffrey P. Bialos. "Congressional Balancing Act Benefits Exporters." *Legal Times,* Aug. 5, 1985, at 17.

"The Strange New World of United States Export Controls Under the International Emergency Economic Powers Act." 18 *Vanderbilt Journal of Transnational Law* 71–108 (1985).

Hein, Werner. "Economic Embargoes and Individual Rights Under German Law." 15 *Law and Policy in International Business* 401–23 (1983).

Henkin, Louis. *Foreign Affairs and the Constitution.* New York: Norton, 1972.

Hersh, Seymour M. *The Price of Power.* New York: Summit Books, 1983.

Holden, Alfred C. "Export Credit Insurance and the FCIA." 14 *Uniform Commercial Code Law Journal* 140–5 (1981).

House Select Committee to Investigate Covert Arms Transactions with Iran and Senate Select Committee on Secret Military Assistance to Iran and the Nicaraguan Opposition. *Report of the Congressional Committees Investigating the Iran–Contra Affair.* H.R. Report 433, S. Rep. No. 216, 100th Cong., 1st Sess. 418. Washington, D.C.: U.S. Government Printing Office, 1987.

Hudec, Robert E. *The GATT Legal System and World Trade Diplomacy.* New York: Praeger, 1975.

Hufbauer, Gary Clyde, and Howard F. Rosen. *Trade Policy for Troubled Industries.* Washington, D.C.: Institute for International Economics, 1986.

Selected bibliography

Hufbauer, Gary Clyde, and Jeffrey J. Schott. *Economic Sanctions Reconsidered: History and Current Policy.* Washington, D.C.: Institute for International Economics, 1985.

Hunt, Cecil. "Multilateral Cooperation in Export Controls – The Role of CoCom." 14 *University of Toledo Law Review* 1285–97 (1983).

International Finance. Annual Reports of the National Advisory Council on International Monetary and Financial Policies for Fiscal Years 1977–1986. Washington, D.C.: U.S. Government Printing Office.

International Monetary Fund. *Direction of Trade Statistics: Yearbook 1987.* Washington, D.C., 1987.

  The International Monetary Fund 1972–1978 (Margaret Garritsen de Vries, ed.). Washington, D.C., 1985.

  The International Monetary Fund: An Introduction. Washington, D.C., Apr. 1982.

International Trade Commission. *Review of the Effectiveness of Trade Dispute Settlement Under the GATT and the Tokyo Round Agreements,* ITC Pub. 1793. Washington, D.C.: U.S. International Trade Commission, 1985.

  U.S. Embargoes on Agricultural Exports: Implications for U.S. Agricultural Industry and U.S. Exports, Pub. No. 1461. Washington, D.C.: U.S. International Trade Commission, Dec. 1983.

Jackson, John H. "Governmental Disputes in International Trade Relations: A Proposal in the Context of GATT." 13 *Journal of World Trade Law* 1–21 (1979).

  World Trade and the Law of GATT. Charlottesville, Va.: Michie, 1969.

Jackson, John H., and William J. Davey. *Legal Problems of International Economic Relations: Cases, Materials & Text.* St. Paul, Minn.: West, 1986.

Jackson, John H., Jean-Victor Louis, and Mitsuo Matsushita. *Implementing the Tokyo Round.* Ann Arbor: University of Michigan Press, 1984.

Jentleson, Bruce W. *Pipeline Politics: The Complex Political Economy of East–West Trade.* Ithaca, N.Y.: Cornell University Press, 1986.

Johnstone, James M., and Jon Paugh. "The Arab Boycott of Israel: The Role of United States Antitrust Laws in the Wake of the Export Administration Amendments of 1977." 8 *Georgia Journal of International & Comparative Law* 661–84 (1978).

Kaye, Harvey, Paul Plaia, Jr., and Michael A. Hertzberg. *International Trade Practice.* New York: McGraw-Hill, 1985.

Keler, Marianne M. "The Export–Import Bank." 11 *Law and Policy in International Business* 355–74 (1979).

Kerns, Hikaku. "An Outfall in the East." 117 *Far Eastern Economic Review* 43–7 (July 23, 1986).

Kissinger, Henry. *The White House Years.* Boston: Little, Brown, 1979.

Knorr, Klaus. *The Power of Nations: The Political Economy of International Relations.* New York: Basic Books, 1975.

Koschik, David N. "Foreign Policy Motivated Credit Restrictions: Potential Bases of Authority and a Practical Analysis." 16 *Law and Policy in International Business* 539–95 (1984).

Kostecki, M. M. *East–West Trade and the GATT System.* New York: St. Martin's Press, 1978.

Kuyper, Pieter Jan. "Community Sanctions against Argentina: Lawfulness under Community and International Law." In *Essays in European Law and In-*

Selected bibliography

tegration (David O'Keeffe and Henry G. Schermers eds). Deventer, Netherlands: Kluwer Law and Taxation Publishers, 1982.

Legg, Keith R. "Congress as Trojan Horse? The Turkish Embargo Problem, 1974–78." In *Congress, the Presidency and American Foreign Policy* (John Spanier and Joseph Nogee eds.). Elmsford, N.Y.: Pergamon, 1981.

Lichtenstein, Cynthia C. "The U.S. Response to the International Debt Crisis: The International Lending Supervision Act of 1983." 25 *Virginia Journal of International Law* 401–35 (1985).

Lillich, R. B. "Requiem for Hickenlooper," 69 *American Journal of International Law* 97–100 (1975).

Lipson, Charles. *Standing Guard: Protecting Foreign Capital in the Nineteenth and Twentieth Centuries.* Berkeley: University of California Press, 1985.

Lissakers, Karin. "Bank Regulation and International Debt." In *Uncertain Future: Commercial Banks and the Third World* (Richard E. Feinberg and Valeriana Kallab eds.). New Brunswick, N.J.: Transaction Books, 1984.

Lofgren, Charles A. "*United States v. Curtiss-Wright Corporation*: An Historical Reassessment." 83 *Yale Law Journal* 1–32 (1973).

Losman, Donald L. *International Economic Sanctions: The Cases of Cuba, Israel, and Rhodesia.* Albuquerque: University of New Mexico Press, 1979.

Lowenfeld, Andreas F. *Public Controls on International Trade.* New York: Bender, 1983.

Trade Controls for Political Ends. New York: Bender, 1983.

Malloy, Michael. "The Iran Crisis: Law Under Pressure." *Wisconsin International Law Journal* 15–98 (Symposium 1984).

Marcus, Maeva. *Truman and the Steel Seizure Case: The Limits of Presidential Power.* New York: Columbia University Press, 1977.

Marcuss, Stanley J. "The Antiboycott Law: The Regulation of International Business Behavior." 8 *Georgia Journal of International and Comparative Law* 559–80 (1978).

Marcuss, Stanley J., and D. Stephen Mathias. "U.S. Foreign Policy Export Controls: Do They Pass Muster Under International Law?" 2 *International Tax & Business Lawyer* 1–28 (1984).

Marcuss, Stanley J., and Eric L. Richard. "Extraterritorial Jurisdiction in United States Trade Law: The Need for a Consistent Theory." 20 *Columbia Journal of Transnational Law* 439–83 (1981).

Marks, Lee R., and John C. Grabow. "The President's Foreign Economic Powers After *Dames & Moore v. Regan*: Legislation by Acquiescence." 68 *Cornell Law Review* 68–103 (1982).

Matsushita, Mitsuo. "Export Control and Export Cartels in Japan." 20 *Harvard International Law Journal* 103–25 (1979).

Maynes, Charles William. "Logic, Bribes, and Threats." 60 *Foreign Policy* 111–29 (Fall 1985).

Medlicott, W. N. *The Economic Blockade.* London: Her Majesty's Stationery Office; Longmans, Green, 1952 and 1959.

Mikva, Abner J., and Gerald L. Newman. "The Hostage Crisis and the 'Hostage Act.'" 49 *University of Chicago Law Review* 292–354 (1982).

Miller, John C. *Origins of the American Revolution.* Stanford, Calif.: Stanford University Press, 1962.

Miller, Judith. "When Sanctions Worked." 39 *Foreign Policy* 118–29 (1980).

Morison, Samuel Eliot and Henry Steele Commager. *The Growth of the American Republic*, 5th ed. New York: Oxford University Press, 1962.

Selected bibliography

Morse, Duane D., and Joan S. Powers. "U.S. Export Controls and Foreign Entities: The Unanswered Questions of Pipeline Diplomacy." 23 *Virginia Journal of International Law* 537–67 (1983).

Moyer, Homer E., and Linda A. Mabry. "Export Controls as Instruments of Foreign Policy: The History, Legal Issues, and Policy Lessons of Three Recent Cases." 15 *Law and Policy in International Business* 1–171 (1983).

Murphy, John F. *Punishing International Terrorists: The Legal Framework for Policy Initiatives.* Totowa, New Jersey: Rowman & Allanheld, 1985.

Murphy, John F., and Arthur T. Downey. "National Security, Foreign Policy and Individual Rights: The Quandary of United States Export Controls." 30 *International & Comparative Law Quarterly* 792–834 (1981).

National Academy of Sciences. *Scientific Communication and National Security.* Washington, D.C.: National Academy Press, 1982.

National Academy of Sciences Panel on the Impact of National Security Controls on International Technology Transfer. *Balancing the National Interest.* Washington, D.C.: National Academy Press, 1987.

National Advisory Council on International Monetary and Financial Policies. *International Finance*, annual reports for 1977 through 1985. Washington, D.C.: U.S. Government Printing Office.

Nonproliferation and U.S. Foreign Policy (Joseph A. Yager, ed.). Washington, D.C.: Brookings Institution, 1980.

Note and Comments of the European Community on the Amendments of 22 June 1982 to the U.S. Export Administration Regulations, August, 1982. Reprinted in 21 *International Legal Materials* 891–9 (1982).

Note. "Analysis and Application of the Anti-Boycott Provisions of the Export Administration Amendments of 1977." 9 *Law & Policy in International Business* 915–57 (1977).

Note. "An Interim Analysis of the Effects of the Jackson–Vanik Amendment on Trade and Human Rights: The Romanian Example." 8 *Law & Policy in International Business* 193–221 (1976).

Note. "The International Emergency Economic Powers Act: A Congressional Attempt to Control Presidential Emergency Power." 96 *Harvard Law Review* 1102–20 (1983).

Note. "The National Emergency Dilemma: Balancing the Executive's Crisis Powers with the Need for Accountability." 52 *Southern California Law Review* 1453–1511 (1979).

Note. "The 1981 OPIC Amendments and Reagan's 'Newer Directions' in Third World Development Policy." 14 *Law & Policy in International Business* 181–213 (1982).

Note. "The Policies Behind Lending Limits: An Argument for a Uniform Country Exposure Ceiling." 99 *Harvard Law Review* 430–49 (1985).

Note. "Predictability and Comity: Toward Common Principles of Extraterritorial Jursidiction." 98 *Harvard Law Review* 1310–30 (1986).

Note. "State and Local Anti-South Africa Action as an Intrusion upon the Federal Power in Foreign Affairs." 72 *Virginia Law Review* 813–50 (1986).

Note. "The United States–Iran Hostage Agreement: A Study in Presidential Powers." 15 *Cornell International Law Journal* 149–201 (1982).

Oakley, Robert B. "Combating International Terrorism," statement before two subcommittees of the House Foreign Affairs Committee on March 5, 1985. Reprinted in 85 *Department of State Bulletin* 73–8 (June 1985).

Selected bibliography

Office of Technology Assessment. *Strategic Materials: Technologies to Reduce U.S. Import Vulnerability.* Washington, D.C., 1985.

Technology and East–West Trade: An Update. Washington, D.C., 1979.

Pierre, Andrew J. *The Global Politics of Arms Sales.* Princeton, N.J.: Princeton University Press, 1982.

Public Report of the Vice President's Task Force on Combatting Terrorism. Washington, D.C.: U.S. Government Printing Office, 1986.

Renwick, Robin. *Economic Sanctions.* Cambridge, Mass.: Center for International Affairs, 1981.

Report of the President's Special Review Board. Washington, D.C., 1987.

Sanford, Jonathan E. *U.S. Foreign Policy and Multilateral Development Banks.* Boulder, Colo.: Westview Press, 1982.

Saunders, Harold H. "Beginning of the End." In *American Hostages in Iran* (Paul H. Kreisberg, ed.). New Haven, Conn.: Yale University Press, 1985.

Schmitt, Roland W. "Export Controls: Balancing Technological Innovation and National Security." *Issues in Science and Technology* 117–26 (Fall, 1984).

Schmitthoff, Clive M. *The Export Trade: A Manual of Law and Practice.* London: Stevens, 1975.

Schoultz, Lars. *Human Rights and United States Policy Toward Latin America.* Princeton, N.J.: Princeton University Press, 1981.

Schwarze, Jürgen. "Towards a European Foreign Policy: Legal Aspects." In *Towards a European Foreign Policy* 69–96. (J. K. de Vree, P. Coffey, and R. H. Lauwaars, eds.). Dordrecht, The Netherlands: Martinus Nijhoff, 1987.

Sears, Louis M. *Jefferson and the Embargo.* New York: Octagon Books, 1966.

Shihata, Ibrahim F. I. "Destination Embargo of Arab Oil: Its Legality Under International Law." 68 *American Journal of International Law* 591–627 (1974).

Sick, Gary. *All Fall Down.* New York: Random House, 1985.

Sigmund, Paul E. "Latin America: Change or Continuity?" 60 *Foreign Affairs* 629–57 (1981).

"The 'Invisible Blockade' and the Overthrow of Allende." 52 *Foreign Affairs* 322–40 (1974).

Smith, Allan D. "The Japanese Foreign Exchange and Foreign Trade Control Law and Administrative Guidance: The Labyrinth and the Castle." 16 *Law and Policy in International Business* 417–76 (1984).

Sommerfield, Stanley L. "Treasury Regulation of Foreign Assets and Trade." In *A Lawyer's Guide to International Business Transactions* (Walter Sterling Surrey and Don Wallace, Jr., eds.). Philadelphia, Pa.: American Law Institute & American Bar Association Committee on Continuing Professional Education, 1977.

Spann, Girardeau. "Spinning the Legislative Veto." 72 *Georgetown Law Journal* 813–18 (1984).

Spector, Leonard S. *The New Nuclear Nations.* New York: Vintage Books, 1985.

Spindler, J. Andrew. "The Growing Entanglement of International Banking and Foreign Policy." 8 *TransAtlantic Perspectives* 3–6 (May 1983).

The Politics of International Credit. Washington, D.C.: Brookings Institution, 1984.

Stanislawski, Harold. "The Impact of the Arab Economic Boycott of Israel on

Selected bibliography

the United States and Canada." In *The Utility of International Economic Sanctions* (Leyton-Brown David, ed.). London: Croom Helm, 1986.

Stein, Eric, Peter Hay, Michael Waelbroeck, and Joseph Weiler. *European Community Law and Institutions in Perspective*. Charlottesville, Va.: Michie, 1975 and 1985 supplement.

Steiner, Henry J. "Pressures and Principles – The Politics of the Antiboycott Legislation." 8 *Georgia Journal of International & Comparative Law* 529–58 (1978).

Stern, Paula. *Water's Edge: Domestic Politics and the Making of American Foreign Policy*. Westport, Conn: Greenwood Press, 1979.

Stone, Geoffrey R., Louis M. Seidman, Cass R. Sunstein, & Mark V. Tushnet. *Constitutional Law*. Boston: Little, Brown, 1986.

Subcommittee on Europe and the Middle East of the House Committee on Foreign Affairs, 97th Cong., 1st Sess. *An Assessment of the Afghanistan Sanctions: Implications for Trade and Diplomacy in the 1980's* (Comm. Print. 1981) (report prepared by the Congressional Reference Service).

"The Politics of Procedure: An Examination of the GATT Dispute Settlement Panel and the Article XXI Defense in the Context of the U.S. Embargo of Nicaragua." 19 *Law and Policy in International Business* 603–25 (1987).

Torem, Christopher, and Robert J. Donatucci. "Overseas Private Investment Corporation: The 1978 Amendments and the Future of OPIC." 11 *Law & Policy in International Business* 321–55 (1979).

Tribe, Laurence H. *Constitutional Choices*. Cambridge, Mass.: Harvard University Press, 1985.

Trimble, Phillip R. "Foreign Policy Frustrated – *Dames & Moore*, Claims Court Jurisdiction and a New Raid on the Treasury." 84 *Columbia Law Review* 317–85 (1984).

U.S. Department of Agriculture. *Embargoes, Surplus Disposal, and U.S. Agriculture*. Washington, D.C., 1986.

U.S. Department of Defense. *Technology Security Program*. Washington, D.C. 1986.

U.S. Department of the Treasury. *United States Participation in the Multilateral Development Banks in the 1980s*. Washington, D.C.: U.S. Government Printing Office, 1982.

U. S. General Accounting Office. *International Trade: Libyan Sanctions*. U.S. Government Printing Office, 1987.

"U.S. Measures Against Polish Government and Soviet Union." 76 *American Journal of International Law* 379–84 (1982).

von Clausewitz, Claus. "On the Nature of War." In *War, Politics, and Power* (Edward H. Collins, ed.). Chicago: Regnery, 1962.

Wallace, Don, Jr. "The President's Exclusive Foreign Affairs Power Over Foreign Aid." 1970 *Duke Law Journal* 293–328, 453–94.

Weissbrodt, David. "Human Rights Legislation and U.S. Foreign Policy." 7 *Georgia Journal of International & Comparative Law* 231–87 (1977).

Whiteman, Marjorie M. *Digest of International Law*. Washington, D.C.: Department of State.

Wilson's Ideals (Paul S. Padover, ed.). Washington, D.C.: American Council on Public Affairs, 1942.

Yoshitsu, Michael M. "Iran and Afghanistan in Japanese Perspective." 21 *Asian Survey* 501–14 (May 1981).

Selected bibliography

Zamora, Stephen. "Voting in International Economic Organizations." 74 *American Journal of International Law* 566–608 (1980).

Zoller, Elizabeth. *Enforcing International Law Through U.S. Legislation.* Dobbs Ferry, N.Y.: Transnational, 1985.

Index of cases

Index of cases

General Index